Rich

Songs, Carols
and
other Miscellaneous Poems

Elibron Classics
www.elibron.com

Elibron Classics series.

© 2006 Adamant Media Corporation.

ISBN 0-543-93487-X (paperback)
ISBN 0-543-93486-1 (hardcover)

This Elibron Classics Replica Edition is an unabridged facsimile
of the edition published in 1908 by Kegan Paul, Trench, Trübner & Co., Ltd.,
London.

Elibron and Elibron Classics are trademarks of
Adamant Media Corporation. All rights reserved.

This book is an accurate reproduction of the original. Any marks, names, colophons, imprints, logos or other symbols or identifiers that appear on or in this book, except for those of Adamant Media Corporation and BookSurge, LLC, are used only for historical reference and accuracy and are not meant to designate origin or imply any sponsorship by or license from any third party.

Early English Text Society.
Extra Series, CI.

Songs, Carols,
and
other Miscellaneous Poems,

FROM THE BALLIOL MS. 354,
RICHARD HILL'S COMMONPLACE-BOOK.

EDITED BY

ROMAN DYBOSKI, Ph.D.

LONDON:
PUBLISHED FOR THE EARLY ENGLISH TEXT SOCIETY
By KEGAN PAUL, TRENCH, TRÜBNER & CO., LIMITED,
DRYDEN HOUSE, 43, GERRARD STREET, SOHO, W.
1907 (*issued in* 1908).

Price Fifteen Shillings.

Early English Text Society.

Committee of Management:
Director: DR. FREDERICK J. FURNIVALL, M.A.
Treasurer: HENRY B. WHEATLEY, ESQ.
Hon. Sec.: W. A. DALZIEL, ESQ., 67 VICTORIA ROAD, FINSBURY PARK, N.
Hon. Secs. for America: { North & East: Prof. G. L. KITTREDGE, Harvard Coll., Cambr., Mass.
{ South & West: Prof. J. W. BRIGHT, Johns Hopkins Univ., Baltimore.

REV. DR. ANDREW CLARK, M.A.
PROF. ISRAEL GOLLANCZ, D.LIT.
SIDNEY L. LEE, M.A., D.LIT.
HENRY LITTLEHALES, ESQ.
REV. PROF. J. E. B. MAYOR, M.A.
DR. J. A. H. MURRAY, M.A.
PROF. NAPIER, M.A., PH.D.
EDWARD B. PEACOCK, ESQ.
ALFRED W. POLLARD, M.A.
REV. PROF. WALTER W. SKEAT, LITT.D.
DR. HENRY SWEET, M.A.
DR. W. ALDIS WRIGHT, M.A.

(*With power to add Workers to their number.*)

Bankers:
THE UNION OF LONDON AND SMITH'S BANK, 2, PRINCES STREET, E.C.

THE Early English Text Society was started by Dr. Furnivall in 1864 for the purpose of bringing the mass of Old English Literature within the reach of the ordinary student, and of wiping away the reproach under which England had long rested, of having felt little interest in the monuments of her early language and life.

On the starting of the Society, so many Texts of importance were at once taken in hand by its Editors, that it became necessary in 1867 to open, besides the *Original Series* with which the Society began, an *Extra Series* which should be mainly devoted to fresh editions of all that is most valuable in printed MSS. and Caxton's and other black-letter books, though first editions of MSS. will not be excluded when the convenience of issuing them demands their inclusion in the Extra Series.

During the forty-four years of the Society's existence, it has produced, with whatever shortcomings, and at a cost of nearly £30,000, an amount of good solid work for which all students of our Language, and some of our Literature, must be grateful, and which has rendered possible the beginnings (at least) of proper Histories and Dictionaries of that Language and Literature, and has illustrated the thoughts, the life, the manners and customs of our forefathers and foremothers.

But the Society's experience has shown the very small number of those inheritors of the speech of Cynewulf, Chaucer, and Shakspere, who care two guineas a year for the records of that speech. 'Let the dead past bury its dead' is still the cry of Great Britain and her Colonies, and of America, in the matter of language. The Society has never had money enough to produce the Texts that could easily have been got ready for it; and many Editors are now anxious to send to press the work they have prepared. The necessity has therefore arisen for trying to increase the number of the Society's members, and to induce its well-wishers to help it by gifts of money, either in one sum or by instalments. The Committee trust that every Member will bring before his or her friends and acquaintances the Society's claims for liberal support. Until all Early English MSS. are printed, no proper History of our Language or Social Life is possible.

The Subscription to the Society, which constitutes membership, is £1 1s. a year for the ORIGINAL SERIES, and £1 1s. for the EXTRA SERIES, due in advance on the 1st of JANUARY, and should be paid by Cheque, Postal Order, or Money-Order, crost 'Union of London and Smith's Bank,' to the Hon. Secretary, W. A. DALZIEL, Esq., 67, Victoria Rd., Finsbury Park, London, N. Members who want their Texts posted to them, must add to their prepaid Subscriptions 1s. for the Original Series, and 1s. for the Extra Series, yearly. The Society's Texts are also sold separately at the prices put after them in the Lists; but Members can get back-Texts at one-third less than the List-prices by sending the cash for them in advance to the Hon. Secretary.

Original and Extra Series Books, 1907–1909.   3

☞ The Society intends to complete, as soon as its funds will allow, the Reprints of its out-of-print Texts of the year 1866, and also of nos. 20, 26, and 33. Dr. Otto Glauning has undertaken *Seinte Marherete;* and Dr. Furnivall has *Hali Meidenhad* in type. As the cost of these Reprints, if they were not needed, would have been devoted to fresh Texts, the Reprints will be sent to all Members in lieu of such Texts. Though called 'Reprints,' these books are new editions, generally with valuable additions, a fact not noticed by a few careless receivers of them, who have complained that they already had the volumes.

March 1908. A gratifying gift is to be made to the Society. The American owner of the unique MS. of the Works of John Metham—whose Romance of Amoryus and Cleopas was sketcht by Dr. Furnivall in his new edition of *Political, Religious and Love Poems*, No. 15 in the Society's Original Series—has promist to give the Society an edition of his MS. prepared by Dr. Hardin Craig of Princeton, and it will be issued this year as No. 132 of the Original Series. The giver hopes that his example may be followed by other folk, as the support hitherto given to the Society is so far below that which it deserves.

The Original-Series Texts for 1907 were, No. 133, Part I of the *English Register of Oseney Abbey, by Oxford*, edited by the Rev. Andrew Clark, LL.D., and No. 134, Part I of the *Coventry Leet Book*, copied and edited for the Society by Miss M. Dormer Harris —helpt by a contribution from the Common Council of the City,—which is publisht by the Society as its contribution to our knowledge of the provincial city life of the 15th century.

The Texts for 1908 and 1909 will be chosen from Part II of the *Coventry Leet Book*, copied and edited by Miss M. Dormer Harris ; Capgrave's *Lives of St. Augustine and St. Gilbert of Sempringham*, edited from the unique MS. by Mr. J. J. Munro ; *The Wars of Alexander* from the unique Thornton MS. edited by J. S. Westlake, M.A., and L. A. Magnus, Ll.B. ; Part II of *The Brut*, edited by Dr. F. Brie ; Part III of the *Alphabet of Tales*, edited by Mrs. M. M. Banks ; Part III of the *English Register of Godstow Nunnery:* and Part II of the *English Register of Oseney Abbey*, edited by the Rev. Dr. Andrew Clark. Future Texts will be Part III of Robert of Brunne's *Handlyng Synne*, edited by Dr. Furnivall, with a Glossary of Wm. of Wadington's French words in his *Manuel des Pechiez*, and comments on them, by Mr. Dickson-Brown ; Part II of the *Exeter Book*—Anglo-Saxon Poems from the unique MS. in Exeter Cathedral—re-edited by Israel Gollancz, M.A. ; Part II of Prof. Dr. Holthausen's *Vices and Virtues;* Part II of *Jacob's Well*, edited by Dr. Brandeis ; the Alliterative *Siege of Jerusalem*, edited by the late Prof. Dr. E. Kölbing and Prof. Dr. Kaluza; an Introduction and Glossary to the *Minor Poems of the Vernon MS.* by H. Hartley, M.A.; Alain Chartier's *Quadrilogue*, edited from the unique MS. Univ. Coll. Oxford No. 85, by Prof. J. W. H. Atkins ; and the *Early Lyrical Poems* in Harl. MS. 2253, re-edited by Miss Hilda Murray. Canon Wordsworth of Marlborough has given the Society a copy of the Leofric Canonical Rule, Latin and Anglo-Saxon, Parker MS. 191, C. C. C. Cambridge, and Prof. Napier will edit it, with a fragment of the englisht Capitula of Bp. Theodulf: it is now at press.

The Extra-Series Texts for 1907 were No. C. *The Harrowing of Hell*, three parallel Texts, with *The Gospel of Nicodemus*, four parallel Texts, re-edited by Prof. Hulme ; and No. CI. *Songs and Carols* from Richard Hill's Balliol MS., edited by Dr. Roman Dyboski.

The Extra-Series Texts for 1908, &c., will be chosen from *Lydgate's Troy Book*, Parts II and III, ed. by Dr. Hy. Bergen ; Lydgate's *Minor Poems*, with a settlement of the Lydgate Canon, ed. by Dr. H. N. MacCracken ; *The Owl and Nightingale*, two parallel Texts, edited by Mr. G. F. H. Sykes; Dr. Erbe's re-edition of *Mirk's Festial*, Part II ; Dr. M. Konrath's re-edition of *William of Shorcham's Poems*, Part II ; Prof. Erdmann's re-edition of Lydgate's *Siege of Thebes* (issued also by the Chaucer Society); Prof. I. Gollancz's re-edition of two Alliterative Poems, *Winner and Waster*, &c., ab. 1360; Dr. Norman Moore's re-edition of *The Book of the Foundation of St. Bartholomew's Hospital, London*, from the unique MS. ab. 1425, which gives an account of the Founder, Rahere, and the miraculous cures wrought at the Hospital ; *The Craft of Nombrynge*, with other of the earliest englisht Treatises on Arithmetic, edited by R. Steele, B.A. ; and Miss Warren's two-text edition of *The Dance of Death* from the Ellesmere and other MSS.

These Extra-Series Texts ought to be completed by their Editors : the Second Part of the prose Romance of *Melusine*—Introduction, with ten facsimiles of the best woodblocks of the old foreign black-letter editions, Glossary, &c., by A. K. Donald, B.A. (now in India); and a new edition of the famous Early-English Dictionary (English and Latin), *Promptorium Parvulorum*, from the Winchester MS., ab. 1440 A.D.: in this, the Editor, the Rev. A. L. Mayhew, M.A., will follow and print his MS. not only in its arrangement of nouns first, and verbs second, under every letter of the Alphabet, but also in its giving of the flexions of the words. The Society's edition will thus be the first modern one that really represents its original, a point on which Mr. Mayhew's insistence will meet with the sympathy of all our Members.

Later Texts for the Extra Series will include *The Three Kings' Sons*, Part II, the

4 Texts preparing: The Extra-Series Texts for 1909, &c. Deguilleville.

Introduction, &c., by Prof. Dr. Leon Kellner; Part II of *The Chester Plays*, re-edited from the MSS., with a full collation of the formerly missing Devonshire MS., by Mr. G. England and Dr. Matthews; Prof. Jespersen's editions of John Hart's *Orthographie* (MS. 1551 A.D.; blackletter 1569), and *Method to teach Reading*, 1570; Deguilleville's *Pilgrimage of the Sowle*, in English prose, edited by Mr. Hans Koestner. (For the three prose versions of *The Pilgrimage of the Life of Man*—two English, one French—an Editor is wanted.) Members are askt to realise the fact that the Society has now 50 years' work on its Lists,—at its present rate of production,—and that there is from 100 to 200 more years' work to come after that. The year 2000 will not see finisht all the Texts that the Society ought to print. The need of more Members and money is pressing. Offers of help from willing Editors have continually to be declined because the Society has no funds to print their Texts.

An urgent appeal is hereby made to Members to increase the list of Subscribers to the E. E. Text Society. It is nothing less than a scandal that the Hellenic Society should have over 1000 members, while the Early English Text Society has not 300!

Before his death in 1895, Mr. G. N. Currie was preparing an edition of the 15th and 16th century Prose Versions of Guillaume de Deguilleville's *Pilgrimage of the Life of Man*, with the French prose version by Jean Gallopes, from Lord Aldenham's MS., he having generously promist to pay the extra cost of printing the French text, and engraving one or two of the illuminations in his MS. But Mr. Currie, when on his deathbed, charged a friend to burn *all* his MSS. which lay in a corner of his room, and unluckily all the E. E. T. S.'s copies of the Deguilleville prose versions were with them, and were burnt with them, so that the Society will be put to the cost of fresh copies, Mr. Currie having died in debt.

Guillaume de Deguilleville, monk of the Cistercian abbey of Chaalis, in the diocese of Senlis, wrote his first verse *Pèlerinaige de l'Homme* in 1330-1 when he was 36.[1] Twenty-five (or six) years after, in 1355, he revised his poem, and issued a second version of it,[2] a revision of which was printed ab. 1500. Of the prose representative of the first version, 1330-1, a prose Englishing, about 1430 A.D., was edited by Mr. Aldis Wright for the Roxburghe Club in 1869, from MS. Ff. 5. 30 in the Cambridge University Library. Other copies of this prose English are in the Hunterian Museum, Glasgow, Q. 2. 25; Sion College, London; and the Laud Collection in the Bodleian, no. 740.[3] A copy in the Northern dialect is MS. G. 21, in St. John's Coll., Cambridge, and this is the MS. which will be edited for the E. E. Text Society. The Laud MS. 740 was somewhat condenst and modernised, in the 17th century, into MS. Ff. 6. 30, in the Cambridge University Library:[4] "The Pilgrime or the Pilgrimage of Man in this World," copied by Will. Baspoole, whose copy "was verbatim written by Walter Parker, 1645, and from thence transcribed by G. G. 1649; and from thence by W. A. 1655." This last copy may have been read by, or its story reported to, Bunyan, and may have been the groundwork of his *Pilgrim's Progress*. It will be edited for the E. E. T. Soc., its text running under the earlier English, as in Mr. Herrtage's edition of the *Gesta Romanorum* for the Society. In February 1464,[5] Jean Gallopes—a clerk of Angers, afterwards chaplain to John, Duke of Bedford, Regent of France—turned Deguilleville's first verse *Pèlerinaige* into a prose *Pèlerinage de la vie humaine*.[6] By the kindness of Lord Aldenham, as above mentiond, Gallopes's French text will be printed opposite the early prose northern Englishing in the Society's edition.

The Second Version of Deguilleville's *Pèlerinaige de l'Homme*, A.D. 1355 or -6, was englisht in verse by Lydgate in 1426, and, thanks to the diligence of the old Elizabethan tailor and manuscript-lover, John Stowe, a complete text of Lydgate's poem has been edited for the Society by Dr. Furnivall. The British Museum French MSS. (Harleian 4399,[7] and Additional 22,937[8] and 25,594[9]) are all of the First Version.

Besides his first *Pèlerinaige de l'homme* in its two versions, Deguilleville wrote a second, "de l'ame separee du corps," and a third, "de nostre seigneur Iesus." Of the second, a prose Englishing of 1413, *The Pilgrimage of the Sowle* (with poems by Hoccleve, already printed for the Society with that author's *Regement of Princes*), exists in the Egerton MS. 615,[10] at Hatfield, Cambridge (Univ. Kk. 1. 7, and Caius), Oxford (Univ. Coll. and Corpus), and in Caxton's edition of 1483. This version has 'somewhat of addicions' as Caxton says, and some shortenings too, as the maker of both, the first translator, tells us in the MSS. Caxton leaves out the earlier englisher's interesting Epilog in the Egerton MS. This prose englishing of

---

[1] He was born about 1295. See Abbé GOUJET's *Bibliothèque française*, Vol. IX, p. 73-4.—P. M. The Roxburghe Club printed the 1st version in 1893.
[2] The Roxburghe Club's copy of this 2nd version was lent to Mr. Currie, and unluckily burnt too with his other MSS.
[3] These 3 MSS. have not yet been collated, but are believed to be all of the same version.
[4] Another MS. is in the Pepys Library.
[5] According to Lord Aldenham's MS.
[6] These were printed in France, late in the 15th or early in the 16th century.
[7] 15th cent., containing only the *Vie humaine*.
[8] 15th cent., containing all the 3 Pilgrimages, the 3rd being Jesus Christ's.
[9] 14th cent., containing the *Vie humaine* and the 2nd Pilgrimage, *de l'Ame*: both incomplete.
[10] Ab. 1430, 106 leaves (leaf 1 of text wanting), with illuminations of nice little devils—red, green, tawny &c.—and damnd souls, fires, angels, &c.

the *Sowle* has been copied and will be edited for the Society by Mr. Hans Koestner. Of the Pilgrimage of Jesus, no englishing is known.

As to the MS. Anglo-Saxon Psalters, Dr. Hy. Sweet has edited the oldest MS., the Vespasian, in his *Oldest English Texts* for the Society, and Mr. Harsley has edited the latest, c. 1150, Eadwine's Canterbury Psalter. The other MSS., except the Paris one, being interlinear versions,—some of the Roman-Latin redaction, and some of the Gallican,—Prof. Logeman has prepared for press a Parallel-Text edition of the first twelve Psalms, to start the complete work. He will do his best to get the Paris Psalter—tho' it is not an interlinear one—into this collective edition; but the additional matter, especially in the Verse-Psalms, is very difficult to manage. If the Paris text cannot be parallelised, it will form a separate volume. The Early English Psalters are all independent versions, and will follow separately in due course.

Through the good offices of the Examiners, some of the books for the Early-English Examinations of the University of London will be chosen from the Society's publications, the Committee having undertaken to supply such books to students at a large reduction in price. The net profits from these sales will be applied to the Society's Reprints.

Members are reminded that *fresh Subscribers are always wanted*, and that the Committee can at any time, on short notice, send to press an additional Thousand Pounds' worth of work.

The Subscribers to the Original Series must be prepared for the issue of the whole of the Early English *Lives of Saints*, sooner or later. The Society cannot leave out any of them, even though some are dull. The Sinners would doubtless be much more interesting. But in many Saints' Lives will be found valuable incidental details of our forefathers' social state, and all are worthful for the history of our language. The Lives may be lookt on as the religious romances or story-books of their period.

The Standard Collection of Saints' Lives in the Corpus and Ashmole MSS., the Harleian MS. 2277, &c. will repeat the Laud set, our No. 87, with additions, and in right order. (The foundation MS. (Laud 108) had to be printed first, to prevent quite unwieldy collations.) The Supplementary Lives from the Vernon and other MSS. will form one or two separate volumes.

Besides the Saints' Lives, Trevisa's englishing of *Bartholomæus de Proprietatibus Rerum*, the mediæval Cyclopædia of Science, &c., will be the Society's next big undertaking. An Editor for it is wanted. Prof. Napier of Oxford, wishing to have the whole of our MS. Anglo-Saxon in type, and accessible to students, will edit for the Society all the unprinted and other Anglo-Saxon Homilies which are not included in Thorpe's edition of Ælfric's prose,[1] Dr. Morris's of the Blickling Homilies, and Prof. Skeat's of Ælfric's Metrical Homilies. The late Prof. Kölbing left complete his text, for the Society, of the *Ancren Riwle*, from the best MS., with collations of the other four, and this will be edited for the Society by Dr. Thümmler. Mr. Harvey means to prepare an edition of the three MSS. of the *Earliest English Metrical Psalter*, one of which was edited by the late Mr. Stevenson for the Surtees Society.

Members of the Society will learn with pleasure that its example has been followed, not only by the Old French Text Society which has done such admirable work under its founders Profs. Paul Meyer and Gaston Paris, but also by the Early Russian Text Society, which was set on foot in 1877, and has since issued many excellent editions of old MS. Chronicles, &c.

Members will also note with pleasure the annexation of large tracts of our Early English territory by the important German contingent, the late Professors Zupitza and Kölbing, the living Hausknecht, Einenkel, Haenisch, Kaluza, Hupe, Adam, Holthausen, Schick, Herzfeld, Brandeis, Sieper, Konrath, Wülfing, &c. Scandinavia has also sent us Prof. Erdmann and Dr. E. A. Kock; Holland, Prof. H. Logeman. who is now working in Belgium; France, Prof. Paul Meyer—with Gaston Paris as adviser (alas, now dead);—Italy, Prof. Lattanzi; Austria, Dr. von Fleischhacker; while America is represented by the late Prof. Child, by Dr. Mary Noyes Colvin, Miss Rickert, Profs. Mead, McKnight, Triggs, Perrin, Craig, &c. The sympathy, the ready help, which the Society's work has cald forth from the Continent and the United States, have been among the pleasantest experiences of the Society's life, a real aid and cheer amid all troubles and discouragements. All our Members are grateful for it, and recognise that the bond their work has woven between them and the lovers of language and antiquity across the seas is one of the most welcome results of the Society's efforts.

[1] Of these, Mr. Harsley is preparing a new edition, with collations of all the MSS. Many copies of Thorpe's book, not issued by the Ælfric Society, are still in stock.
Of the Vercelli Homilies, the Society has bought the copy made by Prof. G. Lattanzi.

The Original Series of the "Early English Text Society."

ORIGINAL SERIES.

1. Early English Alliterative Poems, ab. 1360 A.D., ed. Rev. Dr. R. Morris. 16s. — 1864
2. Arthur, ab. 1440, ed. F. J. Furnivall, M.A. 4s. — ,,
3. Lauder on the Dewtie of Kyngis, &c., 1556, ed. F. Hall, D.C.L. 4s. — ,,
4. Sir Gawayne and the Green Knight, ab. 1360, ed. Rev. Dr. R. Morris. 10s. — ,,
5. Hume's Orthographie and Congruitie of the Britan Tongue, ab. 1617, ed. H. B. Wheatley. 4s. — 1865
6. Lancelot of the Laik, ab. 1500, ed. Rev. W. W. Skeat. 8s. — ,,
7. Genesis & Exodus, ab. 1250, ed. Rev. Dr. R. Morris. 8s. — ,,
8. Morte Arthure, ab. 1440, ed. E. Brock. 7s. — ,,
9. Thynne on Speght's ed. of Chaucer, A.D. 1599, ed. Dr. G. Kingsley and Dr. F. J. Furnivall. 10s. — ,,
10. Merlin, ab. 1440, Part I., ed. H. B. Wheatley. 2s. 6d. — ,,
11. Lyndesay's Monarche, &c., 1552, Part I., ed. J. Small, M.A. 3s. — ,,
12. Wright's Chaste Wife, ab. 1462, ed. F. J. Furnivall, M.A. 1s. — ,,
13. Seinte Marherete, 1200-1330, ed. Rev. O. Cockayne: re-edited by Dr. Otto Glauning. [Out of print. — 1866
14. Kyng Horn, Floris and Blancheflour, &c., ed. Rev. J. R. Lumby, D.D., re-ed. Dr. G. H. McKnight. 5s. ,,
15. Political, Religious, and Love Poems, ed. F. J. Furnivall. 7s. 6d. — ,,
16. The Book of Quinte Essence, ab. 1460-70, ed. F. J. Furnivall. 1s. — ,,
17. Parallel Extracts from 45 MSS. of Piers the Plowman, ed. Rev. W. W. Skeat. 1s. — ,,
18. Hali Meidenhad, ab. 1200, ed. Rev. O. Cockayne, re-edited by Dr. F. J. Furnivall. [At Press. — ,,
19. Lyndesay's Monarche, &c., Part II., ed. J. Small, M.A. 3s. 6d. — ,,
20. Hampole's English Prose Treatises, ed. Rev. G. G. Perry. 1s. [At Press. — ,,
21. Merlin, Part II., ed. H. B. Wheatley. 4s. — ,,
22. Partenay or Lusignen, ed. Rev. W. W. Skeat. 6s. — ,,
23. Dan Michel's Ayenbite of Inwyt, 1340, ed. Rev. Dr. R. Morris. 10s. 6d. — ,,
24. Hymns to the Virgin and Christ; the Parliament of Devils, &c., ab. 1430, ed. F. J. Furnivall. 3s — 1867
25. The Stacions of Rome, the Pilgrims' Sea-voyage, with Clene Maydenhod, ed. F. J. Furnivall. 1s. — ,,
26. Religious Pieces in Prose and Verse, from R. Thornton's MS., ed. Rev. G. G. Perry. 2s. [At Press. ,,
27. Levins's Manipulus Vocabulorum, a ryming Dictionary, 1570, ed. H. B. Wheatley. 12s. — ,,
28. William's Vision of Piers the Plowman, 1362 A.D.; Text A, Part I., ed. Rev. W. W. Skeat. 6s. — ,,
29. Old English Homilies (ab. 1220-30 A.D.). Series I, Part I. Edited by Rev. Dr. R. Morris. 7s. — ,,
30. Pierce the Ploughmans Crede, ed. Rev. W. W. Skeat. 2s. — ,,
31. Myrc's Duties of a Parish Priest, in Verse, ab. 1420 A.D., ed. E. Peacock. 4s. — 1868
32. Early English Meals and Manners: the Boke of Norture of John Russell, the Bokes of Keruynge, Curtasye, and Demeanor, the Babees Book, Urbanitatis, &c., ed. F. J. Furnivall. 12s. — ,,
33. The Knight de la Tour Landry, ab. 1440 A.D. A Book for Daughters, ed. T. Wright, M.A. [Reprinting. ,,
34. Old English Homilies (before 1300 A.D.). Series I, Part II., ed. R. Morris, LL.D. 8s. — ,,
35. Lyndesay's Works, Part III.: The Historie and Testament of Squyer Meldrum, ed. F. Hall. 2s. — ,,
36. Merlin, Part III. Ed. H. B. Wheatley. On Arthurian Localities, by J. S. Stuart Glennie. 12s. — 1869
37. Sir David Lyndesay's Works, Part IV., Ane Satyre of the Three Estaits. Ed. F. Hall, D.C.L. 4s. — ,,
38. William's Vision of Piers the Plowman, Part II. Text B. Ed. Rev. W. W. Skeat, M.A. 10s. 6d. — ,,
39. Alliterative Romance of the Destruction of Troy. Ed. D. Donaldson & G. A. Panton. Pt. I. 10s. 6d. ,,
40. English Gilds, their Statutes and Customs, 1389 A.D. Edit. Toulmin Smith and Lucy T. Smith, with an Essay on Gilds and Trades-Unions, by Dr. L. Brentano. 21s. — 1870
41. William Lauder's Minor Poems. Ed. F. J. Furnivall. 3s. — ,,
42. Bernardus De Cura Rei Famuliaris, Early Scottish Prophecies, &c. Ed. J. R. Lumby, M.A. 2s. — ,,
43. Ratis Raving, and other Moral and Religious Pieces. Ed. J. R. Lumby, M.A. 3s. — ,,
44. The Alliterative Romance of Joseph of Arimathie, or The Holy Grail: from the Vernon MS.; with W. de Worde's and Pynson's Lives of Joseph: ed. Rev. W. W. Skeat, M.A. 5s. — 1871
45. King Alfred's West-Saxon Version of Gregory's Pastoral Care, edited from 2 MSS., with an English translation, by Henry Sweet, Esq., B.A., Balliol College, Oxford. Part I. 10s. — ,,
46. Legends of the Holy Rood, Symbols of the Passion and Cross Poems, ed. Rev. Dr. R. Morris. 10s. — ,,
47. Sir David Lyndesay's Works, Part V., ed. Dr. J. A. H. Murray. 3s. — ,,
48. The Times' Whistle, and other Poems, by R. C., 1616; ed. by J. M. Cowper, Esq. 6s. — ,,
49. An Old English Miscellany, containing a Bestiary, Kentish Sermons, Proverbs of Alfred, and Religious Poems of the 13th cent., ed. from the MSS. by the Rev. R. Morris, LL.D. 10s. — 1872
50. King Alfred's West-Saxon Version of Gregory's Pastoral Care, ed. H. Sweet, M.A. Part II. 10s. — ,,
51. The Life of St Juliana, 2 versions, A.D. 1230, with translations; ed. T. O. Cockayne & E. Brock. 2s. ,,
52. Palladius on Husbondrie, englisht (ab. 1420 A.D.), ed. Rev. Barton Lodge, M.A. Part I. 10s. — ,,
53. Old-English Homilies, Series II., and three Hymns to the Virgin and God, 13th-century, with the music to two of them, in old and modern notation; ed. Rev. R. Morris, LL.D. 8s. — 1873
54. The Vision of Piers Plowman, Text C: Richard the Redeles (by William, the author of the Vision) and The Crowned King; Part III., ed. Rev. W. W. Skeat, M.A. 18s. — ,,
55. Generydes, a Romance, ab. 1440 A.D., ed. W. Aldis Wright, M.A. Part I. 3s. — ,,
56. The Gest Hystoriale of the Destruction of Troy, in alliterative verse; ed. by D. Donaldson, Esq., and the late Rev. G. A. Panton. Part II. 10s. 6d. — 1874
57. The Early English Version of the "Cursor Mundi"; in four Texts, edited by the Rev. R. Morris, M.A., LL.D. Part I, with 2 photolithographic facsimiles. 10s. 6d. — ,,
58. The Blickling Homilies, 971 A.D., ed. Rev. R. Morris, LL.D. Part I. 8s. — ,,
59. The "Cursor Mundi," in four Texts, ed. Rev. Dr. R. Morris. Part II. 15s. — 1875

The Original Series of the "Early English Text Society." 7.

60. **Meditacyuns on the Soper of our Lorde** (by Robert of Brunne), edited by J. M. Cowper. 2s. 6d. 1875
61. **The Romance and Prophecies of Thomas of Erceldoune**, from 5 MSS.; ed. Dr. J. A. H. Murray. 10s. 6d. ,,
62. **The "Cursor Mundi,"** in four Texts, ed. Rev. Dr. R. Morris. Part III. 15s. 1876
63. **The Blickling Homilies**, 971 A.D., ed. Rev. Dr. R. Morris. Part II. 7s. ,,
64. **Francis Thynne's Embleames and Epigrams**, A.D. 1600, ed. F. J. Furnivall. 7s. ,,
65. **Be Domes Dæge** (Bede's *De Die Judicii*), &c., ed. J. R. Lumby, B.D. 2s. ,,
66. **The " Cursor Mundi,"** in four Texts, ed. Rev. Dr. R. Morris. Part IV., with 2 autotypes. 10s. 1877
67. **Notes on Piers Plowman**, by the Rev. W. W. Skeat, M.A. Part I. 21s. ,,
68. **The "Cursor Mundi,"** in 4 Texts, ed. Rev. Dr. R. Morris Part V. 25s. 1878
69. **Adam Davie's 5 Dreams about Edward II.**, &c., ed. F Furnivall, M.A. 5s. ,,
70. **Generydes**, a Romance, ed. W. Aldis Wright, M.A. Part II. 4s. ,,
71. **The Lay Folks Mass-Book**, four texts, ed. Rev. Canon Simmons. 25s. 1879
72. **Palladius on Husbondrie**, englisht (ab. 1420 A.D.). Part II. Ed. S. J. Herrtage, B.A. 15s. ,,
73. **The Blickling Homilies**, 971 A.D., ed. Rev. Dr. R. Morris. Part III. 10s. 1880
74. **English Works of Wyclif**, hitherto unprinted, ed. F. D. Matthew, Esq. 20s. ,,
75. **Catholicon Anglicum**, an early English Dictionary, from Lord Monson's MS. A.D. 1483, ed., with Introduction & Notes, by S. J. Herrtage, B.A.; and with a Preface by H. B. Wheatley. 20s. 1881
76. **Aelfric's Metrical Lives of Saints**, in MS. Cott. Jul. E 7., ed. Rev. Prof. Skeat, M.A. Part I. 10s. ,,
77. **Beowulf**, the unique MS. autotyped and transliterated, edited by Prof. Zupitza, Ph.D. 25s. 1882
78. **The Fifty Earliest English Wills**, in the Court of Probate, 1387-1439, ed. by F. J. Furnivall, M.A. 7s. ,,
79. **King Alfred's Orosius**, from Lord Tollemache's 9th century MS., Part I, ed. H. Sweet, M.A. 13s. 1883
79 b. *Extra Volume.* Facsimile of the Epinal Glossary, ed. H. Sweet, M.A. 15s. ,,
80. **The Early-English Life of St. Katherine** and its Latin Original, ed. Dr. Einenkel. 12s. 1884
81. **Piers Plowman**: Notes, Glossary, &c. Part IV, completing the work, ed. Rev. Prof. Skeat, M.A. 18s. ,,
82. **Aelfric's Metrical Lives of Saints**, MS. Cott. Jul. E 7., ed. Rev. Prof. Skeat, M.A., LL.D. Part II. 12s. 1885
83. **The Oldest English Texts, Charters**, &c., ed. H. Sweet, M.A. 20s. ,,
84. **Additional Analogs to 'The Wright's Chaste Wife,'** No. 12, by W. A. Clouston. 1s. 1886
85. **The Three Kings of Cologne.** 2 English Texts, and 1 Latin, ed. Dr. C. Horstmann. 17s. ,,
86. **Prose Lives of Women Saints**, ab. 1610 A.D., ed. from the unique MS. by Dr. C. Horstmann. 12s. ,,
87. **Early English Verse Lives of Saints** (earliest version), Laud MS. 108, ed. Dr. C. Horstmann. 20s. 1887
88. **Hy. Bradshaw's Life of St. Werburghe** (Pynson, 1521), ed. Dr. C. Horstmann. 10s. ,,
89. **Vices and Virtues**, from the unique MS., ab. 1200 A.D., ed. Dr. F. Holthausen. Part I. 8s. 1888
90. **Anglo-Saxon and Latin Rule of St. Benet**, interlinear Glosses, ed. Dr. H. Logeman. 12s. ,,
91. **Two Fifteenth-Century Cookery-Books**, ab. 1430-1450, edited by Mr. T. Austin. 10s. ,,
92. **Eadwine's Canterbury Psalter**, from the Trin. Cambr. MS., ab. 1150 A.D., ed. F. Harsley, B.A. Pt. 1. 12s. 1889
93. **Defensor's Liber Scintillarum**, edited from the MSS. by Ernest Rhodes. B.A. 12s. ,,
94. **Aelfric's Metrical Lives of Saints**, MS. Cott. Jul. E 7, Part III., ed. Prof. Skeat, Litt.D., LL.D. 12s. 1890
95. **The Old-English version of Bede's Ecclesiastical History**, re-ed. by Dr. Thomas Miller. Part I, § 1. 18s. ,,
96. **The Old-English version of Bede's Ecclesiastical History**, re-ed. by Dr. Thomas Miller. Part I, § 2. 15s. 1891.
97. **The Earliest English Prose Psalter**, edited from its 2 MSS. by Dr. K. D. Buelbring. Part I. 15s. ,,
98. **Minor Poems of the Vernon MS.**, Part I., ed. Dr. C. Horstmann. 20s. 1892
99. **Cursor Mundi.** Part VI. Preface, Notes, and Glossary, ed. Rev. Dr. R. Morris. 10s. ,,
100. **Capgrave's Life of St. Katharine**, ed. Dr. C. Horstmann, with Forewords by Dr. Furnivall. 20s. 1893
101. **Cursor Mundi.** Part VII. Essay on the MSS., their Dialects, &c., by Dr. H. Hupe. 10s. ,,
102. **Lanfranc's Cirurgie**, ab. 1400 A.D., ed. Dr. R. von Fleischhacker. Part I. 20s. 1894
103. **The Legend of the Cross**, from a 12th century MS., &c., ed. Prof. A. S. Napier, M.A., Ph.D. 7s. 6d. ,,
104. **The Exeter Book** (Anglo-Saxon Poems), re-edited from the unique MS. by I. Gollancz, M.A. Part I. 20s. 1895
105. **The Prymer or Lay-Folks' Prayer-Book**, Camb. Univ. MS., ab. 1420, ed. Henry Littlehales. Part I. 10s. ,,
106. **R. Misyn's Fire of Love and Mending of Life** (Hampole), 1434, 1435, ed. Rev. R. Harvey, M.A. 15s. 1896
107. **The English Conquest of Ireland**. A.D. 1166-1185, 2 Texts, 1425, 1440, Pt. I, ed. Dr. Furnivall. 6s. ,,
108. **Child-Marriages and -Divorces, Trothplights**, &c. Chester Depositions, 1561-6, ed. Dr. Furnivall. 15s. 1897
109. **The Prymer or Lay-Folks Prayer-Book**, ab. 1420, ed. Henry Littlehales. Part II. 10s. ,,
110. **The Old-English Version of Bede's Ecclesiastical History**, ed. Dr. T. Miller. Part II, § 1. 15s. 1898.
111. **The Old-English Version of Bede's Ecclesiastical History**, ed. Dr. T. Miller. Part II, § 2. 15s. ,,
112. **Merlin**, Part IV : Outlines of the Legend of Merlin, by Prof. W. E. Mead, Ph.D. 15s. 1899
113. **Queen Elizabeth's Englishings of Boethius**, Plutarch &c. &c., ed. Miss C. Pemberton. 15s. ,,
114. **Aelfric's Metrical Lives of Saints**, Part IV and last, ed. Prof. Skeat, Litt.D., LL.D. 10s. 1900
115. **Jacob's Well**, edited from the unique Salisbury Cathedral MS. by Dr. A. Brandeis. Part I. 10s. ,,
116. **An Old-English Martyrology**, re-edited by Dr. G. Herzfeld. 10s. ,,
117. **Minor Poems of the Vernon MS.**, edited by Dr. F. J. Furnivall. Part II. 15s. 1901
118. **The Lay Folks' Catechism**, ed. by Canon Simmons and Rev. H. E. Nolloth, M.A. 5s. ,,
119. **Robert of Brunne's Handlyng Synne** (1303), and its French original, re-ed. by Dr. Furnivall. Pt. I. 10s. ,,
120. **The Rule of St. Benet**, in Northern Prose and Verse, & Caxton's Summary, ed. Dr. E. A. Kock. 15s. 1902
121. **The Laud MS. Troy-Book**, ed. from the unique Laud MS. 595, by Dr. J. E. Wülfing. Part I. 15s. ,,
122. **The Laud MS. Troy-Book**, ed. from the unique Laud MS. 595, by Dr. J. E. Wülfing. Part II. 20s. 1903
123. **Robert of Brunne's Handlyng Synne** (1303), and its French original, re-ed. by Dr. Furnivall. Pt. II. 10s. ,,
124. **Twenty-six Political and other Poems** from Digby MS. 102 &c., ed. by Dr. J. Kail. Part I. 10s. 1904
125. **Medieval Records of a London City Church**, ed. Henry Littlehales. Part I. 10s. ,,
126. **An Alphabet of Tales**, in Northern English, from the Latin, ed. Mrs. M. M. Banks. Part I. 10s. ,,

8 *The Extra Series of the "Early English Text Society."*

127. An Alphabet of Tales, in Northern English, from the Latin, ed. Mrs. M. M. Banks. Part II. 10s. 1905
128. Medieval Records of a London City Church, ed. Henry Littlehales. Part II. 10s. ,,
129. The English Register of Godstow Nunnery, ed. from the MSS. by the Rev. Dr. Andrew Clark. Pt. I. 10s. ,,
130. The English Register of Godstow Nunnery, ed. from the MSS. by the Rev. Dr. A. Clark. Pt. II. 15s. 1906
131. The Brut, or Chronicle of England, edited from the best MSS. by Dr. F. Brie. Part I. 10s. ,,
132. John Metham's Works, edited from the unique MS. by Dr. Hardin Craig. ,,
133. The English Register of Oseney Abbey, by Oxford, ed. by the Rev. Dr. A. Clark. Part I. 15s. 1907
134. The Coventry Leet Book, edited by Miss M. Dormer Harris. Part I. 15s. ,,
135. The Coventry Leet Book, edited by Miss M. Dormer Harris. Part II. [*At Press.* 1908
136. The Brut, or Chronicle of England, edited by Dr. F. Brie. Part II. [*At Press.* ,,
  or Capgrave's Lives of St. Augustine and St. Gilbert of Sempringham, edited by J. J. Munro. [*At Press.* ,,

EXTRA SERIES.

The Publications for 1867-1907 (*one guinea each year*) *are:*—

I. William of Palerne; or, William and the Werwolf. Re-edited by Rev. W. W. Skeat, M.A. 13s. 1867
II. Early English Pronunciation with especial Reference to Shakspere and Chaucer, by A. J. Ellis, F.R.S. Part I. 10s. ,,
III. Caxton's Book of Curtesye, in Three Versions. Ed. F. J. Furnivall. 5s. 1868
IV. Havelok the Dane. Re-edited by the Rev. W. W. Skeat, M.A. 10s. ,,
V. Chaucer's Boethius. Edited from the two best MSS. by Rev. Dr. R. Morris 12s. ,,
VI. Chevelere Assigne. Re-edited from the unique MS. by Lord Aldenham, M.A. 3s. ,,
VII. Early English Pronunciation, by A. J. Ellis, F.R.S. Part II. 10s. 1869
VIII. Queene Elizabethes Achademy, &c. Ed. F. J. Furnivall. Essays on early Italian and German Books of Courtesy, by W. M. Rossetti and Dr. E. Oswald. 13s. ,,
IX. Awdeley's Fraternitye of Vacabondes, Harman's Caveat, &c. Ed. E. Viles & F. J. Furnivall. 5s. ,,
X. Andrew Boorde's Introduction of Knowledge, 1547, Dyetary of Helth, 1542, Barnes in Defence of the Berde, 1542-3. Ed. F. J. Furnivall. 18s. (Part I. is No. XXXII, 1878, 8s.) 1870
XI. Barbour's Bruce, Part I. Ed. from MSS. and editions, by Rev. W. W. Skeat, M.A. 12s. ,,
XII. England in Henry VIII.'s Time: a Dialogue between Cardinal Pole & Lupset, by Thom. Starkey, Chaplain to Henry VIII. Ed. J. M. Cowper. Part II. 12s. (Part I. is No. XXXII, 1878, 8s.) 1871
XIII. A Supplicacyon of the Beggers, by Simon Fish, 1528-9 A.D., ed. F. J. Furnivall; with A Supplication to our Moste Soueraigne Lorde; A Supplication of the Poore Commons; and The Decaye of England by the Great Multitude of Sheep, ed. by J. M. Cowper, Esq. 6s. ,,
XIV. Early English Pronunciation, by A. J. Ellis, Esq., F.R.S. Part III. 10s. ,,
XV. Robert Crowley's Thirty-One Epigrams, Voyce of the Last Trumpet, Way to Wealth, &c., A.D. 1550-1, edited by J. M. Cowper, Esq. 12s. 1872
XVI. Chaucer's Treatise on the Astrolabe. Ed. Rev. W. W. Skeat, M.A. 6s. ,,
XVII. The Complaynt of Scotlande, 1549 A.D., with 4 Tracts (1542-48), ed. Dr. Murray. Part I. 10s. ,,
XVIII. The Complaynt of Scotlande, 1549 A.D., ed. Dr. Murray. Part II. 8s. 1873
XIX. Oure Ladyes Myroure, A.D. 1530, ed. Rev. J. H. Blunt, M.A. 24s. ,,
XX. Lovelich's History of the Holy Grail (ab 1450 A.D.), ed. F. J. Furnivall, M.A., Ph.D. Part I. 8s 1874
XXI. Barbour's Bruce, Part II., ed. Rev. W. W. Skeat, M.A. 4s. ,,
XXII. Henry Brinklow's Complaynt of Roderyck Mors (ab. 1542): and The Lamentacion of a Christian against the Citie of London, made by Roderigo Mors, A.D. 1545. Ed. J. M. Cowper. 9s. ,,
XXIII. Early English Pronunciation, by A. J. Ellis, F.R.S. Part IV. 10s. ,,
XXIV. Lovelich's History of the Holy Grail, ed. F. J. Furnivall, M.A., Ph.D. Part II. 10s. 1875
XXV. Guy of Warwick, 15th-century Version, ed. Prof. Zupitza. Part I. 20s. ,,
XXVI. Guy of Warwick, 15th-century Version, ed. Prof. Zupitza. Part II. 14s. 1876
XXVII. Bp. Fisher's English Works (died 1535), ed. by Prof. J. E. B. Mayor. Part I, the Text. 16s. ,,
XXVIII. Lovelich's Holy Grail, ed. F. J. Furnivall, M.A., Ph.D. Part III. 10s. 1877
XXIX. Barbour's Bruce. Part III., ed. Rev. W. W. Skeat, M.A. 21s. ,,
XXX. Lovelich's Holy Grail, ed. F. J. Furnivall, M.A., Ph.D. Part IV. 15s. 1878
XXXI. The Alliterative Romance of Alexander and Dindimus, ed. Rev. W. W. Skeat. 6s. ,,
XXXII. Starkey's "England in Henry VIII's time." Pt. I. Starkey's Life and Letters, ed. S. J. Herrtage. 8s. ,,
XXXIII. Gesta Romanorum (englisht ab. 1440), ed. S. J. Herrtage, B.A. 15s. 1879
XXXIV. The Charlemagne Romances:—1. Sir Ferumbras, from Ashm. MS. 33, ed. S. J. Herrtage. 15s. ,,
XXXV. Charlemagne Romances:—2. The Sege off Melayne, Sir Otuell, &c., ed. S. J. Herrtage. 12s. 1880
XXXVI. Charlemagne Romances:—3. Lyf of Charles the Grete, Pt. I., ed. S. J. Herrtage. 16s. ,,
XXXVII. Charlemagne Romances:—4. Lyf of Charles the Grete, Pt. II., ed. S. J. Herrtage. 15s. 1881
XXXVIII. Charlemagne Romances:—5. The Sowdone of Babylone, ed. Dr. Hausknecht. 15s. ,,
XXXIX. Charlemagne Romances:—6. Rauf Colyear, Roland, Otuel, &c., ed. S. J. Herrtage, B.A. 15s. 1882
XL. Charlemagne Romances:—7. Huon of Burdeux, by Lord Berners, ed. S. L. Lee, B.A. Part I. 15s. ,,
XLI. Charlemagne Romances:—8. Huon of Burdeux, by Lord Berners, ed. S. L. Lee, B.A. Pt. II. 15s. 1883
XLII. Guy of Warwick: 2 texts (Auchinleck MS. and Caius MS.), ed. Prof. Zupitza. Part I. 15s. ,,
XLIII. Charlemagne Romances:—9. Huon of Burdeux, by Lord Berners, ed. S. L. Lee, B.A. Pt. III. 15s. 1884
XLIV. Charlemagne Romances:—10. The Four Sons of Aymon, ed. Miss Octavia Richardson. Pt. I. 15s. ,,
XLV. Charlemagne Romances:—11. The Four Sons of Aymon, ed. Miss O. Richardson. Pt. II. 20s. 1885
XLVI. Sir Bevis of Hamtón, from the Auchinleck and other MSS., ed. Prof. E. Kölbing, Ph.D. Part I. 10s. ,,
XLVII. The Wars of Alexander, ed. Rev. Prof. Skeat, Litt.D., LL.D. 20s. 1886
XLVIII. Sir Bevis of Hamton, ed. Prof. E. Kölbing, Ph.D. Part II. 10s. ,,
XLIX. Guy of Warwick, 2 texts (Auchinleck and Caius MSS.), Pt. II., ed. Prof. J. Zupitza, Ph.D. 15s. 1887

The Extra Series of the " Early English Text Society." Works preparing. 9

L. **Charlemagne Romances** :—12. Huon of Burdeux, by Lord Berners, ed. S. L. Lee, B.A. Part IV. 5s. 1887
LI. **Torrent of Portyngale**, from the unique MS. in the Chetham Library, ed. E. Adam, Ph.D. 10s. ,,
LII. **Bullein's Dialogue against the Feuer Pestilence**, 1578 (ed. 1, 1564). Ed. M. & A. H. Bullen. 10s. 1888
LIII. **Vicary's Anatomie of the Body of Man**, 1548, ed. 1577, ed. F. J. & Percy Furnivall. Part I. 15s. ,,
LIV. **Caxton's Englishing of Alain Chartier's Curial**, ed. Dr. F. J. Furnivall & Prof. P. Meyer. 5s. ,,
LV. **Barbour's Bruce**, ed. Rev. Prof. Skeat, Litt.D., LL.D. Part IV. 5s. 1889
LVI. **Early English Pronunciation**, by A. J. Ellis, Esq., F.R.S. Pt. V., the present English Dialects. 25s. ,,
LVII. **Caxton's Eneydos**, A.D. 1490, coll. with his French, ed. M. T. Culley, M.A. & Dr. F. J. Furnivall. 13s. 1890
LVIII. **Caxton's Blanchardyn & Eglantine**, c. 1489, extracts from ed. 1595, & French, ed. Dr. L. Kellner. 17s. ,,
LIX. **Guy of Warwick**, 2 texts (Auchinleck and Caius MSS.), Part III., ed. Prof. J. Zupitza, Ph.D. 15s. 1891
LX. **Lydgate's Temple of Glass**, re-edited from the MSS. by Dr. J. Schick. 15s. ,,
LXI. **Hoccleve's Minor Poems**, I., from the Phillipps and Durham MSS., ed. F. J. Furnivall, Ph.D. 15s. 1892
LXII. **The Chester Plays**, re-edited from the MSS. by the late Dr. Hermann Deimling. Part I. 15s. ,,
LXIII. **Thomas a Kempis's De Imitatione Christi**, englisht ab. 1440, & 1502, ed. Prof. J. K. Ingram. 15s. 1893
LXIV. **Caxton's Godfrey of Boloyne, or Last Siege of Jerusalem**, 1481, ed. Dr. Mary N. Colvin. 15s. ,,
LXV. **Sir Bevis of Hamton**, ed. Prof. E. Kölbing, Ph.D. Part III. 15s. 1894
LXVI. **Lydgate's and Burgh's Secrees of Philisoffres**. ab. 1445—50, ed. R. Steele, B.A. 15s. ,,
LXVII. **The Three Kings' Sons, a Romance**, ab. 1500, Part I., the Text, ed. Dr. Furnivall. 10s. 1895
LXVIII. **Melusine**, the prose Romance, ab. 1500, Part I, the Text, ed. A. K. Donald. 20s. ,,
LXIX. **Lydgate's Assembly of the Gods**, ed. Prof. Oscar L. Triggs, M.A., Ph.D. 15s. 1896
LXX. **The Digby Plays**, edited by Dr. F. J. Furnivall. 15s. ,,
LXXI. **The Towneley Plays**, ed. Geo. England and A. W. Pollard, M.A. 15s 1897
LXXII. **Hoccleve's Regement of Princes**, 1411-12, and 14 Poems, edited by Dr. F. J. Furnivall. 15s. ,,
LXXIII. **Hoccleve's Minor Poems**, II., from the Ashburnham MS., ed. I. Gollancz, M.A. [*At Press.*
LXXIV. **Secreta Secretorum**, 3 prose Englishings, by Jas. Yonge, 1428, ed. R. Steele, B.A. Part I. 20s. 1898
LXXV. **Speculum Guidonis de Warwyk**, edited by Miss G. L. Morrill, M.A., Ph.D. 10s. ,,
LXXVI. **George Ashby's Poems**, &c., ed. Miss Mary Bateson. 15s. 1899
LXXVII. **Lydgate's DeGuilleville's Pilgrimage of the Life of Man**, 1426, ed. Dr. F. J. Furnivall. Part I. 10s. ,,
LXXVIII. **The Life and Death of Mary Magdalene**, by T. Robinson, c. 1620, ed. Dr. H. O. Sommer. 5s. ,,
LXXIX. **Caxton's Dialogues, English and French**, c. 1483, ed. Henry Bradley, M.A. 10s. 1900
LXXX. **Lydgate's Two Nightingale Poems**, ed. Dr. Otto Glauning. 5s. ,,
LXXXI. **Gower's Confessio Amantis**, edited by G. C. Macaulay, M.A. Vol. I. 15s. ,,
LXXXII. **Gower's Confessio Amantis**, edited by G. C. Macaulay, M.A. Vol. II. 15s. 1901
LXXXIII. **Lydgate's DeGuileville's Pilgrimage of the Life of Man**, 1426, ed. Dr. F. J. Furnivall. Pt. II. 10s. ,,
LXXXIV. **Lydgate's Reason and Sensuality**, edited by Dr. E. Sieper. Part I. 5s. ,,
LXXXV. **Alexander Scott's Poems**, 1568, from the unique Edinburgh MS., ed. A. K. Donald, B.A. 10s. 1902
LXXXVI. **William of Shoreham s Poems**, re-ed. from the unique MS. by Dr. M. Konrath. Part I. 10s. ,,
LXXXVII. **Two Coventry Corpus-Christi Plays**, re-edited by Hardin Craig, M.A. 10s. ,,
LXXXVIII. **Le Morte Arthur**, re-edited from the Harleian MS. 2252 by Prof. Bruce, Ph.D. 15s. 1903
LXXXIX. **Lydgate's Reason and Sensuality**, edited by Dr. E. Sieper. Part II. 15s. ,,
XC. **English Fragments from Latin Medieval Service-Books**, ed. by Hy. Littlehales. 5s. ,,
XCI. **The Macro Plays**, from Mr. Gurney's unique MS., ed. Dr. Furnivall and A. W. Pollard, M.A. 10s. 1904
XCII. **Lydgate's DeGuileville's Pilgrimage of the Life of Man**, Part III., ed. Miss Locock. 10s. ,,
XCIII. **Lovelich's Romance of Merlin**, from the unique MS., ed. Dr. E. A. Kock. Part I. 10s. ,,
XCIV. **Respublica**, a Play on Social England, A.D. 1553, ed. L. A. Magnus, LL.B. 12s. 1905
XCV. **Lovelich's History of the Holy Grail**, Pt. V. : The Legend of the Holy Grail, by Dorothy Kempe. 6s. ,,
XCVI. **Mirk's Festial**, edited from the MSS. by Dr. Erbe. Part I. 12s. ,,
XCVII. **Lydgate's Troy Book**, edited from the best MSS. by Dr. Hy. Bergen. Part I. 15s. 1906
XCVIII. **Skelton's Magnificence**, edited by Dr. R. L. Ramsay, with an Introduction. 7s. 6d. ,,
XCIX. **The Romance of Emaré**, re-edited from the MS. by Miss Edith Rickert, Ph.D. 7s. 6d. ,,
C. **The Harrowing of Hell, and The Gospel of Nicodemus**, re-ed. by Prof. Hulme, M.A., Ph.D. 15s. 1907
CI. **Songs and Carols** from Richard Hill's Balliol MS., edited by Dr. Roman Dyboski. 15s. ,,
CII. 1908
CIII.
CIV. **Lydgate's Troy Book**, edited from the best MSS. by Dr. Hy. Bergen. Part II. [*At Press.* 1909

EARLY ENGLISH TEXT SOCIETY TEXTS PREPARING.

Besides the Texts named as at press on p. 12 of the Cover of the Early English Text Society's last Books, the following Texts are also slowly preparing for the Society :—

ORIGINAL SERIES.

The **Earliest English Prose Psalter**, ed. Dr. K. D. Buelbring. Part II.
The **Earliest English Verse Psalter**, 3 texts, ed. Rev. R. Harvey, M.A.
Anglo-Saxon Poems, from the Vercelli MS., re-edited by Prof. I. Gollancz, M.A.
Anglo-Saxon Glosses to Latin Prayers and Hymns, edited by Dr. F. Holthausen.
All the **Anglo-Saxon Homilies and Lives of Saints** not accessible in English editions, including those of the Vercelli MS. &c., edited by Prof. Napier, M.A., Ph.D.

Works preparing for the "Early English Text Society."

The Anglo-Saxon Psalms; all the MSS. in Parallel Texts, ed. Dr. H. Logeman and F. Harsley, B.A.
Beowulf, a critical Text, &c., edited by a Pupil of the late Prof. Zupitza, Ph.D.
Byrhtferth's Handboc, ed. by Prof. G. Hempl.
Early English Confessionals, ed. Dr. R. von Fleischhacker.
The Seven Sages, in the Northern Dialect, from a Cotton MS., edited by Dr. Squires.
The Master of the Game, a Book of Huntynge for Hen. V. when Prince of Wales. (*Editor wanted.*)
Ailred's Rule of Nuns, &c., edited from the Vernon MS., by the Rev. Canon H. R. Bramley, M.A.
Early English Verse Lives of Saints, Standard Collection, from the Harl. MS. (*Editor wanted.*)
A Lapidary, from Lord Tollemache's MS., &c., edited by Dr. R. von Fleischhacker.
Early English Deeds and Documents, from unique MSS., ed. Dr. Lorenz Morsbach.
Gilbert Banastre's Poems, and other Boccaccio englishings, ed. by Prof. Dr. Max Förster.
Lanfranc's Cirurgie, ab. 1400 A.D., ed. Dr. R. von Fleischhacker, Part II.
William of Nassington's Mirror of Life, from Jn. of Waldby, edited by J. A. Herbert, M.A.
More Early English Wills from the Probate Registry at Somerset House. (*Editor wanted.*)
Early Lincoln Wills and Documents from the Bishops' Registers, &c., edited by Dr. F. J. Furnivall.
Early Canterbury Wills, edited by William Cowper, B.A., and J. Meadows Cowper.
Early Norwich Wills, edited by Walter Rye and F. J. Furnivall.
Early Lyrical Poems from the Harl. MS. 2253, re-edited by Miss Hilda Murray.
Alliterative Prophecies, edited from the MSS. by Prof. Brandl, Ph.D.
Miscellaneous Alliterative Poems, edited from the MSS. by Dr. L. Morsbach.
Bird and Beast Poems, a collection from MSS., edited by Dr. K. D. Buelbring.
Scire Mori, &c., from the Lichfield MS. 16, ed. Mrs. L. Grindon, LL.A., and Miss Florence Gilbert.
Nicholas Trivet's French Chronicle, ed. from Sir A. Acland-Hood's unique MS. by F. W. Clarke, M.A.
Early English Homilies in Harl. 2276 &c., c. 1400, ed. J. Friedländer.
Extracts from the Registers of Boughton, ed. Hy. Littlehales, Esq.
The Diary of Prior Moore of Worcester, A.D. 1518-35, from the unique MS., ed. Henry Littlehales, Esq.
The Pore Caitif, edited from its MSS., by Mr. Peake.
Trevisa's english Vegetius on the Art of War, MS. 30 Magd. Coll. Oxf., ed. L. C. Wharton, M.A.
Poems attributed to Richard Maydenstone, from MS. Rawl. A 389, edited by Dr. W. Heuser.
Knighthood and Battle, a verse-Vegetius from a Pembroke Coll. MS., Cambr., ed. Dr. R. Dyboski.

EXTRA SERIES.

Bp. Fisher's English Works, Pt. II., with his Life and Letters, ed. Rev. Ronald Bayne, B.A. [*At Press.*
Sir Tristrem, from the unique Auchinleck MS., edited by George F. Black.
John of Arderne's Surgery, c. 1425, ed. J. F. Payne, M.D.
De Guilleville's Pilgrimage of the Sowle, edited by Prof. Dr. Leon Kellner.
Vicary's Anatomie, 1548, from the unique MS. copy by George Jeans, edited by F. J. & Percy Furnivall.
Vicary's Anatomie, 1548, ed. 1577, edited by F. J. & Percy Furnivall. Part II. [*At Press.*
A Compilacion of Surgerye, from H. de Mandeville and Lanfrank, A.D. 1392, ed. Dr. J. F. Payne.
William Staunton's St. Patrick's Purgatory, &c., ed. Mr. G. P. Krapp, M.A.
Trevisa's Bartholomæus de Proprietatibus Rerum, re-edited by Dr. R. von Fleischhacker.
Bullein's Dialogue against the Feuer Pestilence, 1564, 1573, 1578. Ed. A. H. and M. Bullen. Part II.
The Romance of Boctus and Sidrac, edited from the MSS. by Dr. K. D. Buelbring.
The Romance of Clariodus, and **Sir Amadas,** re-edited from the MSS. by Dr. K. D. Buelbring.
Sir Degrevant, edited from the MSS. by Dr. K. Luick.
Robert of Brunne's Chronicle of England, from the Inner Temple MS., ed. by Prof. W. E. Mead, Ph.D.
Maundeville's Voiage and Travaile, re-edited from the Cotton MS. Titus C. 16, &c., by Miss M. Bateson.
Avowynge of Arthur, re-edited from the unique Ireland MS. by Dr. K. D. Buelbring.
Guy of Warwick, Copland's version, edited by a pupil of the late Prof. Zupitza, Ph.D.
Awdelay's Poems, re-edited from the unique MS. Douce 302, by Prof. Dr. E. Wülfing.
The Wyse Chylde and other early Treatises on Education, Northwich School, Harl. 2099 &c., ed. G. Collar, B.A.
Caxton's Dictes and Sayengis of Philosophirs, 1477, with Lord Tollemache's MS. version, ed. S. I. Butler, Esq.
Caxton's Book of the Ordre of Chyualry, collated with Loutfut's Scotch copy, by Miss Alice H. Davies.
Lydgate's Dance of Death, ed. Miss Florence Warren.
Lydgate's Lyfe of oure Lady, ed. by Prof. Georg Fiedler, Ph.D.
Lydgate's Life of St. Edmund, edited from the MSS. by Dr. Axel Erdmann.
Richard Coer de Lion, re-edited from Harl. MS. 4690, by Prof. Hausknecht, Ph.D.
The Romance of Athelstan, re-edited by a pupil of the late Prof. J. Zupitza, Ph.D.
The Romance of Sir Degare, re-edited by Dr. Breul.
The Gospel of Nichodemus, edited by Ernest Riedel.
Mulcaster's Positions 1581, and Elementarie 1582, ed. Dr. Th. Klaehr, Dresden.
Walton's verse Boethius de Consolatione, edited by Mark H. Liddell, U.S.A.
Sir Landeval and Sir Launfal, edited by Dr. Zimmermann.
Rolland's Seven Sages, the Scottish version of 1560, edited by George F. Black.
Partonope of Blois, edited from the complete MS., &c., by Dr. A. T. Bödtker.
Early English Fabliaux, a Collection, edited by Prof. George H. McKnight, Ph.D.

Songs, Carols,
and
Other Miscellaneous Poems.

Early English Text Society.
Extra Series, No. CI.
1907.

BERLIN: ASHER & CO., 13, UNTER DEN LINDEN.
NEW YORK: C. SCRIBNER & CO.; LEYPOLDT & HOLT.
PHILADELPHIA: J. B. LIPPINCOTT & CO.

Songs, Carols,
and
other Miscellaneous Poems,

FROM THE BALLIOL MS. 354,
RICHARD HILL'S COMMONPLACE-BOOK.

EDITED BY
ROMAN DYBOSKI, Ph.D.

LONDON:
PUBLISHED FOR THE EARLY ENGLISH TEXT SOCIETY
By KEGAN PAUL, TRENCH, TRÜBNER & CO., LIMITED,
DRYDEN HOUSE, 43, GERRARD STREET, SOHO, W.
1907 (*issued in* 1908).

Extra Series, CI.

RICHARD CLAY & SONS, LIMITED, LONDON AND BUNGAY.

TO

DR. F. J. FURNIVALL

ON FEBRUARY 4, 1908,

BEING THE DAY ON WHICH HE COMPLETES
THE EIGHTY-THIRD YEAR OF A LIFE MEMORABLE
IN THE ANNALS OF ENGLISH PHILOLOGY,

THIS BOOK OF SONGS
IS GRATEFULLY AND ADMIRINGLY DEDICATED

BY THE EDITOR.

PREFACE.

IN publishing this volume, it is my duty to gratefully state manifold obligations: first of all, to the authorities of both Balliol College and the Bodleian Library, for facilitating the use and copying of the MS. in the reading-room of the latter; to its sub-librarian, Mr. Falconer Madan, for palaeographical instruction; to Dr. James Morison, Oxford, for kindly collating proofs with the MS.; to Dr. J. H. Wylie as well as my American friends Professor F. M. Padelford (of Washington State University) and Dr. H. N. MacCracken (of Harvard) for useful information on particulars;—finally, and above all, to Dr. Henry Bradley and Dr. F. J. Furnivall, for help and encouragement in every way. Dr. Bradley's valuable contributions to my glossary are recorded in it; of Dr. Furnivall's experienced hand it will be easy to discern characteristic touches on almost every page of the book.

Fond remembrances of a hundred proofs of kindness and hospitality are connected for me with the names of the two great English scholars last mentioned; and it is to express a deep feeling of gratitude for what they and all my other English friends have done by me during my first stay in their country, that I venture to offer this volume, which opens the second hundred of the Extra Series, as a birthday present to the Founder of the Early English Text Society.

ROMAN DYBOSKI.

Vienna, Feb. 1, 1908.

CONTENTS.

	PAGE
INTRODUCTION :	
Richard Hill's Children, 1518-26	xiii
,, ,, City Freedoms, 1508-1511	xv
His MS., Balliol 354	xvi
Poems printed here :	
§ 1. Sacred Songs and Carols	xvii
§ 2. Religious Poems and Prayers in Verse	xxii
§ 3. Didactic, Moral and Allegorical Poems	xxiii
§ 4. Historical Poems	xxiv
§ 5. Ballads and Worldly Songs. Humorous pieces	xxv
§ 6. Proverbs, Sentences and Rules in Verse and Prose	xxvii
Parts of the MS. not printed in the present volume	xxviii
The Prose Pieces in Richard Hill's MS.	xxx
Table of Contents of the Balliol MS. 354	xxxiv

I. SACRED SONGS AND CAROLS :

1. Be mery all þat be present	1
2. Fayre maydyn, who is this barn ?	2
3. Vpon a lady fayre & bright	2
4. In what state þat euer I be	3
5. Yf God send þe plentuowsly riches	3
6. Now let vs syng, both more & lesse	3
7. Whan Jhesu Crist baptised was	4
8. Now we shuld syng & say newell	4
9. Gabriell of hygh degre	5
10. Ther ys a flowr sprong of a tre	6
11. Make we mery in hall & bowr	7
12. Off a rose, a louely rose	7
13. Man, asay, a-say, a-say !	8
14. Now syng we wyth joy and blys	8
15. Mary moder, I you pray	9
16. The Son of the Fader of hevyn blys	9
17. Now syng we, syng we	10
18. Ther ys a chyld borne of a may	10
19. Pray for vs to the prince of peace	11
20. Abowt the feld they pypyd ryght	11
21. Now syng we all in fere	12
22. To blys God bryng vs all & sum	12

x   *Contents.*

		PAGE
23. Ther ys a blossum sprong of a thorn	... ...	12
24. Mary moder, cum and se		13
25. In to þis world now ys cum		14
26. Man þat in erth abydys here		14
27. Make we mery, bothe more & lasse		15
28. The New Year		15
29. The Virgin Mary's Five Joys		15
30. The Jolly Shepherd Wat		16
31. The Farewell of Christmas		18
32. Christ's Questions to his Mother		19
The Virgin and her Son:		
33. Now synge we with angelis		21
34. Lulley, Jhesu, lulley, lulley!		23
35. This enders nyght I sawe a sight		25
Two Moral Songs:		
36. For sothe, I hold hym well & withowt woo		26
37. God þat sittith in trinite		27
38. Syng we with myrth, joye & solas		29
39. Now syng we right as it is		30
40. The Murder of Thomas à Beket		31
41. The Stoning of St. Stephen		32
42. The Boar's Head		33
43. Gawde for thy joyes five		33
44. Christ, an Ear of Wheat		34
45. An Appeal to Saint John		35
46. The Fear of Death		36
47. The fleur de lys, Christ		37
48. I pray you, be mery & synge with me		38
49. Tydyngis trewe, ther be com newe		39
50. "O my harte is wo!" Mary, she sayd so		40
51. To see the maydyn wepe her sonnes passion		41
52. Don't swear by the Mass!		42
53. What, hard ye not, þe kyng of Jherusalem		44
54. Wassaill, wassaill, wassaill, syng we		45
55. He is wise, so most I goo		46
56. An old sawe hath be fownd trewe		47
57. Man, be ware & wise in dede		47
58. Man, meve thy mynd, & joy this fest		48
59. All this tyme this songe is best		49
60. Now syng we, syng we		49
61. Qvene of hevyn, blessyd mot þou be		49
62. Man, be ware, or thou be wo		50
II. RELIGIOUS POEMS AND PRAYERS IN VERSE:		
63. To þe gud angell		51
64. Have pity on me, O God		52
65. Now, mercy, Lord, and gramercy		54

Contents.

		PAGE
66a. Salve, sancta parens! To the Virgin Mary	... ...	57
66b. Hail, Mary!	... ...	59
67a. An holy 'Salue Regina' to God in Englisshe	... ...	60
67b. Wytt hath wonder, & kynde ne can	... ...	61
68. Prayers	... ...	62
69. Ave Maria!	... ...	65
70. The Sacrament of Matrimony	... ...	66
71. The Sacrifice of the Mass	... ...	68

III. DIDACTIC, MORAL AND ALLEGORICAL POEMS:

72. Fortune, by Sir Thomas More:		
(Part I.) The wordis of Fortune to þe people	... ...	72
(Part II.) To them þat tristith in Fortune ...	... ...	73
(Part III.) To them þat seketh Fortune	... ...	78
73. Revertere!	... ...	80
74a. The Duty of Prelates	... ...	81
74b. Know thyself	... ...	82
75. Fortis ut mors dilectio	... ...	84
76. The Seven Deadly Sins	... ...	86
77. The Four Bequests in a Man's Will	... ...	86
78. Farewell! Death comes	... ...	87
79. 'Welfare hath no sykernes'	... ...	88
80a. Die I must	... ...	89
80b. Earth upon Earth	... ...	90
80c. Dr. John Ednam on What's the good of it!	... ...	92
80d. God's Blessing	... ...	92
81a. To dy, to dy!	... ...	92
81b. Death and the Four Ages of Man ...	... ...	93
82. 'Speculum vitae et mortis'	... ...	93

IV. HISTORICAL POEMS:

83. The Lamentacion of the Duches of Glossester	... ...	95
84a. The Lamytacion off Quene Elyzabeth	... ...	97
84b, c. Latin and English Epitaph on Queen Elizabeth	...	99
85. A treatice of London, by W. Dunbar	... ...	100

V. BALLADS AND WORLDLY SONGS. HUMOROUS AND SATIRICAL PIECES:

86. Lully, lulley, lulley, lulley!	... ...	103
87. How! we shall have game & sport ynow ...	... ...	103
88. My twelve oxen	... ...	104
89. A treatise of wyne	... ...	105
90. Good Gossipis mine!	... ...	106
91. Quid vidistis in villa?	... ...	109
92. I will haue the whetston & I may ...	... ...	110
93. The Goodman smites his Wife	... ...	110
94. Old Hogyn and his Girl	... ...	111
95. Of all creatures women be best	... ...	112
96. Women, women, love of women	... ...	113

Contents.

	PAGE
97. When to trust a Woman. Never	114
98. The Juggler and the Baron's Daughter	115
99. The Holly and the Ivy	116
100. Bon jour!	117
101. Ho, butler, ho!	118
102. The Disconsolate Lover	119
103. Jak & his Stepdame, & of the Frere	120

VI. PROVERBS, VERSE-RULES AND MORAL SENTENCES:

	PAGE
104. Diwers good prowerbis	128
105a. Fifty-five Proverbs in English and Latin	129
105b. Latin Proverbs	133
105c. Documentum Aristotilis ad Alexandrum magnum	134
105d. Latin Maxims	134
105e. Names of English Cities	135
105f. Men excelled by Animals	135
105g. Greetings	135
105h. Latin Puns	136
105i. A Prayer to the Virgin	136
105j. How to be welcome	136
105k. The Seven Deadly Sins	136
105l. The Ten Commandments	136
105m. The Seven Works of Piety	136
105n. The Five Senses	136
105o. Verse-making	136
105p. Contrast between Hens and Women	137
105q. For a syngar	137
105r. Further Latin Maxims	137
106. Rules for purchasing land	137
107. Spend money for your Soul while you live	138
108. Directions for Conduct	139
109. Good Advice	139
110. Quatuor complexiones hominum	139
111. Latin and English Maxims	140
112. Proverbial Rhymes	140
113a, b. Maxims	140
113c. Three things make me anxious. English	141
113d. Three things make me anxious. Latin	141
114. Death, Bribery, Adversity	141

APPENDIX.

A Chronicle, 1413–1536	142
NOTES	169
GLOSSARY	191

INTRODUCTION.

The MS., its original owner and date.—The MS., from which the miscellaneous poetical pieces contained in the present volume are all taken, is usually known as "*the commonplace-book of Richard Hill.*" It is a paper codex in oblong folio (11½ × 4½ in.) and quires of eight,—numbered 354 in Balliol College Library, Oxford. The handwriting of the chief poetical pieces is pretty uniform, and was identified by Coxe with that of one John Hyde. The only name, however, that occurs in the MS. itself, is that of its owner Richard Hill, on whose person and circumstances the MS. affords the following information in the shape of memoranda on the birth of his children and previous important events of his own life (apparently entered by himself):—

[leaf 17]   The birth of children of me
    Richard hill þat was borne on hillend / in langley in the
    parishe of huchy[n] in the shire of hartfford
    god make them all his seruantis
    & margret my wyf þat was dowghter to harry wyngar ha-
    [-berdasher dwellyng in bowe parishe in London].[1]

A° 1518 *Memorandum* þat John hill my first child was borne
    the XVII day of novembre a° MCCCCCXVIII
    at hillend afforesayd on the day of seynt
    hewe littera dominicalis C / godfardirs thomas hoo
    of abbotis walden / & he gave IIs.
    Thomas gaskyer of graveley & he gave XXd.
    & my moder Elizabeth hill godmoder
    And godfader at the bisshope / Edmond
    worth of ofley / & he was bisshoppyd in þe
    hows of þe said Master worth þe XIX of desembre 1518

(hora tercia ante nonam)

A° 1520 *Memorandum* that thomas hyll my second child was born
    the XXX day of may a° MCCCCCXX yere at
    VIII of þe clok in þe mornyng littera dominicalis A G
    at Freshe wharff in þe paryshe of saynt buttulff
    godfaders / Thomas Wall salter & he gave IIIs. IIII. (*This whole entry crossed through*)
    george wyngar grocer & he gave . . IIs.
    My lady dame agnes wyngar & gave . IIIs. II . . . .
    & at bishope John lane grocer & he gave IIIs. IIIId.

(þe wedynsday in wytson weke)

[1] Supplied from "table of contentis," leaf 4, back.

xiv   *Richard Hill's Children, 1521–1526.*

              Memorandum that william hill my thyrde child was
              born in briggestret In the parishe of seint margrett*is*
              the XIX day of octobre a° MCCCCCXXI yere
A° 1521   abowt XI of the clokk affore none / godfaders   *(crossed through)*
littera domi- william whaplot fishemo*nger* & he gave XXd
nicali   nycholas Cosyn merchau*n*t taylor he gave XXd
F   Margret preston my syster & she gave I docat IIIIs. VId.
              And at bishoppe John smythe fishemonger

+   Memorandum þat Elizabeth my IIIIth child was born In the parishe of
      seynt andreas vnd*er* shaft / the XVII day of octobre A° 1522
      on the fryday l*itte*ra d*omi*nicalis E / at X of þe clok affore nown
      godfader Master west parish prest of seynt margrett*is* i*n* fishestret
      & he gave VIIId. / godmod*er*s my sist*er* Elizabeth lan*ere*
      & she gave XXd. / my cosyn elze astry vx*or* henrici astry
+   & she gave XXd / & at bishope / Mary sist*er* to elze astry
      & wyff to denys Jacobs of mydillburg

(The entry again crossed through ; additional note:)

      þis elizabeth depa*r*tid þe VII day of aprell A° 1530 in sey[nt] mary hill
            parys*h*e

in þe parish of seint andreas vnder shaft A° 1528

      Memorandum that Kateryn my Vth child was borne et . . the
      shoff monday þat was the VIII day of februari betwen
      II & III of the clokk. þe mornyng A° 1523 / l*itte*ra d*omi*nicalis
      C·B· And this yer owr lady day anu*n*cyacio*n* fell
      on good Fryday / god fad*er* henry lom*ener*
      grocer & he gave IIIs / godmothers my lady dame
      Kateryn haddon & she gave IIIs IIIId / & Mastres
      lett*is* Rise ux*or* simonis Rise / & she gave IIIs IIIId
      And at þe bisshop / Mastres m*ar*gret ward / XIIs [1]
      vx*or* Stephani ward wexchandler

      Memorandum that Symond hill my VIth child was born
      in þe parishe of seynt Andreas vnd*er* shaft the XXIII
      day of aprell A° MCCCCCXXV l*itte*ra d*omi*nicalis A
      which was seynt georg*is* day / & fell on lowe
1525 sonday / betwen IIII & V of the clokk i*n* þe mornyng
      godfaders symond Rise mer*cer* & he gave VIs VIIId
      henry astry mer*cer* & he gave IIIs IIIId godmoder
      My sist*er* Eme Cosyn & she gave IIIs IIIId
      godfader at the bishop / John Rayn . . . talowchan-
      deler of london

(Crossed through ; additional note:)

              mortuus & sepultus in pa*r*ochia *s*a*n*cte marie
              at þe hill iuxta bilyng*is* gate i*n* london
[*leaf* 17b]   +   1526   + abowt V of þe clok in
                          þe mornyng or litill affore

*M^d þat he depa*r*tid to god II^d day of m*ar*cho A° 1527 at wymmoley þe litill [1525, struck through] hart- fordshire*

      Memorandum þat Rob*er*t hill my VIIth child was born
      in þe parishe of seynt Andreas vndershaft
      on þe tuysday which was þe XXVI day
      of Iuyn A° MCCCCCXXVI l*itte*ra d*omi*nicalis G   *(Crossed through,*
      Godfad*er*s John lan*er* groc*er* my brod*er* in lawe   *and side-note*
      & he gave IIIs IIIId in a karolus & XIId silu*er*   *added.)*
      John batt. Coopar & he gave XIId
      Godfader at þe bishop Robert A . . . arshm*er* lorym*er*
      but he occupieth as a frut*er*er.

                          [1] *struck through.*

Richard Hill's City Freedoms, 1508–1511.

[leaf 107]   The day of my hanseyng at Barow.

Memorandum that I was hansed at Barow þe XXth day
of May a° 1508 & þer was paid for my hance   IIs. VIIId. ff.

The day þat I was mad fre in Barow

32s. 6d.   Memorandum þat I Richard Hill was made fre among þe
my costis   merchantis
& all   aventurers of Ynglond in Barow the XXV day
of May a° 1508 & ther I paid for yt   VIIs. VId. ff.

The day þat I received XLs. of my Masters bequest

Memorandum that I received of my lady Wynger þe VIIth day of
Juyn 1508 of M. Wyngar bequest . . . .   XLs. st.

¶
Memorandum þat what a man bieth by the ƻ. in Barow he shall
wyn in Ynglond VI ƻ. in þe C. And þat he bith by þe
C. he shall lese in Ynglond VI ƻ. in the C.
Item þat he bieth by þe ƻ in Andwarpe he shall wyn
in Ynglond IIII ƻ. in þe C. & þat he bieth by þe C he
shall lese in Ynglond VIII ƻ. in þe C as men say.

¶ *(in another ink)*
Memorandum that I was hannsid at Brigius at synsyn
marte in a° 1511 at þe goldyn starre & I paid
for my hannce & my dyner . . .   IIs. IIId. ff.

Memorandum that I was hansid at Andwarpe
in passe marte a° 1511 & I paid
at the pansar in casse strette . . .   XXIId. ff.

Memorandum that y was made free at Yeld hall
the . . .
(a blank)

Memorandum that I was sworn at grocers hall
þe Xth day of Novembre in a° 1511 & þer
I paid to M. wardens clark & bedell . .   IIIs. Xd. st.

Express testimony to Hill's ownership of the book is borne by a note on fol. 176r° (at the end of More's "Lamentation of Queen Elizabeth"): "Iste liber pertineth Rycardo Hill seruant to M. Wynger alderman of London."[1]—"Explicit quod Hill" occurs at the end of some poems.

For an identification of this Richard Hill with a cellarer of this name in the court of Henry VIII, who is very frequently mentioned in the "Letters and papers, foreign and domestic, of the reign of Henry VIII" (ed. Brewer and Gairdner), and whose epitaph is given in Weever's "Ancient Funerall Monuments" (1631, fol.; p. 405, dioc. of London, church of St.

[1] Professor Flügel's conclusion from this passage, that the MS., or at least this part of it, must have been written before the year of John Winger's Mayorship, 1504, because after that date Hill would have styled Wynger "Mayor of L." (*Anglia* 26, 189), seems not to be sufficiently founded, because (as Dr. Wylie informs me) a man never was called "Mayor" outside the actual year of his being in office.

xvi *Richard Hill's MS. ranges from* A.D. 1508 *to* 1536.

Michaels at Queene-Hithe),—no sufficient ground exists either in these records or in the MS.

As to his book, the period of its gradual composition is approximately fixed by some of the above-quoted private memoranda as extending over the earlier part of Henry VIII's reign. The latest distinct date in the whole MS. is that of the last in a series of annalistic historical notes (printed as an appendix to the present volume); it is 1536.[1]

Of the later fate of the MS., an interesting trace is left in the form of 18th century farming accounts (on "bushels of wheat," and the like), partly dated 1731, and entered on fol. 17[b] and in a few other places. They may, as was disrespectfully suggested by a person acquainted with the history of the treatment of MSS., relate to Balliol College property of the time; but no positive information as to how and when the MS. came into the College library was to be obtained; nor is it included in the list of donors and their gifts, prefixed to Coxe's "Catalogus codicum MSS. collegii Balliolensis."—The vellum binding is evidently later than the MS., borders of pages being cut off, and some pasted over, to prevent crumbling off. The original pagination, after fol. 178, grows unintelligibly confused, and after some twelve leaves of such confusion, starts numbering what actually are ff. 191–253 (marked so by the modern hand that has numbered the leaves throughout) as ff. "CLXXIX—IICXXXI," and not that even without a few irregularities; nor does the chaotic "table of the contentis," at the beginning (printed in *Anglia* 26, 96 ff.) give a clue to the original arrangement or contents as different from the present.—For a detailed account of the MS., the reader is referred to the table of its contents placed at the end of this introduction, where he will find it described piece by piece, with the pagination and other peculiarities recorded, omissions in Coxe's Catalogue [2] pointed out, and bibliographical references given to all printed editions of the single pieces from this or other versions of the pieces from other MSS., as far as they have come to the editor's knowledge.

[1] As a matter of fact, the dates 1535 and 1536 do not appear in the MS., but can safely be supplied, as the names of the Lord Mayors and Sheriffs are given.

[2] The MS. has been described before in H. O. Coxe's "Catalogus Codicum MSS. qui in collegiis aulisque Oxoniensibus hodie adservantur," Oxon. 1852; pars I, 2: codices MSS. collegii Balliolensis, p. 110 b ff.; also by Prof. E. Flügel, *Anglia* 26, 94 ff.

Poems only printed here. § 1. *Sacred Songs and Carols.* xvii

Contents of the present volume.—Richard Hill's MS. is an interesting specimen of a type very common when books were dear and scarce, chiefly from the 15th to the 17th century, and which were met with even afterwards, nay, down to the late 19th century in remoter parts of the country: the household book called "*enchiridium*" by the humanists, "*silva rerum*" in some continental countries, and "*commonplace-book*" in England—into which were entered, firstly poems and songs which struck a man as worth transcribing and preserving for family use, and secondly, prose notes of a most varied character on anything of interest that he came across: encyclopaedic scraps of useful knowledge, tracts, commercial and statistical dates and tables, medical and other receipts, puzzles and tricks for amusement, records of important events, public and private, and the like.

Desirable and interesting as it would have been to present a collection of this kind in its whole bulk and boundless variety, this in the present case appeared impossible, for reasons detailed below in the passage on the excluded pieces. In confining myself to a selection of the poetical pieces from the MS. in the present edition, I did not think it necessary to preserve the MS. order of the pieces, but I have arranged them in a few large groups, into which they naturally fell; and only within these groups, which represent the different kinds or types of poetry in the MS., have I strictly followed the succession of the original, partly because further sub-classifying would have led to pedantic monotony, partly because the arrangement of connected pieces in the MS. is sometimes really (unintentionally perhaps) skilful and consistent, as instances occasionally mentioned below will prove. In the following passages, these groups will be discussed and analysed into their elements.

The first and most important of them are the numerous **Sacred Songs and Carols**, the greatest part of which are actually placed together in the MS. (see No. 120 *a*—*zz* in the Table of Contents) and were probably transcribed in one series from a then extant collection. Among those, several different kinds are to be distinguished. First and foremost in number rank the **Christmas Carols** proper. There are several distinct types of them, differing in the poetical treatment of the subject and the point they chiefly envisage. We have, in the first place, carols on the theme, not of xviii *Carols on the Annunciation, and in praise of Mary.*

Christ's birth itself, but of the **Annunciation**, "Advent Carols" as we might call them; some of them, not injudiciously, are placed in the MS. together in a small group at the beginning of the chief bulk of Christmas songs, which they rather usher in, than essentially belong to. Representatives of this type are, in the present collection, No. 8, 9, 17, 49, 53 (where we meet with the feature, not unfrequent, of the two headlines which serve as burden, being out of connection with the contents of the poem, and referring abruptly to another aspect of the chief subject). The structure common to all these is a simple account, following the Scripture, of the angel's visit to Mary and their dialogue with (occasional) lyrical comments on the angel's salutation. Single lines and burdens in Latin, fitted into the metrical scheme, are not uncommon in these and other songs; they can all be traced back to Latin church-hymns in old collections.

From these songs, in which the Virgin alone is the centre and chief subject, we pass naturally to a group of purely **Lyrical Carols**, entirely devoted to the **praise of Mary**, and devoid of any narrative allusions to the events commemorated at Christmas. The codex, besides songs and carols, contains a number of longer religious poems in honour of Mary, *e. g.* No. 69, The Five Joys; 67, Salve Regina—and others, which will be dealt with under section II (Religious Poems and Prayers in verse). Among the carols themselves, such mere songs to Mary are: No. 10 (an allegorical glorification of Mary as the flower from the root of Jesse); 12 (also an allegory, and, as different versions testify, greatly popular); 21 (which shows several points of interest: first, the well-known burden "Alma Redemptoris Mater," secondly the typical introduction of the average allegorical vision: "As I me lay on a nyght," etc., uncommon in a short song;—and thirdly, a scheme not lyrical like the others, but rather narrative, in that it brings the chief scenes of Mary's life briefly before our eyes [1]); 29 (a parallel, in the class of carols, to the numerous longer poems on the Joys of Mary, like No. 69 in our volume); 43 (on the same subject), and finally, 61 (a Supplication to Mary; burden out of keeping with contents, except in st. 2).—Even the highly peculiar form, so widely spread in mediæval religious lyrics, of a song

---

[1] The song, in fact, is an exact parallel, within its class, to the longer verse lives of the Blessed Virgin,—quite as the one next mentioned, is one to another type of longer religious poems.

§ 1. *The Christmas Carols of Richard Hill's MS.* xix

in terms of worldly love, but applied and addressed to the Queen of Heaven, is represented by a specimen: No. 3.[1]

We pass now from these two preliminary groups, to the large central class of **Christmas Carols** in the strictest sense of the word; viz., narrative songs on the birth of Christ, relating the events that accompanied it, and colouring the whole with a tinge of lyrical expression and some touches on the religious and dogmatic associations of the great fact. We find the general structure of these songs typically exemplified in the very first instance we meet with: the carol No. 6. It mentions the Annunciation, but proceeds at once to the chief event, presents most vividly the scene in the stable (without, however, introducing shepherds and kings) and Mary's quiet gladness, throws out, by way of contrast and deeper reflection, a hint at Christ's passion (almost invariably met with, towards the end, in carols of this class), and finishes, as it began, with a joyous outburst of praise, which also, in the form of the burden, runs as an under-strain right through the whole song.—Another song of this type is No. 11, where the Shepherds come in. The mention of Christ's death is very effectively introduced, and the lyrical note of gladness struck in the well-known worldly-joyous headline only, the *finale* being, this time, a penitent supplication.

Of course, not all songs centering in the birth of Christ, show the above-mentioned logical disposition and fulness of narrative detail: some are, in the latter respect, confined to an emphatic statement of the chief fact (though most, as will be seen, add something or other of the accessory circumstances), the rest consisting in lyrical exultations, and moral and dogmatical reflections. Thus, in No. 14, the birth of Christ is only the starting point for a series of thoughts on original sin, redemption, Christ's resurrection and his return on doomsday, ending with a prayer for his grace in life and death. The note of sentiment is again confined to the headlines and the burden. Another half-reflective, half-narrative song is No. 16. In No. 18, which is more purely narrative again, the framework is made up of lines from the hymn "*Veni, Creator Spiritus*," which gives the piece a somewhat striking, original aspect (a similar effect is brought about in the Epiphany carol No. 23 by the introduction of the Easter cry "Alleluia").—

[1] Cf. a number of similar songs to Mary and Jesus in Flügel's "*Neuenglisches Lesebuch*," p. 126–128.

xx *The Carols of Worldly Joy. Shepherd & Dramatic Carols.*

The remaining pieces of this class are: 22 (which alludes to the Murder of the Innocents), 24 (in verses alternately English and Latin), 47 (with its mystic splendour of flower-de-luce), 48, 58 (the angel's message to the shepherds), 59, 60.

Opposed to these narrative and religiously-reflective carols, stands a group of purely and simply lyrical ones, of which mere **worldly joy** and pleasance in Christmas forms the key-note and whole contents. The best examples of this kind are No. 27 (*Make we mery* . . .) and the New-Year's song 28. No. 31, a parting monologue spoken by Christmas in person, also belongs here; and finally the Boar's Head carol, No. 42, which although printed from the same MS. in the "Babees boke," yet appears again in the present volume, because any collection of Christmas Carols would be incomplete without a specimen of this well-known type.

In contrast to these songs of worldly mirth, we find such as present only the serious moral aspect of the fact. One is No. 39, which might be called "Expostulation," and which in its form comes near the Dialogue Carols to be discussed below. The extreme in this serious style is reached by a carol entirely on the subject of Christ's passion (No. 44). Another event in Christ's later life, viz. his baptism, is the subject of No. 7, of which only the heading, strangely unconnected with the contents, justifies inclusion among Christmas carols.

But let us return to real Christmas songs. We next come to a group of them, entirely devoted to the **shepherds**, their joy at the angel's message, and their adoration of the new-born Saviour. No. 58, mentioned above, is in its essence a shepherds' carol; but in true spirit, No. 20, with its characteristic burden "Tyrly tirlow" is an especially good specimen, while No. 30, telling a whole detailed story, is certainly among the best of its kind, and in the unrivalled poetical freshness of the parting dialogue between the Virgin and "herd*i*sman Wat," approaches the excellence of some of the mystery plays.

This takes us over to what may be called "**dramatic carols**," being songs in dialogue form. As with the shepherd, so in No. 2 Mary speaks with an undefined adoring person (addressed by her as "Sir"), to whom she tells the story of Christ's birth and the adoration of the Magi. But the chief carols of this class are dialogues between the Virgin and the child; such as No. 32, where (as I understand the poem) the child Jesus relates to his Mother a

Dramatic Carols. Epiphany & Saints' Carols. Moral Songs. xxi

prophetic vision which he had of his later life and suffering, and asks her anxiously, if it is really to be; 33, where the Child replies to his Mother's inquiries by prophecies of his passion and death; 34, another version of the same; and 35 (whose popularity is testified by numerous other versions), a conversation between Mother and Child full of natural charm. It will be observed, that these four poems, all on a similar plan and model, are placed together in the MS.

Another group of dramatic songs presents to us Mary at the foot of the cross, complaining: Nos. 24, 50.[1] No. 51 describes the same scene in non-dramatic form.

To return once more to the Christmas Carols proper, we must finally mention the few **Epiphany carols** of the collection: the first piece in this volume is one; besides, Nos. 23 and 38 deal almost exclusively with the adoration of the Magi; 1 and 38 contain the old symbolical explanation of the three kings' gifts.

A class of carols necessarily and indissolubly connected with the Christmas songs are those in honour of **Saints**, whose Festivals fall about the time of Christmas. The foremost of them is, of course, the "protomartyr" St. Stephen, whose feast is the day after Christmas, and whom carol No. 41 celebrates. Next comes St. John the Apostle (December 27); carols in his praise are Nos. 19 and 45. Thirdly, there is the "holy blisful martir" St. Thomas Becket, the anniversary of whose death—the 29th of December—falls within the Christmas holidays; this accounts for a carol on his murder by Henry's knights being found among the Christmas songs (No. 40).

There is one more distinct class of songs interspersed among the Christmas carols, yet not belonging to them in anything but the form: these are the "**moral songs**" embodying religious doctrines and teachings of general experience. Turning first to those on dogmatic and ritual subjects, we meet with a specimen in No. 26, a song on the "mirabile misterium" of transubstantiation; another one, No. 52, celebrates the holiness and dignity of the Mass, and warns people from swearing by it. (For other poems on the Mass, see No. 70 in the second section, and the account of Lydgate's "Virtues of the Mass" in the passage on the excluded pieces.)

[1] For a French song of a similar type (monologue-complaint of Mary) see Bartsch, *Chrestomathie de l'ancien français*, 4th ed., p. 149.

xxii § 1. *Moral Songs.* § 2. *Religious Poems & Prayers in Verse.*

Songs on general moral topics are: first of all, some on the much-sung theme of the fear of death and doom (which is also the subject of several longer poems in the present collection, see third section): thus, the song No. 4, of which the framework—a bird speaking to the poet—is that of a large and well-known class of longer didactic poems, cf. for example No. 78,—rings with the impressive and widely-used burden (familiar to every reader of Dunbar) "*Timor mortis conturbat me.*" Similar in burden and subject is No. 46 ("*Terribilis mors conturbat me*"). Next in popularity to this ranks, among moral subjects, that of the vanity of worldly wealth and splendour: and "*Divitiae si affluant, nolite cor apponere*" (No. 5) represents it among the songs.—Other songs on various subjects of this group are: one on penitence and mercy (No. 13); one on the terrors of Doomsday (No. 15), with headlines addressed to the Virgin, which makes it fit in among the carols; then, there is one on the worldly wisdom of self-content (No. 36), and (immediately following in the MS.) a complaint of the vices reigning in the world, and the want of grace and lovingkindness (No. 37).—Of a group of three moral songs, placed together in the MS. (No. 55–57), the first two are short *compendia* of various precepts; the third is on the particular lesson of trying a friend before we need him, and shows again (as No. 4 above) the popular form of a wise bird's teaching. Finally, the last of all the songs proper in the MS., No. 62, is also of the didactic category; it deals with the sin of pride as an origin of evil and misfortune.

The songs, in their great variety of subjects and moods, having struck, like a prelude, all the chief notes in the poetry of the period, as represented in Hill's collection, we now pass to the several groups of longer poems in the MS. which have been included in the present edition.

The second section, headed "**Religious Poems and Prayers in verse,**" consists of a number of (anonymous) specimens of late Middle-English religious lyrics of Lydgate's school and epoch, all of them rather uniformly typical in contents as well as in form (this for the most part being the 8-line stanza *ababbcbc*, or, as in the first instance, *ababab*). The verses to the good angel which open the section (No. 63), the two parallel poems on God's mercy, with the burdens "*miserere mei deus*" and "marcy, lorde, and

§ 2. *Religious Poems.* § 3. *Didactic and Allegorical Poems.* xxiii

gramarcy" (Nos. 64 and 65), and the collection of prayers in rhyme-royal stanzas (68), give no occasion for further remarks; nor does the paraphrase of "*Salve Regina*" (67),[1] probably transcribed with some other pieces standing next to it in the MS., from a printed quarto of Caxton (see the note on the poem). Besides this, there are three longer poems addressed to the Virgin: the two hymns, comprised under No. 66, being variations on one subject (as also the two afore-mentioned pieces, 64 and 65, are) and both distinguished by the use of alliteration: the latter of them is paralleled in a collection analogous to this part of the Balliol poems (Furnivall's "Hymns to the Virgin and Christ"); the third hymn to Mary (No. 69), somewhat more of a song than the rest, is on the subject of the joys (as carols 29 and 43)[2] and heads, in the MS., the chief bulk of songs and carols (No. 120 in the catalogue table), with which it was evidently transcribed from a common source and at the same time, as writing and ink testify.

Poems on purely ritual subjects are: No. 70, on the sacrament of matrimony, and 71, on hearing Mass (cf. the carol No. 52, and the account of Lydgate's poem below).

As the poems of the second section correspond to the religious carols, so do the **didactic, moral and allegorical** ones of the third to the class distinguished as "moral songs." The first of them (No. 72), Sir Thomas More's youthful poem (or rather Induction to a projected poem) on Fortune, is not much out of the common track of the numerous productions of this kind, but is still interesting enough by its association with an author who in his own person experienced the shocks of Fortune's mutability so cruelly, and whose tragical death is duly recorded in the very same MS. (see historical notes, printed in the appendix).

There follow some less significant pieces: No. 73 (*Revertere*) being a very short version of a piece printed in its fuller form elsewhere; then two fragments, the one of a satire on the clergy, the other of a moral poem "Know thyself," both written in the same hand and ink on the two pages of one leaf in the MS., as if

---

[1] For Latin songs (with Italian and French parallels) of this wide-spread type, see Mone, *Lat. Hymnen des Mittelalters*, II, p. 203 ff., Nos. 487–495).
[2] With the typical Latin end-lines of stanzas, the same in all songs on the subject, down from St. Bonaventura's Latin "*Corona S. Mariae*" (see No. 454 and 460 in Mone's *Lateinische Hymnen*, vol. II).

xxiv § 3. *Poems on Death. A Latin piece.* § 4. *Historical Poems.*

the latter were the continuation of the former (No. 74); a poem on the power of love (No. 75), again in the form of a bird's teaching, and adorned with alliteration; and in No. 76, we have a representative of the type so very common in the early modern period of all European literatures, of the "Dance of the Seven Deadly Sins."

Another group of poems, which follows next, deals with the idea of *death* and the vanity of all earthly things. The first of them (No. 77) is called "The Testament of the Christian" in the "Reliquiae Antiquae," where it was printed from another MS. The next (78, immediately following in the MS.) is a farewell to the world and friends. In 79, not death, but the "*vanitas vanitatum*" of worldly prosperity is the theme, the burden being "Welfare hath no sikerness," the allegorical form again, as in so many cases before, a bird's address to the poet. No. 80 is one of the numerous variations—almost invariably represented in any MS. of that kind and time—on "Earth out of earth," the typical form and contents of which are so beautifully summarised in a Melrose Abbey epitaph often quoted:

"The earth goeth on the earth glist'ning like gold,
The earth goeth to the earth sooner than it wold;
The earth buildeth on the earth castles and towers,
The earth sayeth to the earth, all shall be ours."[1]

The last poem of this little group is No. 81, on the suddenness and remorseless power of death, and the stages of human life.

At the end of the whole didactic section I have ventured to place, as a fit close, an extremely curious piece of mediaeval Latin rhyme (No. 82), on the transitoriness of this world's glory,[2] to the immense popularity of which (attested by seven MSS. in English libraries) the fact of its being preserved in as late a MS. as the Balliol one, bears new and interesting witness, and which is in itself worth including in a collection like the present.

The next section consists of the two **historical poems** of the MS.,

[1] For bibliography of the poem, see the catalogue table. Douce, in his "Dance of Death" (1833), quotes Latin verses very like those prefixed to our poem, from a Latin poem ascribed to W. Map; but I don't find it in Wright's ed.

[2] On the authorship of this piece, attributed by some to Walter Map, by others to Jacobus de Benedictis (the author of "Stabat Mater Dolorosa"), and by others still to St. Bernard of Clairvaux, see B. Haureau, *Des poèmes latins attribués à saint Bernard*, Paris 1890, p. 27 f.

§ 4. *Two Historical Poems. Dunbar's London.* § 5. *Ballads.*

both of them in the form of Complaints of unhappy Princesses. The first of them is a "Lamentation" of Eleanor (Cobham) Duchess of Gloucester, wife of the "good Duke Humphrey," on the occasion of her condemnation (for attempting to bring about by witchcraft the death of the young king Henry VI) and her ensuing penance in the streets of London (on November 13, 1441). The poem, probably composed soon after the event, has been printed in Wright's "Political Poems" and fully commented upon in his introduction.—The second of the two poems is another youthful work of Sir Thomas More (whose "Fortune" was mentioned above): an elegy on the death (Febr. 11, 1503) of Elizabeth of York, Henry VII's wife, in the form of a monologue of the dead queen, containing in its first part a general complaint on the instability of worldly wealth and splendour (she died at the early age of 38), and in its second part addressed as a farewell to Henry ("whose mourning, if sincere, was short," Lingard remarks), to her daughter Margaret, Queen of Scotland (married to James IV), to Henry's mother, to her daughter-in-law Katherine (widow of Prince Arthur, dead ten months before his mother), to her three children left at home, her sisters, the lords and ladies of the court, and the "comyns."

To these historical poems I have added, as historical in contents and associations, the "**Praise of London**" by **William Dunbar** (No. 85), "made," as the MS. correctly states, "at Mr. Shaa table when he was mayre," that is, in Christmas week 1501, when the Scottish poet was present in London with the Embassy then negotiating the marriage between James IV and Henry VII's daughter Margaret,—and said to have been composed (or recited), at a banquet given by the Lord Mayor Sir John Shaw to the ambassadors.[1] The ornate stanzas are preserved in two English MSS. besides the present one, which gives new proof of the popularity of the Scottish poet's verses among the flattered citizens of the English metropolis.

The fifth section of the volume collects under the heading "**Ballads and worldly songs. Humorous and satirical pieces**" miscellaneous profane poems of the MS., most of them of a more

---

[1] For a fuller account of the banquet anecdote (from the Cotton MS.) and other historical particulars, see D. Laing's elaborate notes on pp. 272-275 and 297-300 of his *Supplement to the Poems of William Dunbar*, Edinburgh, 1865.

xxvi § 5. *Ballads & Worldly Songs. Festive ones. Against Shrews.*

or less humorous character. The opening piece, however (No. 86), is altogether serious and of extreme interest. This ballad in song-form, probably fragmentary, written in exquisitely neat *thin* characters on a half-page of the MS., presents to us—after a typical introduction (describing a person borne away by a falcon to some visionary place)—a scene (a wounded knight, bleeding evermore, on a bed in a hall, a lady kneeling and weeping, a stone by the bed-side with the inscription "Corpus Christi") which reminds us most strikingly of some features of the Holy Grail legend: of Perceval's meeting, on his wanderings, with King Amfortas' daughter, then with the King himself, who still looks up to the Graal for healing of his ever-bleeding wound,—in the French and German epics on the Quest.[1]

We next pass to two songs (87, 88), a hunting-carol which is also preserved in one of the most precious relics of Wynkyn de Worde's press, and the song of the "XII oxen,"—both of which most vividly bring to our mind the olden times when all England sang at work and play, in wood and field.

We now enter the regions of mirth, with the Anglo-Latin verses on the virtues of wine (No. 89), full of monkish fun in their Scriptural moralizations on the excellences of the vine and its fruit. If this song—not unique in its kind, as it seems, for one similar in contents and form is found *e. g.* in Sandys's "Festive Songs," No. VII—breathes the air of the convent-cellar, the next piece (90) takes us to the old English tavern, where we meet with a merry company of "gossips," women regaling themselves at a kind of picnic, to which every one contributes her share of eatables and her "shot" to pay the drinks, and indulging in a free exchange of confidential observations on their unconscious husbands, and some of the less peaceful scenes in connubial life. Two other texts[2] of this vivid poetical sketch of ancient life and manners have appeared in recent collections, one of them being a wholly different version, where a harper comes in to amuse the women.

The next piece "*In villa*" (91), directed against the shrew-ishness and self-will of women, opens a series of short poems, all

[1] According to Prof. Flügel, the poem is to be interpreted as an allegory of Christ's passion, who here, as in the "Ancren Riwle," appears as a "knight."
[2] For analogues, Prof. Flügel points to *Piers Plowman*, text C, VII, and Skelton's *Elynour Rummyng* (ed. Dyce 1, 99); also Gower's French *Mirour de l'Omme*, l. 26080 ff.

§ 5. *Women's shrewishness. Boy & Friar.* § 6. *Proverbs, etc.* xxvii

written together in one hand, and evidently at one time, on the last ten pages of the MS. These are: a burlesque or lying-song (93), a tragi-comical story of domestic wrangles between goodman and goodwife (94), a coarse song on a motive like Chaucer's Miller's Tale (94), three satires against women (95, 96, 97), the first of them in the popular form of the ironical *encomium* (with the destroying burden "*Cuius contrarium verum est*"), the last one in a series of preambles (in 7-line stanzas).[1] The next piece (98) is narrative again : how the fair baron's daughter was beguiled by a "joly juggeler"; the next (99), adds one more to the numerous versions of the popular "Contentions" between Holly and Ivy; then follow: convivial invitations to singing (100), a drinking song (101). Between this and the next, the birched schoolboy's monologue (printed in Dr. Furnivall's "Babees boke"); and lastly, an ironical love-complaint with the delightful burden "whan I slepe, I can not wake."

At the end of this section (No. 103), I have placed the one long piece from the MS. that appears in the present collection; it is a text of the widely-spread folk-tale[2] of the Boy, his Stepmother and the Friar, whom he made dance in the hawthorn-bush,—of which English versions, from old prints and MSS., appear in a great many recent collections of early popular poetry (see Bibliography), and of which two texts of the same class with the Balliol one—viz. without the law-court scene at the end, have been edited (with unfulfilled hope for more) by the late Prof. Zupitza in *Herrig's Archiv*.

In a last section (VI), I have collected various small pieces from the MS., which do not aspire to literary merit and interest, being **proverbs, sentences, and rules in verse and prose.** The one large group among them (No. 105), written in a very small hand on 4¼ consecutive pages of the MS., is a curiously confused heap of odds and ends of popular wisdom in moral verse and phrase, chiefly English proverbial sentences with renderings in Latin (would-be) hexameters; and the handful of proverbs (No. 104), partly written in ciphers, is full of the freshness of living use. The other bits

---

[1] For similar preambles, see the *Bannatyne MS.*, published by the Hunterian Club (Glasgow), vol. IV, pp. 776 f. (Nos. 291–292).
[2] For the general history of this tale in tradition and literature, see Prof. J. Bolte's essay "*Das Märchen vom Tanze des Mönches im Dornbusch*" in the "*Festschrift zum V. Neuphilologentag*" (1892), and his additional article in *Herrig's Archiv*, 90, p. 289.

and scraps of verse-rules, printed in this section, and mostly taken from odd corners of the MS.'s pages, where they have filled blanks between the longer entries, could probably be easily paralleled from similar miscellanies (as, in fact, Nos. 108 and 109 are from Caxton, see note).

In the **Appendix**, finally, appears an annalistic chronicle of the chief events from 1413 to 1536, growing fuller towards the end, as the writer drew from his own experience, with the names of Mayor and Sheriffs prefixed to each year's notes. It ranks with similar records kept by many London citizens of the time, specimens of which have been edited by Prof. Gairdner in various volumes of the Camden Society (*e. g.* No. XXVIII, new ser.); and though it is not likely to add greatly to our historical knowledge of the period, yet being one of the usual ingredients of household books like Richard Hill's, it has been thought worth including in a volume intended to represent some of such a book's chief and typical features.

Parts of the MS. not included in the present volume.—Of these I shall consider the **poetical pieces** first. Exclusion was natural in the case of the large **selection of Tales from Gower's** "**Confessio Amantis**" (44 leaves, Nos. 10–20 and 71 [1]). The critical value and comparative position of this text among the numerous other ones of the popular work have been carefully investigated and expressly defined by Prof. Macaulay in the preface to his admirable edition (where also he describes some other MSS. containing selections from Gower like the present). No systematic principle in the choice of the stories is to be discovered, and perhaps the selecting of them was not done by the writer of the MS. himself. The striking features of the texts are: the careful elimination of the dialogue between *Confessor* and *Amans* by means of omissions and little alterations, often only by generalising the address (" you " for " thou "); and secondly, modernisation of the language, not only with respect to forms and endings (which is a matter of course, and sadly hampers the metre), but also in a lexicographical way, by substituting words more generally used in Hill's time, for such of Gower's as had become obsolete or less intelligible. In fact, a collation of the texts from this point of view

[1] In this passage on the excluded pieces, the numbers in parentheses refer to those in the tabular index of the MS.'s contents at the end of this introduction.

(as it has been made by the editor) throws some very interesting light on the history of use and disuse of words.

Two other pieces as naturally excluded from the present edition, are the complete versions the MS. contains of the "**Seven Sages**" (No. 9) and the "**Siege of Rouen**" (42). The proper place for these two is, of course, not a volume like the present, but the respective parallel-text editions, "devoutly to be wish'd," of these well-known poems. The Balliol text of the "Seven Sages" has been fully dealt with in Dr. Killis Campbell's dissertation on this romance; of the "Siege of Rone" it may suffice to say here, that it seems a somewhat careless copy of a fairly good version, and is well worth attention.

Another one of the longer poems of the MS., the verse legend (No. 44) of Pope Gregory's "**Trentale**" (thirty masses) to redeem his mother's soul, adheres generally to the Cotton MS. version of the poem, edited by Dr. Furnivall in the 15th volume of the Society's Original Series.

Fifthly, there are two **Books of Courtesy**; the one of them (No. 46) is a tract on behaviour at table in English verse with a French interlinear translation, and an Anglo-French conversational manual, vocabulary, formulas of letters (see also No. 76), etc., clustering round it: the English verse of this being known (from other MSS.) through the "Babees boke," and the English, together with the French version, from publications in German periodicals. The whole complex, including phrases and vocables, is identical in substance, though not in arrangement, with Wynkyn de Worde's "*lytell treatyse to speke Englysshe and Frenche*" (of which Dr. Oelsner is preparing a reprint for the Society), and being chiefly of lexicographical and phraseological interest, has been published by myself (with some readings of Wynkyn de Worde's and Pynson's prints added) in a German magazine devoted to Modern English Lexicography (Professor Kellner's "*Bausteine*").—The other Book of Courtesy in verse, entitled "*Lytill John,*" has been printed in full, along with Caxton's and an Oriel Coll. MS. version, in the E. E. Text Soc.'s third Extra Series volume.

To these Books of Courtesy we may subjoin the two shorter pieces "*How the wyse man tawght his son*" (No. 59) and "*Stans puer ad mensam*" (60), which, being both well known from various versions printed in the 32nd and other volumes of the Society, have not been thought worth editing here from texts which do not xxx *Poems not printed here. Richard Hill's Prose Pieces.*

exhibit any peculiar and interesting features. As to "*Stans Puer*," in fact, the Balliol text seems to be copied from Caxton's print (see the note on "*Salve Regina*," No. 67 in this volume). The next piece to be mentioned is the lengthy and rather tedious poem of Lydgate "**The Vertues of the Masse**" (No. 55), which, although extant only in a private fifty-copies reprint of Wynkyn de Worde's edition, and being amplified in our MS. by two epilogues, has yet been kept back from this volume (perhaps to the relief of some readers), as being more fit for a collective one of Lydgate's poetry. For the same reason, another long poem by Lydgate, "**The Chorle and the Byrde**" (No. 67), easily accessible in Halliwell's selection, from whose version the Balliol one differs in the main only by the absence of one stanza, does not appear here.

Another piece (which Coxe ascribed to Lydgate) possesses a certain interest as presenting a transitional stage midway between the common Middle-English allegorical vision and the early Modern English dramatic Morality (No. 85); it has been printed from a fuller text than the incomplete Balliol one, in Dr. Furnivall's "Hymns to the Virgin and Christ" under the title "**The Bids of Virtues and Vices for the Soul of Man**."

Finally, the poem justly termed by Professor Flügel "the pearl of Hill's whole collection," being probably the earliest extant complete text of "**The Nutbrown mayde**" (No. 106), must be supposed to be within easy reach of the reader, having been printed, together with the Percy Folio version, in Furnivall and Hales's edition of it. Hill may have copied it during his residence at Antwerp (cf. p. xv), from Arnold's Chronicle (printed there about 1502).

In concluding this section, I may note that I possess transcripts of some of these pieces excluded from the present volume, and intend to publish them occasionally.

We now pass to the **prose contents** of Hill's MS. It may be said at once that they are a perfect mine of materials for the history of English commerce, statistics, popular medicine, social and religious life, customs, sports and amusements, and that a miscellaneous volume of them, to match the present poetical one, could not fail to be of the highest interest to the student of English *realia*.

To give a characterising general survey of these mixed entries, we must divide them into subject-groups.

The Prose Pieces and Entries in Richard Hill's MS. xxxi

Firstly, then, of prose pieces of a **literary** character, the MS. contains but one, which appears at its very beginning: the tale of **Godfridus of Rome** and his three sons from the "Gesta Romanorum" (No. 4), well known as the germ of the *Fortunatus* story, adhering, in the Balliol text, rather closely to the bottom-page one (Addit. MS. 9066) in Herrtage's edition.

A second class is formed by two long **treatises** in English prose, both on practical subjects: the one **on the Managing and Breaking of Horses** (No. 7), the other " **of graffyng** " **Trees** (37), this last of the same kind as, though longer than the Porkington one in Halliwell's Warton Club Miscellany. Apart from the interest they possess for the history of the matters they treat of, they would also be of considerable lexicographical value for the technical terms of both arts.

The extensive group of **Religious and ecclesiastical** entries (for the most part in Latin) consists of: No. 2 (Latin Graces, edited in the "Babees Book" volume, and most ingeniously disentangled there by the late Henry Bradshaw), 6 (a list of Feasts, and Rules for Curates), 40 (" Tabila Cristiane religionis," a Latin treatise of nine pages), 41 (a Latin verse paraphrase of the Ten Commandments), 77 (Formulas for Questions to be asked by the Confessor), 91 (a Latin Prayer by St. Augustine), 112 (a list, apparently unfinished, of London Parish-Churches), and, finally, odd jottings down of biblical names at the bottom of fol. 165 v° (" Ést tuus, Anna, patér Izacár, Nasaphát tua máter ") and 221 v° (" Rebecca. Sefora. Abigina. Susanna. Zael ").

The class naturally largest and most interesting in a London citizen's household book, is formed of the **commercial** entries, fully illustrative of weights, measures, prices, trades and their regulations, business statistics, arithmetic and correspondence. They are the following: No. 1 (places where fairs are kept, and their days); 25 (statistics of a taxation); 26 (the size of "tall-wood "—see Halliwell's Dictionary—and Essex billets in London); 27 (some general statistics of England) ; 31 (two forms for Letters of Attorney) ; 34 (names of the Crafts officially entered), 35 (extracts from the Statutes of the Realm, being the rules for " craft*is*men vytelers," viz. millers, bakers, brewers, butchers, fishers, cooks and innkeepers) ; connected with these, the ordinances for bakers (36) ; and in conjunction with these xxxii *The Prose Pieces, Recipes, &c., in Richard Hill's MS.*

again, the copious statistics on the Size of Bread in London (37); 78 (a large bulk of notes on Weights, Coins, Prices of different wares, chiefly Wool, with a pictorial table of Merchants' Stamps, mysteriously called "*The Cures of Mader*," at the end); immediately following this (79), a long treatise on *Agryme* or *Algorysme*, i.e. arithmetic, chiefly commercial; 90 (a Table of Weights, and a "Reckoning of Lead" with a table), 109 (Regulations for Taverners), 114 ("a good Remembrans & Knowlage of þe pownd troy weight" and its difference in England and Flanders), and finally, the memorandum at the bottom of fol. 225 v°, on what $\frac{2}{3}$, $\frac{5}{8}$, $\frac{5}{15}$ of a shilling come to.

The two entries illustrative of **customs and manners** strictly, No. 28 (household stuff used at the Lord Mayor's banquet) and 92 (Rules of precedence in going or sitting) have both appeared in the Society's "Early Meals and Manners" volume.

Another class are **encyclopaedic** notes on things considered curious or useful to know (*de omni re scibili*), such as the Seven Ages of the World and of Man (No. 24), the four "Complexions" or Temperaments (74, Latin verses; No. 110 in section VI of this volume); 80 (a jumble of Rules for cipher-writing and miscellaneous notes), 84 (a *calendarium saeculare*) and 115 (names of Christian Monarchs).

The seventh group is formed of household **medical receipts**, plentifully interspersed over top and bottom nooks and corners, and spare pages; the numbers are (with the diseases in brackets): 33 (indigestion), 43 (paralysis), 45b (tooth-ache), 47 (stone), 72 ("for a cutt"), 83a (for a woman with child), 113 (sciatica, etc.), 116 and 117 (*diversa*), 122b (*pro vene*[no]*so aere pestilencie*; cf. sub 48: "For the pestelence"); 146 (*diversa*, partly pale and effaced; last leaf of the MS.).—To these, we may add some veterinary receipts, mostly mingled up with those for men: 36 (for a 'fowndyd'—rectè 'fownderyd'?—and over-ridden horse), 48a (for a poisoned dog), and the first three items of 146 (for horses again).

Besides medical, there are **chemical, cooking** and other household precepts, such as: No. 5 (to brew beer, etc., see index), 30 (an "oyle" and an "oyntment" for harness), cf. 123 (to scour mail-harness), 82 (to colour water divers ways, to colour and inlay cloth, etc.), 83b (to make green ginger and "soryppe" [syrup]), 95 (to make ink), 110 (to kill rats), 128 ("to mak water lyme").

Lastly, as a ninth group, there are arithmetical **puzzles, riddles, tricks** with cards and other amusements of the kind : Nos. 45a, 58 (puzzles), 75 ("St. Thomas' lots," the same superscription to 121), 93 (a trick with cards), 94 (puzzles partly written in ciphers, cf. the first group of proverbs in section VI of this vol.), 108 ("*mirabilia*"; various tricks), 111 (card-tricks), 119 (riddles), 122a, 124, 125, 126 (puzzles).

The **language** of a collection like Hill's, being a modern transcript made without care for strict uniformity, of late Middle-English and early Modern English texts from the most multifarious sources, probably very different in spelling, word-forms, and age, would not seem capable of comprehensive systematic treatment in a separate chapter of the Introduction. Some of the more frequent or consistent peculiarities of spelling (such as *a* for *o* in protonic prefixes; the constant exchange between *w* and *v*) will be found recorded in the glossarial and the textual notes on the most striking cases.

The text of the MS., rendered quite faithfully (except capitals and punctuation) without any emendatory alterations, will be found evidently corrupt or unintelligible in several passages, some of which I was obliged to leave unexplained. The notes given at the end, before the glossary, consist chiefly of parallel texts and different readings from modern publications of ancient poetical collections resembling that of Richard Hill.

TABLE OF CONTENTS

of the Balliol MS. 354.

In *Anglia*, vol. XXVI (*neue Folge*, XIV) 1903, p. 94-285, Prof. Ewald Flügel has published a descriptive account of the MS., with annotated texts of what are, in the following index, Nos. 3, 21, 22, 23, 29, 46 (*Boke of Curtasie* only), 49, 50, 51, 52, 53, 54, 61, 62, 63, 65, 66, 68, 69, 71, 73, 87, 88, 89 (partly), 96, 98, 99, 100, 102, 103, 104, 105, 107 (partly), 118, 119 (partly), 120 *a–zz* (except *s*), 131-145. Other publications of single pieces from this and other MSS. are referred to in the bibliographical notes of the following list, where also all those that appear in the present volume, are marked with asterisks (*) and cross-references indicating their place in the book. The numbering of the pieces in Coxe's *Catalogus codicum MSS. collegii Balliolensis* (= *C.*), where different from mine, and the pagination of the MS., where showing any peculiarities, are recorded in brackets. Beginning and end of each piece are given. Where a piece has no title in the MS., its contents are indicated in square brackets [ ].

1. fol. 1ᵃ rº– The cheff placis wher faires be kept in Ynglond.
   1ᵃ vº   *Beg.*: ... in die catthedra sancti Petri at seynt Nedis.
   End: ... in the wedynsday in esterwek Huchyn.

2. fol. 2ᵃ rº– The grace þat shuld be said affore mete & after
   2ᵃ vº.   mete | all the tymes in the yere.
   Beg.: Benedicite. Dominus. Oculi enim in te sperant Domine.
   End: Benedicamus domino. Deo gracias.
   Printed E. E. T. S., orig. ser. 32, p. 382-396 (*with scheme of arrangement by Henry Bradshaw*).

3. fol. 3ᵃ rº– The table of the contentis within this bok whiche
   4ᵃ vº   is a boke of dyueris tales & balettis & dyueris
   (*fol. 3 inverted*)   reconyngis, etc.
   Beg.: First the tale of Godfridus of Rome & his III sonnes ff. I.
   End: ¶ Item to make gren gynger and þe seroppe ff. CLXXXI.

4. fol. 1 rº-3 vº [*The tale of Godfridus of Rome and his three sons*].
   (*here MS. pagination sets in; a recent one goes on with "5-7"*)   *Beg.*: Godfrydus regned in Rome that had III sonnes.
   End: ... he leved after in joy & endid his lyf in pease. Explicit.
   Printed in Herrtage's edition of "The Early English Versions of the Gesta Romanorum"

Contents of Richard Hill's Balliol MS. 354.   xxxv

(*E. E. T. S., Extra Series,* 33, p. 180 f.) *from MS. Harl.* 7333 *and Addit.* 9066 (*to which latter the Balliol MS. adheres more closely*), *with variations of Kk.* I. 6. *Cambr. The "Moralite" is omitted in Ball.*

5. fol. 3 v°–5 r°
(*recent pagination* 7 [v°] -9)

The crafte to brewe bere.—The costis to make sope.—The craft to make a water to haue spottis owt of wollen clothe.—The form of mesure to mete londe by.—To make vynegre shortly.—To make parseley grow in an owr space able for to cutte.—Reynysshe wyne.—The reconyng of wyne a burdeux.—The craft to make gunpowder.—The weight of Exsex & Suffolk chese in Ynglong & þe weight in Andwarpe & Barowgh.—The costis to mak heryng & sprottis at the coste.—To mak red sprottis at þe coste.—The maner to make ynke.— To make a pekyll to kepe fresshe storgen.—A reseyte for ypocras.—For clary.—The craft to make ypocras. —The craft to make clary.—The craft to make braket.—The craft to make orchall for dyers.—The craft to make cork for dyers.—The maner of weight & bying of iron.

6. fol. 5 v°– 6 v°
(*rec. pag.* 9, 10, *and stops*)

"In hac tabula continentur festa *et* dies pro quibus singulis diebus ciues *et* inhabitantes ciuitatis London *et* suburborum eiusdem deo *et* curatis singulis annis offerre teneantur," *together with rules and ordinances for curates.*

7. fol. 7 r°– 13 v°
(*follows blank page, numbered* ff xvi,*on the other side modern farmer's entries of* 1731.)

The boke of merchalsie (*title about the middle of first page, preceded by passage on* "propertees" *of the horse*). ("*Treatise on the breaking and managing of horses, with medicines and modes of treatment.*" *Coxe.*)
Beg.: An hors hathe XXV propertees wherof he hath IIII of a lyon (*etc., half a page, then*:) The boke of merchalsie here shall begyn . . .
End: " . . . and mase (?) it fayre a way with þe hete" (*in* "Capitulum XVᵐ: For to do a way þe lampas.").

8. fol. 17 r°–v° The birth of children of me Richard Hill, *etc.* (*see introduction, p. xiii*).
Beg.: a° 1518. Mᵈ þat John Hill my first child was borne . . .
End: . . . but he occupieth as a fruterer.

9. fol. 18 r°– 54 v°
Here begynneth þe prologes of the VII sagis or VII wise masters which were named as here after followith.
Beg.: In olde days ther was a man.
End: Amen amen for charyte. Thus endith of the VII sages of Rome which was drawen owt of crownycles & owt of wrytyng of old men & many a notable tale is ther in as ys beffore sayde. Quod Richard Hill.

xxxvi   *Contents of Richard Hill's Balliol MS. 354.*

	(See Killis Campbell, *A study of the Romance of the Seven Sages with special reference to the Middle English versions*, Publ. of the Mod. Lang. Assoc. of America, vol. XIV [new series VII], p. 1–117; vide p. 39 f., p. 60 f.).
10.–20. (and 70)	[*A selection of stories from Gower's "Confessio Amantis."*]
	See "*The English Works of John Gower*," ed. by G. C. Macaulay (E. E. T. S., Extra Ser. 81 f.), introduction, p. clxvi.
10. fol. 55 r°– 70 v°	The tale of Antiochus and Appolynes of Tyre. *Beg.:* Of a Cronyque in dayes gon. *End:* For many a man thorow fals lust his lyf hath lore. (*Gower, C. A.*, ed. Macaulay, VIII, 271–2028.)
11. fol. 70 v°– 79 r°	The tale of Tybory Constantyne, Ytaly his wyf & his dowghter Constance. *Beg.:* A worthy kynge of Cristis lawe. *End:* Which to this matere is accordynge. (*G., C. A.*, II, 587–1612.)
12. fol. 79 r°– 81 v°	The tale of Phylip of Masedown kyng & his two sonnes Demetrius & Perseus. *Beg.:* In a Crownyk as ye shall wytt. *End:* Or ellis for sothe ye be not wyse. Explicit. (*G., C. A.*, II, 1613–1865.)
13. fol. 81 v°– 83 v°	The tale of Adryan of Rome & Bardus the pore man. *Beg.:* To speke of on vnkynd man. *End:* And every trewe creature it hateth. (*G., C. A.*, V, 4937–5162.)
14. fol. 83 v°– 84 v°	The tale of Pyrotous & Ypotasie þe fayre mayde. (*incl. Galba and Vitellius*). *Beg.:* This fynd I wrytt in poiesy. *End:* And so shalt þou kepe the best from payn. (*G., C. A.*, VI, 485–595.)
15. fol. 84 v°– 86 v°	The tale howe pore Lazar lay at the lordis gate. *Beg.:* Of Cristis word who so it rede. *End:* Hath made full many a wise man erre. (*G., C. A.*, VI, 975–1238.)
16. fol. 86 v°– 89 v°	The tale of Constantyne the gret emperowr. *Beg.:* A monge the bokes of Latyne. *End:* Gode geve vs grace that to attayn. (*G., C. A.*, I, 3187–3507.)
17. fol. 89 v°– 91 v°	The tale of Nabeghodonosor howe he dremed of the grett tree. *Beg.:* Ther was a kynge of myche myght. *End:* Hit shall down fall & over throwe. (*G., C. A.*, I, 2785–3066.)
18. fol. 91 v°– 93 r°	The tale of kyng Alysander þat cam to Diagynes wher he sat in his tonn.

Contents of Richard Hill's Balliol MS. 354.

        Beg.: A philosiphre of which men told.
        End: Which vs be hoveth for to wit.
        (*G.*, *C. A.*, III, 1201–1330.)

19. fol. 93 r°– 94 v°   The tale of Pyram*us* & Thesbee which slew th*em* self vpon *on* swerd.
        Beg.: I rede a tale & tellith this.
        End: But cawsith a man to fall in rage.
        (*G.*, *C. A.*, III, 1331–1502, 1655-1672; *printed from the Balliol MS. by E. Flügel in "Anglia"* XII, 16 ff.)

20. fol. 94 v°– 96 r°   The tale of kyng Mide how all þat he towched was gold (*unfinished, 3½ pp. left blank*).
        Beg.: Bachus which is the god of wyne.
        End: To gold they torne all at ones.
        (*G.*, *C. A.*, V, 141–312.)

*21. fol. 98 r°– 100 v° (108 *in the* (*present vol.*)   Jak & his stepdame & of the frere.
        Beg.: God that died for vs all.
        End: Holy God in his empere.
        Printed: 1. *from Porkington MS. in Hallivell's Early Engl. Miscellanies (Warton Club, 1855)*; 2. *from a Cambridge MS. in Th. Wright's "The tale of the Basyn and The Frere and the Boy," London, Pickering, 1836;* 3. *from the Percy Folio MS. in Furnivall-Hales's edition (vol.* IV); 4. *from MS. Rawlinson C.* 86 *by J. Zupitza, Herrig's Archiv,* 90, 56 ff.—*From early prints (of Wynkyn de Worde, E. Allde, and others, on which see Zupitza and Flügel*), *in*: 5. *Ritson's Pieces of Ancient Popular Poetry,* 1791, *and* 6. *Hazlitt's Remains of Early Popular Poetry,* III, 54.—7. *From the Balliol MS., with readings of all m o d e r n editions: Anglia* 26, 104 ff. (*E. Flügel, see above*).

*22. fol. 100 v° (106 *in present vol.*)   [*Rules for purchasing land.*]
        Beg.: Who so will beware in purchasynge.
        End: Þou shalt a gayn thy money see.
        Printed from MS. Lambeth 306, *fol.* 203, *in E. E. T. S., orig. ser.* vol. 15, p. 24 (*also on* p. xxvi *of J. Gairdner's introduction to "Three Fifteenth-Century Chronicles," Camden Soc., new ser. No.* 28).

*23. fol. 101 r°– v° (89 *in present vol.*)   A treatise of wyne.
        Beg.: The best tre yf ye take entent.
        End: Vbi non siscient amplius.
        Printed from Wright's MS. (now Eng. Poet. e. 1., *Bodl.*) *in his " Songs and Carols" (Percy Soc.,* 23) p. 53 ff.; *the Balliol version partly in Flügel's "Neuenglisches Lesebuch," p.* 149.

24. fol. 101 v°– 102 r°   Þe VII ages of þe world from Adam forward. The VII ages of man lyveyng in the world.

xxxviii   *Contents of Richard Hill's Balliol MS. 354.*

         Beg.: In the begynnyng god made hevyn & erth.
         End: The VIIth age ys crepill & lastith vnto dethe.

25. fol. 102 r°– v°   The charge of euery ward in London at a XV.
         Beg.: The ward of Chepe taxed in London at LXXII£. XVIs. & in þe escheker alowed LXXII£.
         End: The sum of the hole XV taxed in London XICXVIII marke Vs. IIIId. & in the cheker accomptid for XIC marke.—The sum of a hole XV in Ynglond ys XXXVIII M¹.IXCXXX£ IXs. Explicit.

26. fol. 103 r°   The assise of talewode & Essex billet in London.
         Beg.: First þat talewood hold & conteyn in length. . . .
         End: . . . the said bilet of on shide *etc.*

27. fol. 103 r°   The nombre of parishe chirches townes bisshoperiches & sheres in Ynglond & þe compas of the londe.
         Beg.: Ther ben in Ynglond of parishe chirches . . .
         End: . . . a bowte III M¹CCCLX myles.

28. fol. 103 r°– v°   Here folowith suche howshold stuff as must nedis be occupied at þe mayres fest yerely kepte at þe Yelde hall *(margin:* þe butlers charge*).*
         Beg.: First V diaper table clothes.
         End: for þe hire VIIId. þe garnyshe of pewter.
         Printed *E. E. T. S., orig. ser.* 32, p. 378-380.

*29. fol. 103 r°– 106r° (72 *in present vol.*)   The wordis of Fortune to þe peple *(by Sir Thomas More).*
         Beg.: Myne high estate power & auctoryte.
         End: As ar þe jugementis of astronomye.
         Printed in the folio edition of More's English Works, 1557, and recently, from a copy in Lambeth Palace Library, in Huth-Hazlitt's " Fugitive Poetical Tracts " (priv. prtd., 1875), first ser. (1493–1600), No. XIII.

fol. 106 v°   The ordinance for þe assise & weight of bred in þe cite of London *(three paragraphs, crossed through; marginal reference* "post fol. CXVIII," *where indeed the piece is found [No.* 39 *below]).*

30. fol. 106 v°   An oyle for harnes.—An oyntment for harnes.
         Beg.: Take a penyworth of oyle.
         End: " and than put wex & rosen þer to and let it be still *etc.*"

31. *(Coxe under* 30*)* fol. 106 v°– 107 r°   The forme of makyng of letters of attorney.—An oþer letter of attorney.
         Beg.: Be it knowen to all men by theis presentis. . . .
         End: . . . to relece & quytaunce make of & vpon þe premisses *etc.*

Contents of Richard Hill's Balliol MS. 354. xxxix

*32. (Coxe 31) fol. 107 r°
(see introduction, p. xi)
: The day of my hanseyng at Barow (*and other personal memoranda of Richard Hill*).
Beg.: M^d that I was hansed at Barow.
End: and þer I paid to M. wardens clark & bedell IIIs. Xd. st.

33. (om. Coxe) fol. 107 r°
: To clarifie the stomacke (*receipt*, 7 *lines*).
Beg.: Take a quantitie of vineger.
End: & with the grace of god it will healpe thee.

34. (32 C.) fol. 107 v°
: Thes ben the names of all þe craftis of euery mistere named abled & enuellyd in þe chambre of London as her after seryously it appereth | in primus (*follow names of 75 crafts, then* "vacue sunt iste" *and* 16 *names more*).
Beg.: Mercers | Grocers | Drapers | . . .
End: Mylwrightis | Tanners | Stryngers |

35. (C. 32) fol. 108 r°–v°
: Here folow parte of þe statutes of Ynglond how euery craftisman vyteler shall be ruled. — Myllers.— Bakers.— Brewers.— Bochers.— Fishers.— Cookis.— Inholders.
Beg.: Myllers. First þe sise of þe myller is . . .
End: . . . pillary & after to forswer þe towne.

36. (om. C.) fol. 108 v°
: For a hors þat is fowndyd & ouer ridyn þat his skyn clevith to his sidis (*receipt*, 8 *lines*).
Beg.: Take venecryk (?) long peper | grens & lycoris . . .
End: & with in XXIIII owris it shall ease hym.

37. (C. 33) fol. 109 r°–117 r°
: Of graffyng ("*Treatise on graffyng trees, compiled from different authors*," *Coxe, who quotes names of the different authors from the MS.*).
Beg.: The maner of tretise is manyfold and so comyn þat at the tyme . . .
End: . . . to haue a gardeyn in shorte tyme etc.
Explicit quod Richard Hill.

38. (C. 34) fol. 117 r°– v°
: An ordynance for bakers.
Beg.: By þe discrecion & ordynance of owr lorde þe kyng . . .
End: . . . & þat oþer half to þe vse of þe master of þe bakers.

39. (C. 35) fol. 118 r°–122 r°
: The assise of Bred with in London.
Beg.: The quarter whet at IIIs. | after Vs.
End: for euery XXd. 1 oz. for euery Xd. ½ oz. and so forthe.

40. (C. 36) fol. 122 r°–126 r°
: Tabila Cristiane religionis valde vtilis et necessaria cuilibet Christiano: quam omnes scire tenentur (*in Latin*).
Beg.: "Vltima enim sunt hec," etc. "Diffinicio articuli fidei. Articulus fidei," etc.
End: ". . . per tuam misericordiam libera nos. | Explicit tabula ad Christiane religionis disciplinam."

41. (C. 37) fol. 126 r°–127 r°
: Isti sunt versus continentes X precepta legis (*Latin hexameters*).

Beg.: "Primum preceptum: vnum cole deum. Qui colit extra deum sanctos quodcumque creatum" etc.
End: Demum mandatum: nec rem cupias alienam. Explicit.
(*Blank of one page and a half.*)

42. (*C.* 38) fol. 128 r°–138 v° The siege of Rone.
Beg.: God that dyed vpon a tree.
End: Say we all Amen for charyte.
Edited: (1) *ll.* 1–955, *from MS.* "*Bodl.* 124" (?), *by Conybeare in* "*Archaeologia*" *XXI,* p. 48 ff.; (2) *ll.* 636–1312, *from MS. Harl.* 2256 (*with readings of Harl.* 753, *and notes*) *by Sir F. Madden,* "*Archaeologia*" *XXII,* 361 ff.; (3) *a very mutilated version* (*incomplete*) *from the Percy Folio MS.: Furnivall-Hales, III,* 533–541; (4) *the complete version from MS. Egerton* 1995 (*with chief readings of some others*) *by J. Gairdner in* "*The Historical Collections of a Citizen of London in the XV*th *Century*" (*Camden Soc., new ser.* 17; 1876).

43. (*om. C.*) fol. 138 v°, *bottom* For anybody þat is takyn in þe on side all lame & sumwhat swart & thowgh he haue yelow pympilles (*receipt,* 6 *lines*).
Beg.: Tak oyle of camamyll, & oyle of dyll . . .
End: . . . "and vse this tyll he be hole, *etc.*"

44. (*C.* 39) fol. 139 r°–140 v° Trentale Sancti Gregorii pape.
Beg.: I fynde wretyn a noble story.
End: Amen amen for charyte. Explicit Trentale Sancti Gregorii (*ferocious comment at bottom of page:* This talle of pope gregorius is a lye & þat a monsterows on a decea-... [*rest illegible, lower half of third line cut off; Flügel reads:* . . . -uer of Sathan to deceave him or a devise of his owne . . .]).
Printed: (1) *from MS. Cotton, Caligula A* II (*with chief variations of Lambeth* 306) *by Dr. Furnivall, E. E. T. S., orig. ser.* 15, p. 83; (2) *in two versions, from* 5 *MSS., by Dr. A. Kaufmann, Erlanger Beiträge zur engl. Philologie II,—the version A, to which the Balliol text belongs, being Furnivall's Cotton one, collated with two copies in the Vernon MS., and the Lambeth MS.*

45. (*om. C.*) fol. 140 v°, *bottom* (*a*) Questyon. I by IC shepe for IC s^t. what is þat a shepe? (!)
(*b*) For the tothe ache (5 *lines*).
End: lay ye down on the same side.

46. fol. 141 r°–141 v° (*a*) (*C.* 40) [*Phrases and vocables in English and French*].

Contents of Richard Hill's Balliol MS. 354. xli

fol. 142 r⁰–143 r⁰   (b) (C. 41) The boke of curtasie (in Engl. verse, with French interlinear translation; Anglo-French vocables written along the margin).

fol. 143 v⁰   (c) (om. C.) [Formula of a business letter (see also No. 76), in English and French, and names of wares in the two tongues.]

a.	b.	c.
Beg.: vng. 1	Litill children here may ye lerne. . . .	Right worshippull Sire . . .
End: a sleve | vng mance	& in his last end with þe swete Jhesus | et en la dereniere fin auec le doux Jhesus. Here endith þe boke of Curtasie.	& resonabli profer hym þat they be worthe.

Printed: (1) "the boke of curtasye" from MSS. Harl. 541, and Egerton 1995, on the even pages from 16 to 24, of Dr. Furnivall's "Babees boke" (E.E.T.S., orig. ser. 32); from an Edinb. MS. (with description and readings of other MSS. and early prints) by Prof. K. Breul, "Engl. Studien," 9, 51; from the Balliol MS. "Anglia" 26, 151 (Flügel);—(2) the whole complex from the Balliol MS. (collated with W. de Worde's and R. Pinson's substantially identical booklets) by R. Dyboski in Prof. Kellner's "Bausteine, Zeitschrift für neuenglische Wortforschung" (Berlin, Langenscheidt, 1906, vol. I, 329–352).

47. (om. C.) fol. 143 v⁰, bottom.

A medycyne for þe stone (6 lines).–For þe stone (6 lines).
Beg.: Tak saxnifrage \| philypendela . . .
End: "& drynk it with ale or wyne etc."

48. (om. C.) (seven small leaves, half the length of the other, two of them written upon, rest blank, inserted [do not affect the MS. pagination]).

A medicen for a doge that ys poysent (6+3 lines).— Some reckoning of 6 "agges."—(fol. v⁰) For the pestelence (22 lines).
Beg.: Take a pece of chesse as myche as a good wall nott.
End: this shall saue hym by the grace of Gode a men.

*49. (C. 42) fol. 144 r⁰ (63 in pres. vol.)

To þe gud angell.
Beg.: O angell dere wher euer I go.
End: To þe plesaunce of god both day & nyght.

*50. (C. 43) fol. 144 r⁰–145 r⁰ (64 in pres. vol.)

[Miserere mei deus.]
Beg.: O dere god pereles prince of pece.
End: Off miserere mei deus.

*51. (C. 44) fol. 145 r⁰–146 r⁰ (65 in pres. vol.)

['Verses to the Father, and the Virgin,' Coxe. Burden: marcy lorde & gramarcy.]
Beg.: As I walked here by west.
End: With marcy lorde & gramarcy.

xlii   *Contents of Richard Hill's Balliol MS. 354.*

*52. (C. 44)   [*Verses on the Sacrament of Matrimony.*   Burden :
fol. 146 r°–v°   Quod deus coniunxit homo non separet]
(70 in pres. vol.)   *Beg.:* Benedicta sit sancta trinitas.
                           End: Quod deus coniunxit homo non separet.

*53. (C. 44)   [*Two hymns to the Virgin:*]
fol.146 v°–147 v°   (a) Hayle lovely lady laymand so lyght.
(66 in pres. vol.)   (b) Hayle be thow Mary moder of Cryst.
                                     a.   b.
                           Beg.: Hayle lovely lady.   Hayle be thow Mary.
                           End: Salue sancta parens. Pro salute fidelium.
                           (b) *Printed from Lambeth MS. 853 in Dr.
                           Furnivall's " Hymns to the Virgin and Christ,"
                           E. E. T. S., orig. ser.* 24 [1867, 1895], *p.* 4, 5.

*54. (C. 44)   Man yff thou a wyseman arte (14 *lines*).
fol. 147 v°   *Beg.:* Man yff thou . . .
(107 in pres. vol.)   *End:* They will bryng the behynde.

55. (C. 45)   [*Lydgate's Poem on the Virtues of the Mass (with
fol. 148 r°–155 v°   prologue and two epilogues).*]
                           Beg.: O ye folkis all which haue devocion.
                           End: Which for your sake werid a crown of
                              thorn. Amen.
                              *Printed (from an old edition by Wynkyn de
                              Worde) in " Fugitive Tracts written in verse,
                              which illustrate the condition of religious
                              and political feeling in England and the
                              state of society there during two centuries."
                              First series,* 1493–1600 (*ed. Huth-Hazlitt,
                              London* 1875, *privately printed*).

*56. (C. 46)   Incipit [" Revertere."]
fol. 155 v°   *Beg.:* In a tyme of a somers day.
(73 in pres. vol.)   *End:* And than ys best Revertere.   Explicit
                              Revertere.
                              *Printed in a fuller version from Lambeth MS.
                              853 in Furnivall's " Hymns to the Virgin
                              and Christ,"* 1867 (1895) (*E. E. T. S., orig.
                              ser.* 24), *p.* 91.

*57. (C. 46)   [*Two fragments of poems,* 6+4 *stanzas*]
fol. 156 r°–v°   *Beg.:* As I gan wandre in on evenyng
(74 in pres. vol.)   *End:* & hevyn blis shall be your mede.
                           Explicit know thi self (wysely I red *added in paler
                              ink*).

58. (om. C.)   A questyon (*arithmetical puzzle*).
fol. 156 v°,   *Beg.:* Item I bidde my felow lay III rowys of
bottom   cownters.
                           End: . . . " and ther livith 9, etc."

59. (om. C.)   How the wyse man tawght his son.
fol. 157 r°–158 r°.   *Beg.:* Lystyn lordyngis & ye shall here.
                           End: That for vs bare a crown of thorn.
                           Explicit how the wyse man tawght his son.
                              Printed : (1) *E. E. T. S., orig. ser.* 32 (*Babees
                              boke*), *p.* 48–52 (*see Forewords, p.* lxxi), *from
                              MS. Lambeth* 853 ; (2) *in three versions,*

Contents of Richard Hill's Balliol MS. 354.

        in R. Fischer's dissertation, "Erlanger Beiträge zur engl. Philologie," II; readings of Balliol text given in footnotes to text β (p. 35–42).

60. (C. 47)   Stans puer ad mensam.
fol. 158 v°–159 r°   *Beg.:* My dere chyld fyrst thy self inabel.
       End: Yff owght be amys put þe fawte in Lydgate.
         Printed: (1) *from MS. Jesus Coll., Cambr. Q.* Γ. 8, *in "Reliquiae Antiquae"* I, 156 ; (2) *from MSS. Harl.* 2251 *and Lambeth* 853, *on pp.* 26–33 *of E. E. T. S., orig. ser.* 32 (*Babees boke*) ; (3) *from Ashmole MS.* 61 *in E. E. T. S., extra ser.* VIII, 56–64 ; (4) *On Caxton's old print, see Blades, Life and Typography of W. Caxton* (1861), II, 49.

*61. (om. C.)   [*Rhyming rules,* 5 *lines.*]
fol. 159 v°, top   *Beg.:* Aryse erly | serve god devoutly.
(108 *in pres. vol.*)   *End:* And be ther jocondly | slepe suerly.
         Printed by Caxton together with No. 60.

*62. (C. 48)   An holy salue regina in englisshe.
fol. 159 v°   *Beg.:* Salue with obeysance to god in humblesse.
(67 *in pres. vol.*)   *End:* Salue ever as fayer as we can suffyce.
         Printed by Caxton together with No. 60.

(om. C.)   [*Four verses on Mary.*]
fol. 159 v°,   *Beg.:* Wytt hath wonder & kynde ne can.
bottom   *End:* For myght hath maystry & skyll goth vnder. Laus deo.
         Similar verses, in English and Latin, printed in "Reliquiae Antiquae," p. 127 (*Sloane MS.* 3534), 205 (*Harl.* 541), 257 (*Bodl.* 623).— *Also in Caxton's print.*

*63. (om. C.)   [*Verses on wealth.*]
fol. 160 r°   *Beg.:* Who so off welth takyth non hede.
(109 *in pres. vol.*)   *End:* Yff þou knyté or þou know than yt ys to late.

(*No.* 60–63 *incl. probably a wholesale transcript of Caxton's quarto volume, described by Blades, Life and Typography of W. C.* (1861–3), II, 49–51.)

64. (C. 49)   Here begynnyth lytill John.
fol. 160 r°–165 r°   *Beg.:* Lytell John sith your tender enfancye.
       End: Kepe your quayre þat yt be not ther bayte.—Here endyth a lytyll treatyse called þe boke of curtesy or litill John.
         Printed (with Caxton's Text and an Oriel MS. version) in vol. III *of the E. E. T. S.'s Extra Series.*

*65. (C. 50)   [*A ballad.*]
fol. 165 v°   *Beg.:* Lully lulley lully lulley | þe fawcon hath
(86 *in pres. vol.*)   born my mak away.
       End: Corpus Christi wretyn þer on.
         Printed in Flügel's "Neuenglisches Lesebuch," p. 142.

xliv   *Contents of Richard Hill's Balliol MS. 354.*

*66. (C. 51)
fol. 165 v°
(No. 1 in pres. vol.)

[Song] "Owt of þe est . . ." (headlines and burden: Be mery all þat be present | Omnes de Saba venient).
Beg.: Owt of þe est a sterre shon bright.
End: That on the rode was rent.
Printed in Flügel's "Neuenglisches Lesebuch," p. 122.

67. (C. 52)
fol. 166 r°–169 v°

Þe chorle & þe byrde (by Lydgate).
Beg.: Problemes of olde lyknes & fygvres.
End: With supportacion of hys benyngnyte.
Printed from MS. Harl. 116, on pp. 179–193 of Halliwell's "Selection from the Minor Poems of Lydgate," Percy Soc. II (1840) (stanzas 49 and 50 wanting in the Balliol MS.).
Two old prints by Caxton, see Blades' work, II, 60-61.

*68. (C. 53)
fol. 169 v°–170 v°
(83 in pres. vol.)

The lamentacion of the duches of Glossester (title in margin).
Beg.: Thorow owt a pales as I can passe.
End: All women may be ware by me (burden).
Printed in Th. Wright's "Political Poems and Songs . . . from the Accession of Edw. III to that of Ric. III" (Chronicles and Memorials of Great Britain and Ireland, vol. XIV, 1861); II, 205-208; see his Introduction, p. liii.

*69. (C. 54)
fol. 170 v°–171 v°
(75 in pres. vol.)

On a dere day (burden "Fortis vt mors dileccio").
Beg.: On a dere day by a dale so depe.
End: Fortis vt mors dileccio.

70. (C. 55)
fol. 171 v°–175 r°

["The Three Questions".]
Beg.: A kynge sumtyme was yonge & wyse.
End: Now god þat dyed on a tre | Geve vs grace no worse to be | Amen amen for charyte.
Gower, Confessio Amantis, I, 3067–3402 (ed. Macaulay), see above, No. 10 ff.

*71. (C. 56)
fol. 175 r°–176 r°
(84 in pres. vol.)

The lamytacion off quene Elyzabeth (with an epitaph in Latin and English added).
Printed in the blackletter folio of Sir Thomas More's English Works, 1557, on fol. 4 and 5.
Beg.: Ye þat put your trust in confydence.
End: & owr Kyng Hary long lyff & pease.
Explicit. Iste liber pertineth Rycardo Hill seruant to M. Wynger alderman of London.

*72. (om. C.)
fol. 176 r°, bottom

A good medycyne for a cutt.
Beg.: Take a pynte of good ale.
End: make þer of plasters & lay to it etc.

*73 (C. 57)
fol. 176 r°–178 v°
(73 a = No. 2 in the pres. vol.)

[Songs, religious and profane.]
(a) Fayre maydyn (burden: Mater ora filium vt post hoc exilium | Nobis donet gaudium beatorum omnium).
Beg.: Fayre maydyn who is this barn.
End: In hevyn on high to haue a place.

Contents of Richard Hill's Balliol MS. 354. xlv

(73 b = No. 3 in pres. vol.)
    Printed in Flügel's "Neuenglisches Lesebuch" (Halle 1895), p. 111.
(b) Vpon a lady (burden: Newell newell newell newell | I thank a maydyn euery dele).
    Beg.: Vpon a lady fayre & bright.
    End: For on her I thynk & say right nowght.
    Printed "Neuenglisches Lesebuch," p. 126.

(c = 4 in pres. vol.)
(c) As I me walked (burden: Timor mortis conturbat me).
    Beg.: As I me walked in on mornyng.
    End: In what place or contrey can I not say.

(d = 87 in pres. vol.)
(d) As I walked (burden: We shall haue game & sport ynow).
    Beg.: As I walked by a forest side.
    End: How | We shall haue game & sport ynow.
    Printed from the Douce Fragment 94 b, Bodl., of Wynkyn de Worde's Carols of 1521, by E. Flügel in "Anglia," XII, 587.

(e = 5 in pres. vol.)
(e) Diuisie·si affluant | nolite cor apponere (burden: nolite cor apponere).
    Beg.: Yf God send þe plentuowsly riches.
    End: Þerfore þe best þat I can syng or say.

(= 6 in pres. vol.)
(f) Now let vs syng both more & lesse | Of Cristis commyng Deo gracias (burden: deo gracias).
    Beg.: A virgyn pure | this is full sure.
    End: Of Christis commynge Deo gracias.
    Flügel, Neuenglisches Lesebuch, p. 117.

(g = 7 in pres. vol.)
(g) Jhesus autem hodie | egressus est de virgine (burden: Hic est filius meus dilectus ipsum audite).
    Beg.: Whan Jhesu Crist baptised was.
    End: At owr last end we pray þe say than.
    Printed from MS. Add. 5665, Brit. Mus., in "Archiv für das Studium der neueren Sprachen," vol. 106, p. 274 (ed. B. Fehr.)

(h = 88 in pres. vol.)
(h) I haue XII oxen (burden: Sawyste thow not myn oxen þou litill prety boy).
    Beg.: I haue XII oxen þat be fayre & brown.
    End: Sawiste not þou myn oxen þou litill prety boy.
        (a, b, f, g, printed by Flügel in "Festschrift für Rudolf Hildebrand," Leipzig 1894, p. 52 ff.)

*74. (om. C.) fol. 178 vº
(110 in pres. vol.)
Quatuor complexiones hominum (in Latin hexameters).
    Beg.: Largus amans hillaris ridens rubiique coloris.
    End: Frigidus et siccus parum apetit et parum potest.

75. (C. 60) fol. 178 vº
(here MS. pagination stops, and is continued in Arabic figures and modern hand)
Seynt Thomas Lottis (a puzzle).
    Beg.: Post duo. post unum. post tres. composite quinque.
    End: . . . by a preve ye shall knowe.

Contents of Richard Hill's Balliol MS. 354.

76. (C. 61) fol. 179 r°
(old hand: "ff. 7")

[*Formula of a merchant's business letter, in English and French.*]
Beg.: Right dere & wellbelouid gossep.
End: . . . pour lez bons et aggreables seruyces que maves faiz plusyeurs fois. escript etc.
(See No. 46. Edited in Prof. Kellner's "Bausteine.")

77. (C. 62) fol. 179 r°–181 v°
(old hand "ff. 7—ff. 8 —ff. 9")

Interrogaciones et doctrine quibus quilibet sacerdos debiat interrogare suum confitentem.
Beg.: Hec sunt multa vtilia pro confessoribus.
End: . . . postea absoluetur a suis peccatis. Finis deo gracias.

78. (C. 63, 64) fol. 182 r°– 185 v°
("ff. 10, ff. 20, ff. 30, ff. 40")

[*Table of weights.*]—[*Prices of wine.*]—For to know how many ardettis ys a crown of gold in Burdeux.—Weightis.—The reconyng of wollis in Ynglond.—The reconyng of fellis in Ynglond.—*Weight and price of* a nayle woll at Calys.—Dyuerse reconyngis of Custommes of wolles & woll felles.—The prisis of wollis in Calis.—The reconyng off mercery ware & þe reconyng of the coyne & measure.—Nota quod annus solaris constat 365 diebus, etc.—Item in libra argenti sunt 960 quadrantes, etc.—Quatuor grana frumenti faciunt policem, etc.—Thes ben the Cures of mader (*pen-drawings of merchants' stamps*).—A bale of fustyan, etc.
Beg.: Sotill C is V ℔lb.
End: A Corff of vtnall threde | of combes.

79. (om. C.) fol. 186 r°–189 v°
(old hand: "ff. 50, [ff. 60,] ff. 70") (follows blank of one page and a half)

A Good Informacion of Agryme (*arithmetical treatise, partly Latin, partly English*).
Beg.: Hec sunt figure algorismi.
End: (*an example*) He þat bestoweth C markis in eggis after XXX a peny | & sellith C for a peny what makith he of his C markis. Solucio XX£.
(*Blank left for further examples.*)

80. (om. C.) fol. 190 v° and 191 r°
(old hand "ff. 90," "ff. CLXXIX")

[*Tables of letters for secret writing.*]—[*Memoranda:*] "In a peny is XXIIII mytis," etc. "To know veryly how many ardettis ys a crown of gold in Bu[r]dewz."— "Mem. þat . . . makith o ynglishe and o o o makith 1 d," etc.—Eli bath etc. (*names of bishopricks*).—[*Alphabet for cipher writing.*]

*81. (om. C.) fol. 191 v°
(104 in pres. vol.)

Diue[r]s good prowerbes (*written with ciphers for some letters*).
Beg.: Whan I profer the pig open the poke.
End: He that hath nede mvst blowe at the cole.

82. (C. 65) fol. 192 r°–v°
("ff. CLXXX")

For to make tawny water.—To make colowr for a harte.—To make blake water.—To make an other blake.—To make an oþer maner rede.—To lay gold in steynyng.—To make gren water.—To make whit water.—To make blak water.—To make rede water.—To make redde water.—To make yelow water.—Ad

Contents of Richard Hill's Balliol MS. 354.   xlvii

faciend*um* aquam viridum.—For to steyn vppon wolen cloth.—To lay gold in steynyng.—To lay syluer on a clothe.—To make blak.—Mod*us* colorandi rubi*um* Roo.—Ad frangend*um* vincula.
Beg.: Take rede water & blewe water of evyn porcion . . .
End: Accipe cor carpe *et* puluerisa frica vincula *et* frangerent*ur.*

83. (*om. C.*) fol. 192 v°–193 r° ("ff. CLXXXI")
(a) A medycyne for the payn þat a woman hath in þe hedde whan she is yong (?) *with* child.—A medycyne for a woman beyng yong *with* child | havyng a payn *in* þe back | & for the side.
(b) To make gren gynger.—For to make the soryppe.
Beg.: "Tak a hondfull of comyn," *etc.*
End: . . . and the IIIIth parte of an vnce of longe pepper.

84. (*om. C.*) fol. 193 v°
A perpetual calendar table.

85. (*C.* 66) fol. 194 r°–199 r° ("ff. CLXXXII–ff. CLXXXVII")
How that mankynd doth begynne (" *The life of man, corrected by Conscience, by Lydgate ?, in eight-line stanzas,*" *Coxe*) (*defective at end*).
Beg.: How that mankynd doth be gynne.
End: For my tethe they fall me fro.
Printed from MS. Lambeth 853 in Furnivall's "*Hymns to the Virgin and Christ,*" *etc., E. E. T. S., orig. ser. No.* 24 [1867] (*reprtd.* 1895), p. 58 ff. (*complete version, with* 21 *stanzas more than Balliol; but after l.* 392, *Ball. has one stanza not found in L.*).

*86. (*C.* 67) fol. 199 r° (77 *in pres. vol.*)
Terram terra tegat. demon peccata resumat | Mundus res habiat. spiritus alta petat.
Beg.: In IIII poynt*is* or I hens departe.
End: Vnto hevyn on high my sowle I bequeth.
Printed from MS. Lansd. 762, *in* " *Reliquiae Antiquae,*" I, 260 f. ("*The Testament of the Christian*").

*87. (*C.* 68) fol. 199 r°–v° (78 *in pres. vol.*)
Farewell this world.
Beg.: Farewell this world I take my leve for euer.
End: That shede his blode for my redempcion.
One stanza (5) *printed from MS. Lansdowne* 762 *in* "*Reliquiae Antiquae,*" I, 268.

*88. (*C.* 69) fol. 199 v°–200 r° ("ff. CLXXXVIII") (85 *in pres. vol.*)
A treatice of London (*by William Dunbar*).
Beg.: London thow art of townes a per se.
End: London þou art the flowr of cities all.
Printed from MS. Lansd. 762 *in* "*Reliquiae Antiquae,*" I, 205; *in Schipper's edition of* "*The Poems of William Dunbar*" (*No.* 14); *in D. Laing's edition* (*Supplement*), *p.* 277 (*from MS. Cotton. Vitellius A* XVI). *The Balliol version in Herrig's* " *Archiv*" 101, 144, (*see ib.* 90, 151, *and* 91, 241.)

xlviii   Contents of Richard Hill's Balliol MS. 354.

*89. (O. 70) fol.   [*Moral rules in verse, proverbial sentences, etc. in English
200 r°–202 r°   and Latin.*]
("ff. CLXXXVIII–   *Beg.*: A good scoler yf þou wilt be / A rise erly
ff. CLXXXX")   & worship þe trinite.
(105 *in pres. vol.*)   *End*: Dum canis os rodit sociari pluribus odit.

90. (C. 71, 72)   (*a*) [*Table of weights.*]
fol. 202 r°–v°   (*b*) A good trew reconnyng of lede (*with a table*).
("ff. CLXXXX")   *Beg.*: A tonne of yron . . .
             End: . . . VIs. VIIId.

91. (C. 73) fol.   Sequitur oracio eximii doctoris *Sancti* Augustini.
203 r°–v°   *Beg.*: Dulcissime domine Jhesu Christe verus
("ff. CLXXXXI.")   deus.
             End: Qui viuis *et* regnas *in* secula seculorum.
             Amen.

92. (C. 74) fol.   The ordre of goyng or sittyng.
203 v°   *Beg.*: A pope hath no pere (*struck through*).
             End: A yeman of good name.
             Printed on p. 381 *of vol.* 32, *E. E. T. S., orig. ser.*

93. (C. 75) fol.   A prety questyon (" *a trick with cards,*" *Coxe*).
203 v°   *Beg.*: Take XII cardis.
             End: þat ye thowght that ys 7.

94. (*om. C.*) fol.   Questions that be hard to bring to a conclusion for
204 r°   him that hath not herd them (*four arithmetical
("ff. CLXXXXII")   puzzles, with ciphers for some letters, as No.* 81 *and*
             80 *above*).
             Beg.: Ther was a man that went to the market.
             End: and this is a trewe rule for ewer et sithera.

95. (C. 76) fol.   The craft to make ynke dyueris maners (6 *receipts, the
204 v°   last one added later*).
             Beg.: To mak russet ynk. Take cristall or glas
             & grynde.
             End: but it will not be very good.

*96. (C. 77) fol.   [" *Exhortation to hearing mass*" (*Coxe*).]
205 r°–v°   *Beg*: Loke on þis wrytyng man for þi devocion.
("ff. CLXXXXIII")   *End*: Wher god *in* fowrm of bred his body doth
(71 *in pres. vol.*)   present. Explicit quod Hill.

*97. (*om C.*) fol.   [*Proverbial rules in English and Latin* (7 *lines*).]
205 v°, *bottom*   *Beg.*: Si prestabis non rehabebis.
(111 *in pres. vol.*)   *End*: . . . thowgh he begge or borow a loff of
             his neyghbowr.

*98. (C. 78) fol.   As I fared thorow a forest free.
206 r°–v°   (*burden* Welfare hath no sykernes.)
("ff. CLXXXXIIII")   *Beg.*: A I fared . . .
(79 *in pres. vol.*)   *End*: For welfare hath no sikernes.

*99. (C. 79) fol.   Hoow gossip myne gossip myn
206 v°–207 v°   Whan will we go to þe wyne
("ff. CLXXXXIIII v°–   (*burden*: good gossipis myn).
CLXXXXV " v°)   *Beg.*: I shall you tell a full good sport.
(90 *in pres. vol.*)   *End*: For thyngis vsed will not be refused.
             Printed from Wright's MS. in his " *Songs and Carols,*"

Contents of Richard Hill's Balliol MS. 354. xlix

Percy Soc. 23, p. 91 (*an entirely different version reprinted from Ritson's "Ancient Songs" in Wr.'s notes; see also Ritson-Hazlitt*, 1877, II, 117). *Balliol version partly in Flügel's "Neuengl. Lesebuch*," p. 149.

*100. (*C*. 80–81) fol. 207v°-208r° (" CLXXXXV v°- CLXXXXVI " r°) (80 *in pres. vol.*)

(*a*) Vado mori (4 *Latin distichs*).
(*b*) Erth owt of erth (16 *four-line stanzas*).
(*c*) *Six Latin verses on world's vanity* ("Quod doctor Johannes Ednam").
(*d*) *Two Latin verses*.

    Beg.: Vado mori Rex sum quid honor quid gloria mundi.
    End: Sic descendat super nos dei benediccio.

    Bibliography of "Earth upon Earth": (1) *printed from MS. Harl.* 913, *fol.* 62 r°, *in* "*Reliquiae Antiquae*," II, 216, *and in Furnivall's* "*Early English Poems and Lives of Saints*" (*Philological Soc., Berlin* 1862, *p.* 150).

    (2) *from the Porkington MS. in Halliwell's "Early English Miscellanies," Warton Club,* 1855, *p.* 39.—*H., in his note.p.* 94, *points to versions of the poem in MSS. Seld. sup.* 53, *Rawl. C.* 307, *Rawl. Poet* 32, *Lambeth* 853, *and Thornton* (*Lincoln Cathedral*).

    (3) *from Lambeth MS.* 853 *on p.* 88 *of* "*Hymns to the Virgin and Christ*," *ed. Furnivall* (*E. E. T. S.* 1867, *No.* 24).

    (4) *from the Thornton MS. in Perry's* "*Religious Pieces in Prose and Verse*," *E. E. T. S.* 1867, *No.* 26, *p.* 95.

    (5) *from a Stratford church window, by Reeves, in* "*Mod. Lang. Notes*," 9, 204; *ibid.* 270 *b ff. bibliography of the poem by Kittredge.*

    (6) *a version in MS. Egerton* 1995, *fol.* 55, *mentioned in Gairdner's edition of* "*Siege of Rouen*," *Camden Soc., new series*, XVII, 1876 (*introd.*).—*See also Flügel,* "*Anglia,*" 26, 216; *Sir W. Dasent, Life of Richard Cleasby (prefixed to Cleasby-Vigfusson's Icelandic Dictionary*), *p.* lxv (*the Melrose Abbey epitaph*).

*101. (*C*. 81) fol. 208 v° (" CLXXXXVI " v°) (82 *in pres. vol.*)

Cur mundus militat ("*Speculum vitae et mortis*").
    Beg.: Cur mundus militat sub vana gloria.
    End: Cur mundus militat sub vana gloria. Speculum vite et mortis.
Printed from 7 *MSS. in Wright's edition of* "*The Latin Poems commonly attributed to Walter Mapes*" (*Camden Soc.* XVI, 1841).

*102. (*om. C.*) fol. 208 v°, *bottom*
CAROLS.

[*A preamble in English* (10 *lines*).]
    Beg.: He þat oweth mych & hath nowght.
    End: þe longer he levith þe lesse he hath.

d

Contents of Richard Hill's Balliol MS. 354.

("CLXXXVI" v°)
(112 in pres. vol.)
    Cf. four verses in "*Reliquiae Antiquae,*" I, 316 (*from MS. Harl.* 2252, *fol.* 2 *a.*)

*103. (C. 83) fol. 209 r°–v°
("ff. CLXXXVII")
(68 in pres. vol.)
    Prayers in verse: Vnto the Fader. Vnto þe sonne. Vnto þe holy gost. Vnto the trinite. Vnto owr lady. Vnto þe angellis. Vnto þe propre angell. Vnto John Baptist. Vnto þe appostillis. Vnto þe martires. Vnto the confessowrs. Vnto all holy monkis & erimitis. Vnto þe virgyns. Vnto all sayntis.
    Beg.: O most blessid fader omnipotent.
    End: Kepe vs from syn & to thy mercy call.

*104 (om. C.) fol. 210 r°
("ff. CLXXXVII")
(!)
(81 in pres. vol.)
    To dy, to dy, what haue I offendit þat deth is so hasty.
    Beg.: O marcyfull god maker of all mankynd.
    End: Deth strykith with sword | & seyth man it shalbe thus.

*105. (C. 84) fol. 210 r°
("ff. CLXXXVII")
(80 in pres. vol.)
    [*The Seven Deadly Sins.*]
    Beg.: I bost I brage ay with the best (superbia).
    End: Thowgh I in hell þer for ay be (lvxvria).
    Printed from MS. Jesus Coll., Cambr., Q. г. 3 in "*Reliquiae Antiquae,*" I, 36 f.

106. (C. 85) fol. 210 v°–213 v°
("CLXXXVII" v°–"ff. II C" v°)
    The Nutbrown Mayde.
    Beg.: Be it right or wronge.
    End: And serue but hym alon. Explicit quod Richard Hill. Here endith þe nutbrown mayde.
    Printed at the bottom of pp. 174–186 in vol. III of Furnivall and Hales's "Percy Folio."

*107. (C. 86) fol. 213 v°, *bottom*
("ff. IIC" v°)
(113 in pres. vol.)
    [*Rules in verse (last four lines in Latin).*]
    Beg.: Kepe well X and flee from sevyn.
    End: In magis flebo quia nescio quo removebo.

108. (C. 87) fol. 214 r°
("ff. IICI")
    Sequuntur mirabilia (*tricks*).
    Beg.: Ad faciendum unumquemque hominem duo capita.
    End: (*last trick:*) Ad faciendum lepores et animalia currere per domum. (*ends:* . . . et fac inde candelam et illumina.)

109. (C. 88) fol. 214 r°
("ff. IICI")
    The assise of taverners in Ynglond.
    Beg.: entred . . . Also þe sise of a taverner is þat he tak non excesse . . .
    End: . . . to be juggid accordyng to þe form of þe statute.

110. (om. C.) fol. 214 v°
("ff. IICI" v°)
    A medycyne to kyll rattis (*four different prescriptions*).
    Beg.: Tak powder arsmarte, (*etc.*)
    End: this erbe must be gadered abowt mydsomer.

111. (C. 89) fol. 214 v°
("ff. IICI" v°)
    (*a*) A question.
    (*b*) An other demand with þe cardis hartis | treyffoyles | dyamondis | & spadis.

112. (C. 90) fol. 215 r°–216 v°
    The names of all parishe chirches with in London & þe subarbes | & who be patronis.

Contents of Richard Hill's Balliol MS. 354.   li

("ff. IICII"—"203"
[*this number of the old pagination cut off and supplied in pencil by modern hand*])
113. (*C.* 91) fol.
217 r°
("204")

 Beg.: Sent Mary at Bowe dioc*is* Canterbury.
 End: Gylis in the filde (*left unfinished*).

A medycyne for the . . . ake in þe side.—A plaster for the ryght side.—A plaster for his bely.—Flesshe for his mete.—To washe hym.—For his drynk.—For his plaster.—
 Beg.: Take whet bra*n*n II handful.
 End: & sponfull of whit vyng*er* as aforesayd.

114. (*C.* 92) fol.
217 v°
("204" v°)
(*one blank leaf follows*)

Here aft*er* ensueth a good remembrans & knowlage of þe pownd troy weight & by this to know þe defferen*s* & varyans betwyxt þe £. troy in Ynglond & the pownd troy in Flander*s*.
 Beg.: In this behalf it is to vnderstond þat as it hath ben sufficiently proved, [*etc.*]
 End: XXII£. IIs. VId. which ys juste I£ towr & þe vynage. . . .

115. (*C.* 93.) fol.
218 r°
("205" r°)

Names of kyng*is* cristened.
 Beg.: The kynge of Ynglond.
 End: The kyng of leyes north.

116. (*om. C.*)
218 r°
("205" r°)

A medycyne to stoppe a laske.
A medycyne for an ycche.
A medycyne for a cutte.
 Beg.: Tak redde wyne & synamon.
 End: " & make þer of plasters & lay to the sore, etc."

117. (*om. C.*)
fol. 218 v°
("205" v°)

Dyue*r*s medycynes: A medycyne for on þat hath a thorn *in* his yee by mysfortune.—For to hele a gald back of a hors. For to hele a pocke *in* a mans yee or to skowre a mans yee or to take a way reddenes owt of þe yee.—For to hele a brosyd or broken shyn*n* wheþer þe sore be old or newe hurt.—
 Beg.: First take the whyt of an egge . . .
 End: change yt evyn & mornyng til yt be hole. *verum est.*

*118. (*C.* 94) fol.
219 r°
("ff. IICIII")
(69 *in pres. vol.*)

Aue Maria now say we so Mayd & moder were neu*er* no mo.
 Beg.: Gaude Maria Crist*is* moder.
 End: In perhenni gaudio. Explicit de quinque gaudia.
  Printed by Flügel, "Festschrift für R. Hildebrand," p. 56.

119. (*C.* 95) fol.
219 r°
("ff. IICIII")

[*Five short riddles.*]
 Beg.: 8 is my trew love.
 End: LV. CI so hight my leman rede her yf you can.

*120. (*C.* 96, 97)
fol. 219 v°–
231 v°
("IICIII v°–
IICXV" v°)
(*No.* 8–59 *in the present volume*).

[*HYMNS, SONGS AND CAROLS.*]
 (*Printed all except f, h, l, n, q, s, v, y, aa, bb, cc, dd, gg, hh, jj, kk, ll, mm, qq, rr, ss, vv, ww, xx,—by Ew. Flügel in "Festschrift für Rudolf Hildebrand," 1894, pp. 52 ff.; besides in "Anglia" 26 (see note at head of this table), and severally as indicated below.*)

          *

Contents of Richard Hill's Balliol MS. 354.

(a) Now we shuld syng & say newell | Quia missus est angelus Gabriell.—*Beg.*: From hevyn was sent an angell of light.—*End*: & syng newell | quia missus est angelus Gabriell.—*Pr.*: *Flügel's "Neuenglisches Lesebuch," Halle*, 1895, p. 114.—(**8** *in the pres. vol.*)

(b) Nova nova aue fitt ex eva (*burden:* Vt nova . . .).—*Beg.*: Gabriell of hygh degree.—*End:* Ecce ancilla domini.—*Pr.*, *from a MS. in Th. Wright's possession (now Eng. poet. e. 1. Bodl.), in his "Songs and Carols," Percy Soc.* 23, p. 36 f.—(**9.**)

(c) Ther ys a flowr sprong of a tre | The rote of it ys called Jesse | A flowr of pryce | þer ys non such in paradice.—*Beg.*: The flowr ys fresshe & fayer be hewe. *End:* For best of all | þat euer was or euer be shall.—*Flügel, "Neuenglisches Lesebuch,"* p. 115.—(**10.**)

(d) Make we mery in hall & bowr | Thys tyme was born owr savyowr (*burden:* God þat ys owr savyowr). *Beg.*: In this tyme God hath sent. *End:* On vs all to haue pytee.—*A similar song in Wright's "Specimens of old Christmas Carols" (Percy Soc.,* IV), p. 11; *repr. in "Songs and Carols," Warton Club,* IV, 1855, p. 68 (*from MS. Sloane* 2593).—(**11.**)

(e) Off a rose a louely rose | And of a rose I syng a song.—*Beg.*: Herkyn to me both old & yonge.—*End:* And send vs gud lyff & longe.—*A similar song printed as No. 5 in Th. Wright's "Songs and Carols," London* 1836 (*Pickering*); *repr.* 1855, *Warton Club, vol. IV (from MS. Sloane* 2593). *Another text "S. and Car.," Percy Soc.,* 23, p. 21; *the Balliol one in Flügel, "Neuengl. Lesebuch,"* p. 116.—(**12.**)

(f) Man asay asay a say (*burden:* aske þou mercy whill þou may). —*Beg.*: Man haue in mynd how here beforn . . . *End:* & after in hevyn to haue place.—*Printed from MS. Addit.* 5665 *in Herrig's "Archiv,"* 106, p. 275 (*B. Fehr*).—(**13.**)

g) Now syng we wyth joy and blis (*burden: Puer natus est* nobis).— *Beg.*: Mary flowr of flowers all.—*End:* Shryft & hosyll at owr ending. —*Flügel's "Neuengl. Lesebuch,"* p. 116.—(**14.**)

(h) Mary moder I you pray | To be owr help at domys day.—*Beg.*: Att domys day whan we shall ryse. *End:* Þat for vs dyed on gud Fryday.—(**15.**)

121. (*om C.*) fol. 221 r°, bottom ("ff. IICV") Seynt Thomas lottis folow (8 *lines; cf. No.* 75, above). *Beg.*: First II & than I, than III & than V. *End:* Þat ye will have sa . . . . set first.

(i) Verbum patris hodie processit ex virgine (*burden:* processit ex virgine). (**16.**)
Beg.: The son of the fader of hevyn blys.
End: For the to sofer & for to dye.

(j) Now syng we syng we regina celi letare (*burden:* regina celi letare). *Beg.*: Gabryell that angell bryght. *End:* Thou kepe & save vs all from tene.—*Cf. Wright, "Songs and Carols" (Percy Soc* .23), p. 33.— (**17.**)

(k) Conditor alme siderum eterna lux credencium, etc.—*Beg.*: Ther ys a chyld borne of a may.—*End:* To hys blis to bryng them all.—*Cf. the song from Sloane MS.* 2593 *in Wright's "Songs and Carols" (Warton Club,* IV, 1855), p. 79.—(**18.**)

Contents of Richard Hill's Balliol MS. 354. liii

122. (*om C.*) fol. *a.* Questio (5 *lines*).
221 vº, *bottom*   *Beg.*: þer were XII persones.   *Last line*
("ff. IICV vº ")   " solicio."
          b. Pro vene[no]so aere pestilencie.
          Beg.: Rec. II partes opt¹.
          End : probatum fuit Oxonie.
          c. Rebecca.¹ Sefora.² Abigina.³ Susanna.⁴ Zael.⁵

(l) Pray for vs to the prince of peace (*burden :* Amice Christi Johannes.
—*Beg. :* To Crystis own derlyng. *End :* Pray we to hym þat he vs not for sake.—*Printed from Wright's MS. in his* "*Songs and Carols*" (*Percy Soc.* 23), p. 60 ; *from MS. Add.* 5665 *in Herrig's* "*Archiv,*" 106, p. 273 (*B. Fehr*) *; from a Cambr. MS. roll in Maitland-Rockstro,* "*English Carols,*" 1891, p. 25.—(**19.**)

(m) Tyrly tirlow tirly tirlow / so merily the sheperdis be gan to blow (*burden* " terly terlow "). *Beg.:* A bowt the feld they pypyd ryght.— *End :* The whych was never defyled.—*Printed from Wright's MS. in* "*Songs and Carols,*" *Percy Soc.* 23, p. 95 ; *from the Balliol MS. in Flügel's* "*Neuenglisches Lesebuch,*" p. 117.—(**20.**)

(n) Now syng we all in fere (*burden :* Alma redemptoris mater).— *Beg. :* As I me lay on a nyght.—*End :* Tyll after she sawe hym ryse vp right.—(**21.**)

(o) To blis god bryng vs all & sum | Christe redemptor omnium.— *Beg.* : In Bedlem in that fayer cyte. *End :* Be all mery in thys howse.— *Cf. Wright,* "*Songs and Carols*" (*Percy Soc.* 23), p. 52.—(**22.**)

(p) Alleluya, alleluia (*burden :* Deo patri sit gloria). *Beg. :* Ther ys a blossum sprong of a thorn. *End :* þat this was Jhesu full of myght.—(**23.**)

(q) Thys blessyd babe (*burden :* Mary moder cum & se | Thy swet son nayled on a tre.—*Beg.:* Thys blessyd babe þat thou hast born. *End :* He toke hys deth with parfitt gud will.—*Compare the song No.* VIII *in Wright's* " *Specimens of old Christmas Carols* " (*Percy Soc.* IV), (*repr. Warton Club,* IV, 1855) (*MS. Sloane* 2593). *See also* "*S. and C.,*" *Percy Soc.* 23, p. 38.—*The Balliol version in Flügel's* "*Neuenglisches Lesebuch,*" p. 112.—(**24.**)

(r) In to þis world now ys cum Christe redemptor omnium. *Beg.:* O worthy lord & most of myght. *End :* Grant vs thy blis euerlastyng.—(**25.**)

(s) Man þat in erth (*burden :* Mirabile misterium | In forme of bred ys godis son).—*Beg. :* Man þat in erth abydys here. *End :* Dyed for vs vpon a tre.—(**26.**)

(t) Make we mery bothe more & lasse (*burden :* For now ys þe tyme of Crystymas. *Beg. :* Lett no man cum in to this hall.—*End :* For now ys þe tyme of Crystmas.—*Printed in Flügel's* "*Neuenglisches Lesebuch,*" p. 123.—(**27.**)

(u) Lyft vp your hartis (*burden :* What cher gud cher gud cher gud cher | Be mery & glad this gud newyere).—(**28.**)

(v) Ay ay ay ay Gaude celi domina.—*Beg. :* Mary for the loue of the. —*End :* God & man & so he ys for ay | Assendit super sidera.—*Printed from Wright's MS. in his* " *Songs and Carols,*" *Percy Soc.* 23, p. 68 f.— (**29.**)

liv *Contents of Richard Hill's Balliol MS. 354.*

(w) The sheperd vpon a hill (*burden*: Can I not syng but hoy | Whan the joly sheperd made so mych joy). *Beg.*: The sheperd vpon a hill he satt.—*End*: Vt hoy | For in his pipe he mad so myche joy.—*Printed in Flügel's "Neuenglisches Lesebuch,"* 117.—(**30**.)

(x) Here haue I dwellyd (*burden*: Now haue gud day now haue gud day | I am Crystmas & now I go my way.—*Beg.*: Here haue I dwellyd with more & lasse. *End*: Yet for my sake make ye gud chere.—*Flügel, "Neuenglisches Lesebuch,"* p. 126.—(**31**.)

---

123. (*om C.*) fol.   The craft to skowre mayle harnes (10 *lines*).
224 v°, *bottom*   *Beg.*: Take your mayle & put it in an armerers
("IICVIII," v°)   barell.
                      End: and so let it lye.

(y) I was born in a stall (*burden*: Shall I moder shall I do soo | Shall I dye for manys sake | And I never synned ther to.—*Beg.*: I was born in a stall.—*End*: And send vs all good reste.—*Printed in Flügel's "Neuenglisches Lesebuch,"* p. 121.—*Cf. the similar poems of Jacob Ryman, published by Zupitza in Herrig's "Archiv," vol.* 89, p. 228–236 (*Nos.* 62–67).—(**32**.)

(z) A babe is born (*burden*: Now synge we with angelis | Gloria in excelcis).—*Beg.*: A babe is born to blis vs brynge.—*End*: To put a way all hevynes.—(**33**.)

---

fol. 225 v°,   ⅔ *partis* of a shillyng how many pens . . . 8d. |
bottom   ⅔ *partis* of a shillyng | 7d. ob. || $\frac{7}{16}$ *partis* ys 3d
("ff. IICIX" v°) | & quat.

(aa) So blessid a sight (*burden*: Lulley Jhesu lulley lulley | Myn own dere moder syng lulley).—*Beg.*: So blessid a sight it was to see.—*End*: Myn own dere moder syng lulley.—*Printed in Flügel's "Neuenglisches Lesebuch,"* p. 119.—(**34**.)

(bb) A lovely lady (*head-lines*: This enders nyght I sawe a sight . . . etc.).—*Beg.*: A lovely lady sat & sange.—*End*: & I shall syng lulley by by lully lulley.—*Printed in a Northern version (from a MS. in the Adv. Libr.), "Reliquiae Antiquae,"* II, 76. *Another text in Wright's "Songs and Carols" (Percy Soc.* 23), p. 12. *Version of MS. Add.* 31922 *in "Anglia,"* XII, 270 (*Ew. Flügel*). *The Balliol version in Flügel's "Neuenglisches Lesebuch,"* p. 120 ; *ibidem,* p. 119, *a version from MS. Royal, App.* 58 (*the same as in "Anglia"* XII).—(**35**.)

(cc) I was with pope and cardynall (*burden*: For sothe I hold hym well & with owt woo | þat hath ynowgh & can say whoo).—*Beg.*: I was with pope & cardynall.—*End*: That hath ynowgh & can say who.—*See Flügel's "Neuenglisches Lesebuch,"* p. 141.—(**36**.)

---

124. *om. C.*   A question (5 *lines*).
fol. 226 v°, *bottom*   *Beg.*: Ther were XII persones.
("ff. IICX," v°)   *End*: 5 knyghtis 1 fotman & 6 maydyns.

(dd) Vices be wyld (*burden*: God þat sittith in trinite | Amend this world yf thy will be).—*Beg.*: Vices be wyld & vertues lame.—*End*: And amonge all men in Crystynte.—*Wright, "Songs and Carols," Percy Soc.* 23, p. 96 (*from Wright's MS., now Eng. Poet. e.* 1, *Bodl.*).—(**37**.)

Contents of Richard Hill's Balliol MS. 354.   lv

(ee) Glorius god (*burden:* Syng we with myrth joye & solas | In honowr of this Cristemas).—*Beg.:* Glorius god had gret pyte.—*End:* He will not denye thy sowle to wynne.—(38.)

(ff) This babe to vs (*burden:* Now syng we right as it is Quod puer natus est nobis.)—*Beg.:* This babe to vs now is born.—*End:* He asketh no thynge but þat is his.—*Printed in another version (from a MS. roll in Trinity Coll., Cambr.) in Fuller Maitland and Rockstro's "English Carols of the 15th Century,"* 1891), p. 9.—(39.)

(gg) Lystyn lordyngis (*burden:* A. a. a. a. nunc gaudet ecclesia) (*song on St. Thomas Becket.*)—*Beg.:* Lystyn lordyngis both gret & small.—*End:* Optans celi gawdia.—*Printed from MS. Sloane* 2593 *in Wright's "Songs and Carols" (London, Pickering,* 1836), *repr. Warton Club,* IV, 1855. *The Balliol version in Flügel's "Neuenglisches Lesebuch,"* p. 113.—(40.)

(hh) Whan seynt Stevyn (*burden:* Nowe syng we both all & sum Lapidauerunt Stephanum).—*Beg.:* Whan seynt Stevyn was at Jeruzalem. —*End:* Lapidaverunt Stephanum.—*Flügel, "Neuenglisches Lesebuch,"* p. 113.—(41.)

(ii) The boris hed (*burden:* Caput apri refero Resonens laudes domino).—*Beg.:* The boris hed in hondis I brynge.—*End:* Exiuit tunc de patria.—*Printed E. E. T. S., orig. ser.* 32, p. 398, *and Flügel, "Neuenglisches Lesebuch,"* p. 123.—(42.)

---

125. (*om. C.*) A question (8 *lines*).
fol. 228 r°, *bottom*   *Beg.:* As I went by þe way.
(" ff. IICXII," r°)   *End:* 3 quat. & a ob. qu.

(jj) Gaude to whom Gabryell was sent (*burden:* Gawde for thy joyes five | Mary moder maydyn & wyff).—*Beg.:* Gaude to whom Gabryell was sent.—*End:* But ever florisshe & encrese.—(43.)

(kk) On Cristis day (*burden:* A blessid byrd as I you say þat dyed & rose on Good Fryday).—*Beg.:* On Cristis day I vnderstond.—*End:* Thus they bett Jhesu owr det to pay.—*Printed in Flügel's "Neuenglisches Lesebuch,"* p. 112.—(44.)

(ll) Thow dereste disciple (*burden:* Pray for vs to the trinite | Johannes Christi care.—*Beg.:* Thow dereste disciple of Jhesu Criste.—*End:* Cum venerit iudicare.—(45.)

(mm) Alas my hart will brek in thre (*burden:* Terribilis mors conturbat me).—*Beg.:* Illa juventus that is so nyse.—*End:* In celum ther is joy with the.—(46.)

(nn) For his love (*burden:* Synge we all for tyme it is | Mary hath born þe flowre delice).—*Beg.:* For his love þat bowght vs all dere. —*End:* & ther of com the flowr delice.—(47.)

---

126. (*om. C.*)   A question (6 *lines*).
fol. 229 r°, *bottom*   *Beg.:* Ther were II men.
(" ff. IICXIII," r°)   *End:* " & the second had XIIII apples *etc.*"

(oo) In to this world (*burden:* I pray you be mery & synge with me | In worship of Cristys nativite).—*Beg.:* In to this world this day dide com.—*End:* Wher riches ys everlastyngly.—(48.)

Contents of *Richard Hill's Balliol MS*. 354.

(pp) **Tydyngis trewe** (*burden:* Newell newell newell newell | This ys þe salutacion of Gabryell).—*Beg.:* Tydyng*is* trewe | ther be com newe. —*End:* Secu*n*du*m* verbu*m* tuu*m* fiat michi.—*Wright's "Songs and Carols," Percy Soc.* 23, p. 79; *ibid.* p. 62, *the two head-lines and first stanza of this song prefixed, with musical notation, to another song to be sung on the same tune. Another text in* "*The Boke of Brome*" (*a commonplace-book of the 15th century, ed. L. Toulmin Smith,* 1886), p. 122.—(**49.**)

*127. (*om. C.*) [*Three Latin distichs.*]
fol. 229 v°, bottom ("IICXIII," v°) (114 *in pres. vol.*)
Beg.: Regia maiestas omn*is*que terrena potestas.
End: Du*m* Fortuna perit nullus amicus erit.

(qq) Whan þat my swete son (*burden:* O my harte is woo, Mary she sayd so | For to se my dere son dye . & sonnes haue I no mo).—*Beg.:* Whan þat my swete son was XXX^{ti} wynter old.—*End:* Than cam Lungeus with a spere & clift his hart i*n* sonder.—(**50.**)

(rr) Bowght and sold (*burden:* To see the maydyn wepe her sonnes passion | It entrid my hart full depe wit*h* gret compassion).—*Beg.:* Bowght & sold full traytorsly.—*End:* Wher þat thy swet son ys. —(**51.**)

(ss) The masse is of so high dignytee (*burden:* I consayll you bothe more & lesse | Beware of sweryng by þe masse).—*Beg.:* The masse is of so high dignytee.—*End:* Thy sowle i*n* hevyn may haue a place. —(**52.**)

(tt) I shall you tell (*burden:* What hard ye not þe Kyng of Jherusalem | Is nowe born in Bethelem).—*Beg.:* I shall you tell a gret mervayll.—*End:* To þat child Te Deum synge. Te Deum laudam*us.* —(**53.**)

(uu) Now joy be (*burden:* Wassaill wassayll syng we In worshipe of Crist*is* natiuite).—*Beg.:* Now joy be to the trynyte.—*End:* & joy haue they þat make good chere.—(**54.**)

(vv) Be mery & suffer (*burden:* He is wise so most I goo | That can be mery & suffer woo).—*Beg.:* Be mery & suffer as I the vise.—*End:* & shake thy lappe & lat it go.—*Printed in Flügel's "Neuenglisches Lesebuch,"* p. 141; *E. E. T. S., orig. ser.* 32, p. 361.—(**55.**)

(ww) An old said sawe (*burden:* An old said sawe hath be fownd trewe | Cast not away thy*n* old for newe).—*Beg.:* An old said sawe on knowen on kyste. *End:* & ell*is* must þou drynk as thou doste brewe.—(**56.**)

(xx) Man be ware & wise in dede (*burden:* Assay a frend or þou haue nede.—*Beg.:* Thorow a forest þat was so longe.—*End:* Thus she said whan she songe last.—*Printed in Wright's "Songs and Carols," Percy Soc.* 23, p. 28.—(**57.**)

(yy) Man meve thy mynd & joy this fest (*burden:* Verytas de terra orta est).—*Beg.:* As I cam by þe way. *End:* To Jury & Jerusalem | Veritas de terra orta est.—(**58.**)

(zz) All this tyme this songe is best (*burden:* Verbum caro factum est). *Beg.:* This nyght ther is a child born. *End:* Owr helpe owr socowr for to be.—(**59.**)

128. (*om. C.*) fol. 231 v°, bottom ("IICXV" v°)
The craft to mak water lyme. (12 *lines.*)
Beg.: Take good holme lyme.
End: ye may set a cork on euery ende, *etc.*

Contents of Richard Hill's Balliol MS. 354.   lvii

*129. (C. 98.) fol.
232 r°—247 r°
(247 v° blank)
("IIC [XVI]", r°
"IICXVIII"[1],
"IICXIX"—
"IICXXV")
(See appendix to present edition)
 The names of mayeres & sheryffis from the first yere of kyng Henry the Vth (1414–1536, with notes on events).

*130. (C. 99.) fol. 248r°
("IICXXVI")
(91 in pres. vol.)
 In villa in villa Quid vidistis in villa (burden).
  Beg.: Many a man blamys his wyffe perde.
  End: Hys here shall grow thorow his hode In villa.
 Printed from Wright's MS. in his "Songs and Carols," Percy Soc. 23, p. 86.

*131. (C. 100.) fol. 248 v°
("IICXXVI" v°)
(92 in pres. vol.)
 I sawe a doge (burden: Hay Hey hey hey | I will haue the whetston and I may).
  Beg.: I sawe a doge sethyng sowse.
  End: I will haue the whetston & I may.

*132. (C. 101.) fol. 248 v°
("IICXXVI" v°)
(60 in pres. vol.)
 Cryst kepe vs all (burden: Now syng we syng we Gloria tibi domine).
  Beg.: Cryst kepe vs all as he well can.
  End: Qui regnat super aethera.
 Printed by Ew. Flügel in "Festschrift für Hildebrand," p. 82.

*133. (C. 102.) fol. 249 r°
("IICXXVII" r°)
(93 in pres. vol.)
 Alas sayd þe gudman this ys an hevy lyff | & all ys well þat endyth well said the gud wyff (burden: att þe townys end).
  Beg.: A lytyll tale I will you tell.
  End: When on his cheke he ys chekmate.

*134. (om. C.) fol. 249 v°
("IICXXVII" v°)
(94 in pres. vol.)
 Hogyn cam to bowers dore (burden: Hum ha, trill go bell).
  Beg.: Hogyn cam to bowers dore.
  End: or ellis your breth ys wonder strong | hū ha trill go bell.

*135. (C. 103.) fol. 249 v°
("IICXXVII" v°)
(61 in pres. vol.)
 Virgo rosa virginum tuum precor fillium (burden: Gloria tibi domine).
  Beg.: Qvene of hevyn blessyd mott þou be.
  End: That we may to his blis cum.

*136. (C. 103.) fol. 249 v°
(62 in pres. vol.)
 Man be ware or thou be wo | & thynk on pride & lat hym go.
  Beg.: Pryde ys owt & pride ys yn.
  End: . . . down into endles wo.
 Printed from MS. Sloane 2593, among "Moral Songs" in "Reliquiae Antiquae," II, 166 (two stanzas more than in Ball.).

*137. (C. 105.) fol. 250 r°
("IICXXVIII" r°)
(95 in pres. vol.)
 Of all creatures women be best (burden: Cuius contrarium verum est).
  Beg.: In euery place ye may well see.
  End: Ye wold say they be prowde it ys yll said.
 Printed from Wright's MS. in "Songs and Carols," Percy Soc. 23, p. 88.

Contents of Richard Hill's Balliol MS. 354.

*138. (*C.* 106.)
fol. 250 r°–v°
("IICXXVIII" r°-v°)
(96 *in pres. vol.*)

Women women love of women Maketh bare pursis with sum men.
Beg.: Sum be mery & sum be sade.
End: Go shrew wher so euer ye go (*burden*).
Printed from MS. Lambeth 306 in "Reliquiae Antiquae," I, 248; and from Wright's MS. in "Songs and Carols," Percy Soc. 23, p. 89.

*139. (*C.* 107.)
fol. 250 v°
("IICXXVIII" v°)
(97 *in pres. vol.*)

Whan netillis, etc. (*Burden:* Than put in a woman your trust & confidence).—
Beg.: Whan netillis in wynter bere rosis rede.
End: Than put in a woman your trust & confidence.
Printed in a fuller text in Wright's "Songs and Carols," Percy Soc. 23, p. 66.—A similar song on priests' wives in Furnivall's "Ballads from MSS." vol. I, p. 313–315 (Ballad Society, 1868) ("A godlye sang").

*140. (*C.* 108.)
fol. 251 r°
("IICXXIX")
(98 *in pres. vol.*)

Drawe me nere drawe me nere | Drawe me nere þe joly juggelere (*ballad*).
Beg.: Here beside dwellith a(s) riche barons dowghter.
End: Evyn as he was.

*141. (*C.* 109.)
fol. 251 r°–v°
("IICXXIX" r°-v°)
(99 *in pres. vol.*)

Holy berith beris (*burden:* Nay nay ive it may not be iwis | For holy must haue þe mastry as þe maner is).
Beg.: Holy berith beris | beris rede ynowgh.
End: So wold I þat euery man had þat with yvy will hold.
Printed in a different version (from MS. Harl. 5396) in Ritson-Hazlitt, "Ancient Songs" (1877), II, 113.—Songs on the same subject in Wright's volume, Percy Soc. 23, p. 44, 84, 85. The Balliol text "Festschrift für Hildebrand," p. 83.

*142. (*C.* 110.)
fol. 251 v°
("IICXXIX" v°)
(100 *in pres. vol.*)

[*Song with the burden:*] Bon jowre bon jowre a vous | I am cum vnto this hows | vt parla pompe I say.
Beg.: Is þer any goodman here | þat will make me any chere.
End: The worst in this contrey | Bon jowre.

*143. (*C.* 111.)
fol. 251 v°–252 r°
("IICXXIX" v°—
"IICXXX" r°)
(101 *in pres. vol.*)

[*Song with the burden:*] How butler how Bevis a towt | fill þe boll jentill butler & let þe cup rowght.
Beg.: Jentill butler bellamy.
End: With how butler how bevis a towght | fill etc.

144. (*C.* 112.)
fol. 252 r°
("IICXXX")

Hay hay by this day (*burden:* What avayleth it me thowgh I say nay).
Beg.: I wold fayn be a clarke.
End: What vaylith me thowgh I say nay.
"The Birched School-Boy," E. E. T. S., orig. ser. 32, 403 f.

*145. (C. 113.)   [*Ironical love-song, burden:*] Whan I slepe I can not
fol. 252 r°–v°   wake.
("IICXXX" r°–v°)
(102 *in pres. vol.*)   *Beg.* : Lord how shall I me complayne.
    End : That whan I slepe I can not wak. **Finis**.
        *Printed from the Porkington MS. in Halliwell's
        "Early English Miscellanies" (Warton
        Club,* II).

146. (C. 114.)   For a horsback that is gallid.—An other medycyne for
fol. 253 r°–v°   the same.—For an hors þat hathe the facon.—A
("IICXXXI")   medycyne for the colyck.—A medycyne for the gret
    pock*is*.—For the palsy.—For the ston.—For the*m*
    þat may not pysse.—For a woma*n* þat is sek i*n* þe
    hed.—For the fette.—For the heed.—To make on
    slepe.—For þe ague & a gret het & brennyng i*n*
    þe hed.—For þe ague.—To make an orchard
    shortly.
      Beg. : Tak the levis of elder or ye ca*n* not get the
        levis take þe bark.
      End: . . . nygh to þe body of the tree.

I. Sacred Songs and Carols.

1.

Be mery all þat be present,   [leaf 165, back]
Omnes de Saba venient.

(1)
¶ Owt of þe est a sterre shon bright
For to shew thre kyngis light,
Which had ferre traveled day &
    nyght   3
  To seke þat lord þat all hath sent.

(2)
¶ Therof hard kyng Herode anon,
þat III kyngis shuld cum thorow
    his regyon,
To seke a child that pere had non,
  And after them sone he sent.   8

(3)
¶ Kyng Herode cried to them on hye:
"Ye go to seke a child truly ;
Go forth & cum agayn me by,
  & tell me wher þat he is lent." 12

(4)
¶ Forth they went by þe sterres leme,
Till they com to mery Bethelem ;
Ther they fond þat swet barn-teme
  That sith for vs his blode hath
    spent.   16

(5)
¶ Balthasar kneled first a down
& said : " Hayll, Kyng, most of re-
    nown,

And of all kyngis þou berist þe
    crown,   19
  Therfor with gold I the present."

(6)
¶ Melchior kneled down in þat stede
& said : " Hayll, Lord, in thy pryest-
    hede,
Receyve ensence to thy manhede, 23
  I brynge it with a good entent."

(7)
¶ Jasper kneled down in þat stede
& said : "Hayll, Lord, in thy knyght-
    hede,
I offer the myrre to thy godhede, 27
  For thou art he þat all hath sent."

(8)
¶ Now lordis & ladys in riche aray,
Lyfte vp your hartis vpon this day,
& ever to God lett vs pray,
  That on the rode was rent.   32

Explicit.

Est tuus, Anna, pater Izacar,
  Nasaphat tua mater.

CAROLS.   B

2   I. *Sacred Songs and Carols.*

2.

Mater, ora filium, vt post hoc exilium [leaf 177, back]
Nobis donet gaudium beatorum omnium.

(1)
" Fayre maydyn, who is this barn,
That þou beriste in thyn arme ?"
" Sir, it is a kyngis son,
That in hevyn a-bove doth wonne." 4
  Mater, ora[1] [filium, vt post hoc
    exilium   [1 MS. *etc.*]
  Nobis donet gaudium beatorum
    omnium].   6

(2)
"Man to fader he hath non,
But hym self, God alone,
Óf a maydyn he wold be borne 9
To save mankynd þat was forlorn."
  Mater, ora [filium, vt post hoc
    exilium
  Nobis donet gaudium beatorum
    omnium].   12

(3)
" Thre kyngis browght hym presens,
Gold, myrre & frankynsens,
To my son full of myght,   15
Kynge óf kyngis & lorde of myght."
  Mater, ora [filium, vt post hoc
    exilium   ,
  Nobis donet gaudium beatorum
    omnium].   18

(4)
" Fayre maydyn, pray for vs
Vnto thy son, swet Jhesus,
þat he will send vs of his grace
In hevyn on high to haue a place." 22
  Mater, ora filium, [vt post hoc
    exilium
  Nobis donet gaudium beatorum
    omnium].   24

3.

Newell, newell, newell, newell,
I thank a maydyn euery dele.

(1)
Vpon a lady fayre & bright
So hartely I haue set my thowght,
In euery place, wher euer I light,
On her I thynk, & say right
  nowght.
    Newell !   5

(2)
She bare Jhesum full of pite,
þat all þis world with his hond
  hath wrowght,
Soueraynly in mynd she is with me,
For on her I thynk, & say right
  nowght.
    Newell !   10

(3)
Trewe love, loke þou do me right,
  & send grace, þat I to blis be
    browght ;
Mary, moder moste of myght,
  On the I thynk, & say right nowght.
    Nowell !   15

(4)
God þat was on the rode don,
  Grant þat all men to blis be
    browght,
& to Mary I mak my mone,
For on her I thynk, & say right
  nowght.
    Nowell !   20
  Explicit.

4.

In what state þat euer I be,
Timor mortis conturbat me.

(1)
As I me walked on mornyng,
I hard a birde both wepe & synge,
This was þe tenor of her talkynge :
Timor mortis conturbat me.   4

(2)
I asked this birde what he ment ;
He said : "I am a musket gent ;
For dred of deth I am nygh shent,
Timor mortis conturbat me." 8

(3)
Jhesu Cryst, whan he shuld dye,
To his fader lowd gan he crye,
"Fader," he said, "in trynyte,
Timor mortis conturbat me." 12

(4)
Whan I shall dye, know I no day,—
þer-fore this songe synge I may,—
In what place or contrey, can I not say.
Timor mortis conturbat me. 16

5.

Diuisie si affluant, nolite cor apponere. [leaf 178]

(1)
Yf God send þe plentuowsly riches,
Than thank hartely with all meknes,
In thy mynd þis proverbe impresse :
Nolite cor apponere.   4

(2)
And while þou hast it in thy gouernance,
I consaill þe pore men to avance,
Lest deth þe apprese with his cruell lance.
Nolite cor apponere.   8

(3)
& thynk þou must also parte away
From all thy riches, þou mayst not say nay,
þer-fore þe best þat I can syng or say :
Nolite cor apponere. 12
Explicit.

6.

Now let vs syng, both more & lesse,
Of Cristis commyng Deo gracias!

(1)
A virgyn pure, this is full sure,
Gabriell dide her grete,
& all her cure, I am full sure,
Euer dyde endure :
Deo gracias!   5

(2)
A babe was born, erly by þe morn,
& layd betwen þe ox & þe asse,
þe child they knew, þat was born new,
On hym þei blew.
Deo gracias! 10

4   I. *Sacred Songs and Carols.*

(3)
An angell full sone, sang from abone:
"Gloria in excelsis!"
þat lady alon, myght mak no mone
For love of on.
    Deo gracias!   15

(4)
This babe vs bowght, whan we were browght   [case,
In to gret thowght & dredfull
Therfor we syng, both old & yonge,
Of Cristis commynge,
    Deo gracias!   20
    Explicit.

7.
**Jhesus autem hodie
Egressus est de virgine.**

(1)
Whan Jhesu Crist baptised was,
þe Holy Gost dessendid by grace,
þe Faders voice was hard in þat place:
"Hic est filius meus dilectus,
    ipsum audite."   4

(2)
They were III persones in on lord,
þe Son baptised was with on accord,
þe Fader said þis blessid worde:
"Hic est filius meus dilectus,
    ipsum audite."   8

(3)
Considre now, all Cristante,
How þe Fader said because of þe,
þe gret mystery of þe Trinyte:
"Hic est filius meus dilectus,
    ipsum audite."   12

(4)
Now Jhesu, as þou art both God & man,   [leaf 178, back]
& was baptised at flom Jordan,
At owr last end, we pray þe, say than:
"Hic est filius meus dilectus,
    ipsum audite."   16
    Explicit.

8.
Now we shuld syng & say newell,   [leaf 219, back]
Quia missus est angelus Gabriell.

(1)
From hevyn was sent an angell of light
Vnto a cyte that Nazareth hyght,
Vnto a mayd, a bryde so bryght,
And full of blis;
Nomen Maria virginis.   5

(2)
The angell went furth, & nowght he sest;   [drest;
Be-fore that mayden he hym sone
He said: "All hayle, thou art full
And gracius!   [blest
Quia tecum est Dominus."   10

I. *Sacred Songs and Carols.*

(3)
Whan Mary this hard, a-stoned was she, [myght be;
And thowght what thys gretyng
The angell her shewed of grace plente,
And gret solas,
Et dixit: "Maria, ne timeas." 15

(4)
The angell sayd: "Thou maydyn myld,
Thou shalt conceyve & bere a chyld,
Thy maydynhed shall neuer be de- [fyled,
Call hym Jhesus:
Hic erat altissimi filius." 20

(5)
Whan Mary, as bryght as crystall ston,
Thes wordis hard, answered anon,
And asked, how all this myght be done,
And sayd: "How so?
Quia virum non cognosco." 25

(6)
The angell said: "Thou maydyn still,
The Holy Gost shall the fulfill."
The mayd answered with woyse so And sayd mekely: [shryll,
"Ecce ancilla domini!" 30

(7)
Sone after this, this chyld was borne
In Bedleme in a wynters morne.
Now make we mery hym beforne,
& syng newell, 34
Quia missus est angelus Gabriell.

9.
Nova, nova: Aue fitt ex Eva.

(1)
Gabriell of hygh degre,
He cam down from the trynyte,
From Nazareth to Galalye.
vt nova. 4

(2)
He mete a maydyn in a place;
He kneled down be fore her face;
He sayd: "Hayle, Mary, full of grace!"
vt nova. 8

(3)
When the maydyn sawe all this,
She was sore abashed, ywys,
Lest that she had done a-mys.
vt nova. 12

(4)
Then sayd the angell: "Dred not you,
Ye shall conceyve in all vertu
A chyld, whose name shall be Jhesu."
vt nova. 16

(5)
Then sayd the mayd: "How may this be,
Godis son to be born of me?
I know not of manys carnalite."
vt nova. 20

(6)
Then said the angell a-non ryght:
"The Holy Gost ys on the plyght,
þer ys no thyng vnpossible to God Almyght."
vt nova. 24

I. *Sacred Songs and Carols.*

(7)
Then sayd the angell a-non:
"Ytt ys not fully VI moneth a-gon,
Syth seynt Elizabeth co*n*ceyved seynt John."
vt nova. 28

(8)
Then said the mayd a-no*n* a-hye:
"I am God*is* own truly,
Ecce ancilla do*m*ini."
[vt nova.] 32
Explicit.

10.
Ther ys a flowr sprong of a tre, [leaf 220]
The rote of it ys called Jesse,
A flowr of pryce,
þe*r* ys no*n* such i*n* pa*r*adice.

(1)
The flowr is fresshe & fayer be[1] hewe,
Ytt fad*is* never, but euer ys neve;
The blessid stoke þat yt on grew,
Ytt was Mary, that bare Jhe*s*u,
A flowr of g*r*ace;
Of all flowers it ys solas. 6

(2)
The sede of ytt was God*is* sond,
That God hy*m* self sew wit*h* his hond,
In Nazareth, that holy lond;
And a maydyn yt fond, 10
A blessid flowr; [bowr.
Yt spryng*is* neue*r* but i*n* Mary

(3)
On knees Gabriell that maydy*n* gret,
The Holy Gost wit*h* her he mett,
Betwen the*m* two that flowr was sett
And kept yt ys, for yt was dett,
And kyng*is* lede 17
To Bedlem, þe*r* yt bega*n* to spred.

(4)
Whan þat flowr began to spred
And[2] hys blosomys for to woyde,
Ryche & pore of eue*r*y lede 21
Marveled how þat rose myght spred,
Till on a day
Herdme*n* ca*m* þat flowr to asay. 24

(5)
Angels ca*m* owt of ther towr
To loke on that fayer flowr,
Hole yt was in his colowr, 27
And hole yt was in his ardowr
To be-hold,
How such a flowr myght spryng
i*n* mold. 30

(6)
Off lylly whit & rose of ryse,
Of prymrose & of flowr delyce,
Off all flowers, in my devyce,
The flowr of Jesse beryth the pryce,
For most of all
To help owr sowles both gre[t] & small. 36

(7)
I p*r*ayse the flowr of gud Jesse,
Of all the flowers þat eue*r* shall be
Vphold the flowr of gud Jesse, 39
And worship it for ay bewte,
For best of all
Þat eue*r* was or eue*r* be shall. 42
Explicit.

---
[1] MS. he   [2] MS. and &

I. *Sacred Songs and Carols.*

11.

**Make we mery in hall & bowr,
Thys tyme was born owr Savyowr.**

(1)
In this tyme God hath sent
Hys own Son, to be present,
To dwell with vs in verament,
God þat ys owr Savyowr. 4

(2)
In this tyme þat ys be-fall,
A child was born in an ox stall
& after he dyed for vs all,
God [1] [þat ys owr Savyowr]. 8

(3)
In this tyme an angell bryght
Mete III sheperdis vpon a nyght,
He bade them go a-non ryght
To God þat ys owr Saviowr. 12

(4)
In thys tyme now pray we
To hym þat dyed for vs on tre,
On vs all to haue pytee,
God þat ys owr Saviowr. 16
Explicit.

12.

Off a rose, a louely rose, [leaf 220, back]
And of a rose I syng a song.

(1)
Herkyn to me, both old & yonge,
How a rose began to sprynge,
A fayerer rose to my lykyng 3
Sprong perneuer in kyngis lond.

(2)
VI branches ar on þat rose beme,
They be both bryght & shene,
The rose ys called Mary, hevyn
quene, 7
Of her bosum a blossum sprong.

(3)
The fyrst branch was of gret myght,
That spronge on Crystmas nyght,
The streme [2] shon over Bedlem
bryght, [longe.
þat men myght se both brod &

(4)
The II[de] branch was of gret honowr,
þat was sent from hevyn towr,
Blessyd be þat fayer flowr! 15
Breke it shall the fendis bondis.

(5)
The thyrd branch wyde spred
Ther Mary lay in her bede,
The bryght strem III kyngis lede
To Bedlem, þer þat branch þei
fond. 20

(6)
The IIIIth branch sprong in to hell,
The fendis bost for to fell,
Ther myght no sowle þer in dwell,
Blessid be þat tyme þat branch
gan spryng. 24

---

[1] MS. &c.   [2] MS. streme; sterne *Flügel*.

8   I. *Sacred Songs and Carols.*

(7)
The Vth branch was fayer in fote,
þat sprong to hevyn tope & rote,
þer to dwell & be owr bote   27
& yet ys sene in priestis hondis.

(8)
The VIth branch by & by,
Yt ys the V joyes of myld Mary.
Now Cryst saue all this cumpany,
& send vs gud lyff & long.   32
      Explicit.

13.
**Man, asay, a-say, a-say,
And aske thou mercy whyle thou may.**

(1)
Man, haue in mynd, how here beforn
For thy mysded thou wast for-lorn,
To geve the mercy Cryst was born;
Aske þou mercy whill þou may.   4

(2)
Yff thou thy lyff in syn hath lede,
Amend the now & be not dred,
For Crystis mercy furth ys spred : 7
[¹Aske þou mercy whill þou may.]

(3)
Yff thy syn be never so yll,
Yet for no syn thou shalt spyll,
Amend the now yf þat thou will, 11
[¹Aske þou mercy whill þou may.]

(4)
He that hath the hether browght,
He wold that thou mercy sowght,

Aske ytt & he denyth ytt nowght :
[¹Aske þou mercy whill þou may.]

(5)
He that dyed on the rode
& shed for the his precius blod,
He ys both mercyfull & gud :   19
[¹Aske þou mercy whill þou may.]

(6)
Mercy ys spred on the grownd,
Ther for to dwell a lytill stownd ;
Lett vs seke till yt be fownd :   23
[¹Aske þou mercy whill þou may.]

(7)
Ytt for to fynd God geve vs grace,
In this world while we haue space,
& after in hevyn to haue place : 27
[¹Aske þou mercy whill þou may.]
      Explicit.

14.
Now syng we wyth joy and blys :   [leaf 221]
Puer natus est nobis.

(1)
Mary, flowr of flowers all,
Hath born a chyld in an ox stall,
That lorde & prynce ys ouer vs all :
     Puer natus est nobis.   4

(2)
He was born on owre Lady
With owt weme of her body,
Godys own son truly,
     Puer natus est nobis.   8

¹ MS. vt supra.

I. *Sacred Songs and Carols.*

(3)
By an apull of a tre
Bownd men all made were we,
That child was born to make vs fre;
Puer natus est nobis.   12

(4)
That chyld was don on the rode
Wyth hys flesshe & with hys blod,
For owr helpe & for owr gud;
Puer natus est nobis.   16

(5)
The III^de day he rose & to hevyn went,
Wytt & wysedom he vs sent,
For to kepe his cumaundment;
Puer natus est nobis.   20

(6)
He shall cum down at domys day
With blody wovndis, I you say,
As he dyed on Gud Fryday;
Puer natus est nobis.   24

(7)
Now pray we to that hevyn kyng
To send vs all his dere blessyng,
Shryft & hosyll at owr endyng:
Puer natus est nobis.   28
Explicit.

15.
**Mary moder, I you pray
To be owr help at domys day.**

(1)
Att domys day, whan we shall ryse
And cum be fore the hygh Justyce
And geve a cownt for owr seruyce,
What helpyth than owr clothyng
    gay?   4

(2)
Whan we shall cum be fore hys dome,
What will vs helpe? ther all & some
We shall stond as sory grome
Yclad in a full pore a-ray.   8

(3)
That ylke day withowt lesyng
Many a man hys hondis shall wryng,
And repent hym sore for hys lywyng;
Then yt ys to late, as I yow say.

(4)
Ther-for I rede both day & nyght,
Make ye redy to God Almyght,
For in thys londe ys kyng nor knyght
That wott whan he shall wend
    a-way.   16

(5)
That chyld, that was born on Mary,
He glad all thys cumpany,
And for hys loue make we mery,   19
þat for vs dyed on Gud Fryday.
Explicit.

16.
Verbum patris hodie processit ex virgine. [leaf 221, back]

(1)
The Son of the Fader of hevyn blys
Was born as[1] thys day, I will not mys;
Man from thraldom to releve & lose,[2]
    Processit ex virgine.   4

(2)
He was born of a virgyn pure,
Not knowyng a man, as I you sure,
But all only by hevynly cure
    Processit ex virgine.   8

[1] *for* at? But 'as' is still used.   [2] l[is]se *Flügel.*

(3)
Gabryell the angell dyde grett
Mary knelyng in her closett,
Now ys[1] fulfillyd þat sayd the
  profett:
    Processit ex virgine.   12

(4)
Man, be glad![2] thou hast a cavse why
To thanke owr Lord God þat ys on
  hye:
For the to sofer, & for to dye,
    Processit ex virgine.   16
      Explicit.

17.

Now syng we, syng we: Regina celi, letare!

(1)
Gabryell, that angell bryght,
Bryghtter than the son lyght,
From hevyn to erth he toke his
  flyght:
    Regina celi, letare!   4

(2)
In Nazareth, in that cyte,
Be fore Mary he fell on kne,
And sayd: "Mary, God ys with the,"
    Regina celi, letare!   8

(3)
"Hayle be thou, Mary of mytis
  most,
In the shall lyght the Holy Gost,
To saue the sowles þat were lost."
    Regina celi, letare!   12

(4)
Hayle be thou Mary, maydyn shen;
From the fendis that be so kene,
Thou kepe, & save vs all from tene!
    Regina celi, letare!   16

18.

Conditor alme siderum, eterna lux credencium, etc.

(1)
Ther ys a chyld borne of a may
  In saluacion of all vs,
That we shuld worship euery day
  With "Veni Creator Spiritus."   4

(2)
In Bedlem, in that holy place,
  Thys blessid child, born he was;
Hym to serue, he geve vs grace,
  With "Trinitatis vnitas."   8

(3)
The sheperdis hard þat angels songe,
  And worshypped God in trynyte,
Þat so nygh was them a-monge,
  Iam lucis orto sidere.   12

(4)
Eche man be-gan to cry & call
  To hym that syttyth on hye,
To hys blis to bryng them all,
  Jhesu saluator seculi.   16

[1] MS. ytt   [2] MS. ghad

I. Sacred Songs and Carols.

19.

Pray for vs to the prince of peace,
Amice Crysty, Joha*nn*es.

(1)
To Cryst*is* own derlyng,
The whyche was mayd both old & yong,
My hart ys set, a songe to syng,
    Amice Chr*is*ti Joha*nn*es. 4

(2)
For he was so clene a mayd,
On Cryst*is* brest a slepe he layd,
The p*r*ophett*is* of hevy*n* to hy*m* sayd:
    Amice Chr*is*ti Joha*nn*es. 8

(3)
Whan Cryst before Pylat was browght, [nowght,
Thys clene mayd for-soke hym
To dye w*it*h hy*m* was all his thowght,
    Amice Chr*is*ti Joha*nn*es. 12

(4)
Cryst*is* moder was hy*m* be-take,
A mayd, to be a-noder make;
Pray we to hy*m* þ*at* he vs not for-sake,
    Amice Chr*is*ti Joha*nn*es. 16

20.

Tyrly tirlow, tirly t*er*low:
So merily the shep*er*d*is* be-gan to blow.

(1)
A-bowt the feld they pypyd ryght,
So meryly the shep*er*d*is* be-gan to blow;
A-down fro*m* hevy*n* þ*at* is so hygh,—
    Terly terlow, [tirly terlow]! 4

(2)
Angellys ther cam a cumpany
W*it*h mery song*is* and melady,
The shep*er*d*is* a-no*n* that ga*n* a-spye,
    T*er*ly terlow, [tirly terlow]! 8

(3)
"Gloria i*n* excellc*is*," the angels song,
& sayd þ*at* pease was p*re*sent a-mong
To eu*er*y ma*n* þ*at* the feyth wold fong,
    T*er*ly terlow, [tirly terlow]! 12

(4)
The shep*er*d*is* hyed them to Bedlem,
To se that blessyd son beme,
And ther they fond þ*at* glori*us* leme,
    T*er*ly terlow, [tirly terlow]! 16

(5)
Now p*r*ay we to þ*at* meke chyld
And to hys moder þ*at* ys so myld,
The whych was never defyled,
    T*er*ly terlow, [tirly terlow]! 20
    Explicit.

21.
Now syng we all in fere:
Alma Redemptoris mater.

(1)
As I me lay on a nyght,
Me thowght I sawe a semly wyght,
That clepid she was ryght
' Alma Redemptoris mater.'   4

(2)
To her com an angell with gret lyght
And sayd : " Hayle be þou blessid wyght,
To be cleped thou art right
[1] [Alma Redemptoris mater."]   8

(3)
At that word the maydyn bryght
A-non conceyved God Almyght ;
Then knew Mary what she hyght :
[1] [Alma Redemptoris mater.]   12

(4)
Whan Jhesu on the rode was dyght,
Mary was sorofull of that syght,
Tyll after she sawe hym ryse vpright,
Alma Redemptoris mater.   16
Explicit.

22.
To blys God bryng vs all & sum,   [leaf 222, back]
Christe redemptor omnium.

(1)
In Bedlem, in that fayer cite,
A chyld was born of owr Lady,
Lord & prynce þat he shuld be,
A solus[2] ortus cardine.   4

(2)
Chyldren were slayn grett plente ;
Jhesu, for the love of the,
Lett vs neuer dampned be ;
Hostes Herodes ympie !   8

(3)
He was born of owr Lady
With owt wemb of her body,
Godis son þat syttyth on hye,
Jhesu saluator seculi.   12

(4)
As the son shynnyth thorow þe glas,
So Jhesu in her body was,
To serue hym he geve vs grace,
O lux beata trinitas !   16

(5)
Now ys born owr Lord Jhesus,
That mad mery all vs,
Be all mery in thys howse,
Exvltet celum lavdibus !   20
Explicit.

23.
Alleluya, alleluia ! Deo patri sit gloria !

(1)
Ther ys a blossum sprong of a thorn,
To saue mankynd þat was forlorne,
As the profettis sayd be-forne.
Deo patri sit gloria !   4

(2)
Þer sprong a well at Maris fote,
That torned all þis world to bote ;
Of her toke Jhesu flesshe & blod :
Deo patri [[3] sit gloria !]   8

[1] MS. vt supra.   [2] *for* solis   [3] MS. &c.

I. Sacred Songs and Carols.

(3)
From þat well per strake a strem;
Owt of Egipt in to Bedlem a-gayn.
God thorowgh his highnes torned yt
 Deo ¹[patri sit gloria!] 12

(4)
Þer was III kyngis of dyueris londis,
They thowght a thowght þat was strong,
Hym to seke & thanke a-mong,
 Deo ¹[patri sit gloria!] 16

(5)
They cam richely with þer presens,
With gold, myre & frankynsens,
As clerkys² rede in per sequens,
 Deo patri sit gloria! 20

(6)
The eldest kyng of them thre,
He went formest, for he wold se,
What domys man þat this shuld be.
 Deo patri sit gloria! 24

(7)
The medylmest kyng, vp he rose,
He sawe a babe in armys close,
In medyll age he thowght he was.
 Deo patri ¹[sit gloria!] 28

(8)
The yongest kyng, vp he stode,
He made his offryng rych & gud,
To Jhesu Cryst that shed his blod.
 Deo patri sit gloria! 32

(9)
Þer shon a star owt of hevyn bryght,
That men of erth shuld deme a right,
Þat this was Jhesu full of myght.
 Deo patri ¹[sit gloria!] 36
 Explicit.

24.
Mary moder, cum and se   [leaf 223]
Thy swet son nayled on a tre.

(1)
Thys blessyd babe þat thou hast born,
Hys blessyd body ys all to-torne,
To bye vs a-gayn þat were for-lorne,
Hys hed ys crownyd with a thorn.
 Mari ¹[moder, cum and se
 Thy swet son nayled on a tre]. 6

(2)
"Crownyd, alas, with thorn or breer,
Or why shuld my sun thus hang here,
To me thys ys a carefull chere;
Swet son, thynke on thy moder dere."
 Mari ¹[moder, cum and se
 Thy swet son nayled on a tre]. 12

(3)
"Thes wykyd Jewes with ther falshed,
Vnder ther fete they gan hym tred,
They wovndyd hym thorowgh hond & hed,
They left hym not, till he was ded."
 Mari ¹[moder, cum and se
 Thy swet son nayled on a tre]. 18

(4)
"Alas, alas, now may I crye,
Why myght I not with my son dye?
My hart ys replenyshed with petye,
Fulfylled with payn most pytuysly."
 Mari ¹[moder, cum and se
 Thy swet son nayled on a tre]. 24

¹ MS. &c.   ² MS. cherkys

14   I. *Sacred Songs and Carols.*

(5)
Mary moder, greve you not yll,
From hevyn he cam this to fulfyll;
Be-cavse mankynd shuld not spill,

He toke hys deth with parfitt gud
 will.
Mari ¹[moder, cum and se
Thy swet son nayled on a tre]. 30
 Explicit.

25.
In to þis world now ys cum,
Christe redemptor omnium.

(1)
O worthy Lord, & most of myght,
Eterne rex altyssime,
The to honowr me thynkyth ryght,
Iam lucis orto sidere.   4

(2)
As thou art Lord of worthynes,
Conditor alme siderum,
All vs to bryng owt of derknes,
Christe redemptor omnium.   8

(3)
With bemys clere of righttuysnes
Aurora lucis rutilat,
In joy þer-of with all gladnes,
Vox clara ecce intonat.   12

(4)
Now glorius Lord & worthy kyng,
Jhesu saluator seculi,
Grant vs thy blis euerlastyng,
Summi lorgitor primii!   16
 Explicit.

26.
Mirabile misterium :
In forme of bred, ys Godis son.

(1)
Man þat in erth abydys here,
Thov mvst be-leve with-owten dere²
In the sacrament of the auter,
þat God made hym self at hys soper.
 Mirabile!   5

(2)
Thowgh yt seme whit, yt ys rede ;
Yt ys flesshe, yt semyth bred ;

Yt ys God in his manhed,
As he hong vpon a tre.
 Mirabile!   10

(3)
Thys bred ys brokyn for you & me,
Which priestis consecrate, as ye may
Which flesshely man in deite [se,
Dyed for vs vpon a tre.
 Mirabile!   15
 Explicit.

¹ MS. &c.   ² MS. dure

I. *Sacred Songs and Carols.* 15

27.

Make we mery, bothe more & lasse, [leaf 223, back]
For now ys þe tyme of Crystymas.

(1)
Lett no man cum in to this hall,—
Grome, page nor yet marshall,—
But þat sum sport he bryng with-all,
For now ys the tyme of Crystmas.

(2)
Yff that he say he can not syng, 5
Sum oder sport then lett hym bryng,

þat yt may please at thys festyng,
For now ys the tyme of Crystmas.

(3)
Yff he say he can nowght do, 9
Then for my loue aske hym no mo,
But to the stokkis then let hym
  go, 11
For now ys þe tyme of Crystmas.

28.

What cher? Gud cher, gud cher, gud cher!
Be mery & glad this gud New Yere!

(1)
" Lyft vp your hartis & be glad
In Crystis byrth," the angell bad;
Say eche to oder, yf any be sade:
  What cher? 4

(2)
Now þe kyng of hevyn his byrth
  hath take,
Joy & myrth we owght to make,
Say eche to oder, for hys sake:
  What cher? 8

(3)
I tell you all with hart so fre:
Ryght welcum ye be to me;
Be glad & mery, for charite!
  What cher? 12

(4)
The gudman of this place in fere,
You to be mery, he prayth you here,
& with gud hert he doth to you say:
  What cher? 16
  Explicit.

29.

Ay, ay, ay, ay, Gaude celi domina.

(1)
Mary, for the loue of the,
Blyth & glad may we be,
& I shall syng, as ye may se,
  Sua quinque gaudia. 4

(2)
The fyrst joy was sent to the,
Whan Gabryell gretyd the,·

& sayd: "Hayle, Mary, in chastite!
  Officiaris gravida." 8

(3)
The second joy was full gud,
Whan Cryst toke both flesshe &
  blod,
Withowt syn talkyng of mode,
  Inexsa est puerpera. 12

16 I. *Sacred Songs and Carols.*

(4)
The III^{de} joy was of gret myght,
Whan Jhesu was on the rode dyght,
Dede & buryed in all menys syght,
Surrexit die tercia.   16
(5)
The IIIIth joy was withowt ay,
Whan Jhesu to hell toke the way,

& with hym com gret aray
Ad celi palacia.   20
(6)
The Vth joy was on holy Thursday;
Vnto hevyn he toke the way,
God & man ; & so he ys for ay;
Assendit super sidera.   24
Explicit.

30. [The Jolly Shepherd Wat.]

Can I not syng but hoy, [leaf 224]
Whan the joly sheperd made so mych joy.

(1)
The sheperd vpon a hill he satt,
He had on hym his tabard & his hat,
His tarbox, hys pype & hys flagat;
Hys name was called joly, joly Wat ;   4
For he was a gud herdis boy,
  Vt hoy!
For in hys pype he made so mych joy.
  Can I not syng but hoy,[1]
  Whan the joly sheperd made so mych joy.   9

(2)
The sheperd vpon a hill was layd,
Hys doge to hys gyrdyll was tayd ;
He had not slept but a lytill broyd,
But "Gloria in excelcis" was to hym sayd.   13
  Vt hoy!
For in hys pipe he mad so myche joy.
  Can I not syng[2] but hoy,
  Whan the joly sheperd made so mych joy.   17

(3)
The sheperd on a hill he stode,
Rownd a-bowt hym his shepe they yode ;
He put hys hond vnder hys hode,
He saw a star as rede as blod :   21
  Vt hoy!
For in hys pipe he mad so myche joy.   23

[1] Whan . . . joy] &c. MS.   [2] but . . . joy] &c. MS.

I. Sacred Songs and Carols.

Ca*n* I not sing but hoy,[2]
Whan the joly shepe*r*d made so mych joy. 25
(4)
"Now farwell Mall & also Will,
For my love, go ye all styll
Vnto I cu*m* agayn you till,
And eue*r*more, Will, ryng well thy bell." 29
Vt hoy!
For i*n* his pipe he mad so mych joy.
Ca*n* I not syng[1] but hoy,
Whan the joly shepe*r*d made so mych joy. 33
(5)
"Now must I go *þer* Cryst was borne;
Farewell! I cu*m* a-gayn to morn.
Dog, kepe well my shep fro þe corn,
& warn well Warroke, whe*n* I blow my horn." 37
Vt hoy!
For i*n* hys pipe he made so mych joy.
Ca*n* I not sing[1] but hoy,
Whan the joly shepe*r*d made so mych joy. 41
(6)
Whan Wat to Bedlem cu*m* was,
He swet; he had gon faste*r* tha*n* a pace;
He fownd Jhe*s*u in a sympyll place,
Be-twen an ox & an asse. 45
Vt hoy!
For i*n* his pipe he mad so mych joy.
Ca*n* I not syng but hoy,[2]
Whan the joly shepe*r*d made so mych joy. 49
(7)
The shepe*r*d sayd a-no*n* ryght:
"I will go se yon farly syght,
Wher as þe angell syngith on hight
& the star þat shynyth so bryght," 53
Vt hoy!
For i*n* [his] pipe he made so mych joy.
Ca*n* I not sing but hoy,[2]
Whan the joly shepe*r*d made so mych joy. 57

[1] but . . . joy (32, 40)] &c. MS.
[2] Whan . . . joy (25, 49, 57)] &c. MS.

CAROLS.

I. *Sacred Songs and Carols.*

(8)

"Jhesu! I offer to the here my pype,
My scrype, my tarbox & my skyrte;
Home to my felowes now will I skype,
& also loke vnto my shepe."   61
    Vt hoy!
For in his pipe he mad so myche joy.
  Can I not sing but hoy,[1]
    Whan the joly sheperd made so mych joy.   65

(9)

"Now farewell, myne own herdisman Wat!" [leaf 224, back]
"Ye, for God, Lady, even so I hat;
Lull well Jhesu in thy lape,
& farewell, Joseph wyth thy rownd cape!"   69
    Vt hoy!
For in hys pipe he mad so myche joy.
  Can I not sing[2] but hoy,
    Whan the joly sheperd made so mych joy.   73

(10)

"Now may I well both hope & syng,
For I haue bene a[t?] Crystis beryng,
Home to my felowes now wyll I flyng;
Cryst of hevyn to his blis vs bryng!"   77
    Vt hoy!
For in his pipe he mad so myche joy.
  Can I not sing[2] but hoy,
    Whan the joly sheperd made so mych joy.   81
        Explicit.

31.

Now haue gud day, now haue gud day!
I am Crystmas, & now I go my way.

(1)

Here haue I dwellyd with more & lasse
From Halowtyde till Candylmas,
And now must I from you hens passe;
  Now haue gud day!   4

(2)

I take my leve of Kyng & knyght,
& erle, baron, & lady bryght,
To wildernes I must me dyght;
  Now haue gud day!   8

[1] Whan . . . joy (65)] &c. MS.   [2] but . . . joy (72, 80)] &c. MS.

I. Sacred Songs and Carols.

(3)
& at þe gud lord of this hall
I take my leve, & of gestis all.
Me thynke I here, Lent doth call;
    Now haue gud day!   12

(4)
& at euery worthy offycer,
Marchall, panter & butler,
I take my leve as for this yere;
    Now haue gud day!   16

(5)
A-noder yere I trust I shall
Make mery in this hall,
Yf rest & pease in Ynglond may fall;
    Now haue gud day!   20

(6)
But oftyn tymys I haue hard say
Þat he ys loth to part a-way,
Þat oftyn byddyth 'haue gud day';
    Now haue gud day!   24

(7)
Now fare ye well, all in fere!
Now fare ye well for all this yere!
Yet for my sake, make ye gud cher;
    Now haue gud day!   28
    Explicit.

32.

"Shall I, moder, shall I, shall I do soo?   [leaf 225]
Shall I dye for mannys sake,
And I never synned ther-to?"

(1)
"I was born in a stall
Betwen bestis two,
To this world browght in thrall,
To leve in care & woo.   4
    Shall I, moder, [shall I, shall I do
    Shall I dye for mannys sake, [soo?
    And I never synned ther-to?]   7

(2)
Whan I was VIII days elde,
The lawe fulfilled I thoo,
Circumsised as a childe;
Than began all my woo.   11
    Shall I, moder, [shall I, shall I do
    Shall I dye for mannys sake, [soo?
    And I never synned ther-to?]   14

(3)
Thowgh my fader be a kyng,
My-selff I went hym froo,
In to þis world to suffre many a thyng:
See, man, what thow haste do!   18
    Shall [I, moder, shall I, shall I do
    Shall I dye for mannys sake, [soo?
    And I never synned ther-to?]   21

(4)
Man, I am thy frend ay;
Thy self art thy foo;
To my fader, lok thow pray,
& leve thy synnes þat þou hast do.   25
    Shall [I, moder, shall I, shall I do
    Shall I dye for mannys sake, [soo?
    And I never synned ther-to?]   28

(5)
The Ieves were so fell,
Þat to Judas cowld they goo;
They kyssed me, as I you tell,
'Hayle, kyng!' said they tho.   32
    Shall [I, moder, shall I, shall I do
    Shall I dye for mannys sake, [soo?
    And I never synned ther-to?]   35

20   I. *Sacred Songs and Carols.*

(6)
They bond me to a pyler ano*n*,
Honde & fote, both twoo ;
They skorged me wi*th* skorges son ;
The blode ran my body froo.   39
  Shall I, [moder, shall I, shall I do soo ?
  Shall I dye for ma*n*nys sake,
  And I never synned ther-to ?] 42

(7)
They clothed me in a mantell rede,
From the toppe to the too,
Wi*th* a crown of thorn on my hede :
Wi*th* staves they bett it *p*erto.   46
  Shall I, [moder, shall I, shall I do soo ?
  Shall I dye for ma*n*nys sake,
  And I never synned ther-to ?] 49

(8)
They browght me i*n* to Cayfas hall,
Ther he was bisshop thoo ;
Fals witnes on me they ga*n* call ;
Moder, what shall I doo ?   53
  Shall [I, moder, shall I, shall I do soo ?
  Shall I dye for ma*n*nys sake,
  And I never synned ther-to ?] 56

(9)
I toke þe cros on my bak full still ;
To Caluary than muste I goo ;
I sett it down vpon an hill,
Wi*th* other crossis moo.   60
  Shall [I, moder, shall I, shall I do soo ?
  Shall I dye for ma*n*nys sake,
  And I never synned ther-to ?] 63

(10)
They hangid me vp that tide ;
Hond*is* & fette they naylid also ;
& a theff on eue*r*y side,
To lykyn my body too.   67
  Shall I, [moder, shall I, shall I do soo ?
  Shall I dye for ma*n*nys sake,
  And I never synned ther-to ?] 70

(11)
Wi*th* a spere both sharpe & kene
They clave my hart i*n* two ;
Water & blode *p*er owt ran ;
See, man, what þou haste do !   74
  Shall I, [moder, shall I, shall I do soo ?
  Shall I dye for ma*n*nys sake,
  And I never synned ther-to ?] 77

(12)
Wi*th* a spere both sha[r]pe & hend
They clave my harte i*n* III,
Than yeldyd I vp þe gost & dyed,
þat here all men may see.   81
  Shall [I, moder, shall I, shall I do soo ?
  Shall I dye for ma*n*nys sake,
  And I never synned ther-to ? "] 84

(13)
God þat dyed on the rode,
& spred his armes i*n* þe este,
Send vs all his blessyng,
& send vs all good reste !   88
  " Shall I, moder, [shall I, shall I do soo ?
  Shall I dye for ma*n*nys sake,
  And I never synned ther-to ? "] 91
                Explicit.

I. *Sacred Songs and Carols.*

[33–35. The Virgin and her Son.]

33.

Now synge we wi*th* angelis : ⎫
Gloria in excelcis ! ⎬ fote.
⎭

(1)
A babe is born, to blys vs brynge.
I hard a mayd lulley & synge;
She said : "Dere son, leve thy wepyng,   3
 Thy fader is þe kyng of blis."
  Now sy[n]g we [wi*th* angelis :
  Gloria in excelcis !]   6

(2)
"Lulley," she said & songe also,
"Myn own dere son, whi art þou wo ?
Haue I not do as I shuld do ?   9
 Thy grevance, tell me what it is ! "
  Nowe sy*n*g [we wi*th* angelis :
  Gloria in excelcis !]   12

(3)
"Nay, dere mod*er*, for þe wepe I nowght,
But for þe wo þ*at* shall be wrowght
To me, or I ma*n*kynd haue bowght :   15
 Was neu*er* sorow lik it, ywis."
  Now [synge we wi*th* angelis :
  Gloria in excelcis !]   18

(4)
"Pesse, dere son, tell me not soo,
Þou art my child, I haue no moo ;
Shuld I se me*n* myn own son sloo ?   21
 Alas, my dere son ! what menys þis ? "
  Now [synge we wi*th* angelis :
  Gloria in excelcis !]   24

(5)
"My hondis, moder, þ*at* ye may see,
Shall be nayled vnto a tree ;
My fete all so fast shall be ;   27
 Men shall wepe þ*at* shall se this."
  Now sy*n*g [we wi*th* angelis :
  Gloria in excelcis !]   30

(6)
"A, dere son! hard is my happe,
To see my child þat sokid my pappe,
His hondis, his fete, þat I dide wrappe,   33
    Be so naylid, þat neuer dide amysse."
        Now [synge we with angelis :
        Gloria in excelcis!]   36

(7)
"A dere moder! yet shall a spere
My hart in sonder all to-tere ;
No wondre, yf I carefull were,   39
    & wepe full sore to thynk on this."
        Now [synge we with angelis :
        Gloria in excelcis!]   42

(8)
"A dere son! shall I se this?
þou art my child, & I thy moder ywis,
Whan Gabryell called me 'full of grace,'   45
    He told me no thyng of this."
        [Now synge we with angelis :
        Gloria in excelcis!]   48

(9)
"A, dere moder! thorow myn here,
To thrust in thornes, they will not spare ;
Alas, moder! I am full of care,   51
    That ye shall see this hevynes."
        Now [synge we with angelis :
        Gloria in excelcis!]   54

(10)
"A dere son, leve thy wepyng!
þou bryngyst my hart in gret mornyng ;
A carefull songe now may I syng ;   57
    This tydyngis, hard to me it is."
        Now [synge we with angelis :
        Gloria in excelcis!]   60

(11)
"A! pece, dere moder, I the pray,
    comforte me all þat ye may,

I. Sacred Songs and Carols.

& syng, ' by, by, lulley, lulley,' 63
To put a-way all hevynes."
Now sy*n*g we [wit*h* angelis:
Gloria in excelcis!] 66

34.

Lulley, Jh*e*su, lulley, lulley! } fote. [leaf 226]
Myn own dere moder, syng lulley!

(1)
So blessid a sight it was to see,
How Mary rokked her son so fre!
So fayre she rokked & songe " by, by"; 3
    Myn own dere moder, syng lulley!
        Lulley, [Jhesu, lulley, lulley!
        Myn own dere moder, syng lulley!] 6

(2)
" Myn own dere son, why wepyst þou thus?
Ys not thy fader kyng of blis?
Haue I not do þ*at* in me ys? 9
    Yo*ur* grevance, tell me what it is!"
        Lulley, [Jhesu, lulley, lulley!
        Myn own dere moder, syng lulley!] 12

(3)
" Ther for moder, wepe I nowght,
But for þe woo þ*at* shall be wrowght
To me, or I mankynd haue bowght. 15
    Myn own dere moder, syng lulley!
        Lulley, [Jhesu, lulley, lulley!
        Myn own dere moder, syng lulley!] 18

(4)
Moder, þe tyme ye shall see,
Þe sorowe shall brek yo*ur* hart i*n* three,
So fowle þe Jewes shall fare wit*h* me. 21
    Myn own dere moder, syng lulley!
        Lulley, [Jhesu, lulley, lulley!
        Myn own dere moder, syng lulley!] 24

(5)
Wha*n* I am nakid, they will me take,
& fast bynd me to a stake,
& bete me sore for man*us*[1] sake.   27
   Myn own dere moder, syng lulley !
     Lulley, [Jhesu, lulley, lulley !
     Myn own dere moder, syng lulley !]   30

(6)
Vpon þe crose they shall me caste,
Honde & fote, nayle me faste ;
Yet gall shall be my drynk [at] laste ;   33
Thus shall my lyff passe away.
     Lulley, [Jhesu, lulley, lulley !
     Myn own dere moder, syng lulley !]   36

(7)
A, dere moder ! yet shall a spere
My hart *in* sonder all to-tere ;
No wonder thowgh I carefull were.   39
   Myn own dere moder, syng lulley !
     Lulley, [Jhesu, lulley, lulley !
     Myn own dere moder, syng lulley !]   42

(8)
Nowe, dere moder, syng lulley,
  & put a-way all hevynesse ;
In-to this world I toke þe way,
  A-gayn to I shall me dresse,   46
þ*er* joye is wit*h*owt end ay,
Myn own dere moder, syng lulley !"
     Lulley, [Jhesu, lulley, lulley !
     Myn own dere moder, syng lulley !]   50
         Explicit.

[1] man*is* Flügel.

I. Sacred Songs and Carols.

35.

This enders nyght
I sawe a sight,
A sterre as bryght
As any day;
& euer a-monge,
A maydyn songe:
"Lulley, by, by, lully, lulley!" } fote.

(1)
A lovely lady sat & songe   1
And to her son thus gan she say:
"My son, my lord, my dere derlyng,
Why lig͟gis thou thus in hay?   4
   Myn own dere son,
   How art þou cum,
      Art þou not God verey?   7
   But neuer the lesse
   I will not sees
      To syng 'by, by, lully, lulley.'" 10
þis [enders nyght
I sawe a sight,
A sterre as bryght
As any day;
& euer a-monge,
A maydyn songe:
"Lulley, by, by, lully, lulley!"] 17

(2)
Than spake the child þat was so yong
& thus me thowght he said:
"I am knowen as hevyn kyng,
   In cribbe thowgh I now be layd; 21
      Angellis bright
      To me shall light;
      & of þat sight   24
   Ye may be light,
   & syng 'by, by, lully, lulley.'" 26
þis [enders nyght
I sawe a sight,
A sterre as bryght
As any day;

And euer a-monge,
A maydyn songe:
"Lulley, by, by, lully, lulley!"] 33
(3)
"Jhesu, my son, hevyn kyng, [leaf 226, back]
Why lyest þou thus in stall?
& why hast þou no riche beddyng
   In sum ryche kyngis hall?   37
      Me thynkith by right,
      The lord of myght
      Shuld lye in riche aray;   40
   But neuer the lesse
   I will not sese
      To synge 'by, by, lully, lulley.'" 43
This [enders nyght
I sawe a sight,
A sterre as bryght
As any day;
& euer a-monge,
A maydyn songe:
"Lulley, by, by, lully, lulley!"] 50
(4)
"Mary moder, quene of blis,
Me thynkith it is no lawe,
That I shuld go to þe kyngis,
   And they not to me drawe;   54
   But you shall see
   That kyngis thre
      To me will cum on þe XII day;
      For this beheste,
      Geve me your brest,
      & syng 'by, by, lully, lulley.'" 60

This [enders nyght
I sawe a sight,
A sterre as bryght
  As any day ;
And euer a-monge,
A maydyn songe :
  "Lulley, by, by, lully, lulley!"] 67

(5)

"Jhesu, my son, I pray þe, say,
As þou art to me dere :
How shall I serue þe to thy pay, 70
  & mak the right good chere?
  All thy will
    I wold fulfill, 73
  þou knoweste it well, in fay ;
  Both rokke þe still
  & dance the þer-till,
& synge ' by, by, lully, lulley.' " 77
This [enders nyght
I sawe a sight,
A sterre as bryght 80
  As any day ;
And euer a-monge,
A maydyn songe :
  "Lulley, by, by, lully, lulley !"] 84

(6)

"Mary, moder, I pray þe,
Take me vp on loft,
& in thyn arme
Thow lappe me warm, 88

& dance me now full ofte ;
& yf I wepe,
& will not slepe,
Than syng ' by, by, lully, lulley.'" 92
This [enders nyght
I sawe a sight,
A sterre as bryght
  As any day ;
And euer a-monge,
A maydyn songe :
  "Lulley, by, by, lully, lulley!"] 99

(7)

"Jhesu, my son, hevyn kyng,
Yf it be thy will,
Grant thow me myn askyng,
As reason wold, & skyll : 103
What so euer they be,
þat can and will be
  Mery on þis day,
To blis them brynge,
& I shall syng :
  "Lulley, by, by, lully, lulley.'" 109
This [enders nyght
I sawe a sight,
A sterre as bryght
  As any day ;
And euer a-monge,
A maydyn songe :
  "Lulley, by, by, lully, lulley !"] 116
    Explicit.

36.

**For sothe, I hold hym well & with owt woo,
þat hath ynowgh, & can say 'whoo.'**

(1)

I was with pope & cardynall,
& with bisshoppis & prestis gret & small,
Yet was neuer non of them all

I. Sacred Songs and Carols.

  That had ynowgh, & cowld say ' who.'
   For soth, I hold [hy*m* well & wit*h* owt woo,
   þat hath ynowgh, & ca*n* say ' whoo.']   6

(2)
Now covitise begy*n*neth to wake,
& lechery ys to hym take,
& seyth his joy may not slake,   9
  That hath ynowgh, & ca*n* say ' whoo.'
   For sothe, I hold [hy*m* well & wit*h* owt woo,
   þat hath ynowgh, & ca*n* say ' whoo.']   12

(3)
I was wit*h* emprowr, kyng & knyght,
Wit*h* duke, erle, baron & lady bright,
Yet was no*n* of the*m*, to my sight,   15
  That had ynowgh / & cowld say ' who.'
   For soth, I hold [hy*m* well & wit*h* owt woo,
   þat hath ynowgh, & ca*n* say ' whoo.']   18

(4)
Whan all thyng*is* fall a-way,
Than covetyse begyneth to play,
He is not here / I dare well say,   21
  That hath ynowgh, & ca*n* say ' who.'
   For soth, I hold [hy*m* well & wit*h* owt woo,
   þat hath ynowgh, & ca*n* say ' whoo.']   24
    Explicit.

37.

God þ*a*t sittith in trinite,   ⎫ fote. [leaf 227]
Amend this world, yf thy will be. ⎭

(1)
Vices be wyld & vertues lame,
& vice is [1] torned in to game,
Ther-for correc*i*on is to blame   3
  That so lesith his dignyte.
   God þ*a*t sittith in trinite,
   [Amend this world, yf thy will be.]   6

---

[1] vice is] is is vice MS.

I. Sacred Songs and Carols.

(2)
Pasciens hath tak a flight,
& meladye is owt of sight;
Now eu*er*y boy will cow[n]terfet a knyght,   9
Reporte hym self as good as he.
   God þat [sittith in trinite,
   Amend this world, yf thy will be.]   12

(3)
Pryncipally amonge eu*er*y state,
In cowrte me*n* thynk gret debate,
For pees stondith at the gate,   15
And morneth after charyte.
   God þat [sittith in trinite,
   Amend this world, yf thy will be.]   18

(4)
Envy ys thik, & love ys thyn,
& specyally amonge owr eme-Cristyn,
For love ys wit*h*owt / & envy ys wit*h*in,   21
& so kyndnesse away gan flee.
   God þat [sittith in trinite,
   Amend this world, yf thy will be.]   24

(5)
Fortune ys a m*ar*velus chance,
& envy causith gret distance
Bothe i*n* Ynglond & in France;   27
Exiled ys benyngnyte.
   God þat sittith [in trinite,
   Amend this world, yf thy will be.]   30

(6)
Nowe late vs p*r*ay both on & all,
& specially vpo*n* God call,
To send love & g*r*ace a-monge vs all,   33
And amonge all me*n* in Cristynte.
   God þat sittith [in trinite,
   Amend this world, yf thy will be.]   36
        Explicit.

I. *Sacred Songs and Carols.* 29

38.

Syng we with myrth, joye & solas ⎫
In honowr of this Cristemas! ⎭ fote.

(1)
Glori*us* God had gret pyte,
How longe mans sowle in payn shuld
   be ;
He sent his son to mak vs free,
   Which for man*us* sake,   4
Off a maydyn pure,
Agaynst nature,
Owr flesshe dide take.
   Sy*n*g [we with myrth, joye &
     solas
   In honowr of this Cristemas!] 9

(2)
In Bedlem owr saviowr,   10
With-owt fode, in a manjowre
Was born,—hit was his plesure,—
   Best*is* amonge.   13
Angell*is* hevynly
Made armonye
And joyffull songe.
   Sy*n*ge [we with myrth, joye &
     solas
   In honowr of this Cristemas!] 18

(3)
The VIIIth day he was circonsisid,
Leste Moyses lawe shuld be dispised ;
A name to hy*m* they haue devised,
   Call hym Jh*e*sus ;   22
For Gabryell
His moder dide[1] tell
That it shuld be thus.
   Sy*n*g [we with myrth, joye &
     solas
   In honowr of this Cristemas!] 27

(4)
A newe made sterre, more large &
   clere   28
Tha*n* o*þ*er sterres, than dide appere.
Fro Caldey the felosafers in fere
   In to Bedlem yt browght.   31
Ther it dide stond
Still, till that they fonde
Hym that they sowght.
   Sy*n*g we wi*th* myrthe, [joye &
     soals
   In honowr of this Cristemas!]36

(5)   [² leaf 227, back]
[2]The kyng*is* browght *þ*er offrynge,
Gold *þ*at betokneth a worthy kynge,
I[n]sens, p*r*isthode ; myr, buryinge
   For his manhode.   40
The angell com,
Bade the*m* go home
Not by Herode.
   Sy*n*g we [with myrth, joye &
     solas
   In honowr of this Cristemas!]45

(6)
Trust i*n* God, ma*n*, and in no*n* other;
Mistrust hy*m* not, he is thy bro*þ*er ;
Thow hast a mediatrix of his moder.
   Syke for thy synne,   49
Crye marcy,
He will not denye
Thy sowle to wynne.
   Sy*n*g [we with myrth, joye &
     solas
   In honowr of this Cristemas!]54
     Explicit.

[1] MS. dide did

39.

Now syng we right as it is : ⎫
   'Quod puer natus est nobis.' ⎬ fote.

(1)

This babe to vs now is born ;
Wonderfull[1] werk*is* he hath wrowght ;
He wold not lesse that was forlorn,
   But again he hath vs bowght.   4
     And thus it is, / for soth ywys,
     He asketh no thyng / but þat is his.
        [Now syng we right as it is:
         'Quod puer natus est nobis.']   8

(2)

A dulfull deth to hy*m* was mente,   9
   Whan on þe rode his body was spred,
& as a theff he was ther hente.
   & on a spere his liff was lede.   12
     And thus it is, / for soth ywis,
     He asketh no thynge but þat is his.
        [Now syng we right as it is:
         'Quod puer natus est nobis.']   16

(3)

" Man, why art thow vnkynd to me ?   17
   What woldest thow I did for the more ?
Geve me thy trew harte, I p*r*ay the ;
   Yff thow be dampned, it ruthe me sore."   20
     And thus it is / for sothe ywis,
     He asketh no thyng / but þat is his.
        [Now syng we right as it is:
         'Quod puer natus est nobis.']   24

(4)

" Man, I love the, / whom loveste thowe ?   25
   I p*r*ay the, torne to me agayn,
& thow shalt be as welcom nowe
   As he that never in syn was seyn."   28
     And thus it is / for soth ywys,
     He asketh no thynge but þat is his.
        [Now syng we right as it is:
         'Quod puer natus est nobis.']   32

[1] MS. Worderfull

I. Sacred Songs and Carols. 31

40. [The Murder of Thomas a Beket.]

A, a, a, a! nun*c* gaudet eccl*es*ia. } fote.

(1)
Lystyn, lordyng*is* both gret & small!
I will you tell a wonder tale,
Howe holy chirch was browght in bale
    Cum magna iniuria.
      [A, a, a, a! nun*c* gaudet eccl*es*ia.]

(2)
The gretteste clark in this londe,
Thomas of Canturbury, I vnderstonde,
Slayn he was w*ith* wykyd honde,
    Malo*rum* potencia.
      [A, a, a, a! nun*c* gaudet eccl*es*ia.]

(3)
The knyght*is* were sent from Harry þe kynge,
þ*a*t day they dide a wykid thynge,
Wykyd men, with-owt lesynge,
    Per regis imperia.
      [A, a, a, a! nun*c* gaudet eccl*es*ia.]

(4)
They sowght þe bisshop all a-bowt,
With-in his place, and with-owt,
Of Jh*es*u Crist they had no dowght   [leaf 228]
    Per sua malicia.
      [A, a, a, a! nun*c* gaudet eccl*es*ia.]

(5)
They opened þ*er* mowthes wond*er*ly wide,
& spake to hym w*ith* myche pryde:
"Traytor, here thow shalt abide,
    Ferens mort*is* tedia!"
      [A, a, a, a! nun*c* gaudet eccl*es*ia.]

(6)
Beffore þe auter he kneled down,
& than they pared his crown,
& stered his braynes vp so down,
    Optans celi gawdia.
      [A, a, a, a,! nun*c* gaudet eccl*es*ia.]

1

5

10

15

20

25

30

41. [The Stoning of St. Stephen.]

Nowe syng we both all & sum **:** } fote.
Lapidauerunt Stephanum**.**

(1)
Whan seynt Stevyn was at Jeruzalem,
Godis lawes he loved to lerne :
þat made þe Jewes to cry so clere & clen,   3
Lapidaverunt Stephanum.
    [Nowe syng we both all & sum :
    Lapidauerunt Stephanum.]   6

(2)
The Jewes þat were both false & fell,
Agaynst seynt Stephyn they were cruell,
Hym to sle they made gret ȝell,   9
& lapidaverunt Stephanum.
    [Nowe syng we both all & sum
    Lapidauerunt Stephanum.]   12

(3)
They pullid hym with-owt the town,
& than he mekely kneled down,
While the Jewes crakkyd his crown,   15
Quia lapidaverunt Stephanum.
    [Nowe syng we both all & sum :
    Lapidauerunt Stephanum.]   18

(4)
Gret stones & bones at hym they caste,
Veynes & bones of hym they braste,
& they kylled hym at the laste,   21
Quia lapidaverunt Stephanum.
    [Nowe syng we both all & sum :
    Lapidauerunt Stephanum.]   24

(5)
Pray we all þat now be here,
Vnto seynt Stephyn, þat marter clere,
To save vs all from the fendis fere.   27
Lapidauerunt Stephanum.
    [Nowe syng we both all & sum :
    Lapidauerunt Stephanum.]   30

I. *Sacred Songs and Carols.*

42. [The Boar's Head.]

Caput apri refero, } fote.
Resonens laudes domino.

(1)
The boris hed in hondis I brynge
With garlondis gay & byrdis syngynge,
I pray you all, helpe me to synge,   3
    Qui estis in conviuio.
        [Caput apri refero,
        Resonens laudes domino.]   6

(2)
The boris hede, I vnderstond,
Ys cheff seruyce in all this londe,
Wher-so-ever it may be fonde,   9
    Seruitur cum sinapio.
        [Caput apri refero,
        Resonens laudes domino.]   12

(3)
The boris hede, I dare well say,
Anon after the XIIth day,
He taketh his leve & goth a-way,   15
    Exiuit tunc de patria.
        [Caput apri refero,
        Resonens laudes domino.]   18

43.

Gawde for thy joyes five, } fote.   [leaf 228, back]
Mary, moder, maydyn & wyff!

(1)
Gaude! to whom Gabryell was sent,
    From Nazareth to Galalie,
& said that God omnipotent   3
    Wold haue his son be born of the.
        [Gawde for thy joyes five,
        Mary, moder, maydyn and wyff!]   6

(2)
Gaude! thow bare hym withowt payn,
    & with payn thow saweste hym dy on tre,

34   I. *Sacred Songs and Carols.*

But gaude, whan he rose agayn,   9
  For he appered firste to the.
    [Gawde for thy joyes five,
    Mary, moder, maydyn & wyff !]   12

(3)
Gawde ! thowe thow saweste hy*m* assende
  By his own strenth a-bove the skye,
An hoste of angell*is* down he sent,   15
  & assumpte thy sowle wit*h* thy bodye.
    [Gawde for thy joyes five,
    Mary, moder, maydyn & wyff !]   18

(4)
Gaude ! thy dignyte ys gret ;
  For next vnto the trynyte,
Above all seynt*is*, is thy sete,   21
  & all joye is i*n* þe sight of the.
    [Gawde for thy joyes five,
    Mary, moder, maydyn & wyff !]   24

(5)
Gaude, moder & maydyn pure !
  For thy joyes shall never cesse,—
Ther-of thow art siker & sure,—   27
  But ever florisshe & encrese.
    [Gawde for thy joyes five,
    Mary, moder, maydyn & wyff !]   30
      Explicit.

44. [Christ, an Ear of Wheat.]

A blessid byrd, as I you say, } fote.
þ*at* dyed & rose on Good Fryday.

(1)
On Crist*is* day, I vnderstond,
An ere of whet of a mayd spronge,
XXX[ti] wynter in erth to stond,   3
  To make vs bred, all to his pay.
    [A blessid byrd, as I you say,
    þ*at* dyed & rose on Good Fryday.]   6

I. *Sacred Songs and Carols.*

(2)
This corn was repyn & layd to grownd,
Full sore beten & faste bownd
Vnto a piler with cord*is* rownd, 9
 At his fyngers end*is* þe blod ran owt þat day.
  [A blessid byrd, as I you say,
  þat dyed & rose on Good Fryday.] 12
(3)
This corn was repyn wit*h* gret envye
Vpon þe mownt of Caluary,
Tokyn he shewed on Shere-Thursday, 15
 Mawndy he gaff to his dissiples ther.
  [A blessid byrd, as I you say,
  þat dyed & rose on Good Fryday.] 18
(4)
Jhesu vpon his body the crosse bare ;
Water & blode cam fro*m* hym ther ;
This corn was skorged all in f[e]re, 21
 Tyll it wexed blode rede.
  [A blessid byrd, as I you say,
  þat dyed & rose on Good Fryday.] 24
(5)
A crown of thorn set on his hede,
& he was done on the rode
& betyn, till his body was blody rede, 27
 Thus they bett Jhesu, owr det to pay.
  [A blessid byrd, as I you say,
  þat dyed & rose on Good Fryday.] 30
   Explicit.

45.

  P*r*ay for vs to the trinite, ⎫
  Joh*ann*es, Cristi care !   ⎬ fote.
             ⎭
(1)
Thow dereste disciple of Jhesu Criste,
Most best belovid & beste be-triste,
Which at his last sop*er* did lye on his breste, 3
 Sacra fluenta potare.
  [P*r*ay for vs to the trinite,
  Joh*ann*es, Cristi care !] 6

36   I. *Sacred Songs and Carols.*

(2)
As he in his passion to his dere moder
Toke the for her keper, her son & his broþer,
Pray þat owr hartis may most of all other   9
    Jhesum semper amare.
        [Pray for vs to the trinite,
        Johannes, Cristi care !]   12

(3)
[1] And as þou þe stronge venym which II men had slayn,
Drank withowt hurt, & raysed them agayn,   [1 leaf 229]
Pray þat þe venym of syn may vs not payn,   15
    Non poterit alligare.
        [Pray for vs to the trinite,
        Johannes, Cristi care !]   18

(4)
As þou þe II men ther tresure dide restore,
þat had forsakyn & morned ther fore,
Pray þat we may fals riches forsak for euermore,   21
    Celis tesavrizare.
        [Pray for vs to the trinite,
        Johannes, Cristi care !]   24

(5)
And pray þat we may haue suche grace,
Here so to morne for owr trespas,
þat we may stond siker beffore Cristis face,   27
    Cum venerit judicare.
        [Pray for vs to the trinite,
        Johannes, Cristi care !]   30
            Explicit.

46.

Alas, my hart will brek in thre,
Terribilis mors conturbat me.   } fote.

(1)
Illa juventis that is so nyse
Me deduxit in to vayn devise,
Infirmus sum, I may not rise,
    Terribilis mors conturbat me.   4

I. *Sacred Songs and Carols.*

(2)
Dum juvinus fui, lytill I dred,
Set semper in sinne I ete my bred,
Jam ductus sum in to my bed,
    Terribilis mors [conturbat me.]   8
(3)
Corpus migrat in to my sowle,
Respicit demon in his rowle,
Desiderat ipse to haue his tolle,
    Terribilis mors [conturbat me.]   12
(4)
Christus se ipsum, whan he shuld dye,
Patri suo his manhode did crye:
" Respice me pater, that is so hye ! "
    Terribilis mors [conturbat me.]   16
(5)
Queso jam the trynyte,
Duc me from this vanyte
In celum, ther is joy with the,
    Terribilis mors conturbat me.   20
    Explicit.

47. [The fleur de lys, Christ.]
Synge we alle, for tyme it is : } fote.
Mary hath born þe flowre delice.

(1)
For his love þat bowght vs all dere,
Lystyn, lordyngis, that ben here,
& I will tell you in fere,   3
    Wher-of com þe flowr delyce.
    Syng we [alle, for tyme it is :
    Mary hath born þe flowre delice.]   6
(2)
On Cristmas nyght, whan it was cold,
Owr lady lay amonge bestis bolde,
& ther she bare Jhesu, Josepff tolde,   9
    & ther-of com the flowr delice.
    Syng [we alle, for tyme it is :
    Mary hath born þe flowre delice.]   12

I. *Sacred Songs and Carols.*

(3)
Off þat berith witnesse seynt John,
That it was of myche renown;
Baptized he was in flom Jordan, 15
 & ther-of cam the flowr delice.
  Syng [we alle, for tyme it is:
  Mary hath born þe flowre delice.] 18
(4)
On Good Fryday þat child was slayn,
Betyn with skorges & all to-flayn;
That day he suffred myche payn; 21
 & ther-of com the flowr delice.
  Syng [we alle, for tyme it is:
  Mary hath born þe flowre delice.] 24
   Explicit.

48.

I pray you, be mery & synge with me } fote. [lf 229, bk]
In worship of Cristys nativite.

(1)
In to this world, this day dide com
Jhesu Criste, bothe God & man,
Lorde & seruant in on person, 3
 Born of þe blessid virgyn Mary.
  I pray [you, be mery & synge with me
  In worship of Cristys nativite.] 6
(2)
He þat was riche, withowt any nede,
Appered in this world in right pore wede,
To mak vs, þat were pore in dede, 9
 Riche with-owt any nede, trewly.
  I pray [you, be mery & synge with me
  In worship of Cristys nativite.] 12
(3)
A stabill was his chambre; a crach was his bed;
He had not a pylow to lay vnder his hed;
With maydyns mylk þat babe was fedde, 15
 In pore clopis was lappid þe Lord Almyghty.
  I pray [you, be mery & synge with me
  In worship of Cristys nativite.] 18

I. Sacred Songs and Carols.

(4)
A noble lesson here is vs tawght,
To set all worldly riches at nawght,
But pray we þat we may be theder browght, 21
    Wher riches ys everlastyngly.
I pray [you, be mery & synge with me
    In worship of Cristys nativite.] 24

49.

Newell, newell, newell, newell, } fote.
This ys þe salutacion of Gabryell.

(1)
Tydyngis trewe, ther be com newe,
    Sent from the trynyte
By Gabryell from Nazareth to a cite of Galely : 3
'A clene maydyn, a pure virgyn,
    By her humylite
Hath born the person second in divinite.' 6
    Newell, [newell, newell, newell,
    This ys þe salutacion of Gabryell.] 8

(2)
Whan that he presentid was
    Beffore her fayre visage,
In moste demvre & goodly wise
    He dide to her homage 12
& said : "Lady, from hevyn so hye,
    That lordis herytage,
For he of the now born will be,
    I am sent on the message." 16
    Newell, [newell, newell, newell,
    This ys þe salutacion of Gabryell.] 18

(3)
"Hayll, virgyn celestiall,
    The mekeste þat euer was !
Hayll, temple of the deite !
    Hayll, myrrowr of all grace ! 22
Hayll, virgyn pure ! I the ensure,
    With-in a lytill space 24

40   I. *Sacred Songs and Carols.*

Thow shalt conceyve, & hym receyve
  That shall brynge gret solas." 26
    Newell, [newell, newell, newell,
    This ys þe salutacion of Gabryell.] 28

(4)

Than bespak the virgyn agayn,
  & answered womanly :
" What-so-euer my lord comaundith me,
  I will obbey trewly. 32
    Ecce sum humilima ancilla domini :
    Secundum verbum tuum, fiat michi." 34
    Newell, [newell, newell, newell,
    This ys þe salutacion of Gabryell.] 36
      Explicit.

50.

" O my harte is wo ! " Mary, she sayd so,   [leaf 230]
" For to se my dere son dye ; & sonnes haue I no mo."

(1)

" Whan þat my swete son was XXX^{ti} wynter old,
Than þe traytor Judas wexed very bold ;
For XXX^{ti} platis of money, his master he had sold ;
But whan I it wyst, lord, my hart was cold. 4
  O, my hart is woo ! " [Mary,[1] she sayd so,
  " For to se my dere son dye; & sonnes haue I no mo."] 6

(2)

" Vpon Shere Thursday than truly it was,
On my sonnes deth þat Judas did on passe ;
Many were þe fals Jewes þat folowed hym by trace,
& þer, beffore them all, he kyssed my sonnes face. 10
  O my hart [[2]is wo ! " Mary, she sayd so,
  "For to se my dere son dye; & sonnes haue I no mo."] 12

(3)

" My son, beffore Pilat browght was he ;
& Peter said III tymes he knew hym not perde.

Mary . . . mo."] &c. MS.   [2] is . . . mo."] &c. MS.

I. Sacred Songs and Carols.

Pylat said vnto þe Jewes : 'What say ye ? '
Than they cryed with on voys : ' Crucyfyge ! ' 16
O my hart is woo," [¹ Mary, she sayd so,
"For to se my dere son dye ; & sonnes haue I no mo."]18

(4)

"On Good Friday at þe mownt of Caluary
My son was don on þe crosse, nayled with naylis III,
Of all þe frendis þat he had, neuer on could he see,
But jentyll the evangelist, þat still stode hym by. 22
O my hart [² is wo ! " Mary, she sayd so,
"For to se my dere son dye ; & sonnes haue I no mo."]24

(5)

Thowgh I were sorowfull, no man haue at yt wonder ;
For howge was þe erth-quak, horyble was þe thonder,
I loked on my swet son on þe crosse þat stode vnder ;
Than cam Lungeus with a spere & clift his hart in sonder.
O my [hart is wo ! " Mary, she sayd so,
"For to se my dere son dye ; & sonnes haue I no mo."]30
Explicit.

51.

To see the maydyn wepe her sonnes passion,
It entrid my hart full depe with gret compassion.

(1)

Bowght & sold full traytorsly,
And to a pylar bownde,
The Jewes bet hym full pytuowsly,
  & gave hym many a wownde. 4
    To see þe maydyn wepe [her³ sonnes passion,
    It entrid my hart full depe with gret compassion.] 6

(2)

Full maydynly, full moderly,
Whan she the crosse be-helde,
The teris from her eyen fill ;
  She said : " Alas, my childe ! " 10
    To see þe maydyn wepe³ [her sonnes passion,
    It entrid my hart full depe with gret compassion.] 12

[1] Mary . . . mo."] &c. MS. [2] is . . . mo."] &c. MS.
[3] her . . . compassion] &c. MS.

(3)

With sharpe thornes þe fals Jewes
Crowned his holy hede ;
They naylid hym fast to þe crosse,
 For they wold haue hym dede.   16
  To se þe maydyn wepe [her sonnes passion,
  It entrid my hart full depe with gret compassion.] 18

(4)

Eysell & gall they gave hym to drynk,
& percyd hym to the harte.
His blessid moder & maydyn clene,
 She swowned for his smarte.   22
  To see þe maydyn wepe [her sonnes passion,
  It entrid my hart full depe with gret compassion.] 24

(5)

Now, Mary myld, pray for vs,
& bryng vs to þe blisse,
þat we may be in joy with the,
 Wher þat thy swet son ys.   28
  To see þe maydyn wepe her sonnes passion,
  [It entrid my hart full depe with gret compassion.] 30

52.

**I consayll you, bothe more & lesse,
Beware of sweryng by þe masse.**

(1)

The masse is of so high dignytee,
þat no thyng to it comprehendid may be ;
For ther is present in the trynyte,
 On God in persones thre.   4
  I consaill you both more & lesse,—
  [Beware of sweryng by þe masse.]   6

(2)

The Ierachye of angellis kynde,
All other sayntis had in mynde,

I. Sacred Songs and Carols. 43

þe which to forsak þou art to blynde,
Leve þi sweryng, & spill not þi wynde. 10
    I consaill you [¹ bothe more & lesse,
    Beware of sweryng by þe masse.] 12

(3)
In the masse is more mysterye   [leaf 230, back]
Than dropis in þe see or sterres in þe skye,
Infenyte goodnesse, I tell the whye :
For God & man is offred vp trulye. 16
    I consayll you, both more & lesse,
    [Beware of sweryng by þe masse.] 18

(4)
Why swerist by þe masse, þou man so wode,
Wher is thy helth, thy lyves fode,
Cristis body, his precyus blode,
All thy saluacion, no thynge but good? 22
    I consaill [you, bothe more & lesse,
    Beware of sweryng by þe masse.] 24

(5)
Also thus seyth þe prophete Zakarye,
Witnesse beryng, as þou mayest see ;
& thus he seyth in his prophesye :
þat all swerers dampned shall be. 28
    I consaill [you, bothe more & lesse,
    Beware of sweryng by þe masse.] 30

(6)
Than marcy cry & call for grace,
Here in erthe while þou hast space,
þat whan þe erth hath couered thy face,
Thy sowle in hevyn may haue a place. 34
    I consaill [you, bothe more & lesse,
    Beware of sweryng by þe masse.] 36
        Explicit.

---

[1] bothe . . . masse MS. &c.

53.

**What, hard ye not, þe kyng of Jherusalem
Is now born in Bethelem?** *etc.*

(1)

I shall you tell a gret mervayll,
How an angell, for owr avayll,
Com to a mayd, & said : "All hayll!" 3
  What, hard ye not,[1] [þe kyng of Jherusalem
  Is now born in Bethelem?] 5

(2)

"All hayll," he said, "and full of grace,
God is with the now in this place,
A child þou shalt bere in lytill space." 8
  What, hard [ye not, þe kyng of Jherusalem
  Is now born in Bethelem?] 10

(3)

"A child!" she said : "how may that be?
Þer had never no man knowlage of me."
"Þe Holy Gost," he said, "shall light in the." 13
  What, hard [ye not, þe kyng of Jherusalem
  Is now born in Bethelem?] 15

(4)

"And as þou art, so shall thow be,"
The angell said, "in virgynite,
Beffore & after in euery degree." 18
  What, hard ye not,[1] [þe kyng of Jherusalem
  Is now born in Bethelem?] 20

(5)

The mayd answered þe angell agyn :
"Yf God will, þat this be sayn,
The wordis be to me full fayn." 23
  What, hard [ye not, þe kyng of Jherusalem
  Is now born in Bethelem?] 25

(6)

Now will we all, in reioysynge
Þat we haue hard þis good tydyng,
To þat child Te Deum synge.
  Te Deum laudamus. 29
    Explicit.

[1] þe . . . Bethelem MS. &c.

54.

Wassaill, wassaill, wassaill, syng we,
In worshipe of Crist_is_ natiuite!

(1)
Now joy be [1] to the trynyte,
Fader, Son & Holy Goste,
That on God is in trynite,
Fader of hevyn, of myght_is_ most. 4
 Wassaill, [[2] wassaill, wassaill, syng we,
 In worshipe of Crist_is_ natiuite!] 6

(2)
And joy [be] to the virgyn pure,
þat eu_er_ kepte her vndefiled,
Gru_n_did in g_ra_ce, i_n_ hart full sure,
& bare a child as maydyn myld. 10
 Wassayll, [wassaill, wassaill, syng we,
 In worshipe of Crist_is_ natiuite!] 12

(3)
Bethelem & þe sterre so shen,
þ_at_ shon III kyng_is_ for to gide,
Bere witnesse of this maydyn clene;
The kyng_is_ III offred that tide. 16
 Wassaill, [wassaill, wassaill, syng we,
 In worshipe of Crist_is_ natiuite!] 18

(4)
And sheper_r_dis hard, a[s] wretyn is,
þe joyffull songe þ_at_ þ_er_ was songe,
"Glorya in excelsis!"
Wit_h_ angell_is_ voys it was owt ronge. 22
 Wassaill, [wassaill, wassaill, syng we,
 In worshipe of Crist_is_ natiuite!] 24

(5)
Now joy be to þe blessidfull child
& joy be to his moder dere,
Joy we all of þ_at_ maydyn myld,
& joy haue they þ_at_ mak good chere! 28
 Wassaill, [wassaill, wassaill, syng we,
 In worshipe of Crist_is_ natiuite!] 30
   Explicit.

[1] Now be joy be MS.   [2] _wassaill . . . natiuite_ MS. &c.

55.

He is wise, so most I goo, [leaf 231]
That can be mery, & suffer woo.

(1)
Be mery & suffer, as I the vise,
Wher-euer thow sytt or rise ;
Be well ware, whom thow despise,
 þou shalt kysse who is thy foo.   4
  He is wise, [so most I goo,
  That can be mery, & suffer woo.[1]]   6

(2)
Beware, to whom þou spek thy will,
For thy speche may greve the yll ;
Here & see, & goo than still,
 But well is he þat can do soo.   10
  He is wise, [so most I goo,
  That can be mery, & suffer woo.[1]]   12

(3)
Many a man holdyth hym so stowght,
What so euer he thynk, he seyth it owt ;
But if he loke well a-bowt,
 His tonge may be his most foo.   16
  He is wise, [so most I goo,
  That can be mery, & suffer woo.[1]]   18

(4)
Be mery, now is all my songe,
þe wise man tawght both old & yonge ;
Who can suffer & hold his tonge,
 He may be mery & no thyng woo.   22
  He is wise, [so most I goo,
  That can be mery, & suffer woo.[1]]   24

(5)
Yff any man displese the owght,
Suffer with a mery thowght ;
Let care away & greve þe nowght,
 & shake thy lappe & lat it go.   28
  He is wise, [so most I goo,
  That can be mery, & suffer woo.[1]]   30
   Explicit.

[1] *so . . . woo*] &c. MS.

I. *Sacred Songs and Carols.*

56.

**An old sawe haþ be fownd trewe :
Cast not away thyn old for newe.**

(1)

An old said sawe : " On-knowen, on-kyste " ;
"Wher is lytill love per is lytill tryste " ;
And ever beware of " Had I wyste,"   3
And remembre this sawe, for it is new :
Ellis must we drynk as we brewe.   5

(2)

The peple to plese, sir, it is payn,
Peraventure amonge XX^{ti} not twayn ;
Hold me excused, thowgh I be playn.   8
This sawe is old, remembre it newe,
Or ellis most we drynk as we brewe.   10

(3)

An-other thynge, sir, marke we well,
Two facis in on hode, a fayre castell ;
He seyth hym-self he will not medyll ;   13
Folk fayre lest seche in cowrt to shew,
& ellis most we drynk as we brew.   15

(4)

Thyn old seruantis here thus ar meved ;
The tyme wyll cum they must be releved ;
Geve trust to them þat thow hast preved,   18
& if þou do so, thow shalt not rewe,
& ellis must þou drynk as þou doste brewe.   20
Explicit.

57.

**Man, be ware & wise in dede,
& assay a frend or þou haue nede.**

(1)

Thorow a forest þat was so longe,
   As I rode with mekyll drede,
I hard a birde syngyng a songe :
   "Assay a frend or þou haue nede." 4

(2)

As I stode & hoved still
   & to a tre I tyed my stede,
Euer the birde sat syngyng still :
   "Assay a frend or þou haue nede." 8

48   I. *Sacred Songs and Carols.*

(3)
Me thowght it was a wonder noyse,
& nere hond þe byrde I yede;
Iwis she songe with a lowde voise:
"Assay a frend or þou haue nede." 12

(4)
The birde satt high vpon a tree,
Of feders gray than was her wede:
She sayd: " Do a[s] I bide the,
Assay a frend or þou haue nede." 16

(5)
I behelde her wonder longe; [1f 231,bk]
She said: "Do as I bide the, in dede,
Wheþer þou do right & wronge,
Assay a frend or þou haue nede."20

(6)
I trowe, of me she was a-gaste;
She toke her flight; away she yede;
Thus she said, whan she songe last,
"Assay a frend or þou haue nede."24
Explicit.

58.
Man, meve thy mynd, & joy this fest;
Veritas de terra orta est.

(1)
As I cam by þe way,
I sawe a sight semly to see,
The sheperdis rangyng in a ray,
Vpon þe folde kepynge ther fee, 4
A sterre they said they dide espie
Kastyng the bemes owt of þe est,
And angellis makyng melodye:
"Veritas de terra orta est." 8

(2)
Vpon þat sight they were a-gast,
Sayinge thes wordis as I say the:
"To Bedlem shortly lett vs hast
& ther we shall þe trowthe see." 12
The angell said vnto them all III
To þer comfort, or euer he seste:
"Consolamini, & mery be:
Veritas de terra orta est." 16

(3)
From hevyn, owt of þe highest see,
Rightwisnes hath taken þe way,
With marcy medled plentuowsly,
& so conseyved in a may;   20
Miranda res, this is in fay,
So seith the prophet in his gest:
Now is he born, scripture doth say:
Veritas de terra orta est. 24

(4)
Than passed þe sheperdis from þat place
& folowed by þe sterres beme,
þat was so bright affore þer face,
Hit browght them streight vnto Bethlem; 28
So bright it shon over all þe realme
Tyll they cam þer they wold not
To Jury & Jerusalem :   [rest,
Veritas de terra orta est. 32
Explicit.

I. *Sacred Songs and Carols.* 49

59.
All this tyme this songe is best:
Verbum caro factum est.

(1)
This nyght ther is a child born,
That sprange owt of Jessis thorn;
We must synge & say ther forn:
Verbum caro factum est.   4

(2)
Jhesus is the childis name
& Mary myld is his dame,
All owr sorow shall torn to game:
Verbum caro factum est.   8

(3)
Hit fell vpon high mydnyght,
The sterres shon both fayre & bright,
The angellis song with all per myght:
Verbum caro factum est.   12

(4)
Now knele we down on owr kne,
& pray we to the trynyte,
Owr helpe, owr socowr for to be.
Verbum caro factum est.   16

60.
Now syng we, syng we: Gloria tibi domine. [leaf 248, back]

(1)
Cryst kepe vs all, as he well can,
A solis ortu[s] cardine;
For he ys both God & man,
Qui natus est de virgine.
  Syng we, [syng we: Gloria tibi
    domine.]   5

(2)
As he ys lord, both day & nyght,
Venter[1] puelle baiulat,
So ys Mary, moder of myght,
Secreta que non noverat.
  Syng we, [syng we: Gloria tibi
    domine.]   10

(3)
The holy brest of chastyte,
Verbo consepit filium,
So browght before þe trinite,
Vt castytatis lyllyum.
  Syng we, [syng we: Gloria tibi
    domine.]   15

(4)
Betwen an ox & an asse
Enixa est puerpera;
In pore clothyng clothed he was,
Qui regnat super ethera.
  Syng we, [syng we: Gloria tibi
    domine.]—Explicit.   20

61.
Virgo, rosa virginum, Tuum precor fillium. [leaf 249, back]

(1)
Qvene of hevyn, blessyd mot þou be,
For Godis son, born he was of the,
For to make vs fre.
  Gloria tibi domine!   4

(2)
Jhesu, Godis son, born he was
In a crybe with hay & gras,
And dyed for vs on the crose.
  Gloria tibi domine!   8

[1] Ventus MS.

CAROLS.   E

I. *Sacred Songs and Carols.*

(3)

To owr lady make we owr mone,
þat she may pray to her dere son,
That we may to his blis cum.
Gloria tibi domine! 12
Explicit.

62.

**Man, be ware, or thou be wo,
& thynk on pride & lat hym go.**

(1)
Pryde is owt, & pride ys yn, [syn,
& pride ys þe begynnyng of euery
Of pride shall no man no thyng wyn,
But sorow, care & myche wo. 4

(2)
Wenest þou, man, for thi gay cloth-
To be an emprowr or a kyng, [yng,
Or for thy gret othes swepyng?
Do a-way, man, & thynk not so! 8

(3)
Lucyfer was an angell bright,
[C]ovytowr of godis myght;
[Thoro]w his pride he lost his sight,
[And fell] down in to endles wo. 12
Explicit.

II. Religious Poems and Prayers in Verse.

63.
To þe gud angell. [leaf 144]

(1)

O angell dere, wher-euer I goo,
 Me that am comytted to thyne awarde,
Saue, defende, & govern also,
 That in hewyn with the be my reward ! 4

(2)

¶ Clense my sowle from syn þat I haue do,
 & vertuosly me wysse to godward !
Shyld me from þe fende evermo,
 & fro the paynes of hell so hard ! 8

(3)

¶ O thou cumly angell, so gud & clere,
 þat ever art abydyng with me !
Thowgh I may nother the se nor here,
 Yet devoutely with trist I pray to the. 12

(4)

¶ My body & sowle thou kepe in fere,
 With soden deth departid þat they not be !
For þat ys thyn offes, both fere & nere,
 In every place wher ever I be. 16

(5)

¶ O blessid angell, to me so dere,
 Messangere of God Almyght,
Govern my dedis & thowght in fere,
 To þe plesaunce of God, both day & nyght ! 20
Explicit.

64. [Have pity on me, O God!] [leaf 144.]

(1)

O dere God, pereles prince of pece,
  With all my power I the pray,
Lett not thy myght be marcyles
  To man that thou hast made of clay !   4
Owr kynde ys frayle, yt ys no nay,
  & ever hath bene syne we knew vs.
Therfor vs nedeth euery day,
  Of 'miserere mei, deus.'   8

(2)

For we þat be now fayer & fresshe,
  Shall fade & fall as doth the flowr,
& all the delytis of owr flesshe
  Shall fall in lesse than half an owr.   12
Kyng, prince & emperwre,
  All shall wast that now ys,
& be fayn of suche socowr
  Of ' miserere mei, deus.'   16

(3)

When we be dede & doluen depe,
  & breers growyng a-boue owr brayn,
Then helpith yt noder to wayle ne wepe ;
  To þe world shall we never torn a-gayn ;   20
But, as thyke as dropis of rayn,
  Shall wormes all to-chew[e] vs.
Then can I non other sayn,
  But ' miserere mei, deus.'   24

(4)

Whi lowed we than the wykyd lyff   [leaf 144, back]
  That so short while will be leste,[1]
Sith fader & moder, child & wyff,
  & frendis þat shuld love vs best,—   28
When deth hath draw vs to his neste,
  Then will they a-lone leve vs ;
Then can I se non other trust
  But ' myserere mei, deus.'   32

[1] MS. lefte

II. *Religious Poems and Prayers in Verse.* 53

(5)
Here-on to thynke, may dredfull be,
  Man & woman, & euery wyght,
For dowtles dye shall all we,
    To eche of vs, deth ys dight. 36
Then yt helpith not with hym to fyght,
  Sith he than will so rest vs ;
Ne no cumforte, I you plight,
    But 'miserere mei, deus.' 40

(6)
Then helpith it not with hym to stryve :
  Ayen the deth, lett vs not drede,
The which may lightly over dryff
    The world with his pompe & pryde, 44
Ther ys no money ne no mede,
  With hym to take a day of trwse,
But yff we may speke & spede
    With 'miserere mei, deus.' 48

(7)
For we þat all day fall God fro
  & God for-sake, as men for-sworne,
No wonder ys thowgh we be wo,
    þat thorow slowth we be for-lorne. 52
Then were vs better to be vnborne
  Then folow such vicys, & fle vertuse,
Ne were the grace off God beforne,
    Of 'miserere mei, deus.' 56

(8)
Marcy made God Almyght,
  For men þat be myld of mode,
& ordyned his passyon to be dyght,
    For all synfull manys good ; 60
For ellys to hell we hade bene twyte,
  For any thyng that ever was.
Pray we ever ther-for with ryght,
    With 'miserere mei, deus.' 64

(9)
O lorde God, why takis thou to the
  Deth, for all mankyndis gilt ?

54   II. *Religious Poems and Prayers in Verse.*

Thow hade þe sharpe, & we the smothe ;
Thow hade the poynt, and we the hilt.   68
Of thy penance no thyng we felt,
  & certes by reason owght rewe vs ;
Ther-for we synfull to the yelde,
  With ' miserere mei, deus.'   72

(10)
I se wel, God, thy swet[e] grace ;   [leaf 145]
Owr gret[e] gilt, thou hast for-gon ;
Thy marcy hath pight his place
A-boue thy warkis euerychone.   76
For we shuld be dampned a-non,
  Were not thy marcy þat thow yeffis to vs ;
For we haue cumforte non,
  But ' miserere mei, deus.'   80

(11)
Now Cryst þat cumforted mankynd,
Thou late thy pety spred & spryng !
Owt of the world we shall wend ;
Thow sofer no fend to payn vs bryng.   84
Haue we in mynd þat crownyd kyng,
Jhesus of Nazareth, kyng of Jewys,
& here vs, when we rede or syng
  Off ' miserere mei, deus.'   88
          Explicit.

65. [Now mercy, Lord, and gramercy.]

(1)
As I walked here by west,   [leaf 145]
  Ferre vnder a forest side,
I sawe a wight, went hym to rest ;
  Vnder a bowgh he gan a-bide ;   4
  & thus full ofte to Crist he cryde,
    Lyfftyng vp his hondys on hye :
  " Of pouerte, plesavnce, & of pride,
    Now marcy, Lorde, & gramarcy !   8
(2)
God, as I haue grewed the
  In wykyd worde, will or dede,

II. *Religious Poems and Prayers in Verse.* 55

Almyghty Lord, haue marcy on me,
  þat for my syne thy blode can shed.   12
Off witt & worshipe, will & wede,
  I thank the, Lorde, full inwardly,
& in this world, how so euer I spede,
  Euer marcy, Lorde, & gramarcy !   16

(3)
Gramarcy, Lorde, of all thy gyft
  Of wytt, worshipe, weell & wo !
Vp to the, Lord, my hart I lyft ;
  Lett never my dede twayn vs in too.   20
Marcy for þat I haue mysdo,
  & slee me never sodenly !
Thowgh fortune be my frend or foo,
  Ever marcy, Lorde, & gramarcy !   24

(4)
I am vnkynde, well I know,
  & þou hast showed me gret kyndnes ;
Therfor with humble harte & lowe,
  Marcy, God, & forgevenes   28
For pride & for vnbuxvmnes !
  What so euer thow sendyst, thus say I,   [leaf 145,/back]
In hape, in hele, & in sekenes,
  Ever marcy, Lorde, & gramarcy !   32

(5)
Marcy, for I haue mysspent
  My wyttis ·V·, therfor I wepe ;
To dedely syn full ofte I haue assent ;
  Thy comaundmentis can I never kepe ;   36
To sle my sowle, in syn I slepe,
  & lede my lyff in lechery ;
Fro covytyse I can not crepe :
  Now marcy, Lord, & gramarcy !   40

(6)
Othes grete & gloteny,
  Off wanhope & wykyd will ;
Bakbyte my neythbor for envy,
  & rightwes men to robe & spyll,   44

& for þer good, I wold them kyll
  With symony & perivry.
For all þat ever I haue done ill,
  Now marcy, Lorde, & gramarcy!   48
            (7)
By the lawe, I shuld no lengar leve
  Then I hade done a dedely syne;
Gramarcy, for thou wold for-geve,
  & space geve to amend me yn.   52
Fro wykkyd werke yff I wold twyn,
  To receyve me thou arte redy,
To þat blys þat never shall blyn:
  þer-for marcy, Lorde, & gramarcy!   56
            (8)
O dere God, what shall I say?
How shall I amendys make,
þat plesid the never to thy pay,
  Ne thowght neuer my syn to forsake? 60
Now shryft of mowth my syn shall slake,
  & I will sesse & be sory,
& to thi marcy me betake.
  Now, marcy, Lorde, & gramarcy!   64
            (9)
Gramarcy for þat thow madest me,
  & marcy for that I haue done a-mysse;
My hope, my helpe, ys hole in the,
  & thou hast, Lord, be-hight me this: 68
Who that ys baptyzed, shall haue blis,
  Yff þat he rule hym rightwesly.   [leaf 146]
To fulfill thi will, Lorde, me wysse,
  & ever, marcy, Lorde, and gramarcy! 72
            (10)
Fader, Son & the Holy Gost,
Gramarcy, Lorde, with harte lyght,
For thou wold not þat I were loste;
  The Fader hath gewen me myght: 76
The Son assentis, & hath me hight
  Witte & weell to me; & worshipfully
The Holy Gost to me grace hath dight.
  Now marcy, Lorde, & gramarcy!   80

II. *Religious Poems and Prayers in Verse.*

(11)
This ys the truth þat faylyth never
& proved ys in persones thre ;
Ys, & was, & shall be ever,
 Oonly God in trynyte. 84
Now helpe vs, prynce of all pyte,
At the day whan we shall dye,
Thi swete face þat we may se,
 With marcy, Lorde, & gramarcy! 88
  Explicit.

66*a*. [Salve, sancta parens! To the Virgin Mary.]

(1)
Hayle, lovely lady, laymand so lyght! [leaf 146, back]
Hayle myghtyfull modyr & maydyn myld!
Thow bare withyn thy body bryght,
 That ys thi maker & thy child, 4
 And thy virginite never defyled.
Thow rose & rote of right reuerens,
Hayle witt & welth þat never was fyled!
 Salue, sancta parens! 8

(2)
Hayle glad! whan Gabryell the grete
For cheftan chosen in chastyte,
On knese full kyndly he hym sett ;
 Full solemply thus said he : 12
 "Hayll, grete in grace! God ys with the,
Thow shalt consayve Criste, withowt defens,
To mans behowe. Blessid mot thou be!
 Salue, sancta parens!" 16

(3)
Hayle, empres of hell & hevyn!
With Elyzabeth thy cosyn talkyng,
& tolde her of the angels stevyn :
 Ther was gret worshipe of that metyng. 20

John Baptyst in his moder dide spryng;
For joy of Jhesu he was gaudens.
To the, sofferayn, swetly I syng:
 Salue, sancta parens!   24
   (4)
Hayle, blessid byrde, bote of owr balis! [leaf 147]
In Bedlem thy barne thow bere;
A stare shon swetly then ywysse,
 & III kyngis lede, comyng fro placis fere.   28
They presented thy child all in fere
 With gold, myrre, and frankynsens.
To the I synge, as I dyde ere:
 Salue, sancta parens!   32
   (5)
Hayle, worthiest woman, þat sofred most wo,
In the tyme of thy chyldis passyon!
He soffred dole & dede also,
 To make all mans redempcion.   36
The fyrst word after his resurreccion,
 When he sawe the in his presens,
To the he sayd withe discrecion:
 "Salue, sancta parens!"   40
   (6)
"Hayle, holy moder!" sothely to say,
So said owr Savyowr sufferently
Vnto the, lady, & went away;
 He talked to the no more trvly,   44
All holy church wott well for whi;
 Clarkis declare yt in sequens.
þat makis me move to the, Mary,
 Salue, sancta parens!   48
   (7)
Hayle, crowned quene of hevyn & hell!
Hayle, tru-love to the trynyte!
Thou derlyng dere, dight vs to dwell
 In riche hevyn, that fayer cyte.   52
Thow prynces pereles, of all pyte,
 Putt vs to peas when we passe hens,
þat we may syng & joy to the
 With "Salue, sancta parens!"   56
   Explicit.

II. Religious Poems and Prayers in Verse.

66b. [Hail, Mary!]

(1)

Hayle be thow Mary, moder of Cryst!
Hayle be thou blessed, þat bare a child!
Hayle! thou conceyved all with lyst,
Sone of God, bothe meke & mylde.   4
Hayle, mayden swete, þat never was defyl[ed]!
Hayle well, hayle wyte of all wysedom!
Hayle, fayerer then the flowr in felde!
Aue, regina celorum!   8

(2)

Hayle, cumly quene, cumforte of care!
Hayle, gud lady, fayer & bright!
Hayle be thow, heler of all owr sore!
Hayle be thow, lavmpe þat leymys light!   12
Hayle, fayer may! in the was pight
The joy of man, both all & sum!
Hayle, the pynacle of hevyn on hight!
Mater regys angilorum.   16

(3)

Hayle, cumly quene, cumforte of all! [leaf 147, back]
Hayle, that all owr blysse in brede!
Hayle, that all women do on call,
& namly when they ar hard bestede!   20
Hayle, that all the fendis drede,
& shall do at the day of dome!
With madyn mylke, thy child thou fede,
O Maria, flos virginum!   24

(4)

Hayle be thow, fayerest þat euer God fonde,
That Crist chase to his own bowr!
Hayle be thow, lavmpe þat euer ys lyghtand
To high, to lowe, to riche, to pore!   28
Hayle, spyce swettest of all savour,
That bare Jhesus that ys Godis son!
Hayle, of all women frute & flowr,
Velud rosa vell lillium!   32

II. Religious Poems and Prayers in Verse.

(5)

Hayle be thou, godly graunter of grace!
Hayle, blessyd stere on the see!
Hayle be thow, cumforte in euery case!
Hayle be thow, cheffe of chastyte!   36
Hayle well, hayle witt of all marcye!
Hayle be thou, highest in hevyns blome!
Hayle, jentyll lady! I pray the,
Funde preses ad filium.   40

(6)

Hayle be thou, vergyn of virgyns!
Hayle, blessed lady! & hayle, swete may!
Hayle be thou, moder of dere Jhesus!
Hayle, cheff of chastite, so well thow may!   44
Hayle, blessid lady! to thy son thow say,
That we may cum to his kyngdome;
For me & all Crystyn thow pray
Pro salute fidelium!   48
        Explicit.

67a.

An holy 'Salue Regina' to God in Englisshe.

Salue | with all obeysance to God in humblesse,
Regina | to regne ever more in blysse,
Mater | to Cryst, as we beleue expresse,
Misericordie | vnto all wrechesse;   4
Vita | to quyken, to helpe more & lesse,
Dulcedo | of most plesavnte beavte;
& we say this londe thy dowayr ys,
& perfor we syng : **Et spes nostra salue!**   8

¶ **Ad te,** | most meke & most benynge vergyne,
Clamamus | lowde with woyce tymerovs.
Exvles | made by false fravde serpentyne,
Filii | frayll, carefull & dolorovs,
Eve; | therfor owr lyffe laboryovs.   13

II. Religious Poems and Prayers in Verse.

¶ **Ad te,** | best meane to owr Lord God & ma*n*,
Suspiram_us_ | here i*n* þis see trobelovs,
Gementes | as sorowfull as we can,   16
Et flentes | oft wit*h* teris smerte,
In hac | dolefull, paynfull & lame*n*table
Lacrima_rum_, | wovndyng þe mortall herte,
Valle | restles, grevouse & chavngeable.   20

¶ **Eya ergo,** | mayden most amyable,
Advocata no*st*ra, | owr mediatrice,
Illos tuos | bryghtest & co*m*fortable
Misericordes oculos, | full of joy of pa*r*adyce,   24
Ad nos, | fletyng i*n* the see of tovrment,
Converte | now of sovereyn pyte,

¶ **Et Jh**es*u*m, | owr Lord, p*r*i[n]ce om*n*ipotent,
Be*n*edictu*m*, | full of most hye bownte,   28
Fructu_m_ | of lyff & riche benyngnyte,
Ventris tui, | moost evrovs creatovre,
Nobis post hoc exiliu_m_ **ostende,**
To owr eterne gretest joye & pleasure.   32

¶ **O clemens,** | full [of] m*ar*cyfull rychesse!
O pia, | full of ryche co*m*passyon!
O dulcis, | full of helpe i*n* eche distresse!
Virgo | fayrest way to saluac*i*on!   36
Marya, | a swetest medyac*i*on!

¶ **Salue** | wit*h* owr most lowly se*r*vyce,
Mater | of lyffe & ete*r*ne creacion!
Salue | ever as fayer as we ca*n* suffyce!   40
        Amen!

67*b*.

¶ Wytt hath wonder, & kynde ne can,
How maydyn ys moder, & God ys man.
¶ Leve thy askyng & beleve þat wonder,
For myght hath maystry, & skyll goth vnde*r*.
        Lavs deo!

II. Religious Poems and Prayers in Verse.

68. [Prayers.]

(1) Vnto the Fader. [leaf 209]

O most blessid Fader omnipotent! 1
O light most glorius in thy shynnyng!
O lord & maker of þe firmament!
Graffe & plante[1] by thyn hevynly werkyng
In vs myght & grace, þat in owr lyvyng 5
We may so do, to cum vnto the place,
Wher to þi sayntis þou showest þi swet face. 7

(2) Vnto þe Sonne.

O lord Jhesu Crist, þat by þi gret grace & meknes 8
Com from hevyn, thy people to save,
In to þe vergyn, well of all humblese,
Dessend þou woldeste, & on vs mercy have.
Souereyn Lord! of the euer I crave, 12
My sowle to defend, & body also preserue;
þi grace me tech in vertues the to serue. 14

(3) Vnto þe Holy Gost.

Eternall Lord, thow blessid Holy Goste, 15
Þat of þe Fader & [the] Son prosedes,
Show thy power, whan me nedith moste,
In deffassing of my fowle dedes![2]
Blessid Lord, þat from dampnabill d[r]edes 19
Þat conveyest all them þat to thy marcy seche,
My sinnes forgeve, & be my sowle leche! 21

(4) Vnto the Trinite.

Holy Trynite, blessid & eterne, 22
Ever regnyng in parfight vnite,
Whose power, Lord, no thynk may deserne,
Ne þe joyes nombre of thy dignite,
Thy grace euer in eche necessite 26
Be my socowr, my fawtis to redresse,
& with thyn hond, Lord, euery day me blesse! 28

(5) Vnto owr Lady.

Blessid Lady, virgyn of Nazareth, 29
& moder of Almyghty Lord of grace,

---

[1] MS. Grace & plente, *see notes.*
[2] *Supplied from the Talbot Hours, see notes.*

II. Religious Poems and Prayers in Verse. 63

Which his peple saved hath, by his deth,
From the paynes of infernall place,—
Blessid Lady, knele to-fore his face, 33
& pray thy son to kepe me from losse,
Which with his blod bowght vs on þe crosse. 35

(6) Vnto þe angellis.

Deffend me, holy angellis, & archangellis, 36
& for me pray vnto the deite ;
My vicis all in to vertues for to changes (!)
& þat you my helpers, I pray you, euer be !
Seynt Gabriell, & Raphaell with the, 40
Archangellis all & angellis, I require
To be my defence & helpe in euery fere. 42

(7) Vnto þe propre angell.

Holy angell, to whom pusance deuine 43
Is geven for to kepe, & me gwide,
I the beseche, with þe ordres nyne,
To helpe me to resiste ire, slowth & pride,
& of all seven, þat non may bide 47
In me þat am so tender worowght,
For fraylnes of flesshe is yolden with a thowght. 49

(8) Vnto John Baptist.

Blessid John, þat callid art Baptyste, 50
Of Cristis lawe preved first witnes,
Pray to þat lord þat within thy moder chest
Of grace þe inspired with swetnes,
My defawtis with his marcy to dresse ; 54
And patriarkis & prophettis eke, [leaf 209, back]
Pray for me also, mekly I you beseke. 56

(9) Vnto þe Appostillis.

Peter appostill, & doctor Powll, I pray, 57
Phylyp, Jacob & Bartholomee,
Andrew, James, John & Thomas ay,
Simon, Jude, Mathew & Mathie,
Barnabe, Marke, Luke & Thadde, 61
With euery appostill & evangeliste,
Pray for me to þe lord of all triste. 63

II. Religious Poems and Prayers in Verse.

(10) **Vnto þe martires.**
Stephen, George, Chr*is*tofre & Cleme*n*t, 64
Denis, Gerveis, Lawrens, Fabian,
Albon, Mavrice, Vrban & Vi*n*cent,
Evstas, Line, Thom*a*s, Sebastyan,
Cornelis, Sixte, Cosine & Damian, 68
Victor, Lambert, my synnes to defface
& all þe m*ar*tirs, pray to þe Lord for grace! 70

(11) **Vnto þe co*n*fessowrs.**
Siluest*er*, Leo, M*ar*tyn & Benedicte, 71
Gregory, Avstyn & Seynt Nycholas,
Germayn, Julian, þ*a*t harboreth at nyght,
Ambrose, Anthony, þ*a*t gret power has,
Edward, Leonard, Philbert & Bonefas, 75
Donston, Jerom, & all co*n*fessowres,
P*r*ay for vs to þe Lord all owres! 77

(12) **Vnto all holy monk*is* & erimit*is*.**
Covent*is* of monk*is*, chanons & charterhows, 78
Celestynes, freres & pryst*is* all,
Palmers, pilgrymes, heremit*is* & all religi*us*,
þ*a*t stond i*n* grace hole, to you I call,
On yo*u*r knees beffore owr Lord to fall, 82
W*ith* prayers help me, fro*m* syn me to deffende,
þ*a*t i*n* to blis my sowle suerly may assend. 84

(13) **Vnto þe virgyns.**
Blessid & meke Magdelen Mary, 85
Kat*er*yn, Anne, M*ar*tha & Appolyne,
Margarete, Agatha, wit*h* Cleothe,
Egipcyan Anastace, & Cristyne,
Genofeve, Cecilie, Barbera, & Maryne, 89
Elen, Agnes, Susan, Bride & Lucie,
P*r*ay for me wit*h* entire humylite. 91

(14) **Vnto All Saynt*is*.**
Appostill*is*, marters & co*n*fessowres, 92
Evangelist*is*, v*e*rgyns & Innocent*is*,
P*r*ay þ*a*t Lord whose power eu*er* indures,
Of his grace to forgeve vs owr offens,
Owr sowles kepe fro*m* syn & pestelens, 96
& to his blis þ*a*t is celestyall,
Of m*a*rcy bryng vs wher lyf is et*er*nall. 98

II. Religious Poems and Prayers in Verse.

(15)

¶ Pray for hole confession with full repentance, 99
& of owr mysdedis right reparacion.
Grant, Lord, thy marcy, & I do penance,
Spare vs to amend, & from dampnacion
Euer vs deffend, from all tribulacion, 103
& for þe meritis of thy sayntis all,
Kepe vs from syn, & to thy marcy call! 105
Explicit.[1]

69.

Ave Maria, now say we so: [leaf 219a]
Mayd & moder were neuer no mo.

(1)

Gaude Maria, Cristis moder!
Mary myld, of the I mene;
Thou bare my Lord, thou bare my broder;
Thou bare a louly child & clene. 4
¶ Thou stodyst full still withowt blyn,
Whan in thy ere that arand was done so;
Tho gracius God the lyght with-yn
Gabrielis[2] nuncio. 8

(2)

Gaude Maria, yglent with grace!
Whan Jhesus, thi son, on the was bore,
Full nygh thy brest thou gan hym brace;
He sowked, he sighhed, he wepte full sore. 12
¶ Thou fedest the flowr þat neuer shall fade,
Wyth maydens mylke, & songe ther-to:
"Lulley, my swet! I bare the, babe,
Cum pudoris lillio." 16

(3)

Gaude Maria! thy myrth was a-way,
Whan Cryst on crose, thy son, gan die
Full dulfully on Gud Fryday,
That many a moders son yt sye. 20

[1] Added in red. [2] MS. Grabrielis

II. Religious Poems and Prayers in Verse.

Hys blode vs browght from care & stryf,
　His watery wovndis vs wisshe from wo,
The thyrd day from dethe to lyff
　Fulget resurreccio.　　　　　　　　　　24

(4)

Gaude Maria, thou byrde so bryght,
　Bryghtter than blossum þat blowith on hill!
Joyfull thou were to se that sight,
　Whan the appostles, so swet of will,　　28
¶ All & sum dide shryk full shryll,
　Whan the fayrest of shape went you fro,
From erth to hevyn he styed full still,
　Motu que fertur proprio.　　　　　　　32

(5)

Gaude Maria, thou rose of ryse!
　Maydyn & moder, both jentill & fre,
Precius prynces, perles of pris,
　Thy bowr ys next the trynyte.　　　　　36
¶ Thy son, as lawe askyth a-right,
　In body & sowle the toke hym to;
Thou regned with hym, right as we fynd,
　In celi palacio.　　　　　　　　　　40

(6)

Now, blessid byrde, we pray the a bone:
　Be-fore thy son for vs thou fall,
& pray hym, as he was on the rode done,
　& for vs dranke asell & gall,　　　　　44
¶ That we may wone withyn þat wall,
　Wher euer ys well withowt wo,
& gravnt that grace vnto vs all
　In perhenni gaudio.　　　　　　　　48
　　　Explicit de quinque gaudia.

70. [The Sacrament of Matrimony.]

(1)

Benedicta sit sancta trinitas　　　　　[leaf 146]
þat all this world hath wrowght at will,

II. Religious Poems and Prayers in Verse

Attque indiuisa vnitas,
 Gravnte vs matrymony to fulfyll,   4
 & lette vs never owr sowles spyll
In adventure which ys eternall deth,
 But euer to take tent thes wordis vntill :
Quod Deus coniunxit, homo ne separet.   8

(2)
Thes wordis by declaracion
 I vnderstond withowt drede :
Wher Cryst hath made a coniunccion,
 Yt may not be dissevered for any nede.   12
Wherfor at your weddyng take þis to your cred[e];
þer may be no disseveraunce duryng your bre[th] ;
 Who so not loweth matrimony, þe gospell may rede :
Quod Deus coniunxit, homo non separet.   16

(3)
Whi shalt þou þi fader leve, a wyff to take
 & her to love a-lonely,
Thi moder, þi broder, þi syster to forsake
 For the sacrament of matrymony ?   20
Whi of II flesshes ys made but on truly,
Whiche may not be departid eth ?
 Take this ever to thi responcion for ay :
Quod Deus coniunxit, homo non separet.   24

(4)
Man, yf þou be intysed by cownsayle of þe fend
 For to take a-noder, & leve thyn own wyffe,
Lyfte vp thy hart to Crist þat ys hend,
 & pray to amend the of thi yll lyff ;   28
& thus, withowt stres of swerd or knyff,
To Crist thi sowle þou shalt bequeth,
 And kepe thes wordis withowt stryff : [leaf 146, back]
Quod Deus coniunxit, homo non separet.   32

(5)
Woman, be buxom to thy husbonde,
 Loveyng hym lowly, as the lawe will.
When þou hast takyn his trowth in to þi hond,
 þou may not for-sake hym for good nor yll.   36

68   II. *Religious Poems and Prayers in Verse.*

<pre>
    Therfor, frely, frend, thy feyth to fulfyll,
  Sekyng with cyrcumstavnce thy husbonde to plese,
    Truly takyng intent thes wordes vntill :
  Quod Deus coniunxit, homo non separet.   40
                      (6)
  This sacrament of mekill pryce
    Ofte tyme ys put to experiment,¹
  Which was fyrst fygured in paradyse,
    Thorow Godis own comaundment,   44
  To kepe vs all in dewe perseverauns
  Off vnite & peas vnto owr dethe,
    & observe with-owt dystavnce :
  Quod Deus coniunxit, homo non separet.   48
                      (7)
  Pray we to Crist, hevyn Kyng,
    þat ys þe fyrst formar of hall & bowr,
  þe sacrament of matrymony, þat worthi thyng,
    þat we may worshype & honowr ;   52
  & styfly to stond in euery stowr
  Agaynst the fende & all his methe,
    & take this worde to owr socowr :
  Quod Deus coniunxit, homo non separet.   56
                   Explicit.
</pre>

71. [The Sacrifice of the Mass.]

(1)

<pre>
  Loke on þis wrytyng, man, for þi devocion !²   [leaf 205]
    Walk here be-side, yf you can esspye
  þer-in any thyng for your exortacion,
    To make yov to here masse more devoutly ;
    & sum-what you may se to þis subsidye,   5
      That heryth masse with devovt entent,
      Wher God, in form of bred, his body doth present. 7
                      (2)
  The masse is an high sacrafice above all oþer,   8
    As a fygure in þe old lawe makith rehersyng.
</pre>

---

[1] MS. expent, *with the stroke through the* p *which indicates* er.
[2] man for þi devocion *over a cancelled* both old & yonge.

II. *Religious Poems and Prayers in Verse.* 69

Whan Abraham from his enymyes recured his bro[ther];
Hym met Melchesadech, both prist & kyng,
With bred & wyne makyng vp his offryng,   12
    As now doth owr priste, confermyng þe presyden[t],
    Wher God, in fowrm of bred, ¹his body doth present.¹

(3)
The blode, sum tyme of geete, or ellis of calff,   15
Was sprente on þe people, to lech þer sore ;
But now þe blode of Crist, by doble halff
Lechith þe people, & clensith well more,
Which dayly at þe avter, his prist beffore   19
    Consecrate with worde & mynde of entent,
    Wher God, in fowrm of bred, ¹his body doth present.¹

(4)
The chirche is callid þe spowse of Jhesu Criste,   22
Þe cavse of þis mariage is þe holy messe,
Wher dayly at þe auter offreth vp þe priste
The son to þe fader, þat is no lesse.
Call, man, for þi peticion, & lok þou not cesse !   26
    Lat þi hart with gret devocion þer-to relent,
    Wher God, in fowrm of bred, ¹his body doth present.¹

(5)
To þis holy offryng all þe celestyall cowrte   29
Makyth gret reuerens & also melodye,
Þe sperytis infernall, all þe hole rowte,
At þat holy dede are in trobill & sorye,
& euer of þer purpose they er put bye,   33
    Wher þis messe is songe with a blessid entent,
    Þer God, in fowrm of bred, his body doth present. 35

(6)
Seynt Austen shewith þe, man, in his gret boke   36
Callid " De ciuitate Dei,"—now lystyn & here !—
What benyfittis, yf þou lyste for to loke,
 þat day that þou the holy messe doth here,
 þou shallt haue, necessary to þi lyveyng here.   40
    Purches than þes prophettis for thy supplement,
    Wher God, in fowrm of bred, his body doth present. 42

¹—¹ MS. &c.

(7)

Thy fode þat day shall not the fayll ; 43
Thyn eyen from þer sight shall not blynd ;
þi light spekyng, eyþer in fabill or tale,
þat veniall synnes do vp wynd,
Shall be forgeven, & pardon fynd, 47
Whan þou þe messe gave hede or entent,
Wher God, in fowrm of bred, his body doth present. 49

(8)

Thy grevouse othes þat be forgett, [leaf 205, back] 50
In heryng of messe ar don a-way ;
An angell also þi steppis doth mete,
& presentith the in hevyn þat same day.
Than þou at þe chirch indever þe to pray, 54
To worship þat gloryows & blessid sacrament,
Wher God, in fowrm of bred, his body doth present. 56

(9)

Thyn age, at messe shall not encrease ; 57
Nor sodeyn deth þat day shall not þe spill ;
And withowt hostill yf þou hap to dissease,
It shall stond perfore ; & beleve þou this skyll,
Than to here messe þou mayste haue will, 61
Thes prophitable benefittis to þe be lent,
Wher God, in fowrm of bred, his body doth present. 63

(10)

The priste in þe holy canon prayeth alsoo 64
For all þat at þe messe stondith a-bowte,
& for all Cristyn people, þat be well moo,
þat labowr þe comen vele in þe world a-bowt ;
Then to pray for thy frend haue þou no dowt ; 68
Yeve thy prayer to þe pristis for thyn expedyment,
Wher God, in fowrm of bred, his body doth present. 70

(11)

And yf any of þi kynn be departid hens, 71
In purgatory for þer synn abydyng payn,
Thy prayer & þe messe may delyuer them thens,
& of þi redempcion make them fayn.

II. Religious Poems and Prayers in Verse.

In hevyn they shall do for þe same, 75
Beffore angellis & sayntis euer splendent,
Wher God, in his glory,[1] his body doth present. 77

(12)
Than þe meedis of þis messe be nobill & gret 78
To lyveers in erth, but after deth myche more ;
For whan deth from þe body þe sowle doth frett,
Than þe nombre of þes messes be anon vp bore
In to hevyn among sayntis, þe trinite beffore. 82
For þat mayst þou joy, man, þat þi cownt is vplent,
Wher God, in his glory, his body doth present. 84

(13)
Now I cownsaill þe, man, do after my rede, 85
Whan þe priste goth to messe, yf þou may, com,
& but sekenes lett þe, site bare with thyn hede,
& knok on þi brest & say : " Cor mundum
Crea in me, Deus, et spiritum ! " 89
Her it forth to þe end with meke entent,
Wher God, in fowrm of bred, his body doth present. 91
Explicit, quod Hill.

---

[1] his glory *over a cancelled* fowrm of bred

III. Didactic, Moral and Allegorical Poems.

72. [Fortune, by Sir Thomas More.]
[Part I.]
The word*is* of Fortune to þe people. [leaf 104]

(1)
Myne high estate, power & auctoryte,
  Yf ye ne know / enserche, & ye shall spie
That riches / worshipe / & dignite,
  Joy / reste / & peace / & all thyng fynally
    That any pleasure or *pro*phet may cu*m* by   5
      To mannys comfort / aid / & sustynaunce,
      Is all at my devise & ordeynance.   7

(2)
¶ Wit*h*owt my favo*ur* þe*r* is no thyng wonne :   8
  Many a mater haue I browght a[t] laste
To good co*n*clusion / þ*at* fondely was begonne,
  & many a purpose bownden sure & faste
    With wyse *pro*vision / I haue ouer-caste ;   12
      With-owt good happe, þe*r* may no wit suffise :
      Bette*r* is to be fortunate than wise.   14

(3)
¶ And therfore hath som me*n* bene or this   15
  My dedly fooys, & wrytyn many a bok
To my dispayre : & oþer cause ther nys,
  But for me lyste not frendly on the*m* loke.
    Thus like the fox thay fare, þ*at* ons forsok   19
      Þe plesant grapis, & gan for to defye the*m*,
      Be-cause he lepte, & cowld not cu*m* by the*m*.   21

(4)
¶ But let the*m* write ! þer labowr is i*n* vayn ;   22
  For well ye wote / myrth / hono*ur* / & riches,
Bette*r* is / than shame / penvry / & payne.

III. Didactic, Moral and Allegorical Poems.

þe nedy wreche þat lyngereth in distresse,
Withowt myn helpe is euer comfortlesse, 26
A very bordon, odyowse & lothe
To all þe world, & to hym self bothe. 28

(5)
¶ But / he þat by my favour may ascende, 29
To myghty power / and excellent degre,
A Comon wele to govern & deffende,—
O, in how blessid condicion stondith he,
Hym-self in honour & felycyte, 33
And over þat may forther & encrease
An hole regyon / in joy / reste & pease. 35

(6)
¶ Now in this poynt þer is no more to say, 36
Eche man hathe of hym self þe gouernance.
Lett euery wight, than, take his own way,
& he þat owt of pouerte & myschance
Lyste for to lyve, & will hym-self enhance 40
In welthe / & riches / cum forth & wayt on me ;
And he þat will be a beggar / let hym be. 42

[PART II.]

To them þat tristith in Fortune.

(7)
Thow þat arte prowde of honour, shape or kyne, 43
þat kepeste vp this wrecchid worldis tresure,
Thy fyngers shyned with gold / thy tawny skyn
With freshe apparell garnysshed owt of mesure,
& weneste to haue Fortune alway at þi plesure, 47
Cast vp thyn yee / & lok how slipper chance
Illudethe her men with change & variance. 49

(8)
¶ Som tyme she loketh as lovely, fayre & bryght, [lf104,bk]
A[s] goodly Venus, moder of Cupide ; 51
She bekketh & smyleth vpon euery wight ;
But þis fayned chere may not abide ;

III. Didactic, Moral and Allegorical Poems.

þer cometh a clowde / & farewell all owr pride !   54
Lyk any serpent she begyneth to swell,
& loketh as fers as any fury of hell.   56

(9)

¶ Yet for al þat, we brytill men ar fayn,   57
So wrechid is owr nature & so blynde,
As sone as Fortune list to lawgh agayn
With fayre contenance & deceytfull mynde,
To crowche & knele, & gape after þe wynde :   61
Not on or twayn, but thowsandis on a rowt,
Lyke suarmyng bees, cum flateryng her a-bowt.   63

(10)

¶ Than as a bayte she bryngith forth her ware,   64
Syluer / gold / rich perle / & precyous stone,
On which þe mased peple gase & stare,
& gape þer-fore, as dogges for the bone ;
Fortune at them lawghith, & in her trone,   68
Amyd her treasure & waveryng riches,
Prowdely she hoveth, as lady & empres.   70

(11)

¶ Faste by her side doth wery Labowr stonde,   71
Pale[1] Fere also / & Sorow all be-wepte,
Dysdeyn / & Hatred / on þat oþer honde,
Eke restles Wacche / from slepe with travayle kept,
Hys eyes dowsy / & lokyng as he slepte.   75
Beffore her stondith Danger & Envye,
Flatery / Disseit / Myscheff / & Tyrannye.   77

(12)

¶ A-bowt her commeth all þe world to begge :   78
He asketh londe / & he to passe wold brynge
This toye & þat : & all not worth an egge ;
He wold in love prosper above all thynge ;
He kneleth down, & wold be made a kynge ;   82
He forseth not, so he may money haue,
Thowgh all þe world accompt hym for a knave.   84

(13)

¶ Lo, thus dyueris heddis, dyueris wittis,   85
Fortune alone as dyueris as they all,

[1] MS. pare

III. *Didactic, Moral and Allegorical Poems.*

Vnstable, here & þer a-monge them flittis,
& at aventure down her giftes fall.
Cacche who so may / she throwith gret & small, 89
Not to all men / a[s] commeth sonne, or dewe,
But, for þe moste parte, all amonge a fewe. 91
(14)
¶ And yet her brotyll giftis may not laste, 92
He þat she gaue them, loketh prowde & hye :
Sho whirleth a-bowt, & plukith a-way as faste,
& geveth them to an other by & by :
& thus from man to man contynvally 96
She vsith to take & geve / & slyly tosse,
On man to wynnyng of an others losse. 98
(15)
¶ & when she robbeth on, down goth his pride : 99
He wepith & wayleth / & curseth her full sore ;
But þat receyveth it, on þat other side,
Is glad / & blessith her a M tymes þer-fore.
But in a whyle, whan she loveth hym no more, 103
She glidith from hym / & her giftis to,
& he her cu[r]seth, as other foolis do. 105
(16)
¶ Alas ! þe folyshe people can not ceace [leaf 105] 106
Ne voyde her trayne / till they þe harme fele.
A-bowt her alway besyly they preace ;
But, Lord ! what he thynkith hym-self wele
That may set onys his hond vpon her whele ; 110
He holdeth faste / but vpward as he stithe,
She whippeth her whele abowt, & þer he lieth. 112
(17)
¶ Thus fell Julius from his myghty power ; 113
Thus fell Darius, þe worthy kyng of Perse ;
Thus fell Alysandre, þe soverayn conquerowr ;
Thus many mo than I may well reherce ;
Thus dowble Fortune, whan she liste reverce 117
Her slipper favour / from them þat in her truste,
She fleith a-way / & layth them in þe duste. 119
(18)
¶ She sodeynly enhanceth them a-lofte, 120
& sodynly myscheveth all þe floke ;

The hede þat late lay easily & softe,
In stede of pilowse, lith after on þe blokk.
& yet,—alas, þe cruell, prowd mokke!— 124
The deynty mowth þat ladyes kissed haue,
She bryngith in case to kysse a knave. 126

(19)
¶ Thus whan she changith her vncertayn coorse, 127
Vp starteth a knave / & down þer fallith a knyght.
The beggar, riche : & þe riche man pore is ;
Hatred to-torned [1] to love ; love to dispight ;
This is her sporte : thus proveth she her myght. 131
Gret bost she maketh / yf on, by her power,
Welthy & wrechid / bothe in an howre. 133

(20)
¶ Pouerte, þat of her giftis will no thyng take, 134
With mery chere she loketh on þe prece,
& seth how Fortunes howshold goth to wrak.
Fast by her stondith þe wise Socrates,
Aristippus / Pithagoras, & many a lese 138
Of old filosophers / & eke agaynst þe sonne
Bekith hym pore Diogenes in his tonne. 140

(21)
¶ With her is Byas, whose contrey lakkid diffence, 141
& whilom of þer foes stode in dowt,
þat eche man hastyly gan to cary thens,
& asked hym why he nowght caried owt,—
"I bere," quod he, "all myn with me abowt : " 145
Wisedom he ment ; no fortunes brotill fees ;
For nowght he contid his, þat he myght lese. 147

(22)
¶ Heracletus eke liste feliship to kepe 148
With glad pouerte / Democretus also ;
Of which þe first can neuer cease but wepe
To see howe thik / þe blynd people go,
With gret labowr to purchase care & wo. 152
þat oþer laweth to se þe folishe apes,
How ernestly they walke abowt þer japes. 154

---

[1] is torned, *Flügel.*

III. Didactic, Moral and Allegorical Poems. 77

(23)

¶ Of this pore secte it is the vsage, 155
Only to take þat nature may susteyn ;
Banysshyng clen all oþer surplusage,
They be content, & of no thyng complayn :
No nygard eke ys of his good so fayn ; 159
But they more plasure haue M fold,
The secrete drawght of nature to behold. 161

(24)

[1] ¶ Set Fortunes seruantis by them self, & ye wull ; 162
That on ys free / þat other ever thrall ; [[1] leaf 105, back]
That on content / þat other never full ;
That on in suerte / þat other lyke to fall :
Who lyst to advise them both, perceyve he shall 166
As gret differens betwen them, as we see
Betwyxt wrechidnesse & felicyte. 168

(25)

¶ Now haue I shewid you both, chese which ye liste : 169
Stately Fortune / or humble Poverte,
þat is to say, now lyeth it in your fiste,
To take you to bondage or free lyberte ;
But in this poynt, & ye do after me, 173
Draw ye to Fortune, & labowr her to please,
Yf that ye thynk yourself to well at ease. 175

(26)

¶ And first vpon þe lovely shall she smyle,[2] 176
& frendly on þe cast her wanderyng eyes,
Enbrace þe in her armes, & for a while
Put the in to a foolis paradise ;
& forth-with all, what-so þou liste devise, 180
She will þe grant it lyberally perhappes ;
But for all þat, beware of after-clappes. 182

(27)

¶ Rekyn you neuer of her favour sure ; 183
Ye may in þe clowdis as easily trace an hare,
Or in drye londe cause fishes to endure,
& make þe brennyng fyre / his hete to spare,
& all this world encompace to forfare, 187
As her to make, by craft of engyne, stable,
That of her nature ys euer variable. 189

[2] MS. smvte

III. Didactic, Moral and Allegorical Poems.

(28)

Serve her day & nyght as reverently 190
  Vpon thy knees as seruant may ;
& in conclusion, þat þou shalt wynne þer-be,
  Shall not be worth thy seruise, I dare say.
& loke / yet what she geveth þe to-day, 194
  With labowr wonne, she shall haply to-morow
Pluk it owt of thyn hond with sorowe. 196

(29)

¶ Wherfor, yf þou in suerte liste to stonde, 197
  Take Poverties parte, & lat prowde Fortune go ;
Receyue no thynge þat cometh from her honde :
  Love maner & vertu, for they be only tho
Which dowble Fortune may neuer tak þe fro : 201
  Than mayst þou boldly desire her tornyng chance ;
She can the noþer hyndre nor avaunce. 203

(30)

¶ But & þou wilt nedis medill with her tresur, 204
  Trust not þer-in / & spend it lyberally.
Bere þe not prowde, nor tak not owt of mesur ;
  Byld not thyn hows high vp in þe skye ;
Non fallith ferre but he þat clymeth hye. 208
  Remembre Nature sent þe hether bare ;
þe giftis of Fortune, cownt them borowed ware. 210

[PART III.]

To them þat seketh Fortune.

(31)

Who-so deliteth to prove & assay, 211
  Of waueryng Fortune þe full vncertayn lot,
Yf þat þe answere plese þe not alway,
  Blame not me, for I comande you not
Fortune to trust, & eke full well ye wot 215
  I haue of her no brydyll in my fiste ;
She renneth lose, & torneth wher she lyste. 217

(32)

The rollyng dise in whom your lukk doth stonde, [leaf 106]
  With whose vnhappy chance ye be so wrothe,

III. Didactic, Moral and Allegorical Poems.

Ye know your-self, cam neuer in myn honde.
Lo, in this pond be fishe & froggis bothe :
Cast in your nett / but, be you leve or lothe, 222
Holde you content, as Fortune liste asigne,
Hit is your own fishyng, & not myne. 224
(33)

¶ And thowgh in on chance, Fortune you affende, 225
Grucche not þer-at / but bere a mery fface :
In many an oþer, she shall it amende ;
Ther is no man so fer owt of her grace,
But he somtyme hath comfort & solace ; 229
Ne non agayn so ferre forth in her favour,
þat fully satysfied is with her behawour. 231
(34)

¶ Fortune ys stately / solempne / prowde / & hye, 232
& riches geveth / to haue seruise þer-fore.
The nedy beggar cacchith an half-peny :
Som man M £ ; som lesse, som more ;
But for all þat, she kepeth euer in store, 236
From euery man, som parcell of his will,
That he may pray þer-fore, & serue her still. 238
(35)

¶ Som man hath good, but children hath he non. 239
Som man hath both / but he can get no helthe ;
Som hath all thre ; but vp to honowrs trone
Can he not crepe, by no maner stelthe.
To som she sendith / children / riches / welthe, 243
Honowr / worship / & reuerens, all his lyff ;
But yet she plucketh hym with a shrewed wyff. 245
(36)

¶ Than, for-as-mych as it is Fortunes gyse, 246
To grant no man all thyng þat he will axe,
But as her-self liste ordre & devisê,
Doth euery man his parte devide & taxe,
I cownsell you, eyther trusse vp your pakkes, 250
& take no thyng at all, or be content
With suche reward as Fortune hath you sent. 252
(37)

¶ All thyngis in this boke þat ye shall rede, 253
Do as ye liste ; þer shall no man ye bynde

80   III. *Didactic, Moral and Allegorical Poems.*

 Them to beleve as surely as your Crede;
  But notwithstondyng, certis, in my mynde,
 I durste well swere / as trew shall ye them fynd 257
  In euery poynt, eche answere by & by,
 As ar þe jugementis of astronomye. 259
   Explicit.

73.

Incipit ['Revertere.']   [leaf 155, back]

(1)

In a tyme of a somers day,
 The sune shon full meryly þat tyde,
I toke my hawke, me for to play,
 My spanyellis renyng by my syde. 4
A fesavnt henne than gan I see;
 My howndis put her to flight;
I lett my hawke vnto her fle,
 To me yt was a deynte syght. 8

(2)

My fawkon flewe fast vnto her pray;
 My hownd gan renne with glad chere;
& sone I spurnyd in my way;
 My lege was hent in a breer; 12
This breer, forsothe, yt dyde me gref;
 Ywys yt made me to turn a-ye,
For he bare wrytyng in euery leff,
 This latyn word: 'Revertere.' 16

(3)

I hayld & pullid this breer me fro,
 & rede this word full meryly;
My hart fell down vnto my to,
 That was before full lykyngly. 20
I lett my havke & fesavnt fare;
 My spanyell fell down vnto my kne;
It toke me with a sighyng sare,
 This new lessun: 'Revertere.' 24

III. *Didactic, Moral and Allegorical Poems.* 81

(4)
Lykyng ys mod*er* of synnes all,
& norse to eu*ery* wykyd dede;
To myche myschef she makyth me*n* fall,
& of sorow þe dawnce she doth lede. 28
This hawke of yowth ys high of porte,
And wildnes makyth hy*m* wyde to fle,
& ofte to fall in wykyd thowght,
And than ys best : 'Revertere.' 32
Explicit Revertere.

74*a*. [The Duty of Prelates.]
(1)
As I gan wandre in on evynyng [leaf 156]
Betwen the cornys, be-syde a balke,
I sawe the dew in dale gan spryng,
& herd me*n* a-bowt þ*er* shepe gan walke. 4
Than on of the*m* to me gan talke,
Full carefully clothed from the cold :
"Thes prelat*is*, full fall thei shuld stalke,
To kepe þ*er* shepe well in the fold. 8
(2)
The sede of synne so thyke ys sowe
Among the clargy, wit*h* pompe & p*r*ide,
& the gras of grace may not growe,
So yo*ur* shepe ar hurt on eu*ery* syde. 12
But the g*r*ace of God be yo*ur* gyde,
To cvre yo*ur* co*n*cyence þat ys so cold ;
Be ware wher þat ye renne or ride,
For yo*ur* shepe be skabbyd in the fold. 16
(3)
The cheff shepe*r*d i*n* this world þat ys,
Shuld be the pope, yf he were meke,
Wit*h* the gospell to amend þat ys a-mys,
To hele hys shepe so shuld he seke, 20
For fere in hell þat his tayle reke,
That suche a charge he take wol*l* ;
Eche p*r*elat, for fere of paynys eke,
Kepe well the shepe of Cryst*is* fold. 24
CAROLS. G

III. *Didactic, Moral and Allegorical Poems.*

(4)

Peter at Rome sum tyme pope was;
 Owr lordis lawe he kepte truly;
He prechid þe gospell, thorow Godis grace,
 þat many a sowle was saved þerby. 28
This made men fle from þer foly,
 To kepe þer sowles from carys cold;
Peter rode never to rially,
 But kept þe shep well in the fold. 32

(5)

The grace of the gospell þat tyme was kyde,
 While þ[ei] toke them to clene lyffe;
That tyme þe gospell was not hide,
 To kyng ne knyght, mayd ne wyffe; 36
For dymes ne offeryngis tho was no stryf;
 Then covytyce walkyd a-way full cold;
Among men charyte than was ryffe,
 Ther shepe were kept well in the fold. 40

(6)

Byshoppis were than stedfast & stabull,
 & fre of good þat God them lente,
& prechid þe gospell withowt fabull,
 In this world wher þat they went. 44
Than prykyd no prelatis to parlament
 With knyghtis, squyers ne yemen bold,
I dare no more say, lest I were shent,
 But I rede you, kepe well Christis fold." 48

74*b*. [Know thyself.]

[*The beginning is not in the MS.* [leaf 156, back]
. . . .]

(1)

Therfor be thyn own frend; 5
 Thynke what þou art in lenth & brede;
For shame lat no pride þe shende,
 And know thy self, wysely I rede. 8

III. Didactic, Moral and Allegorical Poems.

(2)
Yff þou be a man of holy churche,
Know well Jhesu thy saluacion,
That thow may the better worche,
    To stroy all fowle temptacion,   12
    & perfowrm thy proffessyon,
As thy fyrst frendis dede,
To leve in gud contemplacion
    & know thy self, wysely I rede.   16

(3)
Both in nesshe & eke in hard,
Loke thou haue knowlage in kynd,
þat[1] thou mayst be gud vnto God-ward,
    & to all peple also a frend.   20
Do well & thynke vpon thyn end,
    The dowt of deth þat ys to drede;
Do well, & þe feend will fro the wend;
    & know thy self, wysely I rede.   24

(4)
Thynke on perell, how it doth be-gyn,
& how wonderly yt ys dyght;
But fewe know them-self withynne :
    How shuld they know than God Almyght?   28
Thus ar owr tentis to wild ypyght;
    Therfor sorow gynnyth spryng & spred.
For dred of myschef, day & nyght,
    Knowe thy selfe, wysely I rede.   32

(5)
Yff þou wilt know thy-self ywys,
    Thou must do in this manere;
Crye marcy, also haue I blis,
    Ytt ys a nobull lessun to lere.   36
This worde was wretyn withowt were
    For many a man, þat shuld drede;
Therfor I rede þat thow yt lere,
    & hevyn blis shall be your mede.   Amen.   40
       Explicit : "Know thi self, wysely I red."

[1] MS. þat that

75. ['Fortis ut mors dilectio.']

(1) [leaf 170, back]
On a dere day, by a dale so depe,
As I went thorow a wyldernes,
To byrdis I toke full good kepe,
To here them syng, both more &
   lesse. 4
Sum with þer songe mademe to wepe,
& sum me helyd of hevynes,
& sum also songe me a-slepe :
The nyghtyngale þer was ywys. 8
Then, specyally for to expresse,
A tyrtyll trew a-monge all tho,
Sange this songe in sothfastnes :
  'Fortis vt mors dileccio.' 12

(2)
To þat tyrtill I toke entente, [tyde ;
Towchyng the text she told þat
Of yt I mvsed, what yt by-ment ;
The byrde was blith, on bowgh
   dide bide. 16
Then I me busked vnto a bente,
Vnder a tre, all in that tide,
For I wolde wytt, or þat I went, 19
This clavse expressed & specyfyed.
The byrde was prest withowt
   pride,
& said : " For no thyng fle me
   fro,
Or thow conceyve this clavse dis-
   cryved :
'Fortis vt mors dileccio.' 24

(3)
Off the tyxt, this ys the entent,
Expowndyd by experyens :
Withowtyn lake, wher love ys lent,
Off deth yt dredith no defens ; 28

Or ellis, wher love ys fond farvent,
þer ys fownden none offens ;
So ys love yndefecyent, 31
As Salamon sayth in hys sentens,
Yf love fro deth haue diste[m]-
   perens ; [¹ leaf 171]
¹Tyll on thus I concluded them to,
With this clavse in consequence :
'Fortis vt mors dileccio.' 36

(4)
Off this proces for to procede,
At Cryst hym-self I may be-gyn,
Fro hevyn to erth here to take hede,
Howe he discendid to cesse owr syn ;
& afterward yete wolde he bléde 41
His own hart blode, till yt wold blyn,
For no necessite nor for no nede, 43
Ne for no waryson that lay to wyn.
What cavsid hym be-cum thy kyne?
No thynge but love [he] hade
   the to. 46
Then thus I may defyne that dyne :
'Fortis vt mors dileccio.' 48

(5)
This mater mevys yet in my mynde,
Of his moder, that mayd so fre,
That cumly & clere of kyngis kynde,
þat bare hym in virgynyte. 52
With bytter paynys þat he was pynde,
& nayled nakyd vnto a tre ;
An ·C· tymes, I trow, she swounyd,
þat day whilis þat she myght dre.
That dethe was inequalite, 57
In swoune whan þat she fell so ;
Therefore I synge sykerly :
'Fortis vt mors dileccio.' 60

III. Didactic, Moral and Alleyorical Poems. 85

(6)

To the tyrtill þat loveth so trew,
I may reduce this reason right :
Yt ys her kynde, who so yt knew,
Alone to be, she hath her tight. 64
When þat she mysses her make new,
She movrnyng makith, with all her might ;
Thowgh ther be other, all fresshe of hew,
Ther ys non able vnto her sight ;
But till the day her deth be dight,
Wantyng her make, she will no mo;
Thus I say by this byrde so bright:
'Fortis vt mors dileccio.' 72

(7)

Yet I procede to the pellycane,
& by this cavse her kynd to distroy;
& David, on his savter can sayn : 75
She ys most trew of love to try ;
For when þat her byrdis are nigh slayn,
She defferris not for them to dye ;
To shede her hart-blode, then ys she bayn, 79
Wherof they haue ther helpe in hye.
More specyall love I can not spye
Then thus this byrde her-self to þer-for I syng yet sertenly : [slo :
'Fortis vt mors dileccio.' 84

(8)

And mo exampuls haue I sene
Whiche by this clavse I may conclude,
As Dydo, & other by-dene,
& also Medo, that myld of mode ;
This proces also of Polexine, 89
For this clavse ys not exclude ;
Of many mo I may of mayn, [blode,
þat were full bright of birth &
This ys the glose & gyse full good,
With thes exampuls & many mo,
Of this text, I vnderstond :
'Fortis vt mors dileccio.' " 96

(9)

So cam a fawcon with his flight,
& with a byrde a-way dide flye ;
Then all the byrdis with fethers bright
Flede fro þat fawcon fayer & fre ;
Vpon bowgh, þat fawcon light, 101
Hym for to fede vpon his fee ;
Then I sawe, all in my sight, [tre,
The tyrtyll fro hym then toke a
Then spake þat byrde so bright of ble: [woo,
"I must wende, ellis I shall be
But loke, this reason I leve with the :
'Fortis vt mors dileccio.' " 108

(10)

When she bade me this verse export,
Owt of my sight she was a-non ;
Now thus thes reasons I reporte,
As she me tawght, by on & on. 112
Now by assent of all this sort,
Pray we þat byrde so bright as bon,
Which of paradise ys yate & porte.
þat owr dwellyng may be in her wone, 116
With hym that for owr sake was slone
& for many a myllyan mo,
As tellith this tyxt, for love alone :
'Fortis vt mors dileccio.' 120
                Explicit.

76. [The Seven Deadly Sins.]

(1)
Superbia.
I bost & brage ay with þe best;
To mayntayn syn, I am full prest;
Myn own will I will haue ay,
They God & good men all bid nay. 4

(2)
Invidia.
¶ I am full sory in my hart,
For oþer mennys welfare & quart;
I curse & bakbite wikkydly,
& hynder all þat I may, sikerly. 8

(3)
Ira.
¶ I chide & fight, & manas fast;
All my fomen I will down cast;
Mercy on them I will non haue, 11
But vengance strong, so God me save!

(4)
Accidia.
¶ I irke full sore with Godis service;
Good werkis I love not in no wise;
Idilnes & slepe I love best,
For in them I fynd myche rest. 16

(5)
Avaricia.
¶ I covet ay, & wylis of cast,
How þat I may be riche in hast,
Full fast I hold all þat I wynne,
Thowgh my parte be left þer-in. 20

(6)
Gula.
¶ I love my wombe a-bove all thyng;
Þat most to plese, is my lykyng;
I haue no rest, nyght ne day,
Till he be seruid to his pay. 24

(7)
Luxvria.
¶ I love fowle lust & lechery,
Fornicacion & adowtry,
From synfull lyst will I not fle,
Thowgh I in hell þer-for ay be. 28
Explicit.

77. [The Four Bequests in a Man's Will.]

Terram terra tegat; demon peccata resumat; [leaf 199]
Mundus res habiat; spiritus alta petat.

(1)
In IIII poyntis, or I hens departe,
Reason me moveth to make as I maye:
First, vnto the erthe I bequeth his parte.
My wrechid carayn is but fowle claye;
Lyke than to lyke, erth in erthe to laye, 5
Sith it is accordyng, by it I will a-bide,
As for þe first parte of my will, þat erth erth hide. 7

III. Didactic, Moral and Allegorical Poems.

(2)
Myne horyble synnes, that so sore me bynde,　　　8
　With weyght me appresse, þat bene so many-fold,
So many in nombre, so many in kynde,
　The fende, by his instance, to them made me bolde;
From hym they cam, to hym I them yelde wolde,　12
　Wher-for the second parte of my will is this:
That the fende receyve my synnes as his.　　14

(3)
What avaylith good, I ones dede & roten?　　15
　Them all & som I leve, peny & pownde,
Trewly or vntrewly, som I trow mysgoten,
　Thowgh I not of whom, howe, ne in what grownd;
The worldis they be, them in the world I fownd;　19
　And ther-for the thirde parte is clerely my will:
All my worldly goodis, late the world haue still.　21

(4)
Now for the IIIIth poynt, & than haue I doo:　　22
　Nedefull for the sowle me thynketh to provide.
Hens moste I nedis; but whether shall I goo?
　I dowt my demerytes, which peyse on euery side;
But Godis mercy shall I trust to be my gide,　　26
　Vnder whose lycense, yet while I may bretb,
Vnto hevyn on high, my sowle I bequeth.　　28
　　Explicit.

78. [Farewell! Death comes.]

(1)
Farewell this world! I take my leve for euer,　[leaf 199]
　I am arrestid to appere affore Godis face.
O mercyfull God! thow knowest þat I had lever
　Than all this worldis good, to haue an owr space
For to make a-seth for my gret trespace.　　5
　My harte, alas, is brokyn for that sorow;
Som be this day, that shall not be to-morow.　7

(2)
This world, I see, is but a chery fayre;　　8
　All thyngis passith; & so moste I algate.

III. *Didactic, Moral and Allegorical Poems.*

This day I satt full royally in a chayre,
Tyll sotyll deth knokkid at my gate,
And vnavised he said to me, " chekmate " !   12
Loo ! how sodeynly he maketh a devorce !
And wormes to fede, here he hath layde my corse.   14

(3)
Speke softe, ye folkis, for I am layde a-slepe,   15
I haue my dreme ; in truste is myche treason.
From dethis hold fayn wold I make a lepe ;
But my wisedom ys torned in to feble reason.
I see this worldis joye lastith but a season ;   19
Wold God I had remembrid this beforne !
I say no more, but beware of an horne !   21

(4)
This fekyll world, so false & so vnstable, [leaf 199, back]   22
Promoteth his lovers but for a lytill while ;
But at last he geveth them a bable,
Whan his payntid trowth is torned in to gile.
Experyence cawsith me þe trowth to compile,   26
Thynkyng this to late, alas, that I began.
For foly & hope disseyveth many a man.   28

(5)
Farewell, my frendis ! the tide abidith no man ;   29
I moste departe hens, & so shall ye.
But in this passage, the beste songe þat I can,
Is " Requiem Eternam " : I pray God grant it me.
Whan I haue endid all myn adversite,   33
Graunte me in paradise to haue a mancyon,
That shede his blode for my redempcion !—   35
Beati mortui qui in domino morivntur.
Humiliatus sum vermis.

79. [' Welfare hath no sikernes.']

(1)
As I fared thorow a forest free, [lf. 206] Ther I longid, þat songe to here,
Ther byrdis song from yere to yere,   And to behold her federsfresshe,
I hard a birde, was bright of ble,   Full ofte she said with solam chere:
& of swet song, no birde here pere. 4   " Welfare hath no sykernes." 8

III. Didactic, Moral and Allegorical Poems. 89

(2)
This birde, she said in her songe:
"& weele were siker, well were me
This lyff to lede: I not how longe
My fere & I to-geder shall be. 12
I were þe meryeste birde on tre,
& I cowld helpe this heuynes;
But euer I drede it will not be,
For 'welfare hath no sykernes.' 16

(3)
O lorde, þat all thyng well hath wrowght,"
This birde, she said, with notis sh[r]ill,
"& mankynd from bale hath browght,
Yet worldly welth he thynkith to spill. 20
þerfore I movrn both lowde & still;
But nowght it helpith my hevynes.
O Lorde! I take me to thy will,
For 'welfare hath no sikernes.' 24

(4)
Ther is no man þat weele may tryst,
Yf he be kyng with crown on hede;
For whan he weneth to haue it best,
All-þer-nerest he drawith his dede.
This makyth my hart as dull as lede, 29
& euer I morn withowt redresse;
þer may no mornyng stond in stede,
For 'welfare hath no sikernes.' 32

(5)
But what is he þat wonnys in weele,
þat deth in danger dare not take?

Vnto what cowrt myght he appele,
God is dome euer to for-sake?" 36
Thus she said vnto her make:
"Thowgh all thyn hart be gren a[s] grasse,
For dred of deth, yet shall þou wake,
For 'welfare hath no sikernes.' 40

(6)
[1] And man were hayll as birde on bowgh, [¹ leaf 206, back]
& had lordschippis gret of lond & rent,
Me thynkyth þat man hath welth ynowgh,
þat cowld God thank þat all hath sent. 44
The coueytise man was neuer content,
But euer his mynd vpon encrease.
All shall fall, both bowr & rent,
For 'welfare hath no sikernes.' 48

(7)
Welfare had neuer no sikernes, [say;
Nor neuer shall haue, I dare well
I know right well, for tokyns expresse,
But þe blis of hevyn, þat lastith ay." 52
Thus seyth þis byrde, in ty unes gay.
To hym þat made both more & lesse,
To blis, God bryng vs at owr last day, 55
For 'welfare hath no sikernes.'
Explicit.

80a. [Die I must.]

[1] **Vado mori**, rex sum: quid honor, quid gloria mundi?
Est vita mors hominis regia; vado mori. [¹ leaf 207, back]
Vado mori miles; victo certamine belli
Mortem non didici vincere: vado mori. 4

III. *Didactic, Moral and Allegorical Poems.*

Vado mori, medic*us* medica*mi*ne no*n* relevand*us*,
Quicquid agu*nt* medici, resspuo : vado mori.
Vado mori, logic*us*, aliis co*n*cludere noui,
Concludit breuit*er* mors mihi : vado mori.   8

80*b*. [Earth upon Earth.]

(1)
Erth owt of erth is worldly wrowght,
Erth hath gote*n* oppo*n* erth a dygnite of nowght,
Erth vpon erth hat[h] set all his thowght,
How þ*at* erth vpon erth myght be hye browght.   4

(2)
Erth vpon erth wold be a kyng,
But how þ*at* erth shall to erth, he thy*n*kith no thyng ;
Whe*n* erth biddith erth his rent*is* home bryng,
The*n* shall erth for erth haue a hard p*ar*tyng.   8

(3)
Erth vpon erth wy*n*neth castll*is* & towres,
The*n* seyth erth vnto erth : ' þis is all owres ' ;
But whe*n* erth vpo*n* erth hath bildyd his bowres,
Tha*n* shall erth for erth suffre hard showres.   12

(4)
Erth vpon erth hath welth vpon molde,
Erth goth vpon erth glydryng all i*n* golde,
Like as he vnto erth neu*er* torn shuld ;
& yet shall erth vnto erth son*er* tha*n* he wold.   16

(5)
Why þ*at* erth loweth erth, wonder[1] I thynk ;
Or why þ*at* erth will for erth swet or swynk ;
For wha*n* erth vpon erth is browght w*ith*in þe brynk,
Than shall erth for erth suffre a fowle stynk.   20

(6)
As erth vpon erth were þe worthyes IX,
& as erth vpon erth i*n* hono*ur* dide shyne ;
But erth liste not to know how þei shuld enclyn,   23
& þ*er* crow*n*nys leyd i*n* erth, wha*n* deth hath made hys fyne.

(7)
As erth upon erth, full worthy was Josue,   [leaf 208]
Dauyd þe worthy kyng, Judas Machabe ;

[1] MS. worder

III. *Didactic, Moral and Allegorical Poems.* 91

They were but erth vpon erth, non of them thre,
& so from erth vnto erth þei loste þer dignite.   28

(8)
Alisander was but erth, þat all the world wan,
& Ector vpon erth was hold a worthy man,
& Julius Cesar þat þe empire first be-gan ;
& now, as erth within erth, þei lye pale & wan.   32

(9)
Arthur was but erth, for all his renown ;
No more was kyng Charlis, ne Godfrey of Bolown ;
But now erth hath torned þer noblenes vpsodown ;
& thus erth goth to erth, by short conclusion.   36

(10)
Who so rekyn also of William Conquerowr,
Kyng Harry þe first, þat was of knyghthode flowr ;
Erth hath closed them full streytly in his bowr ;
Loo, the ende of worthynes ! here is no more socowr.   40

(11)
Now thei þat leve vpon erth, both yong & old,
Thynk how ye shall to erth, be ye neuer so bold ;
Ye be vnsiker, wheþer it be in hete or cold,
Like as your brother dide beffore, as I haue told.   44

(12)
Now ye folk þat be here, ye may not long endure,
But þat ye shall torn to erth, I do you ensure ;
& yf ye lyst of þe trewth to se a playn fugure,
Go to seynt Powlis, & see þer the portratowr.   48

(13)
All ys erth, & shall be erth, as it shewith ther,
þer-for, or dredfull deth with his dart you dere,
& for to torn in to erth, no man shall it forbere,
Wisely purvey you beffore, & þer-of haue no fere.   52

(14)
Now, sith by deth we shall all pas, it is to vs certeyn,
For of þe erth we com all, & to þe erth shall torn agayn ;
þer-for to strive of[1] grucche, it were but in vayn,
For all is erth, & shall be erth, no thyng more certayn.   56

---

[1] or ?

92   III. *Didactic, Moral and Allegorical Poems.*

(15)
Now erth vppon erth, consydre thow may,
How erth commeth to erth, nakyd all-way.
Why shuld erth vpon erth go stowt or gay,
Sith erth owt of erth shall passe in pore a-ray ?   60
(16)
I consaill you, vpon erth þat wikkidly haue wrowght,
Whill þat erth is on erth, torn vp your thowght,
& pray to God vppon erth, þat all þe erth hath wrowght,
þat erth owt of erth, to blis may be browght.   64
Amen.

80c. [Dr. John Ednam on What's the good of it!]

Si sum diues agris et nobilitate : quid inde ?
Si mea sponsa decens[1] et si formosa : quid inde ?
Si mihi sunt nati, opes et fama : quid inde ?   3
Si sum felix annis, et vixero mille : quid inde ?
Si rota fortune me tollat ad astra : quid inde ?
Tam cito poterunt[2] hec omnia quam nichill inde.   6
Quod doctor Joh[ann]es Ednam.

80d. [God's Blessing.]

Cruor fusus Jhesu Christi crucis in patibilo,
Nos consortes prebuisti celi contubernio,
Sic descendat super nos Dei benediccio.   3

81.

To dy, to dy! what haue I   [leaf 210]
Offendit þat deth is so hasty!

(1)
O marcyfull God, maker of all mankynd,
What meneth dethe in his mynd,
  & I so yonge of age—   3
Now deth is vnkynd ;
For he seyth : "Man! stop thy wynde,"
  þus he doth rage.   6

---
[1] MS. docens   [2] poterent MS. ; poterint *Flügel*.

III. *Didactic, Moral and Allegorical Poems.*

(2)
¶ ✠ So dye shall then
All Crystyn men ;
No man wottith his tyme, ne when,   9
Wherfor thow may,
Yf þou be hye,
Thynk non oþer but þou shalt dye.   12

[Death and the Four Ages of Man.]
(1)
¶ In XX^{ti} yere of age, remembre we euerychon,
þat deth will not be strange, to taste vs by on & on,
✠ so dy With siknes grevows, which makith man to grone,
Deth biddith beware, þis day a man, to-morow non.   16

(2)
¶ In XL yere of age, whan man is stowt & stronge,
Trow ye þat deth dare stryk hym or do hym any wrong?
✠ so dy Yes, for-soth, with worldly deth he vill not spare among,
& seyth : " Man, beware! þou shalt not tary long."   20

(3)
¶ In LX yere of age, then tyme is cum to thynk—
How he will cum to þe hows, & sit on þe bynke,
Comaundyng man to stowpe toward þe pittis brynk ;
✠ so dy Than farewell, worldis joy, whan deth shall bid a man
drynk.   24

(4)
¶ The last age of mankynd is called ' decrepitus,'
Whan man lakkith reason, than deth biddith hym thus :
✠ so dy Owt of þis world his lyf to pas with mercy of Jhesus ;
Deth strykith with sword / & seyth : "Man! it shal be
thus."   28
Explicit.

82. [' Speculum vitae et mortis.']

(1)   [leaf 208]   (2)
Cur mundus militat sub vana gloria,   Quis credat litteris scriptis in glacie?
Cuius prosperitas est transitoria?   Quam mundi fragilis vane substancie!
Tam cito labitur eius potencia   Fallit in premiis, fallit in spacie,
Quam vasa figuli que sunt fragilia. 4 Quis vnquam tenuit tempus fiducie? 8

III. Didactic, Moral and Allegorical Poems.

(3)
Credendum magis est auris falacibus
Quam mundi miseris prosperitatibus,
Falsis in sompniis ac vanitatibus,
Falsis in studiis et voluptatibus. 12

(4)
Dic vbi Salamon olim tam nobilis,
Vell Samson vbi est dux inuincibilis,
Vell pulcher Absolon vultu mirabilis,
Vell dulcis Jonathas multum amabilis ? 16

(5)
Quo Cesar abiit celsus imperio,
Well diues splendidus totus in pran-
Dic vbi Tvlius clarus eloquio [dio?
Vell Aristotiles summus ingenio? 20

(6)
Tot clari proceres, tot retro spacia,
Tot ora presulum, tot regum forcia,
Tot mundi principes, tanta potencia,
In ictu oculi clauduntur omnia. 24

(7)
Quam breue festum est haec mundi gloria ?
Vt vmbra fugiunt ipsius gaudia.

Que tamen subtrahunt eterna premia,
Et ducunt hominem ad rura deuia. 28

(8)
O esca verminum, o massa pulueris,
O ros, o vanitas, vt quid extolleris !
Ignoras penitus, vtrum cras vixeris,
Fac bonum omnibus quam diu poteris.

(9)
Hec carnis gloria, que magni pendi-
Sacris in litteris flos feni dicitur, [tur,
Vell bene folium, quod vento rabitur;
Sic vita hominis a luce trahitur. 36

(10)
Nill tuum dixeris quod potes perdere,
Quod mundus tribuit habet repetere,
Superna cogita, cor sit in ethere,
Felix qui poterit mundum contempnere. 40

(11)
Vt marcent yeme frondes et folia,
Sic mortis frigore tabescunt omnia.
Hinc, cum sit labilis presens leticia,
Cur mundus militat sub vana gloria
Speculum vite et mortis.

IV. Historical Poems.

83.

Hic incipit [leaf 169, back]
The Lamentacion of the Duches of Glossester.[1]

(1)
Thorow-owt a pales as I can passe,
I hard a lady make gret mone;
& ever she syked & sayd: "Alas,
All worldly joy ys from me gone! 4
& thus am I lefte, my self alone,
& all my frend*is* from me can fle,
Alas! I am full woo be-gon!
All women may be ware by me. 8

(2)
All women *þat in* this world be wrowght,
By me they may insampull take,
As I *þat* was browght vp of nowght,
A pri*n*ce had chosyn me to his make. 12
My sofferen lorde so to for-sake,
Yt was a dulfull destenye;
Alas! for to sorow how shuld I slake? 15
All wome*n* may be ware by me.

(3)
I was so high vpon my whele,
Myne own estate I cowld not know;
Therfor the gospell seyth full well:
'Who will be high, he shall be low.'
The whele of fortune, who may it trow?

All ys but veyn & vanyte! 22
My flowris of joy be all down blow;
All wome*n* may be ware by me.

(4)
In worldly joy & worthynes
I was be-sette on eu*er*y side;
Of Glowcester I was duches, 27
A-monge all wome*n* magnyfyed;
[2] As Lucyfer fell down for pryde, [²¹f. 170]
I fell from all felycyte;
I hade no gra*c*e, my self to gyde;
All wome*n* may be ware by me.

(5)
Alas! what was myn adventure,[3]
So sodeynly down for to fall, 34
That hade all London at my cure,[3]
To crok & knele whan I wold call?
Now, Fader of Hevyn celestyall,
Of my co*m*playnt haue pyte! 38
Now am I made sympulest of all:
All wome*n* may be ware by me.

(6)
Be-fore the covnsell of this londe
At Westmynster, vpon a day,
Full rewfully ther dide I stonde;
A worde for me durst no ma*n* say. 44
Owr soverayn lorde, wi*th*owt delay,

---
[1] Title written in a different hand along the margin.
[3] *The final* e's *in* adventure *and* cure *were added in later ink.*

Was ther; he myght both here
 & see,
& to his grace he toke me ay :
All women may be ware by me. 48

(7)
Hys grace to me was euermore gayn,
Thowgh I hade done so gret offence;
The lawe wold I hade bene slayn,
 & sum men dyde ther delygence. 52
þat worthy pry[n]ce of high pru-
 dence,
Of my sorow hade gret petye :
Honour to hym with reverence!
All women may be ware by me. 56

(8)
I come be-fore the spiritualte :
Two cardynals & byshoppis fyve,
 & oder men of gret degre
Examened me of all my lyff; 60
 & openly I dyde me shryff
Of all thyng þat they asked me ;
Than was I putt in penance belyff ;
All women may be ware by me. 64

(9)
Thorow London, in many a strete
Of them þat were most pryncypall,
I went barefote on my fette,
þat sumtyme was wonte to ride
 riall. 68
Fader of hevyn & lorde of all,
As thou wilt, so must yt be ;
The syne of pryde will haue a fall :
All women may be ware by me. 72

(10)
Farewell, London, & haue good day!
At the I take my leve this tyde,
Farewell, Grenwych, for ever & ay!
Farewell, fayer placis on Temys
 syde!   76

Farewell, all welth in the world
 so wide !
I am asigned wher I shal be,
Vnder mens kepyng I must a-bide;
All women may be ware by me. 80

(11)
Farewell, damask & clothes of gold!
Farewell, velwet & clothes in
 grayn !
Farewell, robes in many a folde ! 83
Farewell ! I se you never agayn.
[1] Farewell, my lorde & sufferayn !
Farewell ! yt may no better be;
Owr partyng ys grownd of felyng
 payn :   [¹ leaf 170, back]
All women may be ware by me. 88

(12)
Farewell, my mynstrels, & all your
 songe,
þat ofte hath made me for to
 davnce !
Farwell ! I wott I haue done wronge,
 & I wyte my mysgovernance. 92
Now I lyste nother to pryk nor
 prance ;
My pryde is put to poverte;
Thus both in Englond & in Fravnce
All women may beware by me. 96

(13)
Farewell, all joy & lustynesse !
All worldly myrth I may for-sake,
I am so full of hevynesse, [make.
I wott not to whom my mone to
Vnto hym I will me take,   101
þat for me dyed vpon a tre;
In prayer I will both walke & wake :
All women may be ware by me.

Here endith þe lamytacion of the
 Duches of Glowcetter.

84.

The Lamytacion off Quene Elyzabeth [by Sir Thomas More]. [leaf 175]

(1)
Ye þat put your trust & confydence
In worldly riches & frayll prosperyte,
þat so leve here, as ye shuld never hens,
Remember deth, & loke here vpon me.
 Insampull, I thynk, þer may no better be. 5
  Yourself wote well þat in þis realme was I
 Your quene but late : loo ! here I lye. 7

(2)
Was I not born of old worthy lynage ? 8
 Was not my moder, quene, & my fader, kyng ?
Was I not a kyngis fere in maryage ?
 Hade I not plente of euery plesant thyng ?
 Marcyfull God ! þis ys a strange reconyng ; 12
  Ryches, honour, welth & auncetry,
 Hath me for-sake. Loo ! here I lye. 14

(3)
Yff worship myght haue kept me, I had no[t] g[on], 15
 Yff welth myght me haue serued, I nedid not to f[ere],
Yff money myght haue hold, I laked non,
 But, o, good God ! what avaylith all þis gere ?
 Whan deth commyth, thy myghti mesanger, 19
  Obey we must, þer ys no remedye ;
 He hath me somond. Loo ! here I lye. 21

(4)
Yet was I lately promised oþer wyse ; [leaf 175, back] 22
 This yere to leve in welth & delice.
Lo ! wher-to cumyth thi blandyshyng promyse,
 O false astrologye dyvynatrice,[1]
 Of Godis secrettis makyng the so wyse, 26
  How trew ys for this yere the propheysye :
 The yere yet lastyth, and loo ! now here I lye. 28

(5)
O brytill welth, ay full of bitternes, 29
 Thy synglar plesure ay dowbled ys with payn.

[1] MS. dymynatrice

CAROLS.   H

IV. Historical Poems.

Accompte my sorow fyrst & my distres
  Sondre wyse, & rekyn ther a-gayn
The yoy þat I haue had, I dare not sayn. 33
  For all my honour, indured yet haue I
More wo than welth, & lo, here I lye. 35

(6)

Wher are owr castellis now, & owr towers? 36
  Goodly Richemond, son, art þou gon from me!
At Westmynster þat goodly werk of yours,
  Myne own dere lord, now shall I neuer se.
Almyghty God witsave to grante þat ye 40
  & your children well may edyfye!
My place bilded ys; for lo, here I lye. 42

(7)

A-dewe, my trew spouse, my worthi lord! 43
  The feythfull love þat dide vs to combyne
In maryage & pesybull concorde,
  Vnto your hondis here I clene resyne,
To be bestowed on your children & myne. 47
  Erst were ye fader; now must ye supplye
The moders parte also: lo, wher I lye! 49

(8)

Farewell, my dowghter, lady Margarete! 50
  God wote, full sore yt grevid hath my mynd,
þat ye shuld go wher we shuld seldom mete,
  Now am I gon, & haue left you behynd:
O mortall folke, what we [be] very blynd! 54
  þat we lest fere, full oft yt ys full nye;
Fro you departe I fyrst; lo, here I lye! 56

(9)

Farewell, madam, my lordis worþi moder! 57
  Comfort your son, & be ye of good chere;
Take all in worth, for yt will be non oþer.
  Farwell, my dowghter, late the fere
To prince Arthur, my own child so dere; 61
  Yt botith not for me to wepe & crye.
Pray for my sowle, for now, lo, here I lye. 63

(10)

A-dewe, Lord Harry, my lovely son, a-dewe! 64
  Owr Lord increase your honour & your estate!

IV. *Historical Poems.* 99

A-dewe, my dowghter Mary, bright of hewe!
God make you vertuus, wyse & fortvnate!
A-dewe, swet harte, my lady dowghter Cate! 68
Thou shalte, good babe, suche ys thi destenye,
Thy moder never know, for lo, here I lye! 70
(11)
O lady Cecill, Anne and Kateryne, [leaf 176] 71
Farewell, my welbelouyd systers thre!
O lady Brygyte, dere syster myne,
Lo, here the ende of worldly vanyte!
Lo, well ar you, þat erthly folye fle, 75
And hevynly thyngis loue & magnyfye;
Farewell, & pray for me; for lo, here I lye! 77
(12)
Adewe, my lordis & ladyes all! 78
Adewe, my feythfull seruantis euerychon!
Adewe, my Comyns, whom I neuer sha[ll]
Se in þis world;—wherfor, to the a-lone,
Immortall God, very thre in on, 82
I me commend, to thy infenyte mercy,
Shew to thi seruant now; for lo, here I lye! 84

84*b*. [Latin Epitaph on Queen Elizabeth, wife of Henry VII.]

Extinctum jacet hic genus a plantagine dati,
Et rosa purpurea candida mixta rosis,
Elizabeth, claris Anglorum regibus orta,
Regina ac patrii gloria rara soli,
Edwardi soboles quarti, tibi septimo coniux, 5
Henrici, heu populi cura benigna tui;
Exemplar vite, qua nec prestancior altra
Moribus, ingenio, nec probitata fuit.
Regina[m] Deus eterno dignetur honore
Et regem hic annos viuere gefferos.[1] 10

84*c*. [English Epitaph on Queen Elizabeth.]

Here lith the fresshe flowr of Plantagenet;
Here lith the white rose in the rede sete;

---

[1] *The Latin of this I have purposely left unaltered. For the right readings from Weever, see notes.*

100   IV. *Historical Poems.*

<pre>
Here lith the nobull quen Elyzabeth ;
Here lith the princes departid by deth ;   4
Here lith blode of owr contray royall ;
Here lith fame of Ynglond immortall ;
Here lith of Edward the IIIIth a picture ;
Her lith his dowghter & perle pure ;   8
Here lith þe wyff of Harry, owr trew kyng ;
Here lith þe hart, þe joy & þe gold rynge ;
Here lith the lady so lyberall & gracius ;
Here lith the pleasure of thy hows ;   12
Here lith very loue of man & child ;
Here lith insampull, owr myndez to bild ;
Here lith all bewte, of lyvyng a myrrour ;
Here lith all vertu, good maner & honour ;   16
God grant her now hevyn to encrese,
& owr kyn Harry long lyff & pease !   18
            Explicit.
</pre>

Iste liber pertineth Rycardo Hill,
seruant with M. Wynger, alderman of London.

85.

A treatice of London [by William Dunbar].

(1)

London, thow art of townes a per se,   [leaf 199, back]
 Soverayn of cyties, semlyest by sight,
Of high renown, riches & royalte,
 Of lordis, barones, & many goodly knyght,
 Of most dilectable lusty ladyes bryght,   5
  Of famowse prelates in habytis clerycall,
 Of merchantis full of substance & myght :
  London, thow art þe flowr of cytes all.   8

(2)

Gladdeth a-non, thow lusty Troynouant,   9
 Citie that sumtyme called was New Troye ;
In all this erth, imperiall as þou stante,
 Prynces of townes, of pleasure & joye,
 A rychar restyth vnder no Crystyn Roye,   13

IV. *Historical Poems.* 101

For manly power with craftes naturall
Formeth no fayrer sith the flode of Noye.
London, thow art þe flowr of cyties all!   16

(3)

Geme of all joye, jaspe of jocondyte,   17
  Moste myghty carbuncle of vertu & valour,
Strong Troy in vigure & sterne-vite,
  Of royall cyties rose & geraflowr,
Empres of townes, exalte in honowr,   21
  In beawte beryng þe trone imperyall,
Swete paradise prosellyng in pleasowr;
  London, thow art þe flowr of ceties all!   24

(4)

A-bove all ryvers, thy ryuer hath renown,   25
  Whose boryall stremes plesant & preclare,
Vnder thy lusty walles renneth down,
  Wher many a swan doth swym with wyngis fayre,
Wher many a barge doth sayle & rowe with thayre,   29
  Wher many a shipe doth rest with toppe royall.
O town of townes, patron but compare!
  London, thou art þe flowr of ceties all!   32

(5)

Vppon thy lusty brygge of pylers whight   33
  Ben merchantis full royall to beholde;
Vpon thy stretes goth many a semely knyght
  In velvet gownes & cheynes of fyne golde.
By Julyus Sesar thy Tour fownded of olde   37
  May be the hows of Mars victoryall,
Whose artylary with tonge may not be told.
  London, thow art the flowr of ceties all!   40

(6)

Strong be the walles þat abowt þe stondes,   [leaf 200]
  Wise be the people þat within the dwellis;
Fresshe is thy river with his lusty strandis;
  Blith be the chirches; well sownyng be þe bellis;
Ryche be thy merchantis in substance þat excellis; 45
  Fayre be þer wyffes, right lovesum, whit & small,
Clere be thy virgyns, lusty vnder kellis.
  London, þou art the flowr of ceties all!   48

(7)

Thy famowse mayre, by princely gouernance, 49
　With swerde of justice the ruleth prudently,
No lorde of Paris, Venys, or Florance,
　In dignyte or honour goth hym nygh.
He is examplar, right lodester & gwy, 53
　Pryncypall patrone & rose orygynall,
A-bove all mayres, as master most worthy.
　London, þou art the flowr of cities all! 56

Explicit þe treatise of London, made at M. Shaa table
whan he was mayre.

[*fol.* 3*b. index:* "a litill balet made by London, made at Mr. Shawes table **by a Skote.**"]

V. Ballads and Worldly Songs. Humorous and Satirical Pieces.

86.

Lully, lulley, lully, lulley! [leaf 165, back]
þe fawcon hath born my mak away.

(1)
He bare hym vp, he bare hym down,
He bare hym in to an orchard brown.
Lully, lulley, lully, lulley!
þe fawcon hath born my mak away.   4

(2)
¶ In þat orchard þer was an hall,
þat was hangid with purpill & pall;
Lully, lulley, [lully, lulley!
þe fawcon hath born my mak away.]   8

(3)
¶ And in þat hall þer was a bede,
Hit was hangid with gold so rede;
Lully, lulley, [lully, lulley!
þe fawcon hath born my mak away.]   12

(4)
¶ And yn þat bed þer lythe a knyght,
His wowndis bledyng day & nyght;
Lully, lulley, [lully, lulley!
þe fawcon hath born my mak away.]   16

(5)
¶ By þat bedis side þer kneleth a may,
& she wepeth both nyght & day;
Lully, lulley, [lully, lulley!
þe fawcon hath born my mak away.]   20

(6)
¶ & by þat beddis side þer stondith a ston,
"Corpus Christi" wretyn þer-on.
Lully, lulley, [lully, lulley!
þe fawcon hath born my mak away.]   24
Explicit.

87. [How! we shall have game & sport ynow!]

(1)
As I walked by a forest side,
I met with a foster; he bad me a-bid.
At a place wher he me sett, [leaf 178]
He bad me, what tyme an hart I met,   4

That I shuld let slyppe & say "go bett";
With "hay go bet, hay go bett, hay go bett,"
How! we shall haue game & sport ynow.   7

(2)
I had not stond ther but a while,
Ye, not þe montenance of a myle,
But a gret hart cam rennyng, withowt any gile;
With "þer he goth, þer he goth, þer he gothe"!
How! we shall haue game & sport ynow.   12

(3)
I had no sonner my howndis lat goo,
But the hart was over-throwe,
Than euery man began to blowe,
With "trororo, trororo, trororo,"
How! we shall haue game & sport ynow.   17

88. [My twelve oxen.]

(1)
I haue XII oxen þat be fayre & brown,
& they go a grasynge down by the town,
  With hay, with howe, with hay!
    Sawyste thow not myn oxen, þou litill prety boy? 4

(2)
I haue XII oxen, & they be fayre & whight,
& they go a grasyng down by the dyke,
  With hay, with howe, with hay!
    Sawyste not þou myn oxen, þou lytyll prety boy? 8

(3)
I haue XII oxen, & they be fayre & blak,
& they go a grasyng down by the lak,
  With hay, with howe, with hay!
    Sawyste not þou myn oxen, þou lytyll prety boy? 12

(4)
I haue XII oxen, & they be fayre & rede,
& they go a grasyng down by þe mede,
  With hay, with howe, with hay!
    Sawiste not þou myn oxen, þou litill prety boy? 16
      Explicit.

V. *Ballads and Worldly Songs. Humorous and Satirical Pieces.* 105

89.
A treatise of wyne. [leaf 101]

(1)
The best tre, yf ye take entent,
　Inter ligna fructifera
Ys þe vine tre, by good argument,
　Dulce ferens pondera. 4

(2)
¶ Seynt Luke seyth in his gospell :
　Arbor fructu noscitur ;
The vyne berith wyne, as I you tell,
　Hinc aliis preponitur. 8

(3)
¶ The first that plantid þe vyneard
　Manet in celi gaudio,
His name was Noe, as I am lerned,
　Genesis testimonio. 12

(4)
¶ God gaff vnto hym knowlage & witt,
　A quo procedunt omnia,
First of þe grape wyne for to get
　Propter magna misteria. 16

(5)
¶ Melchisedech made offeryng,
　Dando licorem vinium,
Full myghtyly sacrafying
　Altaris sacraficium. 20

(6)
¶ The first myracle þat Jhesus dide,
　Erat in vino rubio ;
In Cana Galalee þer it be-tide
　Testante evangelio. 24

(7)
¶ He changed water in to wyne,
　Aque rubescunt idrie ;
& bade geve it to archetriclyne,
　Vt gustet tunc primarie. 28

(8)
¶ Lyke as þe rose excedeth all flowres
　Inter cunta florigera,
So doth wyne oper lycowres
　Dans multa salutifera. 32

(9)
¶ Dauid the prophet seyth þat wyne
　Letificat cor hominis ;
Yt maketh men mery, yf it be fyne,
　Est ergo digni nominis. 36

(10)
¶ The malicoli fumosetyve,
　Que generat tristiciam,
Yt causith from þe hart to rise
　Tollens omnem mesticiam. 40

(11)
¶ The first chapter specified
　Libri ecclesiastici,
þat wyne ys¹ musik of cunyng delite,
　Letificat cor clarici. 44

(12)
¶ Sirs, yf ye will se Boyce
　" De disciplina scolarium,"
þer shall ye se withowt mysse,
　Quod vinum acuit Ingenium. 48

(13)
¶ First whan Ypocras shuld dispute
　Cum viris sapientibus,
Good wyne beffore was his persute,
　Acumen prebens sencibus. 52

(14)
¶ Hit quykneth a mans spiritis &
　his mynd, [leaf 101, back]
　Audaciam dat liquentibus ;
Yf þe wyne be good & well fyned,
　Prodeste sobrie bibentibus. 56

¹ ys MS.] and *or* with : *Flügel.—Qu.* as ?

106   V. *Ballads and Worldly Songs.*   *Humorous and Satirical Pieces.*

(15)
¶ Good wyne receyved moderatly
   Mox cerebrum letificat,   [dye,
Naturall het it strengtheth well per-
Omne membrum fortificat.   60

(16)
¶ Dronkyn also soburly,
Degestionem vberans,
Helthe it lengtheth also of þe body,
Naturam humanam prosperans. 64

(17)
¶ Good wyne provokis a man to
   swete
Et plena lavat viscera,
Hit maketh men to ete þer mete,
Facit-que corda prospera.   68

(18)
¶ Hit norissheth age, yf it be good,
Facit vt esset juuinis,
Hit gadereth in hym gentill blode,
Nam venas purgat sangvinis. 72

(19)
¶ Syrs, by all thes causes ye shuld
   Que sunt racionabiles,   [thynk,

þat good wyne shuld be best of all
   drynk,
Inter potus potabiles.   76

(20)
¶ Fille the Cuppe well, belamye,
   Potum iam michi ingere ;
I haue said, till my lippis be drye,
   Vellem nunc vinum bibere.   80

(21)
¶ Gentill blode loveth gentill drynk,
   Nam simile amat simile ;
Had I þe cuppe full by þe brynk,
   Parum manebit bibile.   84

(22)
¶ Wyne-drynkers all, with gret
   honowr
Semper laudate dominum,
þe which sendith þe good licowr
   Propter salutem hominum.   88

(23)
¶ Plente to all þat love good wyne
   Donet Deus homo largius, [hene,
& bryng them sone whan they go
   Vbi non siscient amplius.   92

90.
Hoow, gossip myne, gossip myn,   [leaf 206, back.]
Whan will we go to þe wyne,
Good gossip[is myn ?]

(1)
I shall you tell a full good sport,
How gossippis gader them on a sort,
Ther seke bodyes to comforte   3
   Whan they mete
   In lane or stret,
      God gossipis myn.   6

(2)
But I dare not, for þer dissplesans,
Tell of þes maters half the substance,
But ȝet sum what of þer gouernance, 9

As ferre as I dare,
I will declare,
   Good gossipis myn.   12

(3)
" Good gossip myn, wher haue ye
   be ?
Hit is so long sith I you see ;
Wher is þe best wyne, tell you me !
   Can ye owght tell ? "
   " Ye, full well,
      Good gossippis myn.   18

V. *Ballads and Worldly Songs. Humorous and Satirical Pieces.* 107

(4)
I know a drawght of mery-go-down;
The beste it is in all this town,
But yet I wolde not, for my gown,
 My husbond wyste."
 "Ye may me triste,
  Good gossipp(is) myn." 24

(5)
"Call forth owr gossippis by & by,
Elynore, Johan & Margery,
Margret, Alis & Cecely, 27
 For þei will cum,
 Both all & som,
  Good gossippis myn, a! 30

(6)
And eche of them will sum what bryng
Gose or pigge, or capons wynge,
Pastes of pygynnes, or sum oþer
 thyng; 33
 For we mvste ete
 Sum maner mett,
  Good gossippis myn, a! 36

(7)
Go beffore by tweyn & tweyn,
Wisely þat ye be not seen,
For I mvste home & cum a-gayn,
 To witt, ywis,
 Wher my husbond is,
  Good gossippis myn, a! 42

(8) [¹ leaf 207]
¹A strype or two God myght send me,
Yf my husbond myght here see me."
"She þat is a-ferde, lett her flee;"
 Quod Alis than,
 "I dred no man,
  Good gossippis myn, a!" 48

(9)
"Now be we in þe tavern sett,
A drawght of þe best lett hym fett,

To bryng owr husbondis owt of dett;
 For we will spend
 Till God more send,
  Good gossippis myn, a!" 54

(10)
Eche of them browght forth þer
 disshe,
Sum browght flesshe, & sum
 [browght] fisshe. [wisshe:
Quod Margret meke now with a
 "I wold Anne were here,
 She wold mak vs chere,
  Good gossippis myn, a!" 60

(11)
"How say ye, gossippis? Is þis wyn
 good?" [rode!
"Þat is it," quod Elynore, "by þe
It chereth þe hart & comforteth þe
 Such jonkers amonge [blod.
 Shall make vs leve long.
  Good gossippis [myn, a]!" 66

(12)
Anne bade me fill a pot of Muscadell,
"For of all wynes I love it well;
Swet wynes kepe my body in hele;
 Yf I had it nowght,
 I shuld tak thowght,
  Good gossippis myn, a!" 72

(13)
"How loke ye, gossip, at þe bordis
 end?
Not mery, gossip? God it amend!
All shall be well, els God defend;
 Be mery & glad
 & sit not so sade,
  Good gossip myn, a!" 78

(14)
"Wold God I had don after your
 covnsell,

108   V. *Ballads and Worldly Songs.*   *Humorous and Satirical Pieces.*

For my husbond is so fell,
He betith me lyke þe devill of hell,
And þe more I crye,
þe lesse m*er*cy,
  Good gossippis myn, a !"   84
(15)
Alis wit*h* a lowde voys spak than :
" Evis," she said, " litill good he can,
þ*a*t betith or striketh any woma*n*,
And specially his wyff,
God geve hy*m* short lyff,
  Good gossippis myn, a !"   90
(16)
Margret meke said : "So mot I thryve,
I know no ma*n* þat is a-lyve,
þ*a*t gevith me II strok*is*, bvt he
  haue V :   93
I am not afferd,
Thowgh he haue a berde,
  Good gossippis myn, a !"   96
(17)
On cast down her shot, & went a-way :
" Gossip," q*uo*d Elynore, "what dide
  she pay ?"
" Not but a peny : loo, þ*er*-for I say,
She shall no more
Be of owr lore,
  Good gossippis myn, a !"   102
(18)
" Suche gest*is* we may haue ynow,
þ*a*t will not for þ*er* shot alowe ;
With whom com she, gossip ?"
  " W*it*h you."   105
" Nay," q*uo*d Johan,
" I com aloon,
  Good gossippis myn, a !"   108
(19)
"Now rekyn owr shot, & go we
  hens ;

What cu*m*meth to eche of vs ?' "
  " But IIId."
" P*ar*de, þis is but a small expens
For suche a sorte,
& all but sporte,
  Good gossip*is* myn, a !"   114
(20)
[1]" Torn down þe stret, wha*n* ye cu*m*
  owt,   [¹ leaf 207, back]
& we will cu*m*pas rownd a-bowt."
" Gossip," q*uo*d Anne, " what nedith
  þat dowt ?   117
You*r* husbond is pleased,
Wha*n* ye be eased,
  Good gossipp*is* myn, a !   120
(21)
What-so-eu*er* any man thynk,
We co*m* for nowght but for good
  drynk ;
Now let vs go home & wynke,   123
For it may be seen
Wher we haue ben,
  Good gossipp*is* myn, a !"   126
(22)
This is þe thowght þ*a*t gossippis take :
Ons i*n* þe wek, mery will they
  make,
& all small drynk*is* þei will forsake ;
But wyne of þe best
Shall have no rest,
  Good gossippis myn, a !   132
(23)
Su*m* be at þe tav*er*n III*se* in þe weke,
& so be su*m* eu*er*y day eke,
Or ell*is* þei will gron & mak the*m* sek,
For thy*n*gis vsed
Will not be refused ;
  Good gossipp*is* myn, a !   138
    Explicit.

91.
In villa, in villa, quid vidistis in villa? [leaf 241]

(1)
Many a man blamys his wyffe parde;
Yet he ys more to blame than she,[1]
Trow ye þat any suche ther be
In villa? 4

(2)
Ye, ye, hold your pease, for shame!
By owr Lady, ye be to blame,
Wene you that womenys tongis be
In villa? [lame

(3)
Nay, God for-bede! yt ys naturall
For them to be right lyberall,
Now I report me, overall
In villa. 12

(4)
On thyng for-soth I haue esspyed;
All women be not tong-tyed;
For yf they be, they be by-lyed
In villa. 16

(5)
Yff owght be sayd to them, sertayn,
Wene you þei will not answer a-gayn?
Yes, for euery word, twayn!
In villa. 20

(6)
Now, in gud feyth, the soth to say,
They haue gret cavse, from day to day,
For they may nother sport ne play
In villa. 24

(7)
þer husbondis controll them so streytly;
But ȝet no force for þat hardely;
þer skuse shall be made full craftyly
In villa. 28

(8)
How say ye, women þat husbondis haue?
Will not ye ther honowr saue,
& call them 'lowsy stynkyng knave'?
In villa! 32

(9)
Yes, so haue I hard tell or this,
Not fer owt of this cuntrey ywys,
Of sum of them, men shall not mys,
In villa. 36

(10)
God wot, gret cavse þei haue a-mong;
But dowt ye not, ther hartis be strong,
For they may sofer no maner wrong
In villa. 40

(11)
And yff þei dyde, ther hartis wold brest,
Wher-for in feyth I hold yt best,
Lett them a-lone with evyll rest
In villa. 44

(12)
Ye, husbondis all, with on asent,
Lett your wyffys haue þer yntent,
Or suerly ye will be shent
In villa. 48

(13)
Ytt ys hard a-yenst þe strem to stryve,
For hym þat cast hym for to thryve,
He mvst aske leve of hys wyff,
In villa. 52

(14)
Or ellis by God & by the rode,
Be he never so wyld & wode,
Hys here shall grow thorow his hode
In villa. 56
Explicit.

[1] he ... she] MS. she ... he.

110 V. *Ballads and Worldly Songs. Humorous and Satirical Pieces.*

92.

Hay, hey, hey, hey, [leaf 241, back]
I will haue the whetston, and I may.

(1)
I sawe a doge sethyng sowse,
& an ape thechyng an howse,
And a podyng etyng a mowse,
 I will haue þe whetston, & I may. 4

(2)
I sawe an vrchyn shape & sewe
And a-noder bake & brewe,
Scowre the pottis as þei were newe,
 I will haue þe whetston, & I may. 8

(3)
I sawe a code-fysshe corn sowe,
& a worm a whystyll blowe,
& a pye tredyng a crow,
 I will haue þe whetston, & I may. 12

(4)
I sawe a stokfysshe drawyng a harow,[1]
& a-noder dryveyng a barow,
& a saltfysshe shotyng an arow.
 I will haue þe whetston, & I may. 16

(5)
I sawe a bore, burdeyns bynd,
& a froge, clewens wynd,
& a tode, mvstard grynd,
 I will haue þe whetston, & I may. 20

(6)
I sawe a sowe bere kyrchers to wasshe;
The second sowe had an hege to plasshe;
þe III^{de} sow went to þe barn to throsshe,
 I will haue þe whetston, & I may. 24

(7)
I sawe an ege etyng a pye ;
Geve me drynke, my mowth ys drye;
Yet ys not long syth I made a lye.
 I will haue þe whetston, & I may. 28
  Explicit.

93.

"Alas," sayd þe gudman, "this ys an hevy lyff"; [leaf 249]
"And all ys well þat endyth well," said þe gud wyff.

(1)
A lytill tale I will you tell,
The very trowth, how it befell,
& was trew as þe gosspell.
 Att þe townys end. 4

(2)
Betwen þe gudman & his make,
A lytill stryf be-gon to wake ;
þe wyff was sum-what shrew shake,
 At þe townys end. 8

(3)
He gafe a thyng ther hym lyst,
As son as his wyff yt wyst,
Vp she stode, & bent her fyst,
 At the townys end. 12

(4)
"Thou knave, þou churle," gan she [say,
"In the XX^{te} devyls way,
Who bade the geve my gud a-way
 At the townys end? 16

---
[1] MS. barow.

V. *Ballads and Worldly Songs.* Humorous *and Satirical Pieces.* 111

(5)
þou traytor, þou thef, þou mysguerned
To love þe furst when I began, [man!
I wold þou had be hangyd than
  At þe townys end." 20

(6)
He lent her a strype, two or III,
"Owt, alas!" then cryed she,
"I aske a vengance, thef, on the,
  At þe townys end. 24

(7)
Thou stynkyng coward! so haue I grace,
þou daryst not loke a man in the face,
Now lett them say I know the cace,
  At þe townys ende." 28

(8)
"What, dame, what hast þou but of
& I haue no-thyng of the [me;
But chydyng, brawlyng[1]; evyll mvst þou the
  At þe townys end." 32

(9)
The gudman myght no lengar for-
But smote hys wyff on the ere,[bere,
þat she ouer threw: then lay she ther,
  At þe townys end. 36

(10)
"Alas," she sayd, "I am but dede:
I trow þe brayn be owt of my hed";
& yet þer was no blod shed
  At þe townys end. 40

(11)
"Gett me a priest, þat I were shryve;
For I wot well I shall not lyve,
For I shall dye or to-morow eve
  At þe townys end." 44

(12)
This tale must nedis trew be;
For he þat sawe yt, told yt me;
Aske ferder, & know shall ye,
  At þe townys end. 48

(13)
Now euery man þat ys a-lone,
þat shuld be weddyd to such a on,
I cownsayl hym raþer to haue non
  At þe townys end; 52

(14)
Lest he be knokked a-bowt þe pate;
Then to repent yt ys to late,
When on his cheke he ys chekmate,
  [At þe townys end.] 56
Explicit.

94. [Old Hogyn and his Girl.]

(1)
[2] ¶ Hogyn cam to bowers dore,
Hogyn cam to bowers dore, [²1f. 249, bk.]
  He tryld vpon þe pyn for love,
    Hum, ha, trill go bell!
  He tryld vpon þe py[n] for love,
    Hum, ha, trill go bell! 6

(2)
¶ Vp she rose & lett hym yn,
Vp she rose & let hym yn,

She had a-went, she had worshipped
    all her kyn;
    Hum, ha, trill go bell!
She had a-went, she had worshipped
    all he[r] kyn,
    Hum, ha, trill go bell! 12

(3)
¶ When þei were to bed browght,
Whan thei were to bed browght,
The old chorle he cowld do nowght;

[1] MS. barwlyng.

Hum, ha, trill go bell!
The old chorle he cowld do nowght,
Hum, ha, trill go bell! 18

(4)

¶ "Go ye furth to yonder wyndow,
Go ye furth to yonder wyndow,
And I will cum to you with-in a
Hum, ha, trill go bell! [throw";
"& I will cum to you with-yn a
Hum, ha, trill go bell! [throw";

(5)

¶ Whan she hym at þe wyndow wyst,
Whan she hym at þe wyndow wyst,
She torned owt her ars, & þat he kyst,
Hum, ha, trill go bell!
She torned owt her ars, & þat he kyst,
Hum, ha, trill go bell! 30

(6)

¶ "Ywys, leman, ye do me wrong;
Ywis, leman, ye do me wrong,
Or ellis your breth ys wonder
  strong,"
Hum, ha, trill go bell! 34
"Or ellis your breth ys wonder
Hum, ha, trill go bell! [strong,"
Explicit.

95.

Of all creatures women be best; } fote. [leaf 250]
Cuius contrarium verum est.

(1)

In euery place ye may well see [tree,
That women be trewe as tirtyll on
Not lyberall in langage, but euer in
  secree,[1]
& gret joye a-monge them ys for to be:
Cuius [contrarium verum est.] 5

(2)

The stedfastnes of women will neuer
  be don, [chon,
So jentyll, so curtes they be euery-
Meke as a lambe, still as a stone,
Croked nor crabbed, fynd ye none:
Cuius [contrarium verum est.] 10

(3)

Men be more cumbers a thowsand
  fold; [bold,
& I mervayll how they dare be so
Agaynst women for to hold, [cold:
Seyng them so pascyent, softe &
Cuius [contrarium verum est.] 15

(4)

For, tell a woman all your cownsayle,
& she can kepe it wonderly well;
She had lever go quyk to hell [tell:
Than to her neyghbowr she wold it
Cuius [contrarium verum est.] 20

(5)

For by women, men be reconsiled;
For by women, was neuer man begiled,
For they be of þe condicion of curtes
  Gryzell,
For they be so meke & mylde:
Cuius [contrarium verum est.] 25

(6)

Now say well by women, or ellis be
  still, [will;
For they neuer displesed man by þer
To be angry or wroth they can no
  skill,
For I dare say they thynk non yll:
Cuius [contrarium verum est.] 30

[1] MS. secrete

V. Ballads and Worldly Songs. Humorous and Satirical Pieces.

(7)
Trow ye þat women list to smater,
Or a-gaynst þer husbondis for to clater?
Nay, they had leuer fast bred & water
Then for to dele in suche a mater:
Cuius [contrarium verum est.] 35

(8)
Thowgh all þe paciens in þe world were drownd,
& non were lefte here on the grownd,
Agayn in a woman it myght be fownd,
Suche vertu in them dothe abownd:
Cuius [contrarium verum est.] 40

(9)
To þe tavern they will not goo,
Nor to þe ale-hows neuer the moo,
For, God wot, þer hartis wold be woo
To spende ther husbondis money soo:
Cuius [contrarium verum est.] 45

(10)
Yff here were a woman or a mayd
That lyst for to go fresshely arayed,
Or with fyne kyrchers to go displayed
Ye wold say "they be prowde": it is yll said:
Cuius [contrarium verum est.] 50

96.

Women, women, love of women } fote.
Maketh bare pursis with sum men

(1)
Sum be mery, & sum be sade,
& sum be besy, & sum be bade;
Sum be wilde, by seynt Chade,
 Yet all be not so; 4
  For sum be lewed, & sum be shrewed;
  Go, shrew, wher-so-euer ye go. 6

(2)
Sum be wyse, & sum be fonde;
Sum be tame, I vnderstond;
Sum will take bred at a mannus hond,
 Yet all be not so; 10
  For sum be lewde, & sum be shrewed;
  Go, shrew, wher-so-euer ye go. 12

(3) [¹lf. 250, bk.]
¹ Sum be wroth, & can not tell wher-
Sum be skornyng evermore; [fore;
& sum be tusked lyke a bore;

 Yet all be not so: 16
  For sum be lewed, & sum be shrewed:
  Go, shrewe, wher-so-euer ye go. 18

(4)
Sum will be dronkyn as a mowse;
Sum be croked, & will hurte a lowse;
Sum be fayre, & good in a hows;
 Yet all be not so: 22
  For sum be lewed, & sum be shrewed;
  Go, shrewe, wher-so-euer ye go. 24

(5)
Sum be snowted like an ape;
Sum can nother play ne jape;
Sum of them be well shape;
 Yet all be not so: 28
  For sum be lewed, & sum be shrewed;
  Go, shrewe, wher-so-euer ye go. 30

(6)
Sum can prate withowt hire;
Sum make bate in euery shire;
Sum can play chek-mate with owr sire,
Yet all they do not so :   34
For sum be lewed, & sum be shrewed;
Go, shrew, wher-so-euer ye go. 36
Explicit.

97. Fravs fravde.[1]

[When to trust a Woman.   Never.]

(1)
Whan netillis in wynter bere rosis rede,
& thornys bere figgis naturally,
& bromes bere appyllis in euery mede,
& lorellis bere cheris in þe croppis so hie,
& okys bere datis so plentvosly,   5
And lekis geve hony in per superfluens;
Than put in a woman your trust & confidens.   7

(2)
Whan whityng walk in forestis, hartis for to chase   8
& heryngis, in parkys, hornys boldly blowe,
& flownders, more-hennes in fennes enbrace,
& gornardis shote rolyons owt of a crosse-bowe,
& grengese ride in huntyng, þe wolf to ouer-throwe, 12
& sperlyngis rone with speris in harnes to defence;
Than put in a woman your trust & confidence.   14

(3)
Whan sparowys bild chi[r]ches & stepullis hie,   15
& wrennes cary sakkis to the mylle,
& curlews cary clothes, horsis for to drye,
& semewes bryng butter to þe market to sell,
& woddowes were wodknyffis, theves to kyll,   19
And griffons to goslyngis don obedyence;—
Than put in a woman your trust & confidence.   21

[1] Fravs fravde *added in different hand and ink immediately below the* explicit *of the foregoing piece, but probably, as the contents demand, to be taken for a title to the following one.*

V. *Ballads and Worldly Songs. Humorous and Satirical Pieces.* 115

(4)
Wha*n* crabbis tak wodcok*is* i*n* forest*is* & p*a*rk*is*, 22
& haris ben taken wi*th* swetnes of snaylis,
& camell*is*, wi*th* þer here, tak swalowes & p*er*chis,
& myse mowe corn wi*th* wafeyyng of þ*er* taylis ;
Wha*n* dukk*is* of þe dunghill sek þe blod of Haylis, 26
Wha*n* shrewed wyff*is* to þ*er* husbond*is* do no*n* offens,
Than put i*n* a woma*n* yo*u*r trust & co*n*fidence. 28
Explicit, q*u*od Ric*h*ar*d* Hill.

98. [The Juggler and the Baron's Daughter.]

Drawe me nere, draw me nere, [leaf 251]
Drawe me nere, þe joly juggelere.[1]

(1)
Here beside dwellith a[2] riche barons dowght*er* ;
She wold haue no ma*n* þat for her love had sowght her,
So nyse she was. 3

(2)
She wold haue no ma*n* þat was made of molde,
But yf he had a mowth of gold, to kiss her wha*n* she wold,
So da*n*ger*us* she was. 6

(3)
Ther-of hard a joly juggeler þ*at* layd was on þe gren,
& at this lad*is* word*is*, ywys, he had gret tene :
An angrid he was. 9

(4)
He juggeled to hy*m* a well good stede of an old hors bon,
A sadill & a brydill both, & set hy*m* self þ*er*-on :
A juggler he was. 12

(5)
He priked & pransid both beffore þat ladis gate,
She wend he [had] ben an angell was com for her sake :
A prikker he was. 15

(6)
He pryked & pransid beffore þ*at* ladys towr,
She went he had ben an angell co*m*me*n* from hevyn towre :
A pravns*er* he was. 18

[1] MS. juggelege   [2] MS. as

(7)
XXIIII^{ti} knyghtis lade hym in to the hall,
& as many squyres his hors to the stall,
   & gaff hym mete.   21

(8)
They gaff hym ottis & also hay,
He was an old shrew, & held his hed a-way :
   He wold not ete.   24

(9)
The day began to passe ; þe nyght began to com,
To bede was browght the fayre jentyll woman
   & þe juggeler also.   27

(10)
The nyght began to passe, þe day began to sprynge,
All the brydis of her bowr, they began to synge
   & þe cokoo also.   30

(11)
"Wher be ye, my mery maydyns, þat ye cum not me to?
þe joly wyndows of my bowr lok þat you vndoo,
   þat I may see ;   33

(12)
For I haue in myn armes a duk or ellis an erle."
But whan she loked hym vpon, he was a blere-eyed chorle;
   "Alas!" she said.   36

(13)
She lade hym to an hill, & hangid shuld he be ;
He juggeled hym self to a mele pok; þe duste fell in her eye;
   Begiled she was.   39

(14)
God & owr Lady & swete Seynt Joh[a]n,
Send euery giglot of this town such an-oþer leman,
   Evyn as he was!   42
   Explicit.

99. [The Holly and the Ivy.]

**Nay, nay, Ive, it may not be, iwis,
For holy must haue þe mastry, as þe maner is.**

(1)
¶ Holy berith beris, beris rede ynowgh ;
þe thristilcok, þe popyngay, dance in euery bow[gh] ;
Welaway, sory ivy, what fowles hast thow

V. *Ballads and Worldly Songs. Humorous and Satirical Pieces.* 117

But þe sory howlet þat syngith "How-how"? 4
Na[y, nay, Ive, it may not be, iwis,
For holy must haue þe mastry, as þe maner is.] 6

(2)

¶ Ivy berith beris as blak as any sho,
þer commeth þe woode-coluer, & fedith her of tho;
She liftith vp her tayll, & she cakkis or she go:
She wold not for C. li. serue holy soo: 10
[Nay, nay, Ive, it may not be, iwis,
For holy must haue þe mastry, as þe maner is.] 12

(3)

[1] ¶ Holy with his mery men, they can dance in hall;
Ivy & her jentyl women can not dance at all, [1 lf. 251, bk.]
But lyke a meyny of bullokkis in a water fall,
Or on a whot somers day, whan they be mad all: 16
Nay, [nay, Ive, it may not be, iwis,
For holy must haue þe mastry, as þe maner is.] 18

(4)

¶ Holy & his mery men sytt in cheyres of gold;
Ivy & her jentyll women sytt with-owt in fold,
With a payre of kybid helis cawght with cold;
So wold I þat euery man had, þat with yvy will hold. 22
Nay, [nay, Ive, it may not be, iwis,
For holy must haue þe mastry, as þe maner is.] 24
Explicit.

100. [Bon jour!]

Bonjowre, bonjowre a vous!
I am cum vnto this hows,
Vt parla pompe, I say.

(1)

¶ I[s] þer any good man here,
þat will make me any chere?
& if þer were,
I wold cum nere,
   To wit what he wold say. 5
   A! will ye be wild?
   Be Mary myld,
I trow ye will synge gay!
Bon Jowre! 9

(2)

¶ Be gladly, masters, euery-chon, 10
I am cum my self alone,
To appose you, on by on;
   Let se who dare say nay! 13
   Sir, what say ye?
   Syng on, lett vs see!
Now, will it be
Thys or an other day?
Bon Jowre! 18

118 V. *Ballads and Worldly Songs.* *Humorous and Satirical Pieces.*

(3)

¶ Loo, this is he þat will do þe dede,
He tempereth his mowth; þerfore
 take hede!   [blede,
Syng softe, I say, leste yowr nose
 For hurt yowr self ye may.   22
But, by God þat me bowght,
Your brest is so towght,
Tyll ye haue well cowght,
Ye may not þer-with a-way;
Boniowr!   27

(4)

¶ Sir, what say ye with your face so
 lene?   [ne mene.
Ye syng noþer good tenowre, treble
Vtter not your voice withowt your
 brest be clene,
Hartely I you pray.   31
I hold you excused,
Ye shall be refused,
For ye haue not be vsed
To no good sport nor play.
Bon Jowre!   36

(5)

¶ Sir, what say ye with your fat face?
Me thynkith ye shuld bere a very
 good bace
To a pot of good ale or ipocras,
 Truly, as I you say.   40
Hold vp your hede,
Ye loke lyke lede,
Ye wast myche bred,
Euer more from day to day.
Bon Joure!   45

(6)

Now will ye see, wher he stondith
 behynde?
Iwis, broþer, ye be vnkynd: [wynd,
Stond forth & wast with me som
For ye haue ben called a synger ay.
Nay, be not a-shamed,
Ye shall not be blamed,
For ye haue ben famed
The worst in this contrey.
Bon Jowre!   54
 Explicit.

101. [Ho, butler, ho!]

**How, butler, how! Bevis, a towt!
Fill þe boll, jentill butler,[1] & let þe cup rowght!**

(1)

Jentill butler, bellamy,
Fyll þe boll by þe eye
þat we may drynk by & by,   3
 With how, butler, how! Bevis, a towt!
 Fill þe boll, butler, & let þe cup rowght!   5

(2)

Here is mete for vs all,
Both for gret & for small;

[1] MS. butlet

V. Ballads and Worldly Songs. Humorous and Satirical Pieces. 119

I trow we must þe butlar call, 8
 With how, butler, how! Bevis, a towght!
 Fill þe boll, butler, & lett þe cupe rowght! 10
(3)
I am so dry, I can not spek; [leaf 252]
I am nygh choked with my mete;
I trow þe butler be a-slepe, 13
 With how, butler, how! Bevis, a towght!
 Fill þe boll, butler, [¹ & let þe cup rowght!] 15
(4)
Butler, butler, fill þe boll,
Or ellis I beshrewe thy noll,
I trow we must þe bell toll, 18
 With how, butler, how! Bevis, a towght!
 Fill þe boll, [¹ butler, & let þe cup rowght!] 20
(5)
Iff þe butlers name be Water,
I wold he were a galow-claper;
But if he bryng vs drynk þe raper, 23
 With how, butler, how! Bevis, a towght!
 Fill [¹ þe boll, butler, & let þe cup rowght!] 25
Explicit.

102. [The Disconsolate Lover.]

(1)
Lord, how shall I me complayn
 Vnto myn own lady dere,
For to tell her of all my payn
 That I fele this tyme of the yere? 4
My love, yf þat ye will here,
 Thowgh I can no songis make,
So þis love changith my chere,
 That [whan] I slepe, I can not wake. 8
(2)
Thowgh love do me so mykyll wo,
 I love you best, I make a vowe,
That my shoo byndith my litill too,
 & all my smarte is for you. [1f. 252, bk.]

For-sothe, me thynkith it will me slo,
 But ye sum-what my sorow slake;
But barefot to my bedde I goo,
 & whan I slepe, I can not wak. 16
(3)
Who-so-ever wyst what lyff I lede,
 In myn abseruance in dyuersiteis:
From tyme that I go to my bedde
 I ete no mete tyll that I rise. 20
Ye myght tell it for a gret enprise
 That men thus morneth for your sak;
So mykyll I thynk on your seruice
 That whan I slepe, I can not wak. 24

¹ MS. &c.

120   V. *Ballads and Worldly Songs.*   *Humorous and Satirical Pieces.*

(4)
In the mornyng, whan I shall rise,
  Me lyst right well for to dyne;
But comonly I drynk non ale ywis,
  Yf I may get any good wyne.   28
To mak your hart to me enclyne,
  Suche tormentis to me I take,
Syngyng dothe me so myche pyne,
  That whan I slepe, I can not wak.

(5)
I may vnneth boton my slevis,
  So myn armes wexith more;
Vnder my hele is þat me grevis,
  For at my hart I fele no sore.   36
Euery day my girdyll goth owt a bare,
  I clynge as doth a wheton cake,
& for your love I sigh so sore,
  That whan I slepe, I can not wake.

(6)
þer-for, but ye quyt me well my hire,
  For-soth, I not what I shall done;
& for your love, lady, by this fire,
  Old glovis will I were non.   44

I lawgh & syng & mak no mone,
  I wex as lene as any rake;
Thus in langowr I leve alone,
  & whan I slepe, I can not wak. 48

(7)
My dublet ys narrowar than it was,
  To love you first whan I began;
Hit must be wyder, by my lace,
  In eche a stede by a spanne.   52
My love, sith I becam your man,
  I haue riden thorow many a lake;
On myle-way mornyng I cam;
  Yet whan I slepe, I can not wak. 56

(8)
Thus in langowr I am lent,
  Longe or you do so for me;
Take good hed to myn entent,
  For this shall my conclusion be: 60
Me thynkith I love as well as ye,
  Neuer so quaynt thowgh ye it
By this ensample ye may se, [mak;
  That whan I slepe, I can not wak.
Finis.

103.
Jak & his Stepdame, & of the Frere. [leaf 98]

(1)
God, that died for vs all,
And drank aysell & gall,
  Bryng vs owt of bale!   3
& grant them good lyff & longe,
That will lystyn vnto my songe
  & tende vnto my tale.   6

(2)
¶ Ther was a man of my contree,
þe which wedded wyff is three,
  In prosess of tyme.   9
By the first wyff a child he had,
The which was a propre lade
  & an happy juveyn.   12

(3)
¶ For-soth, his fader loved hym well;
So dide his stepmoder never a dele;
  I tell you as I thynk.   15
All she thowght loste, by the rode,
That dide the boye any goode,
  Off mete or ellis of drynk.   18

(4)
¶ Therfore evill mot she fare,
For ofte she dide hym myche care,
  As ferre forth as she durste.   21
Not half ynowgh þer-of he had,
& for-soth it was right bade,
  & yet she thowght it loste.   24

V. *Ballads and Worldly Songs.   Humorous and Satirical Pieces.* 121

(5)
¶ The goodwyff to her husbond gan
    say:
"Sir, ye moste put this boy a-way,
    I rede you, in haste;   27
In feyth, it is a shrewed lade;
I wold som oþer man hym hade,
    That wold hym better chaste." 30

(6)
¶ The goodman answered her agayn,
& sayd, "Dame, I shall the sayne,
    He ys but yonge of age;   33
He shall abide with me this yere,
Tyll he be more strongere,
    To wynne hym better wage. 36

(7)
¶ We haue a man, a stronge freke,
Which kepeth in þe felde owr
    nete,
    & slepeth half the day;   39
He shall com home, by Mary mylde,
þe boye shall forth in to the fylde,
    And kepe them yf [he¹] may." 42

(8)
¶ The goodwyff was glad & well
    a-ment,
& therto she gaff sone her assent,
    And said: "So it ys beste."   45
Vpon the morow, whan it was day,
Forth went the lytill boye,
    To the fild he was full preste. 48

(9)
¶ Vpon his bak he bare his staff,
Of no man no force he gaff,
    He was mery ynowgh.   51
He went forthe, þe soth to sayn,
Till he cam to the playn;
    His dyner forth he drowgh. 54

(10)
¶ Whan he sigh it was bade,
¹ Full lytill luste þer-to he had
    And put it vp a-non. [¹lf. 98, bk.]
In feyth, he was not wite;
He said: "I will ete but lite
    Till nyght þat I come home." 60

(11)
¶ Vpon the hyll he down satt,
& an old man þer he mett,
    Com walkyng by the way. 63
He said: "God spede, good sonne!"
The boye said: "Sir, welcome";
    The sothe for to say. 66

(12)
¶ The olde was an-hungred sore;
He said: "Son, hast þou any mete
    in store,
That thow may geve to me?" 69
The boye sware, so God hym save,
"Thow shalt see suche as I haue,
    & welcome shalt thow be." 72

(13)
¶ The boye gaff hym suche as he
    had,
& bade hym ete & mak hym glad,
    & said "Welcom, truly!"   75
The old man was glad to plese,
He ete & made hym well at ese,
    & said: "Sir, gramarcy!   78

(14)
¶ For this thow hast geven me,
I shall geve the giftis thre
    That shall not be for-gote." 81
The boy said: "As I trowe,
Hit were best I had a bowe,
    Birdis for to shote." 84

¹ I *MS.*

122   V. *Ballads and Worldly Songs.   Humorous and Satirical Pieces.*

(15)

¶ "Bowe & bolt þou shalt haue blive,
þat shall serue þe all thy lyve,
And euery while mete;   87
Shote wher-so-euer thow wilt,
Thow shalt neuer fayle of it,
The markis shalt thow kepe."   90

(16)

¶ The bowe in hond anon he felt,
& put þe shaftis vnder his belt,
Lightly than he drowgh.   93
He said: "Had I nowe a pipe,
Thowgh it were never so light,
Than were I mery ynowgh."   96

(17)

¶ "A pipe þou shalt haue also;
Trewe mesure shall it go,
I do the owt of dowght.   99
All that euer may it here,
They shall not them-self asstere,
But lepe & dawnce abowte.   102

(18)

¶ Let se, what shall þat other be?
For þou shalt haue gyftis thre,
As I the hight beffore."   105
þe litill boye than lowde lowgh
& said: "By my trowth, I haue
I will desire no more." [y-nowgh,

(19)

¶ The old man said to hym: "A plight,
Thow shalt haue as I the hight,
Ther-fore say on, let see!"   111
The litill boye said full sone:
[1] "I have a stepmoder at home,
She is a shrewe to me; [[1] lf. 98 (sic MS.)]

(20)

¶ Whan my fader geveth me mete,
She wold the devill wold me cheke,
She stareth fast in my face;   117
Whan she loketh on me soo,
Yf she myght late a rape go,
& rynge in all þe place!"   120

(21)

¶ The old man said to hym thoo:
"& yf she loke on the soo,
She shall begyn to blowe;   123
All that euer may her here,
They shall not them self asstere,
But lawgh vpon a rowe.   126

(22)

¶ "Fare well," said the old man;
"Fare [well], sir," þe boye said than,
"I take my leve of the.   129
All myghty God, þat best may,
Spede the both nyght & day!"
"Gramarcy, sir," said hee.   132

(23)

¶ Than afterward, whan it was nyght,
Home went this boye right,
This was hys ordynance;   135
He toke his pipe & began to blowe,
Than all his bestis, on a rowe,
A-bowt gan they dawnce.   138

(24)

¶ The boye went pypyng thorow þe towne,
The bestis folowed by the sowne
Vnto his faders close;   141
Whan he had them ther echone,
He shete them fast in a-non,
In to the hall he goys;   144

(25)

¶ His fader at soper sat,—
The littil boye spyde well þat,—
& spake to hym anon;   147
He said: "Siker, þou art welcome;
Wher be my bestis, good sonne?
Hast thou browght them home?"

V. Ballads and Worldly Songs.   Humorous and Satirical Pieces.

(26)
¶ "Ye, fader, in good fay,   151
I haue kept them all this day,
& I haue them in þe close shett."
A capons lege he cast to hym tho,
& said: "Jak, that was well do;
Boye, thow shalt fare the bett."

(27)
¶ The goodwyff stared fast on Jak,
& anon she lete a gret crake,
Hit range lyke a gonne.   159
Jake said: "Well, ye may witt,
I hope this gonne was well smytt,
As it had be of a stone."   162

(28)
¶ Full angerly loked she on hym tho,
An-oþer ffarte lete she goo,
And fowle she was shent.   165
The goodman said: "By my lyff,
I know not what eileth my wiff;
I trowe her arse be rent."   168

(29)
¶ Than after ye shall here,   [fol. 98, bk.]
To þat hows þer cam a frere
Evyn that same nyght.   171
With hym full sone she was a-quaynt,
& vnto hym she mad her playnt,
& told hym a-non right: 174

(30)   [wonnys,
¶ "I haue [a] boye þat with vs
He ys shrewed for the nones,
He dothe me myche care;   177
I may not ons loke hym on
But I am shamed, by seynt John,
I tell you how I fare!   180

(31)
¶ Mete hym in þe felde to-morowe,
Loke ye bete hym, & do hym sorowe,
& make the boye lame;   183

I-wis, it is a cursed byche,
I trow the boye be som wyche
He dothe me myche shame."   186

(32)
[¶ The freyr sayd: "Y wyll wyte!"
"Y pray the, ser, lete it not be forgete,
For that wold greve me sore."]¹
¶ The frere said: "In good fay,
But I be-lasshe well þat boy,
Trist me never more!"   192

(33)
Vpon þe morow þe boye rose,
Forth in to þe filde he gois,
His bestis gan he dryve.²   195
¶ The frere folowed after at þe gate,
He went he had com to late,
& ran after full rive.   198

(34)
¶ Whan he com in to the londe,
The litill boy ther he fonde
& his bestis echone.   201
He said: "þou, boy, God geve þe shame,
What hast þou don to thy dame?
I rede the, tell me anon.   204

(35)
¶ But þou can excuse the bett,
In feyth, thyn ars shall be hett,
I will no longar a-bide."   207
The [boye] said: "Frere, what ayleth the?
My dame fareth as well as ye,
Thow hast no cawse to chide."

(36)
¶ The boye said: "Frere, wilt þou witt
How feld-byrdis I can shete
& other thyngis all?   213

¹ Supplied from Porkington MS., wanting in Ball.   ² before, cancelled.

I trow, thowgh I be but light
Yonder birde shall I smyte
 & yeve it to the, I shall." 216

(37)

¶ Ther sat a birde on a brere:
"Shote on," quod the frere,
 "That me luste to see." 219
The boye smote it on þe hede,
That it fell down dede;
 Hit myght no lengar flee. 222

(38)

¶ The frere in to þe hegge went
& þe birde vp he hente,
 As it was for to doo. 225
þe boy to his pipe, & began to blowe,
Full hastely, as I trowe,
 & sone he pyped thoo; 228

(39)

[1] ¶ But whan the frere þe pip harde,
Lyke as a made man he ferde, [¹¹ lf. 99]
 & be-gan to lepe a-bowght; 231
A-monge the bowes small & gret
A-bowght hastely gan he lepe,
 But he cowld no-wher owght. 234

(40)

¶ Brambils[2] crached hym in þe face
& eke in many an-other place;
 His body be-gan to blede. 237
He rent his clothes by & by,
His girdill & his chaplary,
 & all his other wede; 240

(41)

The boye blewe, & lowgh amonge,
Howe þe frere lepte & wownd,
 & hoppid wonder hye. 243
Than said þe boye & sware with-
 all:
"In feyth, this is a sport royall
 For any man to see with eye." 246

(42)

¶ Ever the frere helde vp his honde,
& cried vnto þe boye amonge,
 & prayed hym to be still: 249
"& here I plight my trowth to the;
Thow shalt haue non harme of me,
 For I will do the non yll." 252

(43)

¶ The boy said to hym þat tide:
"Than crepe owt on that oþer side,
 & hye the þat thow were goo.
My dame made he[r] playnt to the;
& now I can non other see, [also."
 But þou muste go playn to her

(44)

¶ The frere owt of the hegge went,
All to-ragid & to-rente,
 & torne on euery side; 261
Vnneth he had any clowte
For to wynd his body a-abowte,
 His armes for to hide. 264

(45)

¶ Bothe his fyngers & his face
Were be-cracched in many a place,
 & be-brewed all in blode. 267
Euery man þat myght hym see,
Was full glad hym to flee;
 They went þe frere had ben wode.

(46)

¶ When he cam in to his oste,
Of his jorney he made no boste,
 He was bothe tame & tall. 273
Myche sorow in his hart he had,
For euery man hym dradde,
 Whan he came in to the hall. 276

(47)

¶ The goodwyf said: "Wher haste
 þou be?
In evill places, as semeth me; 278
 Me thynketh by thyne arraye."

[2] MS. Brambild

V. Ballads and Worldly Songs.   Humorous and Satirical Pieces. 125

"Dame," he said, "I haue be wit*h*
    thy sonne;
The devill of hell hym ou*er* come,
    For certyse I ne may."   282

(48)

¶ With that, com in the good man;
"Loo, si*r*," said the goodwif than,
"Here is an evill arraye; [lf. 99, bk]
Thy son, þat is to the dere,
Hath almost slayn this holy frere,
    Alas, alas, & wele-a-waye!" 288

(49)

¶ The goodman said: "Benedicite!
What hath þat boye done to the?
    Tell me with-owt stryff!" 291
The frere said: "By seynt Jhame,
I haue dawnsed in þe devils name";
    Thes word*is* said he blyff. 294

(50)

¶ Thes word*is* said þe goodma*n* than:
"Thow hast ben a wild yong ma*n*,
    & þou haste bene in gret synne."
"Nay," said þe frere, "I shall tell why:
Me-thowght þe pipe went so merily
    That I cowld never blynne." 300

(51)

¶ "That pipe will I here, trewly!"—
The frere said: "So will not I,
    By God & by seynt Jhame!" 303
"That pipe, se*r*tise, will I here."
"Nay, for God," quod the frere,
    "Sure it ys no game." 306

(52)

¶ Than aft*er*, wha*n* it was nyght,
Home come this boye full right,
    As it was for to done. 309
As sone as he com i*n* to þe hall,
Anon his fader gan hym call,
    & sayd: "Com hether anon! 312

(53)

¶ Hark þou boye, now þou art here:
What hast þou done to this frere?
    Tell me with-owt lettyng!" 315
He said: "Fader, In good fay,
I dide no-thyng to hy*m* this day,
    But piped hym a sprynge." 318

(54)

¶ "That pipe truly will I here."
"Nay, for God*is* sak," qu*o*d the frere,
    "That were an evill thynge." 321
"Yes," said þe good wiff, "by God*is*
    grace"!
The frere cried owt & said 'alas'!
    His hond*is* gan he wrynge. 324

(55)

¶ "For God*is* love," qu*o*d the frere,
"& yf ye will the pipe here,
    Bynd me fast to a poste; 327
I-wis I can no bett*er* rede,
For well I wot I shall be dede,
    My lyff ys nygh loste." 330

(56)

Ropis anon they had in honde;
To a post they hym bonde,
    That stode in the hall. 333
Tho that at soper satt,
They had game & lowgh þ*er*-at,
    & said: "þe frere shall not fall."

(57)

¶ Tha*n* bespake the goodman,
To his son he said than:
    "Pipe on what thow wylt!" 339
"All redy, fader," said he, [leaf 100]
"I shall you shewe a mery glee,
    & ye shall haue a fitt." 342

(58)

¶ As sone as the pype went,
þ*er* myght no man hym self stent,
    But began to dawnce & lepe. 345

All þat euer myght it here,
They myght not them self asstere,
But worled on a hepe. 348

(59)

¶ They that at soper sat,
Over þe table anon they lept,
& stered in that stownd. 351
They þat sat on the forme,
They had no leyser them to torne,
But they were born to grownd.

(60)

¶ The goodman was in dispayre;
Strayght he start owt of the chayre
With an hevy chere; 357
Som start over the blokk,
& brak þer shynnes agayn þe stokk,
& some fell in the fyre. 360

(61)

¶ The goodwif cam all be-hynde,
She began to lepe & wynde,
& sharply for to shake. 363
But whan she loked on litill Jake,
Anon her ars to her spake,
& lowde began to crake. 366

(62)

¶ The frere was almoste loste,
He bete his hed a-gayn the poste;
He had no better grace. 369
Ropes rubbed of the skyn,
That þe blode ran down by hym
In many a dyueris place. 372

(63)

¶ The boye went pypyng in þe strete;
After worled all the hepe;
They myght never stynt. 375
They went owt of þe dore so thyke,
That eche leped in other neke,
So wightly owt they went. 378

(64)

¶ Tho that dwellid ther-bye,
That hard þe pipe sikerly,
In placis ther they were sett, 381
A-non they leped ouer the hache,
They had no tyme to vndo þe lache,
They were so lothe to be lett. 384

(65)

¶ They that lay in ther beddys,
Anon they lyfte vp ther hedis,
Bothe the lesse & the more; 387
Into the stret, as I here saye,
In good feyth, they toke þe way,
As nakid as ever they were bore.

(66)

¶ But whan they were gadred all a-bowt
Than ther were a gret rowt
In the myddis of the strete; 393
Som were lame, & myght not go,
[1] But they hopped all a-bowt tho
On hondis & on fete. [¹ leaf 100, bk.]

(67)

¶ The boye said: "Fader, will ye reste?
For in feith I hold it beste
That ye reste here." 399
His fader said: "Whan þou wilt;
In feyth, it is þe merieste fitt
That I had this ·VII· yere." 402

(68)

¶ But whan þe pipe went no more,
Than all they marveled sore
Of the governance. 405
"Seynt Mary," said some,
"Wher ys all þe mirth be-com,
That made vs for to dawnce?"

(69)
¶ Euery man was good of chere,
Save þe goodwyff & the frere;
They were all dysmayd. 411
He that hath not all his will,
Be it good, or be it yll,
He holdith hym not well a-payd.

(70)
¶ Now haue ye hard, all in same,
Howe Jake pleyed with his dame
& piped beffore þe frere. 417

The frere liked not þe boyes lay,
Ther-fore shortly he went a-way,
Som dele with hevy chere. 420

(71)
The goodman norished forth his child;
His stepmoder was to hym full myld,
& fared well all in fere. 423
That Lord you kepe, frendis all,
That drank aysell & gall,
Holy God, in his empere!— 426
Explicit.

VI. Proberbs, Verse-rules and Moral Sentences.

104.
Diwe[r]s good prowerbis.[1] [leaf 191, back]

1. Whan I profir the pig, opin the poke.
2. While the grasse grwith, the hors sterwith.
3. Sone hit sharpith, that thorn will be.
4. It is a sotill mowsse, that slepith in þe cattis ere.
5. Nede makith the old wiff to trotte.
6. A birde in hond is better than thre in the wode.
7. And hewin fall, we shall hawe mani larkis.
8. A shorte hors is son curried.
9. Thowgh peper be blak, it hath a good smak.
10. Of a rwgged colte, cwmeth a good hors.
11. Faire behestis makith folis fain.
12. All thing hath a begining.
13. Wepin makith pese diwers times.
14. Winter etith, that somer getith.
15. He that is warned beffore, is not begiled.
16. He that will not be warned bi his owne fader, he shall be warned bi his stepfader.
17. Pride goth beffore, and shame cometh after.
18. Often times prowith the frwight after the stok that hit cometh off.
19. Hit is a febill tre that fallith at the first strok.
20. Hit fallith in a dai, that fallith not all the iere after.
21. While the fote warmith, the sho harmith.
22. A softe fire makith swete malte.
23. Whan the stede is stolen, shit the stabill dore.
24. Mani hondis makith light werke.

[1] Written with ciphers for some of the letters, viz. (scheme on leaf 190):

a   i   e   o   w
ℏ   3   4   2   ɤɤ

VI. Proverbs, Verse-rules and Moral Sentences.

25. Whan thow hast well don, hange wp thi hachet.
26. It is not all gold that glareth.
27. Often times the arow hitteth the shoter.
28. It is comenly said, that all men be not trew.
29. That natwre geweth, no man can tak awai.
30. This arow cwmmeth newer owt of thin own bow.
31. Betwen two stolis, the ars goth to grwnd.
32. Son crokith the tre, that crokid will be.
33. Whan the hors waloweth, som heris be loste.
34. This dai a man, to-morow non.
35. Seld sene, sone forgotin.
36. Whan the beli is fwll, þe bonis wold hawe rest.
37. Better it is to be wnborne than wntawght.
38. He that no good can nor non will lern,
    If he newer thriwe, who shall him warne?[1]
39. He that all coweitith, often all lesith.
40. Ner hope harte wold breste.
41. Hasti man lakkith newer woo.
42. A good beginning makith a good endinge.
43. Better it is, late than newer.
44. Powerte partith felishipe.
45. Brente honde fire dredith.
46. Non sigheth so sore as þe gloton that mai no more.
47. He mai lightli swim, that is hold wp by þe chin.
48. Clime not to hie, lest chipis fall in thin eie.
49. On skabbid shepe infectith all the folde.
50. All the keis hange not bi on mannis girdill.
51. Better it is, to lese cloth than brede.
52. He that hath nede, mwst blowe at the cole.

105a. [Fifty-five Proverbs in English and Latin.]

1. A good scoler yf þou wilt be,   [leaf 200]
   A-rise erly & worship þe trinite.
      Surge sub aurora, dominum que frequenter adora ;
      Talibus vtaris, si vis bonus esse scolaris.   4
2. Yf thow wilt be light / let thy soper be shorte.
      Si vis esse levis, sit tibi cena breuis.

[1] *The MS. has* warm *with the gloss or* warne *rather.*

VI. Proverbs, Verse-rules and Moral Sentences.

3. O thow riche man / þou shalt not alway leve.
   O diues, diues · non *omni* [1] tempore viues.   8
4. He hath II faces vnder on hode.
   Sub facies vno binas habet ipse galiro.
5. Salt & mele norissheth many a brothell.
   Cum sale farina nutritur plurima scurra.   12
6. Whan thou art at Rome, do after the dome ;
   And whan þou art els wher, do as they do ther.
   Cum fueris Rome / Romano viuito more ;
   Cum fueris alibi, viuito more loci.   16
7. Be it better or be it worse / do after hym þat berith þe purse.
   Seu bene siue male, loculum qui fert imitare.
8. Do well whill þou art here / & þou shalt haue well els wher.
   Fac bene dum super es / et habebis prosperitates.
9. A fole will not geve his babill for þe Towr of London.
   Pegma valet blati plus turri Londoniarum.
10. A skalde man-is hede is sone brokyn.
    Frangitur ex facile caput infantis glabriosa.   24
11. All the world goth by fayre speche.
    Omnia mundana · pertrancit pulcra loquela.
12. The nere þe chirche, the ferder from God.
    Ecclesie quanto prope longior est bono tanto.[2]   28
13. The grettir state, the more wisedom.
    Que status est melior, prudencia sit tibi maior.
14. In whom I trust most, sonnest me deseyvith.
    In quo confido, leniter me decipit ipse.   32
15. Of a lytill sparkyll, commeth a gret fyre.
    De modica magnus scintilla nascitur ignis.
16. A litill & a litill, þe cat etith vp þe bacon fliche.
    Murelicus paruam palatum devorat illam.   36
17. Thowgh peper be blake, hit hath a good smakke.
    Est piper nigrum, quod gratum prestat odorem.
18. Besy in stody be þou, child / & in þe hall, meke & mylde,
    & at þe table, mery & glade / & at bedde, softe
    & sadde.   40
    Sidulus in studio · puer, in templo pius esto,
    Ad mensam letis (!) · ad lectum vade quietis.

[1] MS. o͞ie   [2] MS. *something like* tm̄

VI. *Proverbs, Verse-rules and Moral Sentences.* 131

19. Lende never that thyng, that thow nedest moste.
    Quibus semper eges, rem nullam tradere debes. 44
20. He ys a trew frend, þat loveth me for my love / & not for my good.
    Fidus amicus erit, qui plus me quam mea querit.
21. He þat torneth þe gose, by right shuld haue þe nekke.
    Aucam qui gerit, collum sibi iure requirit. 48
22. A fastyng bely may neuer be mery.
    Jeiunus venter nescit gaudire libenter, vel frequenter. [1 leaf 200, back]
23. [1] Hit is, & euer shall be : a like will drawe to like.
    Est et semper erit : similis similem sibi querit. 52
24. Pride goth beffore, & shame commethe after.
    Fastus procedit ; sequitur pudor et male ledit.
25. Whan Adam delffid & Eve span, who was than a gentilman ?
    Cum vanga quadam · tellurem foderat Adam,
    Ast Eva nens fuerat, quis generosus erat ? 57
26. I say with-owt boste / that the smoke stereth the roste.
    Dico sine pompa, quod fumus violat ossa.
27. He is no good swayn / þat lettith his jorney for þe rayn.
    Qui parcit stille · non est bonus armiger ille. 61
28. Deme no thyng þat is in dowt / till þe trowth be tred owt.
    In dubiis serui melius cape, pessima sperne.
29. Better is a frend in cowrte, than a peny [in] my purse.
    Plus mihi quam bursa amicus regis in aula.[2] 65
30. Whan thow doste any thynge, think on the ende.
    Quicquid agas, prudenter agas, et respice finem.
31. In a thyn table, good chere is best sawse.
    In tinui mensa, satis est sencera voluntas. 69
32. In a busshell of wynnynge, ys not a hondfull of cunnyng.
    In modico[3] rendi, non est vola plena sciendi.
33. He loveth well moton, þat[4] weteth his bred in woll.
    Optat eius carnem, tangens in vellere panem. 73

[2] MS. alla   [3] MS. medico   [4] MS. &

VI. Proverbs, Verse-rules and Moral Sentences.

34. Assay thy frend or thow haue nede.
   Cum non indegias rerum, temtabis amicum.
35. Tonge breketh bon / wher bon he hathe non.
   Ossa terit glossa, tamen in se non habet ossa. 77
36. He is wysse, þat can beware by an oþer manys harme.
   Felix, quem faciunt aliena pericula cautum.
37. Whote wortis make softe crustis.
   Molificant olera, durissima seruida scrusta. 81
38. He that heweth to hye, þe chippis will fall in his ye.
   Qui nimis alte secant, hos quisquile cito cecant.
39. A woman oftymes will do þat she is not bede to do.
   Femina prona rei que proibetur ei. 85
40. He [that] hath nowght, ys nowght sett by.
   Non commendatur qui paupertate grauatur.
41. Whan the whelpe gameth, the old dogge grenneth.
   Dum ludit catulus, frendit canis in-veteratus. 89
42. He þat commeth last to þe pot, ys sonnest wrothe.
   Iratus primo sit, ad ollam qui venit imo.
43. While the gresse growith the hors stervith. 92
   Dum gramen cressit, equus in moriendo quiescit.
44. Of an-other mannes ledder / we cut a longe thonge.
   Corigiam corige longam damus ex alieno.
45. A thynge ferre fett, is good for ladyes.
   Res longe lata, dominabus constat amata. 97
46. When thow hast well doo, hange vp thy hachet.
   Cum bene fecisti, sursum suspende securim.
47. He that spareth to speke, ofte spareth to spede.
   Qui parcit fari, parcit sibi dona parari. 101
48. The mowse goth a-brode, wher þe cat is not lorde.
   Mus deuagatur, vbi catus non dominatur.
49. Ther may no man all men please.
   Nemo potest vere cunctis omnino placere. 105
50. At a lytill hole, a man may se his frende.
   Ad speculor[1] modicum speculator[1] amicus amicum.
51. For my brokyn sleve, men me refuce. 108
   Pro manica fracta, manus est mea sepe retracta.
52. He that is warned ys half armed.
   Qui premunitur desceptus non reperitur.

[1] *Sic* MS.

VI. Proverbs, Verse-rules and Moral Sentences.

53. Selde dyeth the oxe that wepeth for the cok.
   Bos moritur rara qui gallo plorat amara.   113
54. Wynter etythe, that somer getith.
   Brume tempestas[1] vorat hoc quod procreat estas.
55. Hungre maketh harde bones softe.
   Dura licet faba denti[2] sic salus esurienti.   117

105b. [Latin Proverbs.]   [leaf 201]

Tolle peripsimam, post pete pulpam, spernes arulam.
¶ Quere dei regnum prius, et precepta seruato,[3] }
Eius, et addentur a patre cunta tibi.   }
¶ Quicquid agas, sapienter agas, et respice finem.   } 4
Sepe minus faciunt homines, qui multa loquntur }
¶ Mendicat multociens filius potentis;   }
Regnat e contrario, filius egentis.   }
¶ Omnis inops stultus; vbi res, ibi copia sensque. } 8
Si Salamon pawper, stultus reperitur vt alter.   }
¶ Tempore felici, multi nvmerantur amici;   }
Cum fortuna perit, nullus amicus erit.   }
¶ Si paupertatem paciaris, aut anxietatem,   } 12
Stabis vbique foris, et eris miser omnibus horis. }
¶ Qui cupit omnia, perdere[4] plurima sepe videtvr. }
Similator ori decepit amicum suum.   }
¶ Non est peior pestis quam familaris amicus,   } 16
Dulcia non meruit, qui non gustauit amara.   }
Yf thow be happy, kepe thyn own cownsayle.   }
Si fueris felix, semper tibi proximus esto.   }
¶ Omnia si perdas, famam seruare memento;   } 20
Qua semell amissa, postea nullus eris.   }
¶ Est vis in verbis, in petris, est et in herbis. }
Denario plus hiis argentum, vis mea tu scis.   }
¶ Si sapiens fore vis, sex serua que tibi mando. } 24
Quid loqueris et vbi, de quo, cui, quomodo, quando. }
¶ Qui me deridet, sua facta non bene videt.   }
Quicquid agunt homines, intencio indicat omnes.   }
¶ Si tibi copia, seu sapiencia formaque detur,   } 28
Sola superbia destruet omnia si committetur.   }

[1] MS. compestas   [2] MS. denti faba
[3] MS. seruate   [4] MS. prodere

VI. Proverbs, Verse-rules and Moral Sentences.

¶ Multis annis iam paractis, nulla fides est in pactis.   videte
Mell in ore, verba lactis, fel in corde, fraus in factis. cavete
¶ Est qui torquetur, ne fastus ei dominetur.   32 vt Paulus
Est qui torquetur, vt purior inde probetur.   vt Joob.
Est qui torquetur, vt Christus glorificetur.   vt Cecus.
Est qui torquetur, vt perpetuo crucietur.   vt Herodes.
Est qui torquetur, vt crimine purificetur.   36
   vt Maria soror Moysy, & nati Christi quos cotidie Deus flagitat.

105c.

Documentum Aristotilis ad Alexandrum magnum.
Cela secreta / loquere pauca / verax esto. / Non
sis velox ad loquendum. / Iram scinde / liti cede / nulli
deroges / a viuo cave / memento mori. / Mesericordes
esto. / Non te ignoto socies. / Non de facili dictis
credas. / Inimico reconsiliato non des fidem. / De
re amissa irrecuperabili non doleas. / Noli gaudere
de aduersitatibus proximi. / Noli contendere cum potenciore te. / Nunquam secreta tua vxori neque
pueris reveles. / Nam mulieres et pueri id celant[1]
quod ignorant. / Si cupias bonum et honorem serua
predicta.

105d. [Latin Maxims.]

X gratis nisi sis . bis pulcher · ter quoque fortis.
Qua sapiens / quindece sex sanctus amodo non sis.[2]
¶ "Dews-ays" non possunt · "syse-sinke," sed soluere
   nolunt;
Omnibus est notum · "quatur-trey" soluere totum. 4
¶ Dono nill sperans · sed do tibi mvnera querans
   Largior vt largus · erigo pauperibusque.
¶ Intrant portantes, sed non intrant dona rogantes.
   Ipsum nullus amat, qui semper "da mihi" clamat. 8
¶ Si caput est, currit · ventrem coniunge, volabit; ⎱ Musca-
Adde pedem, comede : et sine ventre bibe. ⎰ tum.
¶ Ancer ouem variat · cui vacca potum ministrat.
¶ Clara dies Pauli bona tempora denotat anni.   12
   Si nix vel pluuia, designat tempora cara.

---

[1] MS. celunt.   [2] *So the MS.*

VI. *Proverbs, Verse-rules and Moral Sentences.*

Si fuerint venti, designat prelia genti.
Si fuerint nubile, perient animalia queque; 15
Palida luna pluat, rubia flat, alba[1] serenat. [leaf 201, back]
¶ Femina dum plorat, hominem superare laborat.
Femina res ficta, res subdula, res malidicta.
¶ " Mu " · mutat mores, " li " liberat a loculo res,
" er " odit amantes, nisi sint sibi mvnera dantes. 20
¶ Si quis eris, si credideris, verbis mulieris,
Crede mihi, si credis ei, tu decipieris.
¶ Rusticus est vere · qui turpia de muliere
Dicit; nam vere sumus omnes de muliere. 24
¶ Non est in speculo res que speculatur in illo;
Eminet, et non est in muliere fides.
¶ Currere cogit equum sub milite calcar acutum;
Et puerum studio virga vacare suo. 28
¶ O diues, diues! non omni[2] tempore viues.
Da tua, dum tua sunt; post mortem tunc tua non sunt.
Pauper dispicitur quamvis sit vir racionis.
¶ Si mea penna valet, melior mea lettera fiet. 32
Dextra pars penne leuior breuior debet esse.

105e. [Names of English Cities.]

Witham. Henton. Bewbale. London. Hull. Coventre. insula Mon. grace shen.
Eli. Bath. Carlill. Canterburi. Chichester. Lincoln. Londõn.
Durham. Exeter. Eboraci. Winchester. Wocetter.
Norwich. Rochester. Chestre. Salesburi. presules habet Angula tales.[3]

105f. [Men excelled by Animals.]

Nos aper auditu, linx visu, simia gustu,
Vultor odoratu (a gripe), precellit aranea (a spider) tactu.[4]

105g. [Greetings.]

" Aue " dic veniens de iure, " vale "-que recedens.
Hoc verbum " salue," sensum comprehendit utrumque.

---

[1] MS. albe   [2] oie MS. (cf. p. 130[1]).
[3] Eli etc. (with Anglia for Angula) also on leaf 191 (cf. *Reliquiae Antiquae*, I, 287).
[4] Cf. *Rel. Antiquae*, I, 90 (from a MS. of Halliwell's).

VI. Proverbs, Verse-rules and Moral Sentences.

105*h*. [Latin Puns.]

Non sunt securi qui colla subdunt securi.
Est ea vilis ouis, qui non prestat tribus ouis. *(worth)*
Si non vis calui, fugias consorcia calui. *(be begiled)*
Non bene prandetur, vbi panis abesse videtur.
Est ciphus crather, res ferrea sit tibi crathes.

105*i*. [A Prayer to the Virgin.]

Da michi dona tria, gloriosissima virgo Maria!
Da spacium vite, da divicias sine lite!
Regnum celeste post mortem, da manifeste!

105*j*. [How to be welcome.]

Non bene venit homo, nisi bibit ad hostium stando.

105*k*. [The Seven Deadly Sins.]

Fastus, avaricia, torpido, liuor et ira,
Et gula, luxuria, septem peccata cavenda,

105*l*. [The Ten Commandments.]

¶ Vnum crede deum, ne iuras vane per ipsum.
Sabita sanctifices, habias in honore parentes.
Ne scis occisor, fur, necus,[1] testis inicus,
Alterius nuptam nec rem cupias alienam.

105*m*. [The Seven Works of Piety.]

¶ Visito, poto, cibo, redemo, tego, coligo, condo,
Sunt septem opera pietatis perficiendo.

105*n*. [The Five Senses.]

¶ Gustus et olfactus, auditus, vicio, tactus,
Sunt sensus quinque, quos nobis constat inesse.

105*o*. [Verse-making.]

Rustice quid queris, vt mecum vercificeris;
Vercificator es tu non melior solis ab ortu.

---

[1] *So MS. (for* moechus?).

VI. Proverbs, Verse-rules and Moral Sentences.

105p. [Contrast between Hens and Women.]
Gallus gallinis ter-quinque sufficit vnus,
Sed ter-quinque viri non sufficiunt mulieri.

105q.
For a syngar.
Versus posterior non prius incipiatur
Quam suus anterior perfecto fine fruatur.
Tres sunt qui psalmos corrumpunt nequiter almos,
Quos sacra scriptura dampnat, vetant quoque iura :
"Momelers, foreskippers, ouerskippers" sunt tria
mala.[1]   5

105r. [Further Latin Maxims.]
Si tu sentires, quo vadis et vnde venires,
Nunquam gauderes, sed omni tempore fleres.
Multa me, multa, quia feci crimina multa.
Gutta cauat lapidem non vi sed sepe cadendo,   4
Sic homo fit sapiens, non vi, sed sepe studendo.
A vulgo de dictum, non est falsum neque fictum.
Sepe probat fructus, de qua sit arbore ductus,   [leaf 202]
Sepe probat natus, de qua sit stirpe creatus.   8
Ad siluam pergo venatum cum cane quino ;
Quod capio, prodo ; quod fuget, hoc habio.
Inter stanna duo libitur anus humo.
Cum manibus mando, sine manibus omnia tango. 12
Cor non est letum, quum pulsat ad hostium letum.
Contra verbosos noli contendere verbis.
Fistola dulce canit, volucrem dum decipit anseps.
Esse fabas duras, fames faciunt tibi dulces.
Dum canis os rodit, sociari pluribus odit.   17
    Explicit.

106. [Rules for purchasing land.]
Who-so will beware in purchasynge,   [leaf 100, back]
Consydre the poyntis that ben suynge :
1. First, see þat thy londe be clere
    In tityll of the sellere.   4
2. Se þat he not in preson be,

[1] Cf. similar verses in Rel. Ant. I, 90.

VI. *Proverbs, Verse-rules and Moral Sentences.*

3. & þat he be in good mind or memory ;
4. And þat it stond in no dangere
   Off no womans dower. 8
5. Se wheþer þe tenvre be bond or fre,
6. & se relesse of euery feffe.
7. Se þat thy sellar be of age,
8. & that it lye in no morgage. 12
9. Loke wheþer a tayle of it may be fownd,
10. & whether it stond in statute bownd.
11. Considre what servise longith þer-to,
12. & what quyte-rent þer-of muste go. 16
13. And yf it meve of weddid woman,
    Thynk on couerde baron than,
14. And yf þou myght by any wise
    Gete thy charter of warantise 20
    To thyn eyres & assignes also :
    Thus shall a wise purcheser do.
15. Yn XV yere, yf thow wise be,
    þou shallt a-gayn thy money see. 24

107. [Spend money for your Soul while you live.]

(1)

Man, yff thou a wyseman arte, [leaf 147, back]
Of thy goodis take thy parte,
  Or thow hens wende. 3
Yf thou leve thy parte,
In thy executours awarde,
  Thy parte, no parte ys, at the last end. 6

(2)

Do sum good, man, by thy lyffe,
  Whilis thow hast thy mynde;
Thy children will for-gete the sone,
  Thy wyffe will be vnkynd, 10
Thy executowrs be covytes,
  And take all that they fynde;
Yff thow wilt not, while thow may,
  They will bryng the behynde. 14

VI. *Proverbs, Verse-rules and Moral Sentences.*

108. [Directions for Conduct.] [leaf 159, back]

A-ryse erly ; serve God devoutly ; þe world besili.
Go thi way sadly ; answere demvrely ;
Go to thy mete appetently, & arise temperatly,
& to þi soper soberly, & to thy bede meryly,
And be ther jocondly, & slepe suerly. 5

109. [Good Advice.]

Who so off welth takyth non hede, [leaf 160]
He shall fynd defawt in tyme of nede.

¶ This world is mvtable, so seyth sage,
Therfor gader in tyme, or þou fall to age. 4

¶ In welth be ware of woo, what so þe happes,
& bere þe evyn for drede of after-clappes.

¶ Fortune ys varyant, ay tornyng her whele,
He ys wyse þat ys ware or he harm fele. 8

¶ Better yt ys suffre, & fortune to abyde,
Than hastely to clyme, & sodeynly to slyde.

¶ Know or þou knyte, & then þou mayst slake,
Yff þou knyte or þou know, than yt ys to late. 12

110.

Quatuor complexiones hominum. [leaf 178, back]

sanguineus
Largus, amans, hillaris, ridens rubiique coloris,
Cautus, carnosus, satis audax atque benignus.
  Calidus et humidus, multum appetit et multum potest.

colericus
Versutus, fallax, irascens, prodigus, audax, 4
Astutus, gracilis, pulchar, croceique coloris.
  Calidus et siccus, multum appetit et parum potest.

flema-[t]ecus
Hic sompnolentus, piger et sputamine multus,
Ebes, hinc sensus pinguis, facie color albus. 8
  Frigidus et humidus, parum appetit et multum potest.

VI. *Proverbs, Verse-rules and Moral Sentences.*

Malen-Inuidus et tristis, cupidus, dextreque tenac*is*,
coli*us*. Non expers fraudis, tumid*us* luteiq*ue* color*is*. 11
Frigid*us et* sicc*us*, paru*m* apet*it et* paru*m* potest.
Explicit.

111. [Latin and English Maxims.]

¶ [1] Si prestabis, no*n* rehabebis; si rehabebis, no*n* ta*m*
cito; si ta*m* cito, no*n* ta*m* bonu*m*; si ta*m* bonu*m*,
per*des amicum*. [1 leaf 205, back]

¶ Happe is hard, grace hathe no pere,
Fortune is a nyggard, & frendship is dere.

¶ For, q*ui* plus expendit, than a plowgh may till i*n* a
twelfmoneth : non admiretur, thowgh he begge or
borow a loff of his neyghbowr.

112. [Proverbial Rhymes.]

(1)

He þat ow*ith* mych & hath nowght, [leaf 208, back]
& spendith mych, & gettith nowght,
& lokith i*n* his purse, & fyndith nowght,
He may be right sory & say nowght.

(2)

He þat swerith till no ma*n* trist hym,
& lyeth till no ma*n* beleve hym,
& borow*ith* till no ma*n* will lend hy*m*,
He may go þ*er* no man know*ith* hym.

He þat will venge eu*er*y wreth,
þe longe*r* he levith, þe lesse he hath.

113. [Maxims.]

(*a*)

Kepe well ·X· & flee from sevyn; ⎫
Spende well V, & c*um* to hevyn. ⎭ [leaf 213, back]
He þat in yowth no v*er*tu will vse, ⎫
In age all hono*ur* shall refuce. ⎭

4

VI. *Proverbs, Verse-rules and Moral Sentences.*

(b)

¶ Serve God truly
& þe world besily ;
Ete thy mete meryly,
And euer leve in rest !   8

Thank God highly ;
Thowgh he visit the porely,
He may amend it lygthly,
Whan hym lykethe beste.   12

(c) [Three things make me anxious.   English.]

¶ Whan I thynk on thyngis thre,
Well carefull may I be :
One is, that I shall henne ;
An oþer is, I wot not when.   16
Off the thirde is my most care,
For I shall dwell I wot not wher.
Man ! remembre whens þou com & wher þou shalt ;
& to thyn evyn Cristyn do no wronge ;   20
    For man with-owt marcy, of marcy shall misse ;
    And he shall haue marcy, that marcyfull is.   22

(d) [Three things make me anxious.   Latin.]

Sunt tria que vere faciunt me sepe dolere :
Est primum durum, quia scio me moriturum.
Secundum timio, quia nescio comodo, quando ;
In magis flebo, quia nescio quo removebo.   26

114. [Death, Bribery, Adversity.   Latin.]

¶ Regia maiestas omnisque terrena potestas,   [leaf 229, back]
   Transit absque mora, mortis cum venerat hora.   2
¶ Lex est defuncta, quia judicis est manus vncta ;
   Et propter vngventum, ius est in carcere tentum.
[¶] Tempore felici, multi numerantur amici ;
   Dum fortuna perit, nullus amicus erit.   6

Appendix.

[A CHRONICLE, 1413–1536.]

Kyng Henry the Vth [leaf 232]
A° Domini M¹ IIII C XIII.
**The names of mayers & sheryffis
from the first yere of Kyng Herry the V**th

1414 . . William Crowmer   John Nycoll   } a° I°
                          John Suttun
This yere the Lorde Cobham made a riseyng with many Lollardys.

1415 . . William Crowmere Thomas Aleyn } a° II°
                          John Mychell
This yere the Kyng wan Harflew in Normandy.

1416 . . Nycholas Wotton   Aleyn Everarde } a° III°
                           Thomas Chambrige
This yere in Octobre the Kyng had a batayll at Agyncowrt & wan it.

1417 . . Harry Barton   Robert Whityngton } a° IIII°
                           John Coventre
This yere the Emprowr cam in to Ynglond, & þe Duke of Holond / & this yere the Kyng wan Normandye.

1418 . . Richard Marlow   Herry Rode   } a° V°
                           John Gedney
✠ This yere the Lord Cobham was taken & juged to dethe.

1419 . . William Sevnmok   John Bryan   } a° VI°
                           Rawlyn Barton
This yere was the sege of Roene & Cane, & of many other castellis & townes.

1420 . . Richard Whityngton John Butler } a° VII°
                            Robert Whytyngham
This yere the Kyng was made Regent of France, & weddid Kateryn, dowghter to þe French Kyng.

Appendix. A Chronicle, 1421–1430.   143

1421 . . William Cambrige   John Butler   } a° VIII°
                             John Welles
This yere the Kyng & the Quene londid at Douer, & she was crowned at Westmynster.

1422 . . Robert Chicheley   John Weston   } a° IX°
                             Richard Gosselyn
This yere was Herry þe VI^{te} born at Wyndsore; & this yere dyed the Kyng; & Herry his son regned; & Mortymere brak owt of the Towr a° domini 141 . . .
Kyng Herry the VI^{te} a° domini M^{l}IIIICXX . . .

1423 . . William Waldern   William Estfild   } a° primo
                            Robert Tatersale
This yere Mortymere was hangid, & Newgate new made.

1424 . . William Crowmere   Richard Jhames   } a° II°
                            Thomas Wandreford
This yere the Prince of Portyngale cam in to Ynglond.

1425 . . John Mychell   Symond Seman   } a° III°
                            John at Water
This yere was gret debate betwen the Cardynall of Wynchester & þe Duke of Glowcester.

1426 . . John Coventre   William Myldred   } a° IIII°
                            John Brokley
[1] Kyng H. þe VI^{te} was mad knight at Wycester.[1]

1427 . . John Raynwell   Robert Arnold   } a° V°
                            John Higham
This yere, on Segewik was hangid & quartered.

1428 . . John Gedney   Robert Otley   } a° VI°
                            Henry Frowik
This yere, Will Wawe was hangid and quartered.
[1] Coronacion of K. H. the VI^{te} at Westminster.[1]

Kyng Henry the VI^{te} [leaf 282, back]
Mayres   Sheryffis

1429 . . Henry Barton   John Abbot   } a° VII°
                            Thomas Doffhows

1430 . . William Estfild   Raff Holond   } a$^{[o]}$ VIII°
                            Nicholas Ruff
This yere Kyng Henry þe VI^{te} was crowned at Paris; & a woman armed, called her-selff "le pusill de Dieu," taken in the feld.

[1]–[1] Added between the lines, in paler ink.

144   *Appendix. A Chronicle*, 1431–1442.

1431	. .	Nicholas Wotton	Robert Large } a° IX°
			Walter Chartsey
1432	. .	John Welles	John Adersley } a° X°
			Stephyn Brown
1433	. .	John Parnes	John Olney } a° XI°
			John Paddesley
1434	. .	John Brokley	Thomas Chalton } a° XII°
			John Lynge

This yere was gret frostis & gret pestylence.

1435	. .	Robert Otley	Thomas Barnwell } a° XIII°
			Symkyn Eyre
1436	. .	Henre Frowyk	Robert Clopton } a° XIIII°
			Thomas Catworth

This yere the Duke of Burgon layd sege to Caleys; & þe Duk of York went in to Normandy.

1437	. .	John Michell	William Grigory } a° XV°
			Thomas Morsted
1438	. .	William Estfild	John Chapman } a° XVI°
			William Haylis

This yere London Brige fell down, & mych harme don.

| 1439 | . . | Stephyn Brown | Nicholas Yoo } a° XVII° |
| | | | Hewe Dyk |

This yere was a gret derth of corn; for a quart of whet was at XXVIˢ· VIII ᵈ·, & malt at XIII ˢ· IIII ᵈ·; & the derth began in John Mychellis tyme, & dured tyll harvest in þe tyme of Robert Large.

| 1440 | . . | Robert Large | Robert Marchall } a° XVIII° |
| | | | Philip Malpas |

This yere a pryste was brent at Towr Hill; & a gret fyre at þe Sterre in Bredstret, & mych harme don.

| 1441 | . . | John Paddesley | John Sutton } a° XIX° |
| | | | William Whetnale |

This yere was justes in Smythfild, betwen a knyght of Spayn & Sir Richard Woodwyle.

| 1442 | . . | Robert Clopton | William Combis } a° XX° |
| | | | Richard Riche |

This yere Elinore Cobham dide her penance / & M. Roger Bolyngbrok juged to deth, & his bokes brent at Powles

Appendix. A Chronicle, 1443–1452. 145

Crosse / & after he was drawen, hangid & quartered, for negromancy / & his hed sett at London Brigge.

1443	John Adersley	Thomas Bewmont Richard Northern	a° XXI°
1444	Thomas Catworth	Nicholas Wyford John Norman	a° XXII°
1445	Henre Frowik	Stephyn Foster Hewe Wiche	a° XXIII°

This yere Quene Margret com in to Ynglond, & was wedded to Kyng Henre the VI^{te}, and was crowned on seynt Powles day.

Kyng Henry the VI^{te} [leaf 233]

| 1446 | Symkyn Eyre | John Darby
Geffrey Fildyng | a° XXIIII° |

This yere Powles steple was set on fyre by a tempest, & quenchid with vynegre, with gret coste.

| 1447 | John Olney | Robert Horn
Geffrey Boleyn | a° XXV° |
| 1448 | John Gedney | Thomas Skot
William Abraham | a° XXVI° |

This yere þe good Duke of Glowcetter died at Bury, at[1] a parlament ther kept.

| 1449 | Stephyn Brown | William Cantlowe
William Marow | a° XXVII° |
| 1450 | Thomas Chalton | Thomas Cannyngis
William Hewlyn | a° XXVIII° |

[*The "Nicholas of the Tower"* (*Fabyan*, ed. *Ellis*, 1811, p. 622).]

This yere Normandy was lost / & þe Duk of Sowthfolk slayn in a ship called "þe Nych of Towr." & þe Comens of Kent arrose, with Jak Cade capten, & entrid in to London, & robbed Philip Malpas.

| 1451 | Nicholas Wiford | John Mydilton
William Dere | a° XXIX° |

This yere Gascoyn & Gyan was lost.

| 1452 | William Grygory | Mathew Philip
Cristofre Water | a° XXX° |

This yere þe Duk of York cam in to Kent with myche

[1] *at . . . kept*] added between the lines, in blacker ink.

CAROLS. L

Appendix. A Chronicle, 1453–1460.

peple, & set a fild agayn þe Kyng / & by entreatise of the lordis he cam to þe Kyng pesibly, & went in prosession at Powles.

1453 .. Geffrey Fildyng   Richard Alley } a° XXXI°
                       Richard Lee

1454 .. John Norman   John Walden } a° XXXII°
                       Thomas Cooke

This yere was þe rydyng of craftis layd downe, & rowed to Westmynster in barges.

1455 .. Stephyn Foster   William Taylor } a° XXXIII°
                       John Felde

primo bat^ll albans } This yere was þe first batell of Seynt Albans: þe Duk of Somerset & oþer lordis slayn.

1456 .. William Marow   John Yonge } XXXIIII
                       Thomas Holgrave

1457 .. Thomas Cannyngis   Raff Verney } XXXV
                       John Styward

This yere þe Lord Egremond brak owt of Newgate; & a strif betwen þe Perses & Neviles.

1458 .. Geffrey Boleyn   William Edward } XXXVI
                       John Raynar

This yere myche peple cam with þe Perses to London / & a gret wach to kepe pese in þe cite. Þe Erle of Warwik fowght with Spaynyardis in the see.[1]

1459 .. Thomas Scott   Raff Josselyn } a° XXXVII°
                       Richard Nedeham

Ludlow fild   This yere was a gret fray in Flet stret by men of þe cowrt & þe cite / & a fild at Ludlow; & þe Duk of York & þe Erle of Rutlond [2] fled in to Yrelond / & þe Erle of Marche & þe Erle of Warwik & þe Erle of Salisbury fled to Calis.

1460 .. William Hewlyn   John Plommar } a° XXXVIII°
                       John Stokker

[Not]tyng [h]am [f]ild   This yere was a parlament at Coventre: & þe Duk of York & all his adherentis endiȝted of hie treason / & than cam in þe said lordis from Cales / & went forth to Notyngham feld a-bowt Mydsomer: þe Duk of Bokyngham slayn.

---

[1] þe erle ... see] added between the lines, in paler ink.
[2] Leaf 233, back; headline: Kyng Henry the VI^te Ludlowe fild.

Appendix. *A Chronicle*, 1461–1470.   147

1461 . .	Richard Lee	Richard Flemmyng ⎱ a° XXXIX°
		John Lambard ⎰

This yere a-bowt Cristmas, þe Duk of York [&] þe Erle of Salisbury were slayn at Wakfild; & þe Erle of Marche

Palme Sonday fild [Wa]kfild — gate an oþer fild in þe West contrey / & went forth to þe North fild at Feribrige, & gate þat fild / & was chosen Kyng, & many lordis slayn, with XXXII M[1] men.

Kyng Edward the IIIIth.

| 1462 . . | Hughe Wiche | John Lokke ⎱ a° primo |
| | | George Ireland ⎰ |

This yere þe Erle of Oxford, & þe Lord Awbray his son, were behedid at þe Towr Hill.

1463 . .	Thomas Cooke	William Hampton ⎱ a° II°
		Bartilmew Jhames ⎰
1464 . .	Mathew Philip	Thomas Muschampe ⎱ a° III°
		Robert Bassett ⎰
1465 . .	Raff Josselyn	John Tate ⎱ a° IIII°
		John Stone ⎰

This yere, Kyng Edward maried Quene Elizabeth, & she was crowned at Witsontide next after.

1466 . .	Raff Verney	Sir Harry Wafur ⎱ a° V°
		William Constantyne ⎰
1467 . .	John Yonge	John Bromer ⎱ a° VI°
		Herry Brice ⎰

This yere þe Lord Skalet fowght with the Bastard of Burgon in Smythfild.

| 1468 . . | Thomas Holgrave | Thomas Stalbrok ⎱ a° VII° |
| | | Humfrey Hayford ⎰ |

This yere, the Lady Margret, soster to Kyng Edward, was maryed to Duk Charles of Burgoyn.

| 1469 . . | William Taylor | William Haryot ⎱ a° VIII° |
| | | Symkyn Smyth ⎰ |

[Eg]ecott [f]eld — This yere was þe batell Egecote feld : þe Lord Harbard & his broþer slayn / & þe Lord Ryvers, & Sir John Woodvyle his son, behedid at Coventre; & anon after, þe Kyng went to Mydlam.

| 1470 . . | Richard Lee | Richard Gardyner ⎱ a° IX° |
| | | Robert Drope ⎰ |

148   Appendix. A Chronicle, 1470–1478.

    Kyng Edward the IIIIth   [leaf 234]
    Stannford fild.

[1470] .. This yere was þe fild of Stannford : þe Lord Welles & his son behedid / & þe Duk of Clarans / þe Erle of Warwik fled / & Kyng Edward fled in to Flaunders, etc.

1471 .. John Stokton   John Crosby   ⎱ a° X°
           John Ward   ⎰

This yere Kyng Edward cam agayn in to Ynglond / & londid at Holdernes in þe North contrey / & þe Duk of Clarans his broþer cam to hym, & lefte þe Erle of War-
Bernet fild   wyk / & they went both to Bernet fild, & þer was þe Erle of Warwik & his broþer, Marques Mountegewe, slayn, with many mo, on Ester day. & anon after, þe Kyng Edward
Tewxbury fild   went forth to Tewxbury fild / & þer was Prince Edward, son to Kynge Henre, slayn / & many moo.

1472 .. William Edward   John Shelley ⎱ a° XI°
           John Aleyn   ⎰

1473 .. William Hampton   Thomas Bledlow ⎱ a° XII°
           John Brown   ⎰

1474 .. John Tate   William Stokker ⎱ a° XIII°
           Robert Billisdon ⎰

This yere was a fray in Chepe-side on Mydsomer Nyght beffore the Kynge.

1475 .. Robert Drope   Thomas Hill   ⎱ a° XIIII°
           Edmond Shawe ⎰

This yere þe Kyng went ouer see to Amyas, & þer spak with þe French Kyng on þe brigge, with a royall company off Yngl[i]sshe men, & had yerly sent hym in to Ynglond LII M[1]. crownes.

1476 .. Robert Basset   Hewe Bryce   ⎱ a° XV°
           Robert Colwich ⎰

1477 .. Sir Raff Josselyn   William Horne ⎱ a° XVI°
           Richard Rawson ⎰

& M. Josselyn þe same yere made the diches to be cast / abowt London / & began þe newe walles abowt the cite, etc.

1478 .. Humfrey Hayford   John Stokker ⎱ a° XVII°
           Henre Colet   ⎰

Appendix. *A Chronicle*, 1479–1485.   149

1479 . . Richard Gardyner   Robert Byfild   } a° XVIII°
                             Robert Hardyng

1480 . . Sir Bartilmew Jhames Thomas Ilam   } u° XIX°
                               John Ward
This yere þe Lady Margret, Duches of Burgoyn, cam in to Ynglond; & þe Kyng received her at Grenwich with gret royalte.

1481 . . John Brown   William Bakon   } a° XX°
                         Robert Danyell

1482 . . William Haryot John Tate   } a° XXI°
                         John Wikyng
& Wykyng dyed, & Chawry chosen.
[1] This yere was a derth of whet & oþer wytallis.

1483 . . Edmond Shawe   William Whit   } a° XXII°
                         John Mathew

Kyng Edward dedde ⎫ This yere, þe XXII day of Aprell, died Kyng Edward; & then Richard, Duk of Glowcetter, toke vpon hym þe crown *in July,* by þe cownsaill, helpe & ayde of þe Duke of Bokyngham. & after þat, the said Duke of Bokyngham raysed a gret people agayn þe said Richard Duke of Glowcetter, at Breknok in Wales / & wold haue subdewed hym. / & he was taken by Kyng Richard, & his hed smyten of at Salisbury / & Prince Edward & his broþer taken at Stony Stratford by þe said Kyng Richard.

Kyng Richard the thirde
Breknok fild

Kyng Richard þe III^de

1484 . . Robert Billisdon   Thomas Northlond   } a° primo
                             William Marten
This yer dyed Quene Anne.

swetyng sikenes ⎧ Thomas Hill   ⎫ Thomas Breton   ⎫
                ⎨ Sir William Stokker ⎬ John Chestur   ⎬ a° II°
                ⎩ John Ward   ⎭ Chestur died & Raff ⎪
                                     Astry chosen   ⎭

Kyng Henry þe VIIth

1485   ⎫ This yere Kyng Henry þe VIIth enteryd in to Yyglond at
Kyng   ⎬ Bartilmew tide / & slewe Kyng Richard in þe fild / & then
Richard fild ⎭ cam in þe swetyng seknes / & so M. Hill, Sir William

---
[1] Leaf 234, back; headline: Kyng Edward þe IIIIth.
    Kyng Richard the III^de . . . a° regni regis XXI°.
* . . . * later additions, in blacker ink.

150   Appendix. A Chronicle, 1486–1493.

Stokker, mayres, dyed both in þe space of III wekis with many mo in London / & John Ward chosen.
Kyng crowned þe XXX day of Octobre, & maryed at Candilmas.

1486 . . Hewe Bryce   John Tate   ⎫
                       John Swan   ⎬ a° primo
This yere was a royall justyng at Westmynster / & a busshell of bay salt was sold for IIIs. IIIId. etc.
& the kyng was crownyd at Westmynster

1487 . . Henre Colett   John Percyvale ⎫
                         Hewe Clopton   ⎬ a° II°

Newark fild ⎫ This yere was þe batell of Newark : & þer was slayn þe Erle
& Marten   ⎬ of Lyncoln / & þe Erle Kyldare is broder, & Marten
[S]warte   ⎭ Swarte, with many moo, etc.

1488 . . William Horne   Sir John Fynkell ⎫
                          William Remyngton ⎬ a° III°

1489 . . Robert Tate   William Isaak ⎫
                        Raff Tilney   ⎬ a° IIII°
This yere þe Erle of Northhombrelond was slayn by men of his own contrey; & þe Lord Brok & Sir John Cheyny were sent in to Breton with V M¹. men.

1490 . . William White   Sir William Capell ⎫
                          John Broke   ⎬ a° V°

1491 . . John Mathew   Henre Cote   ⎫
                        Robert Revell ⎬ a° VI°
& Revell dyed, & Pemberton chosen.

1492 . . Hewe Clopton   Thomas Wode   ⎫
                         William Brown ⎬ a° VII°
This yere in Juyn the Kyngis second sonne, namyd Henry, was born at Grenwich.[1]

Kyng Henry the VIIth   [leaf 235]

1493 . . William Martyn   William Purches ⎫
                           William Welbek ⎬ a° VIII°
This yere þe Kyng went ouer see to[2] Boleyn, & cam home affore Cristmas agayn ; & a gret risyng of yong men agayn þe Stiliard.

* . . . * later additions, in blacker ink.
[1] This . . . Grenwich] added at the bottom of the page in paler ink and larger hand.   [2] MS. to to

Appendix. *A Chronicle*, 1494-1500. 151

| 1494 | Raff Astriche | Robert Fabian
John Wyngar | } a° IX° |

This yere þe Lady Yonge was brent.

| 1495 | Richard Chawry | Nicholas Alwyn
John Warner | } a° X° |

This yere was just*is* & torneys at Westmyns*ter*.

| 1496 | Henre Colett | Thom*a*s Knesworth
Henre Somer | } a° XI° |

| 1497 | S*ir* John Tate | S*ir* John Shawe
S*ir* Rich*ard* Haddon | } a° XII° |

This yere þe Western men & Cornyshe men arrose, & cam
Blak ⎫ thorow the contrey ; & they cam to Blakheth, & set a fild
hethe ⎬ agayn the Kyng / & þe Kyng had þe bett*er* þat day / & þe
fild ⎭ Lord Audley, & Flammok jentilman, & þe smyth of Bod-
*on Seynt man, were taken & browght to London / The Lord Audley
Botulf*is* behedid ; his hed set on London Brige / Flammok quartered,
day   & his hed set on London Brigge / and a yong man called
Sat*ur*day*
Perkyn   ⎫ Perkyn Werbek on owr Lady Day Natiuite next after / said
Werbek   ⎭ 'he was Kyng Edward*is* son' · & he was [1][hangid & hedid
            at Tiborn / his hede set on London Brigge].[1]

| 1498 | Willi*a*m Purches | Bartilmew Rede
Thom*a*s Wyndowt | } a° XIII° |

This yere þe Kyng kept his Cristmas at Shene ; & þ*er* was
a gret fyre & myche harme don.
*And this yere P*er*kyn Werbeck sat vpon a skaffold in
Chepe side.*

| 1499 | John P*er*cyvale | Thom*a*s Bradbury
Stephyn Jenyns | } a° XIIII° |

| 1500 | Nycholas Alwyn | Jhames Wilford
Rich*ard* Brond | } a° XV° |

This yere þe King & þe Quene passed ou*er* þe see to Cales,
& þe Duk of Burgon met wit*h* him at seynt Peters wit*h*owt
Cales. Also þe same yere, abowt þe Natiuite of owr Lady,
þe Erle of Warwik, son to þe Duke of Clarans, was behedid
at þe Towr Hill. *& this yere P*er*kyn Warbek was drawen
& hangid.*

* . . . * later additions, in blacker ink.   [1]–[1] [hangid . . . Brigge] *struck out*.

152   Appendix. A Chronicle, 1501–1505.

1501 . .   William Rymyngton John Hawes   } a° XVI°
            William Stede

This yere þer was a derth of corn, tyll þe hoyes cam owt of Flanders, lade with whet, gret plente; & after þat we had ynowgh: thankid be God! & in May next after, was a royall torney of lordis & knyghtis within þe Towr of London beffore þe Kynge / also abowt Ba[r]tilmewtide next after, þe Duke of Sowthfolk fled owt of Ynglond in to Flanders, to the Kyngis gret displesure. etc.

Kyng Henry the VIIth   [leaf 235, back]

1502 . .   Sir John Shawe   Sir Larans Aylmer   } a° XVII[o]
                              Henre Hed

This yere, a-bowt Myghelmas, londid Katerryne, dowghter to þe Kyng of Spayn, & was weddid to Prince Arthur in Novembre, þe Sonday after seynt Martens day, littera dominicalis C/c in Powlis / also on seynt Powlis day next after, was my Lady Margret, þe Kyngis dowghter, maryed par attorney to þe Kyng of Skottis, at Richemond etc. /
Prince   ) And the second day of Aprell next after, died Prince
Arthur dede) Arthur at Ludlow, & is buryed at Worsetter / * & Sir Jhamus Tyrell & Sir John Wyndham behedid at þe Towr Hill.*

[15]03 . .   Sir Bartilmew Rede   Henre Keybill   } a° XVIII°
                                  Nicholas Nynes
þe Quene   ) This yere died þe Quene Elizabeth at þe Towr, & buryed at
dede   ) Westmynster / & þe March was very wete. & gret flodis.
& this yer cam a gret embasset from þe Kyng of Romayns.

[1]504 . .   Sir William Capell   Christofor Hawes } a° XIX°
                                  Robert Wattis
& Wattis died, & Granger chosen.
This yere was a gret fire on London Brigge, & an oþer at þe Frere Austens, *& in Jamys stret,* & an oþer at Seynt Martens gate / & an oþer at Botall wharff.
& a parlament at Westminster & convocacion at Powlis.

1505 .   John Wyngar   Roger Acheley   } a° XX°
                            William Brown

This yere Lewys Cruyn, seruant of Sir Thomas Brandon, began a fray at þe syne of þe Christofre in Chepe. þe Lord

* . . . * later additions, in blacker ink.

Appendix. A Chronicle, 1506, 1507. 153

Marques, þe Lorde of Essex / þe Lord of Kent / Sir T. Gren / & oþer knyghtis tok parte abowt mydnyght / & all was seasid thorow þe polisie of þe marye & sheryffis, & litill harme don, thankid be God ! / & þis yere was a strif at Yelde-hall, for chosyng of þe sheryf; for þe taylors wold haue had M. Fithwilliam, & þe other Comens chose M. Grove, grocer.

[1]506 . . Thomas Knesworth   Richard Shore   } a° XXI°
                               Roger Grove   }
[and his wyff][1]
This yere was þe Duke of Burgon ∧ dryven in to Ynglond; & his wiff, by force of gret wynd as he was saylyng in to Spayn / & londyd at Plymowth, or þer-a-bowt[2] in þe West contrey on Seynt Mawris day, a° XVCVI. & þat nyght was blowen down þe weder-cokk at Powles. / The which Duk met with þe Kyng at Wynsore, & so went to Richmond / & from thens to Baynardis castell in London / & þe Kyng & þe Duk rode to-geþer thorow London / to þe Towr Hill; & þer was shoten many gonnes for his pleasure / & þis yere, Edmond de la Pole, Lord of Sowthfolk, þat was, / was taken & browght in to Ynglond / & so to þe Towr of London. / Item this yere the Kynge sente [3] down a letter myssyve, þat M. Fithwilliam, taylor, shuld be choson sheryff for þe Comons / but the Comons chase M. Johnson, goldsmyth; & þer-fore þe Kyng was gretly dysplesid; and he commandid þe Comons to make a newe eleccion / & so the Comons mad a newe eleccion the Xth day of Octobre & þer chase M. Fithwilliam sheryff / & the same M. Fithwylliam made a fest alone, the Fryday, the XVI day of Octobre / and M. Johnson was discharged / Item, this same yere Sir Richard Haddon was chosen mayre by the Kyngis commandment | Item, þe wedder-cokke of Powlis was sett vp agayn, the XXI day of August 1506; and this yere the Duke of Burgon died, in Spayne, & he had many masses in Ynglond said for his sowle.

1507[4] . . Sir Richard Haddon   William Copynger   } a° XXII°
                                  William Fithwilliam }

Memorandum, þat on seynt Thomas day at nyght, in Crist-

[1] [. . .] inserted, but struck out.
[2] at plymowth, or þer abowt, *added in paler ink to fill up a blank left for it.*
[3] *Leaf* 236, *headline:* Kyng Henry þe VIIth.
[4] Down from this year, hands and colours of ink begin to vary; gaps evidently were left and filled up later, some remained blank, especially among the later entries.

Appendix. A Chronicle, 1508, 1509.

mas, the bakers hows in Hogyn Lane was brent / and þe goodwyff, II maydys, & III oþer seruantis were brent in the fire. / Also this yere dyueris mercers freight a gret shipe with rede heryng at þe coste / & wold haue caryed it vnto Rome / But God purveyed þat þe wynd was clene agayn them / & they were fayn to sell them owt of þe pipes with-in London, at þe Newe Woll Key, for XII heryngis a peny / and þe Duche men cowld sayll to non oþer cost but to London with þer whit heryngis; & fremen sold XII a peny owt of þe barell, both full & shoton / also þer was gret plente of Skottishe samon; but þat was taken vp amonge the fishemongers / Item, in Octobre per cam III galies to Sowthhamton; & II of them departid in to Flanders, & þe thirde was brent vpon þe water by foly.

1508 . . William Brown,   William Butler,
mercer   grocer   a° XXIII₀
Sir Larans Aylmer, Johannes Kyrby,
draper   sissor

This yere, abowt XIIth tyde / Lady Mary, þe Kyngis dowghter, was mad sure, par attorney, to þe yong Kyng of Castile & Duk of Burgon / Item, this yere, the XXII day of Marche, betwen III & IIII of the clok in the mornyng, dyed William Brown, mayre; and for hym chosen Sir Larans Aylmer, draper, þe XXVII day of Marche; & þe same day he was sworn a[t] Yeld-hall; & þe sword was born home affore hym / & he in a gray clok / & þe XXIX day of Marche he toke his charge at þe Towr of London. [No fest!

1509 . . Sir Stephyn Genyns, Thomas Exmewe,
sissor   a . . .
Richard Smyth sissor

þe Kyng dede

This yere, Kyng Henry þe VIIth departid, þe XXI day of Aprell, at Richemont, & was browght to London þe IX day of May honorably, with V M¹. torches & prikke[ts] brennyng at ons, at þe Kyngis cost / & þe cite ordeyn[ed] for as many or mo / brennyng in euery stret as he cam. & þat nyght he remayned at Powlis / vnder an honor[able] herse; / & on þe morow he had III masses by note; / & þe Bisshop of Rochester mad a sermond in þe quir; / & at afternone he

Appendix. A Chronicle, 1510.   155

was remeved to Westmynster with as many [1] new torches
in to þe abbey; & þer he had an honorable hers. / & on þe
morow after, his helmet was offred vp, & III swordis &
III cappis of mayntenance; / & a knyght rydyng in harnes
rode vp to þe high auter, & þer was vnhorsed / & þe Kyng
honorably buried.

¶ Item, þe VI day of Juyn, J. Darby, bowyar, J. Smyth,
carpenter, / & J. Symson, fuller, / ryng-leders of fals questis
in London, rode abowt þe cite with þer facis to þe hors
taylis / & wer set on þe pillary / & browght agayn to New-
gate / & they died all with-in VII days after / for sham. /
Item, þe XIth day of July, þe Kyng was maried prevely, in
his closet at Grenwich, to Katerryn, þe Kyngis dowghter
of Spayn. /

¶ Item, þe XXIII day of Juyn, þe Kyng rode thorow
London with his lordis & knyghtis, & a Canype was born
ouer his hede. / & þe Quen cam rydyng after, in a hors lytter,
kouered with whit / & a whit Canype born ouer her hede, &
diuerse ladies folowyng her in charyottis & on hors bakkis.

¶ Item, þe howsis, as þe Kyng rode, were haggid without
with clothes of gold & aryes / with whit roses & rede hag-
gyng vpon them / & euery cundite ranne wyne / & vppon
euery cundite wer syngars & mynstrellis, & organs in þe
best maner.

Item, þe XXIII day of Juyn, þe Kyng & Quen wer both
crowned at Westmynster with royall solemnite, & þe Maire
of London was made knyght.

¶ Item, þe XXIX day of Julii, departid my lady þe Kyngis
grandame : on whose sowle, Jhesu haue mercy ! & M. Ymson
& M. Dudley were dampned for treson.

[15]10 . .   Thomas Bradbury,   Georg Monox.
mercer. ✠
Sir William Capel,   John Dockett.   } a° II[do]
draper.

This yere, the Xth day of Januar, died Thomas Bradbury,
at VIII of þe cloke at nyght / and the XIIth day of Januar,
Sir William Capell, draper, was chosen Mair, & sworn at
Westminster / & in Januar began þe parlament at West-

---

[1] *Leaf* 236, *back; headline:* Kyng Henry þe VIIIth a° primo.

Appendix. *A Chronicle*, 1511.

m*inster.*/ M. Tat*er* & M. Records, knyght*is* for þe shire / John Bregi*us*, drap*er*, & yong More, burges of þe p*ar*lame*n*t for Londo*n*. / & the IIIIth day of Feu*er*er was XV or XVI howsis brent at Hatters Key i*n* Te*m*mes stret, & XV or XVI Crysty*n* bodyes brent, or mo : þe more pite !

Item, þe p*ar*lament endid þe II[de] day of M*ar*ch folovyng. ¶ Item, þe XIIth day of Ap*er*ell, was cryed a gen*er*all pece betwen þe Kyng of Ynglond & þe French Kyng, for þ*er* lyves, & a yere & on day aft*er*. / Ite*m*, on Myd-somer nyght þe Kyng ca*m* pr*e*vyly to the Kyng*is* Hed in Chepe, in þe rayme[*n*]t of on of his yeme*n* of þe garde, & a hawberd in his neke / & so dep*ar*tid agayn aft*er* þe washe. / & on seynt Pet*er*s nyght the Kyng & þe Quene ca*m* rydyng to the Kyng*is* Hed royally ; / & aft*er* þe washe, dep*ar*tid to þe Towr.

Item, the XVII day of Aug*ust*, M. Ymson & M. Dudley were hedyd at the Towr Hill. / & þe XVII day of Septe*m*bre, at nyght, was a gret fire in Wod stred and next Chepe, & IIII or V howsis brent. / Item, on Seynt Mathe*us* day, M. Fithwilli*am*, ald*er*ma*n*, was chosen sheryff of London a-gayn, and he rode in to [1] the co*n*trey / & wold not be fownd to co*m* to his answer ; wherfor, on Myghelmas evyn, he was disgracid of his clok, & also of his fredo*m* of þe cite, & to fyne M[l]. m*ar*k*is* for his dishobedyens. & þe same day, M. Rest, ald*er*ma*n* & gros*er*, was chosen sheryff, & þ*er* was sworn at Yeld-hall forth-with.

[1 leaf 237]

1511 . . Henry Keybill, groc*er*. John Mylborn, drap*er*. } a° III° John Rest, groc*er*.

* This yer, IX s*er*uant*is* of þe coyff made. *
This yere, on Newyeris day, was born Harry, þe Kyng*is* first chyld, & he dyed wit*h*-in a moneth.
Also, in August, my Lord Haward, S*ir* Edward Haward, & John Hopton, tok II Scottyshe shippis þat robbed on the see, & browght them to London, & þe captayn, callid þe Lyon of Scotland / & all þe oþ*er* Skottis wer*r*e browght to þe Bishope of York*is* place, & þ*er* were kept as p*r*esoners wit*h* gret favo*ur*, & met & drynk ynowgh.

* . . . * later additions, in different ink.

Appendix. A Chronicle, 1512–1515.

1512 .. Roger Acheley, draper. Nicholas Shelton,
mercer.
Robert[1] Myrfyn,
skyner.
} a° III°

This yere þe Mair tok good hed to þe markettis.[2]

1513 .. Wylliam Copynger, Robert Holdernes,
fishemonger. ha[berdasher.]
Sir Richard Haddon, Robert Fenrutter,
mercer. goldsmyth.
} a° V°

This yere dyed M. Copynger / & M. Haddon chosen Mair. Item þis yer þe Kyng went over in to Frans with many lordis; & þer he gate Turwyn, & Torney, & many oþer townis./ & þer was takyn at a skyrmysh, I duke & I erle of Frans, with many moo / & þe duk & þe erle wer browght to London / & wer her in þe cort / till they made ther rawnsom.

Item, this yer þe Skottyshe Kyng cam in to Ynglond with a gret power, whan þe Kyng was in France; & with hym mett þe Erle of Surrey with a gret power; & þer þe Skottyshe Kyng was slayn in þe fild / & his ded body was browght to Rychemont. & at þat fild was my Lord Amerall, with his maryners, callyd 'the black gard.'[2]

1514 .. Wylliam Brown, John Dawys, gro[cer].
mercer.
Sir John Tate, mercer. John Bryggis, draper.
Roger Bafford, mercer.

This yere dyed William Brown, beyng Mair; & for hym chosen Sir John Tate./ Also this yer, aff[ore] Mydsomer, dyed John Dawes, beyng sheryff; & for hym chosen, Roger Bafford, mercer.[2]

[leaf 237, back] ✠ Henrici VIII[1] a° VII°

1515 .. George Monockis, Jhamis Gerford,
draper. mercer.
John Mondy, gold-
smy[th].[2]

[1]–[1] Christian name added in a different hand and paler ink.
[2] Blanks follow, which were not filled up.

Appendix. A Chronicle, 1516–1521.

1516 . . Wyll*iam* Butler, gro*cer*   Henr*e* Worley, gold-   ⎫
                                     smyth.   ⎬ a° VIII°
                              Will*iam* Bayly,   ⎪
                                   drap*er*.[1]   ⎭

1517 . . John Rest, grocer.   Thom*as* Sem*er*, mer*cer*.   ⎫ a° VIII°
                                  John Thrusto*n*, gold-   ⎬
                                  smyth.   ⎭ IX°

This yer*e* was a risyng [of] p*r*entisys on May day; & many of the*m* were hangid i*n* Chepe-side, & i*n* many other plac*is* i*n* Londo*n* / vppon XV parr*e* of galowssys.[1]

1518 . . Thom*as* Exmew, gold-   Thom*as* Baldry,   ⎫
                             smyth.   mer*cer*.   ⎬ a° IX°
                                              Raff Symond*is*, fish-   ⎪
                                              [monger].   ⎭

This yer*e* was an acte made to dryve the come*n* beggars owt of Londo*n*; & offessers made for the same purpose / & þe beggers amyttyd to wer a Seynt Georg*is* crose i*n* a shild.[1]

1519 . . Rob*er*t Myrfyn,   John Alen*n*, mer*cer*.
                         skyn*ner*.   Jham*is*[2] Spen*cer*, vynt*er*.[1]

1520 . . Jham*is* Gerford,   Will*iam* Wilky*n*son,   ⎫
                         mer*cer*.   drap*er*.   ⎬ a° XI°
                                            Nich. Pa*r*triche,   ⎫ a° XII°
                                            gro*cer*.[1]   ⎭

1521 . . John Brygg*is*,   John Keme, mer*cer*.   ⎫
                         drap*er*.   ⎬ a° XIII°
                                           John Skevyngto*n*,   ⎪
                                           tailor.   ⎭

This yer*e* the Duke of Bokyngham was behedid at þe Towr Hill abowt Wytsontid / & was buryed at the Frere Augustyns in London.

Item, þis yer*e* was made x s*er*uant*is* of þe coyff; & þe fest kept at þe Bishop of Elis place i*n* Holborn. *& þe newe ovyns i*n* Sowthwark wer*e* begon to make.*[1]

[1] Blanks for events left and not filled up.
[2] Corrected from "Thomas."
* . . . * later addition, in different ink.

Appendix. A Chronicle, 1522–1524.

1522 .   John Mylborn,   John Breteyn,
         drape*r*.   tailo*u*r.   ⎫
                               Thomas Pergette,   ⎬ a° XIIII°
                               salte*r*.   ⎭

This yere þe Emprowr of Almeyn co*m* to London, þe Fryday, þe VI^te day of Juyn, & the Kyng i*n* his company, & all þe stat*is* of this realme / & XIII[1] pageant*is* made i*n* Londo*n*, which cost (as was said) M¹ li. & mo*re*. & all chanons, freres & prist*is*, i*n* þ*er* best copis, se*n*syng i*n* eu*ery* stret / & craft*is* sto*n*dyng i*n* ordre / & þe Crosse i*n* Chepe new gilt / & þe Cety lent þe Kyng þat same tyme XX M¹ li./ þ*er*-of þe groce*rs* 2000 li. as me*n* said.

1523 . .   John Mondy,   John Rudston,   ⎫   [leaf 238]
         goldsmyth.   drap*er*.   ⎪
                               John Cha*n*ney,   ⎬ a° XIV°
                               skyn*er*, & second-⎪
                               ary of þe Cownt.   ⎭

This yer was kept a p*ar*lame*n*t at þe Blackfreres i*n* London, & endyd at Westmi*n*ster / & ther was gra*n*tid þat me*n* shuld be taxid by þ*er* othes, what they be worth / & pay to þe Kyng of þ*er* good*is*, a s*er*tayn.

It*em*, this yer ca*m* þe Kyng of Denmark i*n* to Ynglond, & his Quene, & had good cher of þe Kyng & lord*is*; & was her skarse a moneth / & so dep*ar*tyd i*n* to Flande*rs*.

¶ And the Duke of Sothfolk, wit*h* a gret power, went ou*er* i*n* to France, & ther lay all the wynt*er*, & wo[n] dyu*er*is towny*s*./ It*em*, þis yere George Monock*is* was chosen Mair, & wold not tak it vpon hy*m*; & þ*er*-for he was co*n*dempned i*n* M¹ mark*is*; & than after, was Thom*as* Baldry chosen.

1524 . .   Thomas Baldry,   Mychaell English, ⎫
         m*er*c*er*.   m*er*s*er*.   ⎬ a° XVI°
                               Nych. Genyns,   ⎪
                               skyn*er*.   ⎭

This yer*e*, i*n* Februar*e*, III of the me*n* þat wold haue made i*n*surrecc*i*on at Coventre / were hangid, drave*n*, & quartered, at Londo*n* / & the rypears sold fish at Lo*n*don Hall i*n* þe Lent./ It*em*, þis yer*e*, after Mydsomer, ca*m* i*n*

---

[1] "many" struck out, the number "XI. II." inserted instead.

160   Appendix. A Chronicle, 1525–1529.

þe Erle of Angwyshe, a Skottish lord, owt of Frans, & his broder / & had good chere, & so departid in to Scotland.

1525 . . Sir Wylliam Bayly, draper. Raff Dodmer, mercer.
William Roche, draper. } a° XVII°

This yere, Francysco, þe Frenche kyng, was takyn beffore Pavya in Ytaly, & þe Kyng of Navern & many oþer lordis & princis takyn & slayn, among whom Richard de la Pole was slayn / on þe day of Seynt Mathewe, þat was þe 24 day of Februare, 1524.

Item, on Seynt Grygoris evyn next after, was a gret marche in London, & many fires, & wyne dronkyn in þe nyght, & þe Maire rode abowt þe cite & to þe Towr Hill / & þer. þe Kyng made a banket, & on Seynt Grygoris day þe Kyng & the Quen wer at Powlis at a solom masse. & þer was "Te Deum laudamus" song solemply, & in somer after was a generall pece cried / betwen Ynglond & France / & a busshell of bay salt was sold for IIII s. VIII d. a moneth affore Cristmas, tyll þer cam shipis owt of France.
* This yere þe Maire tok good hede to the markettis.*

1526 . . John Alyn, mercer. John Cauerton, haberda[sher].
Christofer Askne, draper.[1] } a° XVIII[o]

1527 . . Sir Thomas Semer, mercer. [Stephyn][2] Pecok, hab[erdasher].
Nycholas Lambard, gr[ocer]. } a° 19°

[leaf 288, back]   Henrici VIII

1528 . . Jhamus Spenser, vyntener. John Hardy, haberdasher.
William Holis, mercer. } a° 20°

1529 . . Sir John Rudston, draper. Raff Waryn, mercer.
John Longe, salter. } a° 21°

* . . . * later addition, in different ink. .
[1] Blank left for events.
[2] Blank for Christian name in MS., but cf. below, 1533.

Appendix. *A Chronicle*, 1530–1532. 161

[1529] . . This yere, Raff Rowlet, goldsmyth, was chosen sheryf; & þe Kyng wrot for hym; & so he was escused for þe yere / and than was chosen Watter Champyon, draper.

1530 . . Sir Raff Dodmere, Mychaell Dormer, mercer. mercer. Water Champyon, draper. } a° 22°

This yere, Raff Rowlett, goldsmyth, was chosen sheryf; & he wold not take yt, but went to Sent Albons / & than, on Myghelmas evyn, was chosen Robert Amadas, goldsmyth; & þe Kyng wrot for hym, & so he was eskused./ & than, þe morowe after Myghelmas day, was chosen Richard Choppyn, talowchandeler; & he was sworn by & by at Yeld-hall / & he was changid in to a skarlet gown & clok, & a chayn of gold abowt his nekk, & a hors redy at þe dore; & so went to Westminster.[1]

a° 1531 . Sir Thomas Pargetter, William Dawnse, mercer.
salter. Richard Choppyn,
talowchandeler.

Thys yere, þe IIIIth or V[th] day of Novembre, was a gret wynde þat blew down many howsis in þe contrey / & tylis, & thecche, & trees. And after folowyng was suche a hie tyde þat yt drownyd all þe marsshis on Essex side / & on Kent side in þe yle of Tenet & other placis, & yt dystroyed myche cattell; and also yt dydde myche hurte in þe cost of Flanders, as in Zelond, *etc.*

Item, my lord Cardynall died, & was buried at Leycetter./
Item, þer was on skaldyd in Smythfild, for poysenyng of dyueris men of þe Bisshop of Rochesters howse.[1]

1532 . . Sir Nicholas Lambard, Richard Gresham, mercer.
grocer. Edlbard Altham,
cloth-werker.

This yere, þe IIIIth day of Decembre, Sir Gryffyn Rise was behedid at þe Towr Hill / [&] burned at Crossid Freres; & þe same day, William Huys, his seruant, was drawen to Tyburn / & þer hangid & quartered, & his hed set on þe brigge[2] / & his quarters at IIII gatis.

Item, a-bowt Alhalowtide was suche gret wyndis þat distroyed many shippis; and þer was suche hie floddis þat

[1] *Blanks follow.* [2] London Bridge.

CAROLS. M

overflowid myche lond in Zelond, Flandres, Holond & Brabaand/ with many townys & many peple drownyd./ and at þat tyme, þe Kyng of Ynglond & þe French Kyng were to-gether at Caleis & at Boleyn with gret Royaltie / & manye lordis & knyghtis with them, on both partis.

[Klyng [at C]aleis

Item, þe . . .[1] day of . . . .[1] a prist was hangid at þe Towr Hill for clippyng of gold.

Item, III herytykis brent in Smythfild, þat ys to say: Richard Boyffild, monk / & a powche-maker, & William Bayman, gentilman.

[leaf 239]
1533 . .

H. VIII[1] a⁰ XXV⁰

Sir Stephyn Pecok, haberdassher. Richard Raynoldis, mercer. } a⁰ 25 and John Prist, grocer, sheryff [2]
Richard Pynson, bocher.
John Martyn, bocher.

This yere, the XXIX day of May, the Maire of London, with þe aldermen in scarlet gownys / went in a barge to Grenwiche / with all þe felyshippis in London in bargis with þer baners, as they were wont to bryng þe. Maire to Westmynster / & the bachelers barge hangid with cloth of gold on þe best maner, with a galey to wayt vppon her, & a foyst / with a best þer-in / which shote many gonnes. And ther they fett Quen Anne vp to the Towr of London / & in þe way, on lond, abowt Lymost,[3] were shot many gret chambres of gonnes; & II of þe Kyngis shippis þat lay by Lymoste shot many gret gonnes / and at þe Towr, or she cam on londe, þer was shott vnnumerable many gonnes.

And þe XXXI day of May, which was Wyt-son evyn, she was conveyd in a chariot from þe Towr of London to York Place, callid Whit Hall, at Westminster./ & at her departyng from þe Towr, þer was a shote of gonnes, which was innumerable to menys thynkyng / & þer in London, dyueris paiantis / þat ys to say: oon at Greschirch,
item, oon at Ledon hall,
item, oon at þe gret Comdyt,
item, oon at þe Standarde,
item, þe Crosse in Chepe newe trymmed,
item, at þe condyte at Powlis gate,

at the coronacion of Quene Anne

[1] Blanks in the MS. [2] and . . . sheryff] added along the margin, upper part of letters of the name cut off; supplied from a later passage. [3] Limehouse.

Appendix. A Chronicle, 1534. 163

item, at Powlis gate, a branch of rosis,
item, wit*h*owt at þe Est end of Powlis,
item, at þe condyt in Flet stret.
& she was accompyned first, Frenche me*n* in cran colowred velvet / & I whit sleve, & *per* horses trappid, & whit crossis *per*-on. Than rode jentylmen / tha*n* knyght*is* / & lord*is* in *per* degree / & þer was II hatt*is* of mayntenans, & many chariott*is* / wi*th* lad*is*, & many jent[il] wome*n* on horsback folowyng þe chariott*is*; and all þe co*n*stables in London wer in *per* best a-ray wit*h* whit staves in *per* hond*is*, to mak rome / & to wayt vpon þe Quene as farre as *. . . .*
& ther rode wit*h* her XVI Knyght*is* of the Bathe, & on Whitsonday she was crownyd at Westm*inster* wit*h* gret solempnyte / & just*is* at Weste[m]ynst*er* all þe Wytson halydais / & the fest[1] was kept in Westm*inster* Hall / & þe just*is* affore York Place, callid Whit Hall.

This yere, i*n* þe begy*n*nyng of Septembr*e*, Quene Anne was delyue*r*id of a woma*n* child at Gremwi*c*he, which child was named Elizabeth.[2]

Item, this yere forreyn bochers sold fleshe at Ledon Hall / for þe bochers of þe Cite of Londo*n* denyed to sell beff for ob. the ℔. & motton for ob. & d. qˢ. the pow*n*d accordyng to the acte of p*ar*lament.[3] This yer, in Septembr*e*, John Martyn, sheryf, [dyed] þe *. . .* day of Septemb e / & John Pryst, groc*er*, was chosen sheryf, þe XVIII day of Septembr*e* / to kepe owt tyll Myghelmas.

[leaf 239, back] aᵒ H. r. 25ᵒ

1534 . . Si*r* Chr*is*tofer Ascne, draper.

{ Si*r* Wylli*am* Forma*n*, habe*r*dasher.
  Si*r* Thomas Rytson, m*er*cer.

This yere, þe XXIII day of Novembr*e*, prechid at Powlys Crosse þe Abbot of Hide./ & þer stod on a skaffold, all þe s*er*mond tyme, þe holy maid of Kent callid [Elizabeth] Barton[4] / & II mo*n*k*is* of Ca*n*turbury / & II frere obs*er*uant*is* / & II pryst*is* & II lay men; & after þe s*er*mond / went to þe Tow*r*.

---

[1] MS. ferst [2] The name added in later hand on a blank left for it.
[3] Stowe's *Annales*, ed. 1592, p. 959: "It was this yeere enacted, that butchers should sell their beefe and mutton by weight, beefe for *a halfe penny* the pound, and mutton for *three farthings*," etc. (*obolus*—*obolus* & *denarii quadrans*.)
[4] Blank left in MS. for the Christian name, which I have supplied from Stowe.
— *Blanks in the MS.*

Appendix. A Chronicle, 1534.

¶ Also this yere, on Palme Son-day evyn, which was þe XXVIII day of Marche, was a gret sodeyn tempest of wynd, & brak opyn II wyndowes at Whit Hall at Westminster / and torned vp þe lede of þe Kyngis newe tenes play at York Place, and brak of þe tylis of III goldsmythis howses in Lombard Stret / & foldyd vp þe ledis of Pewterers Hall, & cast yt down in to þe yarde, & blewe down many tylis of howsis in London, & tres abowt Shordyche.

¶ Item, þe first day of Aprell, which was "tenebre" Wedynsday / Wolf & his wyf, þat kylled þe II Lombardis in a bot vppon Temmys, were hangid vppon II gybettis by þe water side, betwen London Brige & Westmynster / and on þe Monday in Ester wek þe woman was buried at the Crossid Freres in London.

¶ Item, þe XX day of Aprell / þe parson of Mary Aldermary Chirch in London was drawen on a hirdyll, from[1] þe Towr of London in to þe Tyborn, & ther hangid & hedid.

Item, II obseruantis freres drawen on a hurdyll / & bothe hangid & hedyd.

Item, II monkis of Canterbury,—on was callid Doctor Borkyng,—drawen on a hurdyll to Tyborn, and ther hangid & hedid.

Item, þe holy maid of Kent, calid Elizabeth[2] Barton, was drawen on a hurdyll alon to Tyborn, & ther hangid & hedyd; & all þer hedis set on London Brigge / & on þe gattis of London.

¶ Item, þe XI day of July, þe lord Dakers of þe North was conveyed from þe Towr of London to Westminster, to receive jugement for treason / but ther he was quyt by a queste of lordis.

¶ Item, all men, Ynglishe & oþer, beyng in Ynglond, were sworn to be trewe to þe Kyng, & his heiris betwen Quen Anne & hym begotten, & for to be begotten.

¶ Item, þe Lord Thomas Garrard off Yrelond behedid þe bishoppe of Dulyne, callid Doctor Alen / as he wold com in to Ynglond.

¶ Item, a generall peace cried betwen þe Kyng of Ynglond & þe Scottyshe Kyng, for þer lyff tyme.

[1] MS. for
[2] "Elizabeth," later insertion on blank left for it; in a previous entry the writer forgot to fill up the blank.

Appendix. A Chronicle, 1535.

¶ Item, þer was a gret sodeyn storme in þe narowe see, & II shippus of þe Selond flete were lost, with clothe & men & all, for they sonke in the see.

[1535] . Sir John Champneys ⎰ Nicholas Leveson, mercer.
⎱ Wylliam Denham, yremonger, beyng alderman.

¶ This yere, in Novembre, cam ouer þe high Admyrall of Fraunce, as inbassatoure from þe Frensh Kyng / & he had gret gyftis / & his costis paid for as longe as he was in the realme.

¶ Item, þe IIIIth day of May, the Prior of the Charter-hows of London, & II other monkis of þe Charter-howsis in oþer placis / & þe father of þe place at Syon, beyng in a gray abbyt, and a prist, which was, as men said, the vycor of Thistyworth / were drawen all from þe Towr of London to Tyborn, & þer hangyd, & þer bowellis brent / þer hedis cut of & quartered, & þer hedis & quarters / som set on London Brigge, and þe rest vppon all þe gatis of London / & at þe Charter-howss gate.

[leaf 240] ¶ Also shortly after, þe Kyng causid his own hed to be nottyd & cut short / so þat his here was not half an ynche long / & so were all þe lordis, & all knyghtis, gentylmen, & seruyng men þat cam to þe corte.

¶ Item, on Wytson evyne was a gret thonder at London.

¶ Item, þe IIII day of Juyn / a man & a woman, born in Flanders, were brent in Smythfild for heresye.

¶ Item, þe XIX day of Juyn, III monkis of þe order of Charter-hous were drawen from þe Towr to Tyborn, & þer hangid & quartered / & þer hedis on þe Brige, and þer quarters on þe gatis.

¶ Item, þe XXII day of Juyn, þe Bishoppe of Rochester was behedid at þe Towr Hill / the hed set on London Brige / & þe body buryed in Barkyng chirch-yard.

¶ Item, þe VI day of Julii / Sir Thomas Mor, þat somtym was Chanseler of Ynglond, was behedid at þe Towr Hill / his hed set on þe Brigge, and þe body buryed in the Towre.

¶ Also this yer þe power & auctoryte of þe pope was vtterly made frustrat & of non effecte within þis realme / & þe Kyng

Appendix. A Chronicle, 1536.

callid 'suppreme hed, vnder God, of þe chirch of Ynglond'./
& þat was red in þe chirch euery Festyvall day / & þe popes
name was scrapid owt of euery masse bok & oþer bokis / &
was callid Bishop of Rome.

¶ Also Thom[a]s Garrard, þat was son & heire to þe Erle of
Kyldare / yelded hym-self in Yrelond to þe lord Lenard,
marques / to be at þe Kyngis pleasure / & the II^{de} day of
Octobre / he was put in þe Towr of London.

[1536] . . Sir John Alyn, mercer.　　Humffrey Monmowthe, draper.
　　　　　　　　　　　　　John Cootis, salter.

At þe begynnyng of þer tyme, þe sheryffis put a-way, eche
of them, VI seriantis & VI yemen, tyll they were compellid
by þe Comon Consaill / to tak them agayn.

¶ Item, þe canell-rakers of London had hornes to blow, to
geve folkis warnyng to cast owt ther duste.

¶ Item, euery man þat had a well within his howse, to drawe
it III tymes in þe we[k], to washe the stretis.

¶ Item, Friday þe XII day of Novembre, was a gret generall
processyon; & begon at Powlis, & went vp to Ledon Hall,
& by Seynt Magnus corner, & so a-longe Temmes stret,
& vp at Walbrok / & so thorowe Bugge Rowe, & so to
Powlis.

And þer went first þe II bedellis of þe beggers, with þer
staves in þer hondis / & after them all þe waytis of London,
playing, & other mynstrellis; and than all þe children of
scoles in London, with bokis in þer hondis, & all þer
masters folowyng. And after them freres & chanons, all
in copes.

Item, after them, þe clarkis & pristis, all in copes.

Item, monkis after, þat ys to say, Westminster, Barmsey,
& all oþer abowt London, all in coopes.

And than IIII abbottis mytered, & III byshoppis mytered /
among whom þe byshop off London went vnder a canype /
with the sacrament / in a crosse þat he bare in his hond, &
sertayn gren torches burnyng abowt þe same / with many
mynstrellis.

And than cam þe Mayre in black velvet, with a coler of
gold abowt his neck / & þe aldermen in scarlett, & all
chaynes of gold; & III commeners þat had ben sheryffis,

Appendix. A Chronicle, 1536. 167

folowed in scarlet, & chaynes of gold abowt þer neck*is* / & tha*n* þe yema*n*ry of þe me*r*sers wen[t] wit*h* þer crymysyn saten hod*is* / and all the Craft*is* in London þ*at* were of any lyver[y] went i*n* þer best lyvery / in-so-myche þ*at* wodmongers went / which was ne[uer] sene beffore, as old men sayd . . . . t . . . . pewterers ca*m* last of all, th . . .

NOTES.

4. (*No. 73 c in the catalogue table at end of introduction*). *Variations from the text in Wright's "Songs and Carols"* (Percy Soc., 23), p. 57.
1 me walked on] went in a mery *W.*   5 he] sche   6 I am a musket both fair and gent *W.*   7 nygh] al   10 lowd gan he crye] he gan sey   13–16 *Instead of these lines, W. has:*

Al crysten pepull behold and se,
This world is but a vanyte,
And replet with necessyte;
    Timor, etc.
Wak I or sclep, ete or drynke,
Whan I on my last end do thynk,

For grete fer my sowle do shrynke;
    Timor, etc.
God graunte us grace hym for to serve
And be at owr end whan we sterve,
And frome the fynd he us preserve;
    Timor, etc.

5. The Latin head-lines are from Psalm 61. 11 (Flügel).

7. (73 *g in catalogue table*). *Variations from the text of MS. Add.* 5665 (as printed by B. Fehr in Herrig's *Archiv*, vol. 106, p. 274):
Heading: Jhesus autem hodie Regressus est a iordane *Add.*   2 by] with   3 þat] the   4 dilect*us om. Add.*   5 in] &   6 was *om. Add.*   14 was] were   at] in iordayne *Add. The Add. MS. version has "*Hic est filius meus*" only, as burden to stanzas* 2, 3, 4, *and* 5 (*where "*ipsum audite*" in Ball. is quite out of place*).

8. 20 erat : so *MS.* ; er[i]t *Flügel.*

9. (120 *b in catal. table*). *Chief variations from the text in Wright's "Songs and Carols"* (Percy Soc. 23), p. 36 :
3 From N. to G.] To N. in G. (cf. 49, 3).   5 He m. a m. in a pl.] He fond the mayd al in hyr place   7 And seyd, Al heyl, full of grace   9 ff. *run in W.:*

Thou shalt conseyve and ber a chyld,
Thouȝ thou with syn wer never defyled ;
Thou hast fond grace, thou Mary myld,
    With *nova.*
The byrd abasshyd of all ble,
Answerd and sayd, How may this be ?
Man thorow kynd towchyd never me,
    With *nova.*
The angell seynd unto that free,
The *holy* gost shal lyȝt in the,
God and man in on shal be,
    With *nova.*

Syx monthys is ner gon,
Syn Elyzab*eth* conseyvyd Johan ;
She that was *barren* [will] a babe have
    With *nova.*   [borne,
The ree . . . . d unto the fere (*Flügel*:
    The [   ] unto ; *Holthausen cj.* : The
    maydyn sayd unto)
Now hys we . . . . e don in me here,
    (*Flügel* : Now hys w[orde b]e don)
And Godes maydyn now se me here,
    With *nova.*

22 The reading *lyȝt* (in Wright's text) seems to be the correct one, "though *plyght* 'promised' makes a sort of sense" (H. Bradley). *The anagrammatic pun on "EVA"—"AVE" in the title, is from a Latin hymn* (Mone, *Lat. Hymnen des Mittelalters*, II, p. 55, No. 363, l. 7) : Verbum bonum et suave | pandit intus in conclave | et ex Eva formans ave, | Evae verso nomine.

10. (120 *c in catal. table*).
19 Whan þat flowr began to spred & hys blosomys for to woyde] Holthausen (*Anglia* 17, 443) suggests "brede" or "sede" (i.e. "go to seed", cf. *Rom. Rose* 4344,

Anelida and Arcite 306) for "woyde." 22 spred] Holthausen suggests "spede,"
to avoid the repetition, but cf. l. 18.   40 for ay bewte *MS.*] for her bewte
Flügel, for hys bewte (cf. l. 21) *Holthausen.*—*Qu.* for al bewte (= for one that is *all beautiful*, cf. Song of Solomon 4. 7: thou art all fair, my love [tota pulchra es, amica mea])?—The allegorical conception of Jesus as the flower from the root of Jesse, is from Isaiah 11. 1.—See also No. 59, l. 2.

11. (120 *d in Catal. table*).
Wright, *Spec. of old Christm. Car.* (Percy Soc. IV), p. 11 (Sloane MS. 2593, leaf 71 r°) (the same *Songs and Carols* 1855, Warton Club IV, p. 68; *a song with the same heading, but otherwise different: ibid.* p. 78).

Man, be glad in hall and bour,
This tyme was born our savyour.

In this tyme Cryst haȝt us sent
His owyn sone in present,
To dwelle with us verement,
   To ben our helpe and socour.
In this tyme ros a sterre cler
Over Bedlem, as bryȝt as fer,
In tokenyng that he hadde non per,
Lord, God, kyng, and emperour.
In this tyme it is be-falle,
He that deyid for us alle,

Born he was in assis stalle,
   Of Mary, that swete flour.
In this tyme kemyn thre kynges,
He kemyn fro fer, with ryche thinges,
For to makyn here offerynges,
   On here knen with gret honour.
In this tyme prey we
To hym that deyid on the tre,
On us have mercy and peté,
   And bryng us alle to his tour!

12. (120 *e in catal. table*).
Wright, Songs and Carols (Percy Soc., vol. 23), p. 21:

Of a rose, a lovely rose,
Of a rose I syng a song.
Lyth and lystyn, both old and ȝyng,
How the rose began to spryng.
A fayyrer rose to owre lekyng
Sprong ther never in kynges lond.
V. branches of that rose ther ben,
The wych ben both feyer and clene;
Of a maydyn, Mary, hevyn qwene,
Ouȝt of her womb the branch sprong.
The branch was of gret honour,
That blyssed Mary shuld ber the flour;
Ther cam an angell ouȝt hevyn toure,
To breke the develes bondes.
The secund branch was gret of myȝt,
Yt sprong up on Cristmes nyȝt,
The sterres shone and lemeȝd bryȝt,
That man schuld se it both day and nyȝt.
The III. branch gan spryng and spred,
III. kynges than to branch gan led,
Tho to owre lady in hyr chyldbed,
Into Bethlem that branch sprong ryȝt.
The IIII. branch it sprong to hell,
The develes powre for to fell,
That no soule therin shuld dwell,
The braunch so blessedfully sprong.
The V. branch it was so so swote,
Yt sprong to hevyn both croppe and rote,
In every ball to ben owre bote,
So blessedly yt sprong.

Wright, Songs and Carols (Warton Club, IV, 1855), p. 16 (*MS. Sloane* 2593):

Of a rose, a lovely rose,
Of a rose is al myn song.
Lestenyt, lordynges, bothe elde and ȝynge,
How this rose began to sprynge;
Swych a rose to myn lykynge
In all this wor[l]d ne knowe I non.
The aungil cam fro hevene tour,
To grete Marye with gret honour,
And seyde sche xuld bere the flour,
That xulde breke the fyndes bond.
The flour sprong in heye Bedlem,
That is bothe bryȝt and schen;
The rose is Mary hevene qwyn,
Out of here bosum the blosme sprong.
The ferste braunche is ful of myȝt,
That sprong on Cyrstemesse nyȝt:
The sterre schon over Bedlem bryȝt,
That is bothe brod and long.
The secunde braunche sprong to helle,
The fondys power doun to felle;
Therin myȝt non sowle dw[e]lle;
Blessyd be the tyme the rose sprong.
The thredde branche is good and swote,
It sp[r]ang to hevene crop and rote,
Therin to dwellyn and ben our bote;
Every day it schewit in prystes hond.
Prey we to here with gret honour,
Che that bar the blyssid flowr,
Che be our helpe and our socour,
And schy[l]d us fro the fyndes hond.

Notes to Nos. 13-19.

13. (120 ƒ in catal. table). The version of MS. Add. 5665 (as edited by B. Fehr in Herrig's *Archiv*, vol. 106, p. 275):

Man asay and axe mercy while þou may
In synne yf þou thi lyffe haue ledde
amende the man & be not adrad.
God for the his mercy hathe sprade
Asay asay.
For thof thy synne be neuer so ille
Amende thy sylue man yf that þou wille
God will not that þou spylle
asay, asay.

For he that the so dere hathe boȝste
mercy he wolde that þou soȝste
Iff *thou* hit axske he nayes hit noȝte
asay asay.
Thy lyffe vn erthe her thus þou spende
Prayn*g* to Jhesu þat þou notte shende
Then ioy & blisse shall be thyn ende
Asay, asay.

17. (120 j in catal. table). Chief variations from *Wright's MS.* (*Songs and Carols*, Percy Soc. 23, p. 33):

2 son] sonne is   5 in that] that gret   6 Mary he fell] a maydyn he kneyld.

For 9-16, *W.* has:

Heyll, Mary, full of grace,
God is with the and ever was;
He hath in the chosyn a place.
    Letare.
Mari was afrayd of that syȝt,
That cam to her with so gret lyȝt.

Than seyd the angell that was so bryȝt,
    Letare.
Be not agast of lest ne most,
In the is conseyvyd the holy gost,
To save the soules that war for-lost.
    Letare.

18. (120 k in catal. table). Text of *Sloane MS.* 2593 (Wright, *Songs and Carols*, Warton Club IV, 1855, p. 79):

Nowel, el, el, el,
Now is wel that evere was woo.

A babe is born al of a may,
In the savasyoun of us,
To hom we syngyn bothe nyȝt and day,
Veni creator spiritus.
At Bedlem, that blyssid p[l]as,
The chyld of blysse born he was;
Hym to serve geve us gras,
O lux beata trinitas.
Ther come thre kynges out of the est,
To worchepe the kyng that is so fre,

With gold and myrre and francincens,
A solis ortus cardine.
The herdes herdyn an aungele cry,
A merye song then sungyn he,
Qwy arn ȝe so sore agast,
Iam ortus solis cardine.
The aungele comyn doun with on cry,
A fayr song then sungyn he,
In the worchepe of that chyld,
Gloria tibi, Domine.

The head-line in Ball. is the first stanza of an old Latin hymn (Mone, *Lat. Hymnen des Mittelalters*, I, p. 49):

Conditor alme siderum,
aeterna lux credentium,
Christe redemptor omnium,
exaudi preces supplicum.

Also as heading to the first song in "*Hymnarium Sarisburiense,*" London, J. Darling, 1851.

Flügel points to Daniel, *Thesaurus hymnologicus*, 1, 74; 4, 118, 368.

19. (120 l in catal. table). Variations from *Wright's MS.* (*Songs and Carols*, Percy Soc. 23, p. 60):

1 To the now own] der   2 The whyche was] That was a   3 a songe to] for to   5 mayd] maye   6 layd] laye   7 The prevyteys of heyn ther he saye *W.*   9 Qwhen   10 Thys] Hys   14 A] **Won**   14 a-noder] anodyris   15 To help that we be nott forsake *W.*

Variations from the text in Maitland-Rockstro's "*English Carols*" (1891, from a roll in Trinity Coll., Cambr.), p. 25:

1 To] To the now   2 The wyche was] that were   3 a songe] to the   5 he

Notes to Nos. 19–21.

was] thou were 6–7 The preuytes of hevene forsothe thou say Qwan on crystys
brest thou lay 10 Thys . . . mayd] Thou . . . maydyn 11 his] thy
13 hym] the 14 a-noder] a maydenys 15 Thou be oure helpe we be not
forsake.

The version of MS. Add. 5665 (as printed by B. Fehr in Herrig's *Archiv*, vol. 106 p. 273):

Pray for vs thow prince of pesse
Amice cristi Johannes

To the now cristes derlyng
prince of pes the weche was mayden
    [bothe olde & yong
mi soule ys sette to syng
  Amice Cri*st*i Johannes
On crists breste aslepe he lay
The pr*i*uets of heuen ther he say
For hes was so clene a may
  Amice Christi Joha*nn*es.

Criste before pylet was bro3ste
The clene maydyn forsoke hym no3ste
To dye w*ith* hym was all his tho3ste
  Amice Chri*st*i Joha*nn*es.
Crists moder was hym be take
A mayden to be a nothers ys make
Tro3ffe there helpe we shall not be forsake
  Amice Cri*st*i Johannes.

20. (120 *m in catal. table*). *Variations from Wright's text* (*Songs and Carols*, Percy Soc. 23, p. 95):

Tyrly tirlow] Tyrle, tyrle (*so throughout*) 2 Even abowt the middes off the nyght *W*. 3 Adown from heven thei saw cum a light *W*. 7 that gan] gane them 10 þat] who 11 the feyth wold fong] to the faith wold long 14 sons beme *W*. 15 leme] streme 20 *Additional two stanzas in W*.:

That we may cum unto his blysse,
Where joy shall never mysse,
Than may we syng in Paradice :
  Tirle, tirle.

I pray yow all that be here,
Fore to syng and mak good chere,
In the worship off God thys yere.
  Tyrle, tirle.

21. (120 *n in catal. table*).

Text of Sloane MS. 2593 (*Wright, Songs and Carols*, Warton Club, IV, 1855, p. 88):

Alma Redemptoris mater.

As I lay upon a ny3t,
My thowt was on a mayde bry3t
That men callyn Mary of my3t,
  Redemptoris mater.
To here cam Gabriel so bry3t,
And seyde, " Heyl, Mari, ful of my3t,
To be cald thou art ady3t
  Redemp."
After that word that mayde bry3t
Anon conseyvyd God of my3t,
And therby wyst men that che hy3t
  R.
Ry3t as the sunne schynit in glas,
So Jhesu in his moder was,
And therby wyt man that che was
  R.
Now is born that babe of blys,
And qwen of hevene is moder is ;
And therfore think me that che is
  R.
After to hevene he tok his fly3t,
And ther he sit with his fader of my3t ;
With hym is crownyd that lady bry3t,
  Redemptoris mater.

Text from a MS. roll in Trinity Coll., Cambr. (p. 9 *of Fuller Maitland and Rockstro*, *English Carols of the XVth Century*, London, Leadenhall Press, 1891):

Alma redemptoris mater.

As I lay vp on a nyth.
My thowth was on a berd so brith
That men clepyn marye ful of myth
  Redemptoris mater.
(L)o here cam gabryel wyth lyth.
And seyd heyl be thou blysful wyth.
To ben clepyd now art thou dyth
  Redemptoris mater.
At that wurd that lady bryth
Anon conseyuyd god ful of myth
Than men wyst well that sche hyth
  Redemptoris mater.
(Q)wan ihesu on the rode was pyth,
Mary was doolful of that syth
Til sche sey hym ryse vp rith,
  Redemptoris mater.
Jhesu that syttyst in heuene lyth,
Graunt vs to comyn beforn thi sith
wyth that berde that is so brith,
  Redemptoris mater.

Notes to Nos. 22–33.

22. (120 *o in catal. table*). Wright, *Songs and Carols* (Percy Soc. 23), p. 52:

In Bedlem, that fayer cyte,	As the sune schynyth in the glas,
Was born a chyld that was so fre,	So Jhesu of hys moder borne was ;
Lord and prince of hey degre,	Hym to serve God gyffe us grace,
Iam lucis orto sidere.	*O lux beata Trinitas*.
Jhesu, for the lowe of the,	Now is he oure Lord Jhesus ;
Chylder wer slayn grett plente	Thus hath he veryly vysyt us ;
In Bedlem that fayer cyte,	Now to mak mery among us,
A solis ortus cardine.	*Exultet celum laudibus*.

The simile "As the sun shineth through the glass, so Jesus in her body was," may have been suggested by the following lines in an old Latin hymn (Mone, *Lat. Hymnen des Mittelalters*, I, p. 63): *Ut vitrum non laeditur | sole penetrante, | sic illaesa creditur | virgo post et ante.*

For the line "*Christe redemptor omnium*," see Daniel, *Thesaurus hymnologicus*, I, 256 (No. 243, 1) ; for "*Hostis Herodes impie*" ibid. I, 147 (120,1).

25. (120 *r in catal. table*). For the Latin lines in this hymn see Daniel's *Thesaurus hymnologicus : Christe redemptor omnium* I, 256 (No. 243, 1) ; *Aeterne rex altissime* I, 196 (No. 162, 1) ; *Aurora lucis rutilat* I, 83 (No. 79, 1) ; *Vox clara ecce intonat*, I, 76 (No. 73, 1). —All the eight Latin lines of the song are also to be found as initial lines of hymns in Chevalier's *Repertorium Hymnologicum* (Louvain,1892–1897).

28. (120 *u in catal. table*).

St. 4, l. 3 : he doth to you say] as this does not rhyme with *here* and *fere*, Holthausen (*Anglia* 17, 444) suggests: "he doth you *lere*." Flügel (*Anglia* 26, 242) observes that "What cher?" of the burden might supply the rhyme, which is rhythmically impossible, unless we read "he **sayth**: 'What cher?'" and then let the **whole** burden follow. For we can hardly suppose that the poet could not find a rhyme in such an easy case as that.

29. (120 *v in catal. table*). Chief variations from the text in Wright's "*Songs and Carols*" (Percy Soc. 23), p. 68 :

Heading in *W*. : Off the 5 joyes of owr lady.
A, a, a, a, gaude celi domina.

4 Sua] Tua   7 And sayd, Mary, ful of charyte *W*.   8 *Ave, plena gracia W*.
(*Officiaris* in Ball. is meant for *Efficieris*).
11 syn talkyng] sorow and changyng   12 Inexsa *est*] Enixa es   14 dyght] pyght
15 *in* all menys] and layd in   17 ff.—

The fourth joy was on Holy Thursday,	Whan he shal deme us al and some,
Whan God to heven tok hys way,	*Ad celi palacia.*
God and man withowten nay,	Mary to serve God gyve us grace,
Ascendit supra sydera.	And grete her with joys in every place,
The fyfth joy is for to come	To cum afor hyr sones face
At the dredful day of dome,	*In seculorum secula.*

30. (120 *w in catal. table*).

59. "skyrte" and "scrype," as the rhyme shows, changed their places by a scribal mistake.

33. (120 *z in catal. table*).

1. A babe is born, to blis vs brynge. Prof. Holthausen (*Anglia*, 17, 444) proposes the alteration : "us blis to brynge." But *brynge* might be subjunctive, and the subject ("he") not repeated from the parallel sentence ; cf. 8 / 22 : Whan Mary . . .

174			*Notes to Nos.* 33–35.

Thes word*is* hard, answered anon.—Or "brynge" might be an infinitive without its "to," because the poet could not squeeze it in (see foll. note).
32 "To see" is in the MS. ; "to" was omitted by Flügel (in "Festschrift für Hildebrand") and supplied by Holthausen ; but in l. 34, where Holthausen also conjectures "To be so naylid" the MS. has only "Be," and here again, as in l. 1, we might have an infinitive without "to" before us.
45 For rhyme's sake, Holthausen proposes to alter "grace" to "bliss."

35. (120 *bb in catal. table*). *This piece is run on in the MS., with verse-ends indicated by strokes* (/).—*Variations from the text in Wright's* "*Songs and Carols,*" Percy Soc. 23, p. 12 :
  headl. 4 any *om. W.*   headl. 7 Lullay, by, by, lullay *W.*
  1 This *W.*   2 and to hyr chyld sayd *W.*
  3 My sone, my broder, my fader deyr *W.*   4 hayd *W.*
       5–7 My swete byrd,
           Thus it ys betyde,
           Thow thou be kyng veray ; *W.*
  10 lully, lulley] lullay *W.* (*so throughout*).
  18–19 The chyld than spak in hys talkyng, and to his moder sayd, *W.*
  20 I bekydde am kyng *W.*   21 thowgh] thar *W.*   now *om. W.*
       23–24 For aungeiles bry3t
           Dene to me ly3t,
           Thou knowest it ys no nay (*this line has dropt out in Ball.*) ;
           (And of that sy3t) etc. *W.*
  25 Thou mayest *W.*   26 And] To *W.*
  34 Now, swet son, syn thou art kyng, *W.*   35 lyest þou thus] art thou layd *W.*
  36 & . . . riche] Why ne thou ordende thi *W.*   37 ryche] gret *W.*
  38 by] it is *W.*   39 The . . . myght] That kyng or knyght *W.*
  40 riche] good *W.*
      41 But . . . lulley] And than among
           It wer no wrong
           To syng, by, by, lullay, *W.*
  51 Mary . . . drawe]
      Mary moder, I am thi chyld, thow I be layd in stall,
      Lordes and dukes shal worrshyp me and so shall kynges all. *W.*
  55 But you shall] 3e shall well *W.*   57 To me will cum] Shal come *W.*
  59 your] thi *W.*   68 Jhesu . . . say] Now tell me, swet son, I the pray, *W.*
  69 As . . . dere] thou art me leve and dere *W.*
  70 shall I serue] shuld I kepe *W.*   71 the right good] the glad of *W.*
  72 For all *W.*   74 knoweste it] wetyste full *W.*
      75 Both . . . till] And for all thys
           I wyll the kys, *W.*
  85 Mary . . . Take] My der moder, whan tym it be, **Thou** take *W.*
  88 & in . . . full ofte] And in thi arme, Thou hyl me warme, And kepe ny3t and day ; *W.*—*There is evident confusion both in W. and Ball., the original scheme being* (*abab ccd eed*) :
        Mary moder, I pray þe,
        Take me vp on loft,
        [And sett me ry3t vpon þi kne,] (*so Edinb. MS., see below*).
        And dance me now full ofte (*or :* & handell me full soft);

Notes to No. 35.

```
                             & in thyn arme
                             Thow lappe (or hyl) me warme
                             And kepe nyȝt and day;
                             & yf I wepe
                             & will not slepe,
                             Than syng ' by, by, (lully,) lulley.'
90 & yf] If W.         91 will] may W.         92 Than] Thou W.
100–103 Jhesu . . . skyll] Now, swet son, syn it is so, that all thyng is at thi
wyll, I pray the graunte me a bone, yf it be both ryȝt and skyll. W.
104 ff. What . . . day] That chyld or man That wyl or kan Be mery upon my day,
W.
107 them] hem W.
```

J. Julian, quoting Wright's version in his "*Dictionary of Hymnology*" s.v. *Carols* (209a), adds: "It is set (in modernised English to an old English air) and beautifully harmonised by Dr. Steggall, in *Christmas Carols, by the Rev. Henry Ramsden Bramley, M.A., and John Stainer, Esq., M.A., Mus. D., No.* 25."

The version of MS. Add. 31922 [*Royal MSS. App.* 58] (as edited by Ew. Flügel in "*Anglia*" XII, 270, and in his "*Ne. Lesebuch,*" p. 119):

Another version, printed from a MS. in the Advocates' Libr., Edinb., in Rel. Ant. II. 76.

Thys ender nyȝth [leaf 50b]
I saw a syȝth
A ster as bryȝth as day
And euer among
A maydyn song[:]
by by baby lullay
Thys vyrgyn clere [leaf 51a]
wythowtyn pere
vnto hur son gane sing[:]
my son my lorde
my fathere dere
why lyest thow in hay[?]
me thenke be ryght
thow kyng & knyght
shulde lye in ryche array[!]
yet none the lesse
I will not cess
to syng by by lullay [!]
   Thys babe full bayne
aunsweryd agayne[,]
& thus me thowght he sayde
I am a kyng
above all thyng
yn hay yff I be layde[!]
for ye shall see
that Kynges thre
shall cum on twelfe day[.]
for thys behest
geffe me [thy] brest [leaf 51b]
& syng by baby lullay[!]
My son I say
wythowttyn nay
thow art my derlyng dere
I shall the kepe
whyle thow dost slepe
& make the goode chere.
	This endurs nyȝt I see a syght,
	A sterre schon bryght as day,
	And everymeng a meden song
	was, By, by, lulley!
	        This [endurs nyght].
	
	This lovely lady sete and song,
	and tyll hur chyld con say,
	"My son, my lord, my fadur deyr,
	why lyns thou thus in hey?
	My none swete byrd, what art thu kyd
	and knowus thi lord of ey?
	Never the lesse I will not sesse
	to syng, By, by, lulley!"
	        This [endurs nyght].
	
	"My aune der son, to the I say
	thou art me lefe and dere;
	How schuld I serve the to pey
	and plese on all manere?
	All thi wyll I wyll fulfylle,
	thou wottes ryȝt well in fay;
	Never the leyse I wyll not sesse,
	to syng, By, by, lulley!"
	        This [endurs nyght].
	
	"My dere moder, when tyme it be,
	ȝe tak [me] up on loft,
	And sett me ryȝt apon ȝour kne,
	And hondul me full soft;
	In ȝour arme ȝe kepe me warme,
	both be nyght and day
	Gyff I wepe and will not slepe,
	to syng, By, by, lulley!"
	        This [endurs nyght].
	
	"My aune dere son, sen it is thus,
	that thou art lord of alle,
	Thou shuld have ordent the sum bydyng

176   *Notes to Nos.* 35–9.

[*MS. Add. 31922*]
And all thy whylle (!)
I wyll fulfill
thou wotyst hyt well yn fay[.]
yet more then thys
I will the kys
and syng by baby lullay[.]

My moder swete
when I haue slepe[,]
then take me vp at last
vppon your kne
thatt [y]e sett me
and handell me full soft
& yn your arme
lap me ryght ‖ warme   [leaf 52a]
& kepe me myght (!) & day
and yff I wepe
and can nott slepe
syng by by baby lullay.

My son my lorde
my father dere
syth all ys at thy wyll[,]
I pray the son
graunte me a bone
yff hyt be ryght & skylle[:]
that chylde or man
may euer come
be mercy on thys day[,]
to blys them bryng
& I shall syng
by by baby lullay[.]

My mother shene
of hevyn quene
your askyng shall I spede[,]
so that thy myrth
dysplease me nott
yn [wordys] ‖ nor in dede[,]   [leaf 52b]
syng what ye wyll
so that ye fullfyll
my ten cōmaundements ay[,]
ay yow for to please
let them not sesse
to syng baby lullay.

[*MS. Advoc. Libr.*]
in sum kynge halle.
Me thenkus aryght [a kyng or a knyght],
shuld be in rich arey,
And ȝett for this I woll not seysse
to syng, By and lulley ! "
                    This [endurs nyght].

" My aune dere son, to the I say,
me thynkus it is no laye,
That kyngus shuld com so fer to the,
and thu not to them deny.
Yow sarwn see the kyngus ·III·
apon the twelfe day,
And for that syȝt ȝe may be lyght,
to syng By, by, lollé ! "
                    This [endurs nyght].

My aune der son, sen it is thus,
at all thyng is at wyll,
I pray the grant me a bone,
gyf it be ryght of skylle.
Chyld or man that will or can,
be mery on this gud day,
To hevun blysse grawnt hit us,
and syng, By, by, lulley ! "
                    This . . .
                    [*D*(avid) *L*(aing)].

36. (120 *cc in catal. table*).
2 " bisshoppis & prestis " over an original " lordys " struck out.—and prestis *om.*
Flügel.

37. (120 *dd in catal. table*).   *Variations from Wright's text* (*Songs and Carols*,
Percy Soc. 23, p. 96):
1 vycyce *W.*   2 is is (*so MS.*)] now be *W.*   4 And besyd his dignite *W.*
14 gret debate] ther is gret bate   15 For] and   20 owr eme-Cristyn] owr kyne
21 withowt] without the dore.

39. (120 *ff in catal. table*).   *Text from a MS. roll in Trinity Coll., Cambr.* (*printed
in* " *English Carols of the XVth Century,*" *ed. Fuller Maitland and Rockstro, London,
Leadenhall Press,* 1891, p. 9):

Notes to Nos. 39–49.

Now may we syngyn as it is
quod puer natus est nobis.

This babe to vs that now is bore.
Wundyrful werkys he hath i-wrowt.
he will not lese that was i-lore
but boldly aȝen it bowth.
And thus it is
ffor sothe i-wys.
he askyth nouth but that is hys.
This chaffare louyd he rith weel.
The prys was hey & bowth ful dere
Qwo wold suffre and for vs feele
As dede that prince was owtyn pere
And thus it is, (etc.).
Hys raunsum for vs hath i-payd.
Of resoun than we owyn to ben hys,

Be mercy askyd and he be prayd.
We may be rith kalange blys.
And thus it is, (etc.).
To sum parpos God made man.
I leve weel to saluacyoun
Qwat was his blood that fro hym ran,
But defens aȝens dampnacyoun ?
And thus it is, (etc.).
Almythy God in trynyte.
The mercy we pray wyth hool herte
Thy mercy may all woo make fle.
And daungerous dreed fro vs do sterte.
And thus it is, (etc.).

40. (120 *gg in catal. table*). Variations from the text in Wright's *Songs and Carols* (London, Pickering, 1836; from MS. Sloane 2593), No. XI:
7 Thomas *om. W.*   9 ma*lorum*] demonis *W.*   11 The kn. w. s.] Knyts kemyn
12 Ther they dedyn a wonder thing *W.*   12, 13 *transposed W.*
14 Feruentes insania *W.*   16 þe bisshop] him *W.*
22 To Thomeys they spokyn mekyl pryde *W.*   *After* 25, *one additional stanza in W.*; *after* 30, *two.*

42. (120 *ii*). See Brand's *Popular Antiquities* in W. C. Hazlitt's new edition (*Faiths and Folklore: a Dictionary*, etc. 1905), s.v. "Boar's head" (I, 59b).—For other versions of the present song, see Wright, Percy Soc. 23, No. 20 and 38 ; Ritson-Hazlitt, *Ancient Songs* (1877), 160, 161 ; *Reliquiae Ant.*, 2, 30 ; (modern ones:) Bullen's *Christmas Garland*, p. 171, 172.—Wynkyn de Worde's text of 1521 edited by Flügel, *Anglia* 12, 587 (repeated "Neuenglische sLesebuch" 123).—Texts of **seven** different versions (in modernised form) on pp. 116-126 of W. H. Husk's *Songs of the Nativity.*

49. (120 *pp in catal. table*). *Chief variations from Wright's text* (*Songs and Carols*, Percy Soc. 23, p. 79).
of Gabryell] off the aungell Gabriell
3 from N. to a cite of G. (cf. No. 9, 3)] to N., cite of G.
6 Hath born] conceyvid   15 For he] The wich
15 now b. will be] borne wold be   25 conceyve ... receyve *transposed W.*
29 ff. *The rest runs in W.*:

Sodenly she, abashid truly, but not al thyng dysmaid,
With mynd dyscret and mek spyryt to the aungell she said :
By what maner shuld I chyld bere, the wich ever a maid
Have lyvid chast, al my lyf past, and never mane asaid ?
Than ageyne to hire certeyn answered the aungell,
O lady dere, be off good chere, and dred the never a dell,
Thou shalt conceyve in thi body, mayden, very God hym self,
In whos byrth heven and erth shal joy, callid Emanuell.
Not it, he seid, VI. monethys past, thi cosyn Elyzabeth,
That was barren, conceyvid sent Johan, tru it is that I tell ;
Syn she in ag, why not in yought mayst thou conceyve as well,
If God wyl, whome is possybyll to have don every dell ?
Thane ageyne to the aungell she answered womanly,
What ever my Lord commaund me do, I wyll obey mekely,
Ecce sum humillima ancilla Domini,
Secundum verbum tuum, she seid, *fiat mihi.*

Variations from the text in the Brome Commonplace-book (ed. L. Toulmin Smith, p. 122): salutacion of] songe of Angell   3 from N. to a cite of G.] to nazaret, sytte of gallalye   5 By] throw   6 person sec.] secund persone   9 that he] he fyrst   11 In] With   13 from] of   15 For he] The wyche   16 on the] of   19–28 om. Brome; rest (with a few variations, as a chyld for sent Johan) as in Wright.

The MS. arrangement of the double lines 3, 6, 33, 34, *has been preserved in my text. In Flügel's, who breaks them up, l. 22 has slipt out.*

54. (120 *uu in catal. table*).

25 blessidfull] Holthausen (*Anglia* 17, 444): "full blessid" or " blessful"; Flügel (*Anglia* 26, 265): "blessid"; but see *New Engl. Dict.* s.v. *blessedful* (5 quotations); *ibid.* from Wright's Percy Soc. Carols: "this braunch so *blessedfully* sprong," and one quot. (from Tindale) for *blessedfulness*.

56. (120 *ww in catal. table*).

13 For the unintelligible phrase "He seyth hym self he will not medyll," Flügel suggests "He sauyth hymself who will not medyll."

57. (120 *xx in catal. table*).—*Chief variations from the text in Wright's Songs and Carols* (Percy Soc. 23), p. 28:
1 Thorow] Under   4 a . . . haue] thi . . . hast (thi *throughout*)
7 sat syngyng still] sang full shryll
10 & nere hond þe byrde] Alwey ner and ner   *Stanzas 4 and 5 transposed W.*
15 Do as I bide the] and thou wylt do after me
22 away she yede] in lenȝth and bred
23 she said, whan she songe] she sang whan she show . . .
24 *A concluding stanza is patched on in W.'s text*:

> Away full fast she gan hyr hyȝe;
> God graunt us well our lyves to lede;
> For thus she sang, whan she gan flye,
> "Asay thy frynd or thou have ned."

58. (120 *yy in catal. table*).
1 "As I cam *walkyng* by þe way" is Holthausen's emendation (for the sake of the metre) (*Anglia* 17, 444).
3 ray] Flügel's "kay" (in "Festschr. für Hildebrand"), altered to *array* by Holthausen, was a mere misprint or error (the *k*'s of the MS. very strongly resemble the *r*'s).—Likewise in 12 þer, not þes, is in the MS.
13 Holthausen would cancel *all*.

66b. (53 *in catal. table*). *Variations from the text of MS. Lambeth* 853, *as printed in* "Hymns to the Virgin and Christ," *etc.*, ed. Furnivall, E.E.T.S. 1867 (1895), Orig. Ser. No. 24, p. 4.
2 Heil þe blessidist þat euere bare child!   3 thou conceyved] þat conceyuedist
5 defyl[ed]] filid   7 fayerer then the flowr] þou flour! heil fairest
10 gud] blessid   11 heler of all owr] saluour of al
12 thow . . . þat] þe . . . of
13–14 Heil þou blessid beerde in whom [Crist] was piȝt ! *F.*   15 of] in
17 cumly] crowned   cumforte] fairest   18 brede] bradde
20 & namly] in temynge   22 at] til
26 That Crist chase] Whiche chees þee   27 be . . . ys] þe lanterne þat is ay
28 To þee schulen loute boþe riche & poore *F.*
30 Heil þat al oure ioye of come ! *F.*   33 graunter] ground

35 be thow, cu*m*forte] of coumfortis 36 Heil þe cheeuest of charitee ! *F.*
38 Heil þ*a*t bare Ihe*s*u, Goddis sone ! *F.* 39 Heil tabernacle of þe trynyte ! *F.*
42 lady] modir   sw*e*te] blessid 43 be thou, moder] norische
44 cheff] cheefest   so well thow may] forsoþe to say
45 Lady, kepe vs so i*n* oure last day *F.* 46 his] þi.

67. (62 *in catal. table*). This poem seems, in its Balliol version, to be perfectly identical with the text printed by Caxton ab. 1479,—as a comparison with the samples of Caxton's text given by Blades, *Life and Typography of W. Caxton* (1861-1863), II, p. 49f., sufficiently shows. Caxton also has the epigrammatic four lines at the end " *Wytte hath wonder . . .,*" etc., and they are followed in his print by "six proverbial couplets," evidently the same with those immediately following in our MS. (No. 63 in catal. table) and printed as No. 109 in the present volume.— Furthermore, the pieces immediately preceding this whole complex in our MS., viz. No. 60 (*Stans puer ad mensam*) and 61 (Rhyming rules, printed as No. 108 in this volume), also appear in Caxton in the same form and arrangement, so that we arrive at the conclusion, that the whole group of pieces, No. 60–63 in our catalogue table, were probably *transcribed in a bulk from Caxton's quarto.*

67*b.* This epigram is quoted by Gascoigne in his *Theological Dictionary* as composed by Reginald Pecock, in the form:

> Wyt hath wonder that reson not tel kan,
> How a Moder is Mayd, and God is Man.
> Leue resone, beleue the wonder.
> Beleue hath mastry, and reson is under.

It had a wide popular currency; cf. an *English Chronicle from* 1377–1461, p. 77 (Camden Society, 1855). [Churchill Babington, ed. of the *Repressor* in *Rer. Brit. Medii Aevi Script.*, 1860, p. liv, note, and p. 623].—Cf. also *Reliquiae Antiquae*, I, 127, 205, 257. (In one of these MSS. the piece is also ascribed to Pecock.)

68. (103 *in catal. table*).
4-5 Prof. Flügel suggests "*giue*" for "*In*" at beginning of l. 5.—But perhaps "In" might be preserved, if we suppose "*grace and plen*t*e*" of l. 4 to be corrupted from "*graf*[*f*]*e and plante*" (the scribe could easily misread *grase* for *grafe* of his original, because of the similarity between *f* and long *s* [*ſ*].

Dr. Henry Noble MacCracken of Harvard Univeisity kindly puts at my disposal two copies of this piece from "the Talbot and Beauchamp Hours, two magnificent Psalters of date 1424, written for Lord Talbot and Margaret Beauchamp on their marriage in that year" (MSS. described by Dr. Montague Rhodes James in his Catalogue of the Second Fifty MSS. of Mr. Henry Yates Thompson), of which I here give the various readings.

At the beginning, there is one stanza which does not appear in Ball.

T (*fol.* 81*a*): Glorieux crosse, that with the holy blood
    Of Crist Jhesu halowed wast by grace,
    Glorieux crosse, so mighti and so good,
    That al vertu by heuenly power has!
    Honowred be thow this day in euery place   5
    In his worship whom Iewes crucified
    With nayles thre, & for vs on the died!

(*Readings of B, fol.* 53*a* : 1 the] thi   2 hallwid   4 hast   6 Jwes)
    The stanza headed Vnto the Fader *in the Balliol MS.* (*there are no headings in T and B*) *runs thus in B* :

Most blessid fader & allmyghti lord,
Maker of heuene, creur of createurs,
Of thi grace owre prayers here acorde,
Wiche we presente to thi merciful cures :
Thi gret power, lord, whiche euer dures,   5
Vs deffende from all synne & blame,
Preserve & kepe by vertu of thi grace!

Readings of T: 1 Post (*sic*)   2 creeur of creaturez   3 owre] my   4 we] I).
Further variations from the Balliol text: 8 O lord] Lord *T, B*   by] of *T, B*   grace
&] *deest T, B*   9 Com from hevyn] From the leven *T*, From the heuen *B*   to]
forto *T, B*   10 In to þe vergyn] In the vierge *T, B*   all *deest B*   11 Dessend
... vs] Descendest (Deffendist *or* Dessendist *B*) wolde on me (vn vs *B*)   12 Thin
holy name from the firy cave *T* (holi ... feri *B*)   13 to] *deest T, B*   also] eek(e)
T, B   14 me] vs *B*   17 me nedith] my neede is *T*, vs need *B*   18 *deest Ball.*]
In deffassing of my fowle dedes *T* (owre *B*)   19 dedes *Ball.*] dredes *T* (-is *B*)
20 þat conveyest all them þat] Convoiest (Conuoist *B*) all that *T*   21 My sinnes]
My deffawtes *T*, Oure deffautis *B*   sowle *deest T, B* (oure leche *B*)   22 Holy]
Saint *T, B*   al *before* blessed *T*   23 regnyng] regnant *T, B*   24 thynk] tonge
T, B   25 þe *deest T, B*   dignite] deite *T, B*   26 eche] oure *B*   27 my socowr]
in myn help *T*, in oure help *B*   28 me *deest B*.—*There follows in T only the stanza
corresponding to the closing one* (15) *of our text.*—29 Lady] Marie *B*   31 by] with
B   32 *deest B*   33 to-fore] byfore *B*   34 to kepe me] oure soule to saue *B*
35 bowght vs] he bought hath   36 Deffende vs saint Michael Archange *B*   37
me] vs   38 changes] change *B*   39 In oure helpe pray the euer be *B*   41 I]
we *B* (requere *B*)   42 To be my] Be owre *B*   43 Holy] Saint *B* (*cf. 22!*)   44
Vs geuyn has for to kepe & guyde *B*   45 all ordres *B*   46 Help vs resist ageyn
etc. B   47 of all] all the *B*   non may] non of tham *B*   48 me] vs   am so t.]
ar of t.mater *B*   49 fraylnes] strengh *B*   51 apreuid *B*   54 to dresse]
redresse *B*   55 And] Al *B*   & saint prophetis *B*   56 Pray for me] Prayeth
mekly] humbly *B*   57 I] we *B*   59 James] Jaques *B*   60 Mathew &] Mathias
B   61 Marke] Mair *B*   & saint Tadee *B*   65 & Fabyan *B*   66 Albon] Nigas
B   68 Cosine] Cosme *B*   69 my] oure *B*   70 & all þe] Al *B*   to] vnto *B*
for] of *B*   73 at] by *B*   76 & all] with all *B*   77 Prayght *B*, vs *deest B*
78 charterhows] chartreux   79 prystis] prestres *B*   80 & all religius] & recleux
81 hole, to you] holly here *B*   82 to *deest B*   83 me₁ *deest B*   84 to blis]
vnto blisse sewrly *B*   may *deest B*   85 maudalaine marie *B*   87 Cleothe]
Theophe *B*   89 cicile, berbe *B*   90 luce *B*   91 Prayeth for me in owre most
humble vce   92 all *after* Apostles *B*   93 virges *B* (*cf. 10!*)   94 Pray þat]
Praieth the *B*   indures] dures *B*   95 to forgeve vs owr] forgif myn *B*   96 My
sawle kepe *B*   syn &] symful *B*   98 vs *deest B*.—*Stanza* 15 *of our text is not in
B.*—99 Pray for *deest T*   100 & of owr] Of my   101 thy] with *T*   & I do]
& medeful *T*   102 Spare vs] Space me *T*   103 vs] me *T*   from] & *T*   104
merite *T*   105 vs] me *T*.

69. (118 *in catal. table*).

43 & pray hym, as he was on the rode done] Holthausen (*Anglia* 17, 443) proposes
" Pray hym as he on the rode was done " (supposing the " & " to have crept in from
the following line).

37 The rhyme "*right—fynd*" points to a corruption (Holthausen, *Anglia*, 17,
444). Holthausen suggests " as we fynd hight " for " right as we fynd " in l. 39 ;
but even "**as we fynd right**" would do : cf. 10/22, and note "sprede" thrice
repeated, ll. 18, 19, 22).

Notes to No. 72. 181

72. (29 *in catal. table*). Printed in the folio edition of Sir Thomas More's English Works, 1557, on fol. 5b, 6, 7, 8 (among the first 8 unnumbered leaves, containing his English Poems). Reprinted from a "coarsely and incorrectly printed tract of eight leaves, small octavo size, with cuts" in Huth-Hazlitt's *Fifty Poetical Tracts* (priv. prtd., London, 1875), first series (1493–1600), No. XIII. (Hazlitt's statement in the Introduction, that the poem was not included in the folio edition of 1557, is probably due to the fact, that of the three copies in the British Museum, only the two marked G[renville] 2423 and C. 11. b. 14–15, possess the eight leaves with the poems, whereas in the third one, marked 3751. f. 3, and supplied in the Reading Room, these—and other leaves—are wanting.) In the collation given below, the folio of 1557 is referred to as "fol.", Hazlitt's reprint as "*H.*"

Headings: Certain meters in English written by Master Thomas More in hys | youth for the boke of. Fortune, and caused them to be printed in the be-|gynnyng of that boke. | (5b) The wordes of Fortune | to the people. | *fol.*

H.: ¶ The Boke of the fayre Gentyl-|woman, that no man shulde | put his truste, or confy-|dence in: that is to say, | Lady Fortune : | flaterynge euery man | that coueyteth to | haue all, and specyally, | them that truste in | her.   she decey-|ueth them | at laste. (*woodcut with border inscription* The Lady Fortune).

¶ The Prologue.

> As often as I cōsydre, these olde noble clerkes,
> Poetis, Oratours, & Phylosophers sectes thre,
> Howe wonderfull they were, in all theyr werkes
> Howe eloquent, howe inuentyue in every degre
> Halfe amased I am, and as a deed tre
> Stonde styll, ouer rude for to brynge forth
> Any fruyte or sentence, that is ought worth.
>
> ¶ Neuertheles though rude I be, in all cōtryuyng
> Of matis, yet sōwhat to make, I nede not to care
> I se many a one occupyed, in the same thynge
> So vnlerned men nowe a dayes, wyll not spare
> To wryte, to bable, theyr myndes to declare
> Trowynge them selfe, gay fantasyes to drawe
> When all theyr cunnynge is not worth a strawe.
>
> ¶ Some ī French Cronycles, gladly doth presume
> Some in Englysshe, blyndly wade and wander
> Another in Laten bloweth forth a darke fume
> As wyse as a great hedded Asse of Alexandre
> Some in Phylosophye, lyke a gagelynge gandre
> Begynneth lustely the browes to set vp
> And at the last concludeth, in the good ale cup.
>
> ¶ Finis Prologus.
>   quod . T. M.

(*woodcut*: "St. John before walls of Patmos, sign of Robert Wyer, see Furnivall's ed. of Andr. Boorde's *Dyet.* 223, 394." *Flügel*.)

> Fortune peruersse
> Qui le monde versse
> Tonst a ton desyre
> Jamais tu nas cesse
> Plaine de finesse
> Et y prens pleasire.
>
> ¶ Par toy vēnent moulx
> Et guerres mortaulx
> Touls inconueniens
> Par mons et par vaulx
> Et aulx hospitaulx
> Meurent tant de gens.
>
> Fortune, O myghty & varyable
> What rule thou claymest, with thy cruel power
> Good folk thou stroyest, and louest reprouable

Notes to No. 72.

Thou mayst not waraunt thy gyft*is* for one houre
Fortune vnworthy men setteth in honoure
Thorowe fortune thinocent ī wo & sorow shricheth
The iust man she spoyleth, & the vniust enrycheth.
¶ Yonge men she kylleth, & letteth olde men lyue
Onryghtuously deuydynge, tyme and season
That good men leseth, to wycked doth she gyue
She hath no differēce, but iudgeth all good reason
Inconstaunce, slypper, frayle, and full of treason
Neyther for euer cherysshynge, whom she taketh
Nor for euer oppressynge, whom she forsaketh.
Finis . . q. T. M.

(*woodcut*)
The wordes of Fortune | to the people.
Qu. Tho. Mo.

PART I. 1 auctoritie *fol.*   2 knewe *H.*
3 worsh. & dign.] worship, welth and dignitie *fol. H.* (dynyte *H.*)
9 a] at *fol. H.* (*cf.* 51)   15 hath] hath ther(e) *fol. H.*
17. oþer . . . nys] no other cause there is *H.*
21 lepte &] lept and yet *fol.* ; lept & lept, and *H.*
24 Better . . . shame] Much better is than *fol.*
25 wreche] wretch *fol.*, wryteth (!) *H.*   28 & to] and eke to *fol.*
35 A region hole in ioyfull rest and peace
38 take] folowe *fol.*
PART II. *After* 42 : ¶ Thomas More to them that | trust in fortune. *fol.—H. as the Ball. MS.* (trusteth).
44 kepeste] Repest *fol.*, helpest *H.*   45 shyned] shrined *fol.*, *H.*
47 alway *om. fol.*   51 A] As *fol. H.* (*cf.* 9).   52 &] and she *fol.*
53 But this chere fayned, may not long abide *fol.* 58 brytill] brotle *fol.*, brothle *H.*
63 flateryng] flickeryng *fol.*, flakerynge *H.*   67 dogges] dogges doe *fol.*
70 hoveth] loueth *H.* (" *Sic ! perhaps for* lowreth *or* loketh " *Hazlitt*).
72 pare *Balliol MS.*, pale *fol. H.*   75 dowsy *MS.* (*cf. glossary*), drowsy *fol.*, *H.*
79 londe] loude *H.*, lande *fol.*   80 toye] ioye *H.*   85 thus] thus ye see *fol.*
90 a] as *fol.*, *H.* (*cf.* 9, 51)   92 may not] long may not *fol.*
97 to t. & g.] to geue and take *fol. H.*   98 of] and of *H.*
101 þat] he that *fol. H.*   102 a M tymes] *so H.*, often tymes *fol.*
107 fele] do fele *fol.*
109 what . . . wele] how he doth thynk hym self full wele *fol.*
115 soverayn] great *fol.*   120 enhanceth them] enhaunce hym
122 softe] full soft *fol.*   124 cruell] most cruell *fol.*
126 case] the case *fol. H.*
127 Thus whē she chaunseth, her vncertayne course *H.*, In chaungyng of her course, the chaunge showth this *fol.*   130 to] is *fol. H.*
132 by] be by *fol. H.*   133 in] within *fol.*   135 she loketh on] looketh vppon
136 howshold goth] how shulde go *H.*   138 lese] lyfe *H.*
140 Bekith] Baketh *H.*   142 stode] stode so *fol. H.*   146 no] not *fol. H.*
150 cease *om. H.*   151 blynd] *so H.*, *fol.* : blynded
152 gret labowr] labour great *fol.*   155 the] comen *fol.*   159 good] golde *H.*
161 drawght] draughtes *fol. H.*   172 you to] *so H.*, here *fol.*
176 smyle *fol. H.*   179 in to] and kepe the in *fol.*   184 þe *om. fol.*
187 &] As *H.*   encompace] in compace *fol.*   191 seruant] any s. *fol. H.*

Notes to Nos. 72–74.

194 & loke yet] And yet loke *H*.
196 owt of thy*n* hond] agayne out of thyne hande *fol.*, out of thy hande agayne *H*.
199 Receyue *fol., H.*; the *Balliol scribe, as in several other places of the MS., puts the medical abbreviation for "recipe"* (r *with a curl*). 200 for they] they *fol.*
207 high] on heyth *fol.* 208 ferre] farre *fol.*, faire *H*.
210 borowed] as b. *H*.
PART III. *After* 210 : ¶ Thoma*s* More to them that seke fortune *fol.*; *no new heading H.* 212 full *om. fol.* 219 wrothe] wrought *H*.
221 fishe] fyshes *H*. 224 Hit is] For it is *fol.* 230 ferre] set *H*.
231 fully satysfied is] is full satisfyed.
235 M £] a M. pounde *H*., a thousande pounde *fol.* 239 hath he] hath *H*.
240 no] none *fol. H.* 242 maner] maner of *fol. H.*
245 plucketh] pyncheth *fol. H.* 250 eyther] eche one *fol., om. H.*
253–255 *fol. in the margin*: He meaneth the boke of fortune.
254 ye] you *fol., H.* 257 shall ye] ye shall *fol. H.*
After 259 : *Thus endeth the preface to the booke of fortune* (in italics) *fol.—H.* : Here Fineth Lady Fortune.

¶ **Fortune speketh.**

Fortune ou est Dauid, et Salmon
Mathusale, Josue, Machabee
Olofernes, Alexandre, et Sampson
Julles Cesar, Hector, Ausy, Pompee
Ou est vlyxes, et sa grant remommee
Artur le roy, Godefroy, Charlemaine
Daires le grant, Hercules Tholomee
Ilz sont tous mors, ce, monde est chose vaine.

¶ Quest deuenu Pharon, le roy Felon
Job le courtois, Thobie, et leur lignee
Aristote, ypocras, et Platon
Iudich, Hester, Boece, Peneloppee
Royne dido, Palas, Juno, Medee
Geneiure, ausse la tresnoble Helaine
Palamides, Tristan, auec son espee
Ilz sont tous mors, ce, mōde est chose vaine.

¶ Imprynte by me Robert Wyer dwellyn-
ge, in Saynt Martyns parysse, in
the Duke of Suffolkes rentes,
besyde Charynge
Crosse.
Ad imprimendum
Solum.

73. (56 *in catal. table*). *Variations from the text of MS.* Lambeth 853 (as printed in Furnivall's *"Hymns to the Virgin and Christ," etc.*, E.E.T.S., No. 24, 1867 [1895], p. 91): *In MS. L., the title is explained*: In Englisch tunge, Turne a3en !
1 tyme] noon tijd   2 meryly] myrie   3 me] al
4 spanyell*is*] spaynel   6 hownd*is*] hou*n*d   her] up ful fair
7 I sente my faukun, y leet hi*m* flee   8 deynte] deinteuose
9 vnto her] to his   10 My hownd ga*n* renue wi*th*] I ran þo wi*th* a ful
12 in] al wi*th*   15 wrytyng] written   16 latyn word] word in latyn
17 halyd] knelid   18 meryly] hendeli   20 before full] woout sitten
23 þanne tok y me wiþ si3ynge sare *F*.
24 *There follow 7 stanzas in MS. L., which are wanting in Ball.*
26 norse to] norischiþ   27 To myche] In feele   me*n*] to
29 hawke] herte   30 wyde] ofte   31 thowght] sort
32 : 4 *more stanzas follow in MS. L.—The piece, as Dr. H. N. McCracken informs me, is also found on fol.* 22a–b *of MS. O.* 9. 38 *of Trin. Coll. Cambr.*

74. (57 *in catal. table*).
7 The line seems corrupt.—Flügel prints : Thes prela*tes* full still ther shuld stalke.

Notes to Nos. 75-84.

75. (69 *in catal. table*).
The **burden** is from Solomon's Song 8. 6.
88 Medo *MS.*—Flügel suggests Mede (= Medea). The mistake probably crept in through "Dydo" of the preceding line.
90 Flügel proposes "Fro this clavse I not exclude," but gives the passage up as hopelessly corrupt. Could "for" and "ys" be retained : "for this clavse" meaning "for this conclusion," "as an example to prove the truth stated in the burden," —and "exclude" being a 15th century form of the past participle (recorded in the *New Engl. Dict.* as *exclud*) ?—The syntax of this whole piece is clumsily intricate.
91 means "Many more I may mention," and Flügel's conjecture "many oþer may" is unnecessary.

76. (105 *in catal. table*). Variations from the text in *Rel. Ant.* I, 136 f. (MS. Jesus Coll. Cambr. Q. Γ. 3):
1 *In R. A.* two lines precede : Who that wyll abyde in helle, He most do as me hym telle. 6 whert *R. A.* 14 Goodenes wyrk I wyll on no wyse.
20 Thowgh] Alle 24 Till] To 27 From] For
This piece is also found in *Trin. Coll. Cambr. MS. B.* 15. 45, *fol.* 101 (*described in M. R. James' catalogue*, vol. II, p. 512), *and one similar to it, in Camb. Univ. F. f. V.* 48, *fol.* 43b to 44a. [*Dr. H. N. McCracken.*]

77. (86 *in catal. table*). Variations from the text of MS. Lansd. 762, as printed in *Rel. Ant.* I, 260 :
10 many] sondry 18 I not of whom, howe, ne] I wot not of whome, howe, nor
20. clerely] of.—"*There are several other MSS. of this Testament, including one in Stow's Add. MS.* 29729 (*Brit. Mus.*), *where there is the colophon:* Explicit quod Robartus Peet." [*Dr. H. N. McC.*]

78. *This appears also on fol.* 67a *of MS. O.* 2. 83, *of Trinity Coll. Cambr.* (3½ *stanzas only*).

79. (98 *in catal. table*). Lines 1–11 were first written down, but 5–6 being left out, and 10–11 transposed, the scribe crossed it all through and began again.
21 "movrn" over "syng" struck through.

82. (101 *in catal. table*). Variations from Wright's text (Camden Soc. XVI, 1841):
5 Plus crede litteris, etc. *W.* 6 vanae fallaciae *W.* 7 fallit] fallax *W.*
7 fallit in spacie] virtutis specie *W.* 8 tenuit] habuit *W.*
9 auris] duris *W.* rebus *Leyser* (*quot. Wr.*).
11–12 falsis] fallax *W.* falsus *Leyser.*
26 fugiunt ipsius] hominis sunt ejus *W.* 30 vt quid] cur sic *W.*
33 que magni penditur] *so cod. Reg.* 8, *B. VI.* (*fol.* 29), *rest* : quae magni dicitur (*but* Harl. 206 : quae sic appenditur). 35 rapitur *W.*
38 habet repetere] intendit rapere *W.*
ll. 41–44 *wanting in W.* (but he mentions four additional leonines in cod. Reg. 8).

83. (68 *in catal. table*).
For historical details, see p. li–liii of Th. Wright's introduction to the second volume of "Political Poems and Songs . . . from the Accession of Edw. III to that of Ric. III." (Rerum Brit. Medii Aevi Scriptores, vol. 14, 1861), where the poem itself is printed on pp. 205–207.

84. (71 *in catal. table*). Variations from the text in the folio edition of Sir Thomas More's English Works, 1557 (on the fourth and fifth of the first eight unnumbered leaves in the copy marked 2423 in the Grenville Library, Brit. Mus.). Title : "A ruful lamentaciō writen by master Thomas More in his youth of the deth of quene Elisabeth

Notes to Nos. 84–87. 185

mother to king Henry the eight, wife to king Henry the seuēth, & eldest dowghter to king Edward the fourth, which quene Elisabeth dyed in child-bed in February in the yere of our Lord. 1503. & in the 18. yere of the raigne of king Henry the seuenth."
1 Ye] O ye 3 leve] lyue 7 loo, here I] and lo now here I (*so throughout*).
9 & *om*. 1557. 13 auncetry] auncestry *1557*.
16 If wyt myght haue me saued, I neded not fere *1557*. 17 hold] holpe *1557*.
19 commyth] is come *1557*. 21 He hath me] Me hath he *1557*.
25 O false astrolagy and deuynatrice *1557*.
26 the] thy selfe *1557*. 27 the] thy (proph.) *1557*.
30 synglar] single ("ay" *om*. *1557*). 32 Sondre] In sondre *1557*.
33 yoy: *sic MS*. 36 &] where are *1557*. 38 goodly] Costly *1557*.
40 witsave *Balliol MS*.] vouchesafe *1557*.
41 & your ch.] For you and your children *1557*. 42 place] palyce *1557*.
43 my trew] myn owne dere *1557*. 44 to] both *1557*. 47 on] vppon *1557*.
48 ye] you *1557*. 48 now] and now *1557*. 49 lo] for lo *1557*.
51 sore] ofte *1557*. 54 what we] that we be *1557*.
55 full nye] most nye *1557*. 59 in] a *1557*.
60 my dowghter] my doughter Katherine *1557*. 61 my] myne *1557*.
62 &] or *1557*. 64 lovely] louyng *1557*. 65 your estate] estate *1557*.
68 lady] little *1557*. 68 Cate] Kate *1557*. 69 good babe] swete babe *1557*.
71 Cecill] Cicyly *1557*. 71 Kateryne] Katheryne *1557*.
73 Brygyte] Briget (Flügel read "bryghte" in the MS.). 75 Lo] Now *1557*.
78 & ladyes] a dew my ladies *1557*.
84 seruant*is* now *MS*.] seruant *fol.* (*perhaps the flourish in Ball. is not meant for* -is, *but merely ornamental*).

The Latin epitaph and its English version are not in the edition of 1557. The Latin verses are given in Weever's "Ancient Funerall Monuments," ed. 1631, p. 476, as "transcribed out of a Manuscript in Sir *Robert Cotton's* Library," *with the following variations from the Balliol MS.*: dati (*Flügel* dicti)] ductum *W.*—purpurea] purpureis—mixta] nupta—ac] &—septimo] septime—Henrici] Henrice—Exemplar] Exemplex—probitata] probitate—gefferos (*sic MS*.)] Nestoreos *W.*

85. (88 *in catal. table*). Variations from the text of MS. Lansdowne 762, as printed in *R(eliquiae) A(ntiquae)*, I, 205, and that of MS. Cotton. Vitellius A. XVI, as printed in Laing's and Schipper's editions of Dunbar (*D*).
2 semlyest] most symbliest *R. A.* by] in *D*. 7 full *om*. *R. A.*
9 a non *Ball.*, *R. A.*; a man *D*. 9 Troynomond *R. A.* (*see glossary.*)
10 called] cleped *D*, *R. A.* 11 stante] stonde *R. A.* 12 joye *Ball.*] of joy *D*.
17 jasper *D*, *R. A.* 19 sterne-vite] strenuytie *D*, treunytie *R. A.* (*see glossary.*)
22 trone] *so R. A. and MS. Cotton*; Crowne Laing, crone *Schipper*.
23 prosellyng] precelling *R. A.*, *D*. 26 boryall] boriall *R. A.*, beryall *D*.
27 down] a-downe *R. A.* 28 doth . . . fayre] swymeth with wynge fare
29 s. and r.] rowe and sayle *R. A.* 29 thayre] are *D*.
31 but] and not *D*, *R. A.* 33 of] with *R. A.* 36 fyne *om*. *R. A.*, *D*.
42 the₁] thy *D*. 42 þat *om*. R. A. 44 be₂] are *R. A.* 46 þer] thy *R. A.*
51 Venys] Denys *R. A.* 52 hym] to hym *D*. 53 examplar] example *R. A.*
The Balliol version has been printed in Herrig's *Archiv*, 101 (1898), 144, and *Anglia*, 26, 199. See also *Archiv*, 90, 151 (Zupitza on the Lansd. MS. 762) and 91, 241 (J. Schipper on the Balliol MS.).

87. (73 *d in catal. table*). *Wynkyn de Worde's text of* 1521 (*as reprinted from the Douce Fragment* 94*b*, Bodl., *in* "*Anglia*" 12, 587 *by Ew. Flügel*) (*also* "*Neuenglisches Lesebuch,*" Halle 1895, p. 151):

Notes to Nos. 87–89.

A caroll of huntynge.

As I came by a grene forest syde
I met with a forster þat badde me abyde
With hey go bet / hey go bet / hey go, howe.
¶ Underneth a tre I dyde me set
And with a grete hert anone I met
I badde let slyppe / and sayd hey go bet
With hey go bet / hey go bet howe.
¶ I had not stande there but a whyle
For the mountenaunce of a myle
There came a grete herte without gyle
There he gothe / there he gothe. &c.
We shall haue sporte and game ynowe.
¶ Talbot my hoūde with a mery taste
All about the grene wode he gan cast
I toke my horne and blewe him a blast
with tro / ro / ro / ro : tro / ro / ro / ro.
With hey go bet / hey go bet. &c.
Ther he goth / there he goth. &c.
We shall haue sport and game ynowe.
¶ Finis.

89. (23 *in catal. table*). Variations from Wright's text (Percy Soc., 23), p. 53 (also given in *Anglia* 26, 134 ff. ; see *ibidem* for parallels in Latin prose).
4 Dulcia *W*. 5 *Cf. Luc.* 6. 44 : unaquaeque enim arbor de fructu suo cognoscitur (*Flügel*). 9 vynnayard *W*. 12 *Gen.* 9. 20. 13 knowyng *W*.
17 *Gen.* 14. 18. 18 vinic*um* *Flügel*. 21 fyrst of myraculs *W*.
23 Galylee *W*. (galyles *MS.* : *Flügel*). 25 the watur *W*.
26 *aque . . . idrie,* stone pitchers [full] of water, *lapideae hydriae,* Joh. 2. 6, 7 (*Flügel*). 34 Ps. [Vulg.] 103. 15 : ut . . . vinum laetificet cor hominis (*Flügel*).
37 ffumosetyse *Flügel,* fumosytesse *W*. 38 generant *W*. 40 mesticiam *W*.
41 specyfyeth *W*. 41 *Eccl.* 40. 20 (not 1 !) : vinum et musica laetificat cor (*Flügel*). 43 delyeth *W*. 43 For "ys" Flügel proposes " and " or " with."
45 boys *W*.—The reference is to a work formerly ascribed to Boethius, from which Flügel quotes (ed. 1570, fol. 1280, cap. 2) : autem modice sumptum intellectum nidetur conferre acumen, non autem modice sumptum rationem perturbat, intellectum hebetat, memoriam eneruat. 47 se wit*h*owt] fynd wit*h*owten *W*.
51 prefute *W*. 53 &] in *W*. 54 loquentibus *W*.

57 *W*.: Good wyne receyvyd moderatly
Mox cerebrum letificat;
Drunkyn also soberly,
Omne membrum fortificat.
Naturall hete well it strenggthes,
Digestionem roborans;
Helth of body also it lengthes,
Naturam humanam prosperans.

67 men to ete þer] a man wel to ete his *W*. 69 age *om. W.*—ll. 69 and 70 had dropt out in Flügel's transcript. 71 It gather to hym *W*.
72 *purgat venas W*. 73 Me thynkyth, syrs, by thes causys *W*.
75 That wyne is best of al drynkkys 76 *notabiles* 77 bealamy *W*.
78 *mihi iam W*. 80 *vinum nunc W*. 82 Nam *om. W.*
83 Fyll the cope by the brynk 84 *bibere W*. 85 all *om. W.*
87 þe good] this *W*. 89 wynes 90 hoc *W*. (hō *MS.,* see Flügel).
91 sone] self hene] hens 92 *siciant W*.

Notes to No. 90.

90. (99 *in catal. table*). *Variations from Wright's text* (*Songs and Carols*, Percy Soc. 23, p. 91):

1 I shall] I will	16 Can yow ought tell full well *W.*	22 wyste] it wyst
25 owr] yowr	33 Fore a galon off wyn thei will not wryng *W.*	62 is it] it is
63 chereth] cherisheth	64 jonkers] jonckettes	75 defend] amend
86 I-wis *W.*	93 haue] shall have	95 thowgh he haue a berde] though I have no berd
97 a-way] her wey	115 whan] where	
118 pleased] be plesyd	119 eased] reisyd	138 *In W., two more stanzas follow:*

Who sey yow, women, is it not soo?
Yes, suerly, and that ye wyll know;
And therfore lat us drynk all a row,
And off owr syngyng mak a good endyng.

Now fyll the cupe, and drynk to me;
And than shal we good felows be,
And off thys talkyng leve will we,
And speak then good olf women.

The version of the Cotton MS. Titus A. XXVI (*incomplete at the beginning*) (*printed in Ritson's "Ancient Songs," ed. Hazlitt, II,* 117, *and in notes to Wright's "Songs and Carols," Percy Soc. 23, p. 104*).

"Lytyll Thanke."

* * * * * * *

Go ye beffore, be twayne and twayne,
Wysly that ye be not i-sayne [agayne
And I shalle (I'll *R.*) go home and com
To witte what dothe owre syre,
 Gode gosyp.

For yyff hit happ he dyd me see,
A strype or to God myght send me,
Yytte sche that is aferre lette her flee,
For that is nowght be this fyre,
 Gode gosyp.

'Tho' (*MS.* That) everyche of hem
 browght ther dysche,
Sum browght fleshe and som browght
 fysche;
Quod Margery meke thann with a wyise;
I wold that Frankelyne the harper were
 here, Gode gosip.

She hade notte so sone the word i-sayd,
But in come Frankelyn at a brayd,
God save youe, mastres, he sayde,
I come to make youe some chere,
 Gode gosyp.

Anon he began to drawe owght his harpe,
Tho the gossyppes began to starte,
They callyd the tawyrner to ffyll the
And lette note for no coste, [quarte,
 Good gosyp.

Then seyd the gossyppes all infere,
Streke up, harper, and make gode chere,
And wher that I goo, fere or nere,
To owre hu[s]bondes make thou no *boste*,
 Good gossip.

Nay, mastres, as mote I thee,
Ye schall newyr be wrayed ffor me,
I had lever her dede to be
As hereof to be knowe,
 Good gosyp.

They ffylled the pottes by and by,
They lett not for no coste trully,
The harpyr stroke up merrely,
That they myght onethe blowe,
 Good gosyp.

They sette them downe, they myght no
 more,
Theyre legges they thought were passyng
 sore,
They prayd the harper kepe sum store,
And lette us drynke a bowght,
 Gode gosyp.

Heye the taverne[r] I praye the,
Go fyll the potteys lyghtyly,
And latte us dry[n]ke by and by,
And lette the cupe goo route,
 Good gosyp.

This ys the thowght that gossypes take,
Onys in the weke they wyll merey make,
And all smalle drynckys they wyll forsake,
And drynke wyne of the best,
 Good gosyp.

Some be at the taverne onys in the weke,
And some be there every day eke,
And ellse ther hartes will be seke,
And gyffe her hosbondys ewyll reste,
 Good gosyp.

When they had dronke and mad them
 glad,
And they schuld rekyn theyn they sad,
Call they tavernere anone they bade,
That we were lyghtly hens,
 Good gosyp.

I swere be God and by Seynt Jayme,
I wold notte that oure syre at home,
[Shold wyt] that we had this game,
Notte for fourty pens,
 Good gosyp.

Gadyr the scote and lette us wend,
And lette us goo home by lurcas ende.
For dred we mete note with owre frend
Or that we come home,
        Good gosyp.
When they had there countes caste,
Everyche of hem spend six pens at the last,
Alas, cothe Syscely, I am agaste,
We schall be schent everychone,
        Good gosyp.
Fro the taverne be they all goone,
And everyche of hem schewythe her wysdom,
And there sche tellythe her husband anone,
Shee had been at the chyrche,
        Gode gosyp.

Off her werke she takythe no kepe,
Sche muste as for anowe go sclepe,
And ells for angeyr (MS. aggeyr) wyll sche wepe,
She may no werkes wurche,
        Good gosyp.
Off her slepe when sche dothe wake,
Faste in hey then gan sche arake,
And cawthe her serwantes abowte the bake,
Yff to here they outhe had sayd,
        Good gosyp.
Off this proses I make an end
Becawse I will have women to be my ffrend,
Off there dewosyon they wold send
A peny for to drynke at the end,
        Gode gosyp.

The song is also printed in Professor Arber's "*Dunbar Anthology*."

91. (130 *in catal. table*.) *Variations from the text in Wright's "Songs and Carols"* (Percy Soc. 23), p. 86 :
vidist*is*] vidisti   1 blamys] blame   2 she . . . he *Ball.*] he . . . she *W.* (*an evident mistake in Ball.*)   13 On thyng for-soth] Every where   15 For yf they be] And if thei were   19 Yes] Yes, by Christ   27 skuse] scewise   30 ther] owr   30–31 saue . . . knave] saves . . . knaves   43 *with* evyll] in the devillis   47 suerly] by my trowth   51 l. of hys w.] off hys wiffe leve   53 &] or

95. (137.) *Variations from Wright's text ("Songs and Carols,"* Percy Soc. 23, p. 88):
Cui*us*] Eius   17 wonderly] wonder   21–22 Fore by women was never man betraied, Fore by women was never man bewreyed *W.*   28 they] women   34 dele] presse   38 a woma*n*] women   43 wold be] shulbe   48 kyrchers] kerchefs   49 yll] evil. In l. 3, the rhyme requires "secree."

96. (138 *in catal. table*). MS. Lambeth 306, fol. 135 ("Song on Woman," *Rel. Ant.* I, 248):

Women, women, love of women
Make bare purs with some men.
Some be nyse as a nanne hene,
   ʒit al thei be nat so ;
Some be lewde, some all be shreude,
   Go schrewes wher thei go.

Sum be nyse, and some be fonde,
And some be tame y undirstonde,
And some cane take brede of a manys honde ;
   Yit all thei be nat so.

Some cane part withouten hire,
And some make bate in eviri chire,
And some cheke-mate withoute sire ;
   Yit all they be nat so.
Some be lewde, and some be schreued :
   Go wher they go.

Some be browne, and some be whit,
And some be tendre as accripe ;

And some of theym be chiry ripe :
   Yit all thei be not so.
Sum be lewde, etc.

Some of them be treue of love,
Benethe the gerdelle, but nat above ;
And in a hode above cane chove ;
   Yit all thei do nat soo.
Sume be lewde, etc.

Some cane whister, and some cane crie ;
Some can flater, and some cane lye ;
And some can sette the moke awrie ;
   Yit all thei do nat soo.
Sume be lewde, etc.

He that made this songe full good, [blode,
Came of the northe and of the sothern
And somewhat kyne to Robyn Hode ;
   Yit all we be nat soo.
Some be lewde, etc.

Notes to Nos. 96-99.

Variations of the Balliol text from Wright's ("Songs and Carols," Percy Soc. 23, p. 89): Heading in W.:

   Women, women, women, women,
   A song I syng even off women.

2 besy] good   13 wroth] angry   32-33 *transposed W.*   34 they do] be
97. (139 *in catal. table*). *Variations from the text in Wright's "Songs and Carols"* (Percy Soc. 23, p. 66). *In W., two lines precede the poem by way of heading:*

   Whane thes thynges foloyng be done to owr intent,
   Than put women in trust and confydent.

3 bromes bere appyll*is*] ges ber perles   4 in þe croppis so hie] abundantly
6 lek*is*] kyskys   in þer sup.] sup.   7 Than put women in trust and confydens *W.*   *After 7, there follows in W. the stanza:*

   Whan box ber papur in every lond and towne;
   And thystuls ber berys in every place;
   And pykes have naturally fethers in ther crowne;
   And bulles of the see syng a good bace;
   And men be the schypes fyschys do trace;
   And in women be fownd no incypyens;
   Than put hem in trust and confydens.

9 in p*a*rkys hornys] ther hornnys in forestes   10 And marmsattes morn in mores and in lakys *W.*   11 rolyons] rokes   12 & grg. r. i*n* h.] And goslynges hunt   13 And sprates ber sperys in armys of defens *W.*   14 Tha*n* put i*n* a woma*n* your] Than put women in. *Here, another additional stanza follows in W.:*

   Whan swyn be conyng in al poyntes of musyke;
   And asses be docturs of every scyens;
   And kattes do hel men be practysyng of fysyke;
   And boserds to scryptur gyfe ony credens;
   And marchans by with horne insted of grotes and pens;
   And pyys be mad poetes for ther eloquens;
   Than put women in trust and confydens.

15 & st. hie] on a hyth   17 clothes horsis for to drye] tymber howsis to dyth
18 semewes bryn*g*] fomaus ber   19 woddowes] wodkokes   theves] cranis
20 griffons] gren fynchys   21 i*n* a woma*n* you*r*] women in
22 crabb*is* tak wodcok*is* i*n* forest*is*] crowves tak sarmon in wodes
23 swetnes of] swyftes and   24 w*i*th þer here] in the eyer   perchis] larkes
25 mowe corn] move mountans   wafeyyng] wagyng   26 And schypmen tak a ryd in sted of saylles *W.*   27 Wha*n* shrewed wyff*is*] And wha*n* wyfvys
28 i*n* a woma*n*] women in. *A final stanza follows in W.:*

   Whan hantlopes sermountes eglys in flyght;
   And swans be swyfter than haukes of the tower;
   And wrennys set goshaukes be fors and myght;
   And musketes mak vergese of crabbes sower;
   And schyppes seyl on dry lond, syll gyfe flower;
   And apes in Westmynster gyf jugment and sentens;
   Than put women in trust and confydens.

99. (141 *in catal. table*). *The text of MS. Harl.* 5396, *as printed in Ritson's "Ancient Songs"* (ed. Hazlitt, 1877, II, 113).

Nay, Ivy, nay,
Hyt shal not be I-wys;
Let Holy hafe the maystry,
As the maner ys.

Holy stond in the halle,
Fayre to behold;
Ivy stond wythout the dore,
She ys ful sore a-cold.
  Nay, Ivy [&c.].

Holy and hys mery men,
The dawnsyn and they syng;
Ivy and hur maydenys,
They wepyn and they wryng,
    Nay, [&c.].

Ivy hath a kybe,
She kaght yt with the colde,
So mot thay haf ae (*sic*),
That wyth Ivy hold.
    Nay, Ivy, 'nay', hyt [&c.].

Holy hat berys,
As rede as any rose,
The foster [and] the 'hunter' (hunters *MS*.)
Kepe hem fro the 'doos' (doo *MS*.)
    Nay, Ivy, nay, hyt [&c.].

Ivy hath berys,
As blake as any slo,
Ther com the oule,
And ete hym as she goo.
    Nay, Ivy, nay, hyt [&c.].

Holy hath byrdys,
A ful fayre flok,
The nyghtyngale, the poppynguy,
The gayntyl lavyrok.
    Nay [&c.].

Gode Ivy,
What byrdys ast thu?
Non but the howlat,
That kreye how, how!
Nay, Ivy, nay,
Hyt shal not [be, I-wys,
Let Holy hafe the maystry,
As the maner ys.]

(See Brand-Ellis, *Popular Antiquities*, I, 68, 519; Brand-Hazlitt, I, 318.)—For other songs on the same subject, see Wright, Percy Soc. 23, Nos. 40, 69, 70.—Cf. also Halliwell's *Nursery Rhymes* 77, 109, and a love-song of Henry VIII in F. M. Padelford, *Early XVIth Century Lyrics* (*Belles-Lettres Series*), Boston, U.S.A., 1907, p. 77 (No. LVIII.), and references in his note (*ib.*, p. 140).

102. (145 *in catal. table*). Variations from the text of *Porkington MS*. (as printed in Halliwell's *Early English Miscellanies*, Warton Club, II, p. 6).

3 her of all] hereof   4 fele] felte   7 þis] yowre   8 that *Ball. MS*.] That whenne *P*.   8 can] may (*throughout*)   12 smarte] lowf, swyt   15 But] That 18 dyn*er*siteis] dyveris wyse   19 From] Now the   22 That men thus morneth] That this morne   25-27 shall rise . . . no*n* ale ywis] ryse schalle . . . noo ale   37 a bare] avore   41 well *om.* Porkgt.   43 this] the 44 Old glovis] Glowys   48 &] That   49 narrowar] more 52 In yche a spas and stede by a spone *P*.   56 Yet] and yet 57 Thus] This   59 myn entent] my tent   62 quaynt] cayey (*i. e.* coy).

103. (21 *in catal. table*). For a complete collation of the present text with all versions printed in recent collections, the reader is referred to Professor Flügel's edition of it in *Anglia*, 26 (*neue folge*, 14), 104-132.

106. (22 *in catal. table*). For variants of MS. Lambeth 306 (E.E.T.S., orig. ser. 15, 24) and explanatory references to Blackstone's Commentaries and Pollock-Maitland's Hist. Engl. Law, see *Anglia* 26, 133 (l. 8: Bl. 2, 136; P.-M. 3, 420;—l. 9: Bl. 2, 60;—l. 10, Bl. 2, 324;—l. 11: Bl. 3, 300;—l. 13: P.-M. 2, 19; Bl. 2, 112;—l. 14: Bl. 2, 160;—l. 16: Bl. 2, 42;—l. 20: P.-M.2, 661.—In l. 18, Flügel proposes *couerture* for *couerde baron*, with a reference to 34 Hen. VIII, c. 22).—*These "Rules" appear also in MS. O. 2. 53. of Trinity Coll. Cambr. fol. 24a.* [*Dr. H. N. McC.*]

108, 109 (*in catal. table*, 61 *and* 63 *respectively*) were probably taken by the writer of our MS., together with "*Salve Regina*" and "*Stans Puer ad Mensam,*" from a quarto volume of Caxton, No. 14 in Blade's list (*Life and Typography of W. Caxton*, 1861-3, II, 49-51). See note on "*Salve Regina*" (**67**a) above.]

Additional note. Unfortunately, I have been no more able to use the collection of *Early English Lyrics* (1250-1550) lately published by E. K. Chambers and F. Sidgwick.

GLOSSARY.

THE references are to page and line, and in cases of possible ambiguity, to page, piece, and line. The explanations kindly contributed by Dr. Henry Bradley are marked [H. B.].—O. E. = Old English; *N. E. D.* = *New English Dictionary*.

abone, above, (O. E. *abufan*), 4/6/11.
abseruance, see *affende*.
abyde, to undergo, suffer, 70/72.
advise, same as *avise*, to consider attentively, 77/166.
affende = *offende*, 79/225. (The MS. has frequent spellings of this kind; cf. *apprese*, 3/5/7, *appose*, 117/100/12, *abseruance*, 119/102/18.)—Flügel reads *assend*, and identifies it with *ashend* (bring to shame).
allther (O. E. *ealra*), of all; *all*-þernerest, most near, 89/28.
almyght (in *God almyght*), almighty.
ament, 121/43, minded?
among, used adverbially; all the while, at the same time, 11/20/10; 13/23/15; 25/35/headline;—alway, 93/19;—from time to time, 107/64; sometimes, 109/37.
apayd, satisfied, 127/414.
appose, to oppose (see *affende*), 117/100/12 (referring to a contest in singing).
apprese, oppress (see *affende*), 3/5/7.
artylary, warlike munitions, implements of war, 101/39.
a(s)say, "to learn or know by experience" (*N. E. D.*, s. v., 11), to have an immediate experience of, to see, 6/10/24;—to try, endeavour, 8/13/headline;—to try, put to the test, 47/57/headline.
asell, 66/44 = *aysell*.
aseth ("*assethe*, from O. Fr., *as*[*s*]*et*, pronounced *asse*þ,"*N.E.D.*), amends, expiation, 87/78/5.
a towt, *a towght*, = Fr. *à tout*? 118/101/headline, 119/101/burden (rhyming with *how* and *rowght*).
aventure: *at av.*, "at a venture," at random, 75/88.

awarde, keeping, care, custody, wardship, 51/2.
a-wene (O. E.* *on-wēnan*), to 'ween,' think, imagine; *pp. a-went*, 111/9.
ay: *withowt ay*, 16/29/17: "there may have been a phrase *withouten eȝe* = Chaucer's 'oute of drede'" [meaning "without doubt"]—[H.B.]
aye, again, 80/14.
aysell, vinegar, 120/2.

bable, bauble; *geveth them a bable*, gives them a (fool's) bauble, makes fools of them, 88/24.
balke, ridge in a field (between the furrows), 81/2.
barn, child, 2/1; *barn-teme* (O. E. *bearn-tēam*), brood, progeny, child, 1/15.
bate, debate, quarrel, 114/32.
bayn (Old Icel. *beinn*), ready, 85/79.
bede, childbed, 7/12/18 (Wright's MS. has *chyldbed*).
beheste, promise, 25/58; **behight**, promised, 56/68.
beke: *bekith hym*, warms himself, 76/140.
belamye (Fr. *bel ami*), term of address; friend, sirrah, 106/77.
belyff = *blive*.
beme, stock, tree, 7/12/5.
bente, field, 84/17.
beryng, birth, 18/75.
besette, placed in, surrounded with—, 95/26.
bestede: *hard bestede*, in woful plight, hard beset, 59/20.
betake, *pp.* assigned, committed, 11/19/13.
betide, *pret.* befell, 105/23.
betriste, *pp.* trusted, confided in, 35/2.

bett, in *go bett,* used as a hunting cry, 104/87/5 ("origin and meaning doubtful," *N.E.D.*);—the **bett,** the better, 123/156.

beware, beware, take warning by, 95/8 (see *N.E.D.* for the contamination of two phrases in this word; for the meaning here occurring, cf. *ib.* I, 3 [*obs.*]).

ble (O. E. *blēo*), colour, 85/105.

blessidfull, blissful, 45/25 (see *N. E. D.* s. v. '*blessedful*').

blive (*belyff*), instantly, 96/63; 122/85.

blyn, cease, end, 56/55; *substantively,* 65/5.

bon: "*bright as bone*" (polished bone or ivory), 85/114.

boryall, 101/26; Cotton MS. *beryall,* "shining like beryl" (Jamieson).

bote, help, aid, salvation, 8/12/27, 12/23/6.

brace, to embrace, press to one's bosom, 65/11.

brede, breadth, 82/2.

brede, *vb.*, used intransitively: was 'bred,' conceived, 59/18.

breth, 67/14, *duryng your breth,* while you live.

broyd (thus spelt; usually *brayd*) O. E. *brægd*), a moment, short while, 16/30/12.

buske, to address, direct one's self (Icelandic *búask*), 84/17.

but, without: *but compare,* without comparison, peerless, 101/31 (other MSS. *and not*).

by and by, indicating succession in an enumeration, 8/29;—in course, in turn, 75/95;—immediately, 118/3.

bydene, together, 85/87.

bye agayn, to redeem, 13/3; **bowght,** *pret.*, 4/6/16.

bynke, bench, 93/22.

byrde (O. E. *brȳd*), lady, maiden, 58/25.

can: *ne can,* knows not, cannot comprehend, 61/1.—*can,* phraseological like *gan,* did, didst, 55/12.

canon, part of the Roman Catholic mass: secret prayers before and after the consecration, 70/64.

carayn, carrion, 86/77/4.

cast, to plan, purpose, intend, 109/50.

Chade: *seynt Chade* (O. E. *Ceddda*), a Northumbrian monk, educated at Lindisfarne, made abbot of Lastingham in Deira in 664, bishop of York, and later of Mercia (died 672); 113/3.

chaplary, scapular, 124/239.

charterhows, Charterhouse monk, Carthusian, 64/78.

chaste, to chastise, moderate, 121/30.

chekmate, mate! (the victor's cry), 88/12; *adj.*, beaten (at chess), 111/55 (used in pun with *cheek*) (see *N.E.D.*, s. v. *check-mate, adj.*)—*play chekmate with owr sire,* cheat even God himself? (see *N. E. D.*, s. v. *check-mate ,subst.*, 1 c. : *to play check-mate with*) (Wright's MS. has *And some cheke-mate withoute sire*) 114/33.

chery fayre: 'cherry-fair,' a fair held in cherry-orchards for the sale of fruit, often the scene of boisterous gaiety and licence; hence used as a symbol for shortness of life and fleeting nature of its pleasures (see *N. E. D.*), 87/78/8.

chest, in the sense of womb, body? 63/52 ("in thy mother's womb"),— or *adj.*, 'chaste' ("within thy chaste mother")? (rhyme: *Baptyste*!).

clewens (plural formed by double ending), clews, 110/18 (O. E. *cliwe,* plur. *cliwan*).

clynge, to dry up, shrink (the reverse is meant), 120/38.

coif, coyf, "the white cap worn by a serjeant-at-law as part of his official dress," hence *seruants of the coyf* (Appendix, passim) see *N. E. D.*, s. v. *coif, sb.*, 3 b.

comprehendid, in the sense of *compared,* 42/2.

coueytise, covetous, 89/45.

cowght, coughed, 118/25.

crach, crib, manger (O. F. *cre[s]che*), 38/48/13.

crached, scratched, 124/235. (Cf. German *kratzen,* to scratch.)

cran-colowred, of the colour of the cranberry?—(*Appendix,* 163/4).

crok, to 'crook,' bend, bow, stoop, crouch, 95/36;—to bend, curve, 129/32.

cure, 3/6/3, *her cure . . . euer dyde*

endure, "all her thought, occupation, ever continued to be 'Deo gratias'" [H. B.].—9/16/7, *by hevynly cure,* by heavenly ministration, agency;—95/35, *at my cure,* under my charge, hence : at my disposal? ("a forced use, perhaps for rime" [H. B.]).

danger, control, power, 89/34.
dangerus, hard to please, 115/6.
debate : *men thynk gret debate,* quarrel in their thoughts, hold discordant opinions, 28/14.
dede, death, 89/28.
defens, *withowt defens,* "unavoidably, inevitably" (*N. E. D.*), 57/14.
defface, to efface, wipe out, 64/69.
defferre, to put off, hesitate, 85/78.
degree : *in euery degree,* throughout, 44/18.
delygence : *dyde ther delygence,* made efforts, did their utmost, to bring it about, 96/52.
dere (O. E. *derian*), to injure, hurt, hit, 91/50 ;—subst. *withowten dere* . (O. E. *daru*), a mere emphasizing phrase (cf. *ay, dred*), 14/26/2.
deserne, discern, comprehend, 62/24.
dett, due, 6/16.
devise, devyce: *vayn devise,* idle thoughts, 36/2 ; *at my devise,* at my disposal, 72/7 ; *in my devyce,* that I can think of ;—vb. : to appoint, 79/248.
dight, dyght: *me dyght,* address myself, direct my steps, 18/7 ; *on rode dyght,* of crucified Christ, *passim ; deth ys dight* : appointed, ordained, 53/36 ; 53/59.
discryved (for *discried,* see Mätzner, s.v. *descrien,* 1), proclaimed, 84/23.
dispayre, disparagement ? 72/17 ; *disprayse,* cj. Flügel.
distance, estrangement, discord, 28/26.
doluen (*pp.* of *delve*), buried.
domysman, judge, 13/23/23.
don, ended, 112/6.
dowsy, stupid, 74/77 ("related to *dozy,*" *N. E. D.,* where see another quotation from Th. More).
dowt, dowght, fear, 31/18, 76/142, 83/22, 108/117 ; *vb.,* 87/25.
dre (O. E. *drēogan*), 'dree,' bear, endure, 84/56.
dred, afraid, 8/13/6.—**drede,** to CAROLS.

doubt, 53/42 ; *without drede,* without doubt, 67/10.
dresse, *refl.,* to direct one's course, take one's way, 24/46 ; *drest hym,* took his way, appeared, 4/8/6.—*to dresse,* to right, put right, 63/54.
drowgh : *lightly than he drowgh,* 122/93, considered by Zupitza as a corruption ; *ryght meryly than he lowe*(*lowgh,*laughed)*Porkington MS.*
dymes (O. F. *dismes,* Lat. *decimas*), tithes, 82/37.
dyne, 'din,' voice, phrase, sentence (forced use, for rhyme), 84/47.

eme-Cristyn (O. E. *efencristena*), "evenchristian" (*Hamlet,* V, i, 32), fellow-Christian, 28/20 ; **evyn Cristyn,** 141/*c*/8.
enclyn, to sink, fall, 90/23.
encompace (*in compace,* see readings), together, in a bulk ? 77/187.
enders : *this enders nyght,* the other night, one, or a few nights ago, 25/headl. (see *N. E. D.* s.v. *ender;* also Flügel, *Neuengl. Lesebuch,* p. 431 f. The word is probably from O. Icel. *endr,* "formerly, else, again").
engyne (*ingenium*), understanding, skill, 77/188.
ensure, assure, 39/49/23.
entent, drift, meaning, 84/25 ; *yntent,* will, 109/46.
eth, easily (O. E. *ēaðe*), 67/22.
evis, y-wis, 108/86.
evrovs, blissful, Fr. *heureux,* 61/30.
expedyment, profit, advantage, 70/69.
export : *she bade me this verse export,* take this lesson with me among men ? 85/109. (Flügel prints *exort* = exhort, preach ?)
expresse, expressly, distinctly, 60/3.
eye : *by the eye,* "in unlimited quantity" (of drink ; see *N. E. D.* s. v. *eye,* 7, b), 118/2.
eysell = *aysell.*

fare : *fowle fare with,* to ill-treat, 23/21.
farly, a derivative of 'fair' ? (O. E. *fægerlīc), 17/51.
fay : *in fay,* i' faith, truly, 26/74.
fayn, used in an objective sense, pleasant, welcome, 44/23.

o

fee, cattle, 48/4; capture, prey, 85/102.
fell, to make fall, bring down, lay low, 7/22.
felosafers, 'philosophers' (the Magi), 29/30.
fere, companion, mate, 98/60 (*late the fere to,* lately the consort of);—*in fere,* together, 12/21/headl., 15/28/13, 35/21, 51/13, etc.
fere, 'fear,' danger, 63/42.
fett, fetch, 107/50.
flagat, a bottle ("*flakette,* botelle, flasco, flasca" *Prompt. Parv.*), 16/3.
flayn, flayed, 38/20.
flom, river, 4/7/14, 38/47/15 (*þe flumm Jorrdan* occurs, as a borrowing from Old French, as early as the *Orrmulum;* see H. Reichmann, *Die Eigennamen im Orrmulum* [Morsbach's *Stud. zur engl. Philol.*, vol. 25], Halle 1906, p. 36).
flyng, hasten, 18/76.
fonde, foolish, 72/10, 113/7.
fong, take, receive, 11/20/11.
forbere, to avoid, escape, 91/51.
force: *no force,* no matter, 109/26; *no force he gaff,* cared not, 121/50.
forfare, to perish, 77/187.
forgo, to go by, pass over, 54/74.
forsake, to evade, escape, 89/36.
forse, to care, 74/83 (cf. *force*).
freke (O. E. *freca*), warrior, man, 121/37.
frett, gnaw away from, gnaw out of—, 71/80.
fumosetyve, bred of fumes, humours? 105/37. (The rhyme and the reading of Wright's text require *fumosetyse.*)
fyne, to purify, clarify, refine, 105/55.
fyne, *sb.,* end, conclusion, 90/24.

galow-claper, 'gallows-clapper,' gallows-bird ("from the swinging of the body to and fro like the clapper of a bell or of a scare-crow," Halliwell), 119/101/22.
gayn, ready, well-disposed, kindly, 96/49 (see *N. E. D.* s.v. *gain,* adj. 2).
geete, goats (old plural), 69/15.
gent, gentle, noble, 3/4/6.
geraflowr, gillyflower, clove-pink or carnation, 101/19.
gest, book : used of the writings of a prophet, 48/58/22 (cf. *prophetene gestes,* quoted from W. of Shoreham by Mätzner).
giglot, "a romping girl," 116/41.
glose, gloss, explanation, illustration (of a thesis by examples), 85/93.
gornard, gurnard (a fish), 114/11.
gramarcy, thanks, 54/65/burden (where it makes a sort of pun with *marcy,* "pity").
graunter *of grace,* one who grants grace, 60/33 (Lambeth MS.: *ground*).
grome, groom, churl, 9/15/7.
gwy, guide, 102/53 (see *N. E. D.* s. v. *guy*).
gyse, manner, way (of events confirming a general truth), 85/93.

Halowtyde, "the season of All Saints, the first week of November" (*N. E. D.*), 18/2.
hardely, hardily, boldly, 109/26.
hat: *I hat,* I am called, 18/67 (O. E. *ic hätte,* Goth. *ek haitada*).
Haylis, 115/26 : "on *the blode of Crist, that is in Hayles,* 'a vial shewn at Hales in Glocestershire, as containing a portion of our blessed Saviour's blood,' see Skeat's note on *Pardoner's Tale,* 652 (Chaucer V, 284 f.)." [H. B.].
hele (O. E. *hǣlu*), health, 107/69.
henne, hence, 141/c/3.
hent, caught, 80/12.
hett, heated, made hot (with blows), 123/206 (hete *Rawlinson MS.*).
hight: *on hight,* aloft, on high, 17/52.
hode: *his here shall grow thorow his hode,* a proverbial phrase, probably meaning "he will fare ill, have no success" (cf. *Peres the Ploughmans Crede,* 423: "His hod was full of holes, & his heer oute"), 109/55.
horne: cuckold's horn (as emblem of world's mutability)? 88/21.
hosyll, eucharist, 9/27.
howge, huge, 41/26.
hye: *on hye,* aloud, 1/9.
hye: *in hye,* in haste, at once, instantly, 85/80.

Ierachye, hierarchy, 42/7.
inequalite, injustice, 84/57.
insampull, example, 95/10.
instance, pressing, urging on, 87/11.

japes, jokes, tricks, trifles, 76/154 ; as a *vb.*, 113/26.
jaspe, jasper (precious stone), 101/17 (the two other MSS. have *jasper*).
jonkers, for *jonkets* (see Wright's text), delicacies (used of drinks), 107/64.
juggelen, to produce by witchcraft, 115/10 ; to change by w., 116/38.
Jury = Jewery, Judaea, 48/31 (Flügel, *Festschr. f. Hildebrand,* had the misprint *Jary,* which puzzled Holthausen : *Anglia* 17, 444).
juveyn, youth, 120/12.

kelle, plur. *kellis,* caul (*i. e.* the gold hair-net of a lady of distinction), 101/47.
kepe, heed, care, attention, 84/3.
kyde, known, manifest, 82/33.
kynde, nature, human understanding, 61/*b*/1 ;—natural disposition, 85/63.
kyrchers, kerchiefs, 110/21.

lake : *withowtyn lake,* without fail, certainly, 84/27.
lappe, skirt of garment, 46/28.
laymand(Northern form of participle, O. E. *lēomiende*), 57/1 (cf. *lyghtand,* 59/27), shining.
leche, leech, physician, 62/21 ; *vb.,* to heal, remedy, 69/16.
lede, 30/12, *pp.,* led forth, made to leave the body ?
lede (O. E. *lēod*), people, nation, 6/21.
√ **leme** (O. E. *lēōma*), ray, beam, light, 1/13, 11/20/15.
lent, arrived, placed, staying, 1/12 (from *lenden*, to land, alight, arrive, sojourn); 84/27 ; of being "fixed" in a state of mind, 120/57.
lere, to learn, 83/36 ; 83/39.
lerne, to teach, 32/2.
lese, *many a l.,* many a lesser one, 76/138.
lesse (Cambr. MS. *lese*), to lose, forsake, abandon, 30/3. (On the other hand, *forsakyn* means "lost," 36/20.)
leste, leased ('our lease of life is so short') ? 52/26. (cf. *seste,* 48/58/14).
lesyng (O. E. *lēasung*), lie ; *withowt lesyng,* in truth, 9/15/9, 31/13. (In the Anglo-French vocabulary of the MS. this phrase, evidently no more understood, is rendered by *sanz perdre.*)
lett, hinder, prevent, 71/87 ; *withowt lettyng,* 125/315, without hesitation, putting off ; *lett,* hindered, 126/384.
leve or lothe, lief or loth, glad or sad, 79/222 ; *lever,* rather, 87/3.
light = *lyte,* little, 124/214.
lisse (which the rhyme requires for *lose* of the MS.), to relieve, release, comfort, soothe (O.E. *liŏsian*), 9/16/3.
liste : *liste not to know,* deigned not to take notice 90/23.
lore, creed, religion, sect, sort, 108/101.
lowse : *hurt a lowse,* proverbial for "display one's anger even on the smallest object" ? 113/20.
lulley, *vb.,* to sing 'lulley,' lull a child asleep with a cradle-song, 21/2.
lykyn, liken, make alike, give equal rank, 20/67.
lyst, wisdom, prudence (*with lyst* merely serves to fill up the verse and add emphasis), 59/3.

maintenance, *cap of m.,* "a cap borne as one of the insignia of office before the sovereign of England at the coronation, and before mayors of some cities" (*N.E.D.*); appendix, passim.
make (O. E. *ge-maca*), fere, mate, companion, fellow, 11/19/14.
make, to make my will, testament, 86/77/2.
malicoli, melancholy, 105/37.
maner, custom, what is mannerly, proper, due, 116/99/headline.
mawndy (Lat. *mandatum*), the washing of the Apostles' feet by Christ ; also used for the Lord's Supper itself (Mätzner) ; 35/16. (Hence *Maundy-Thursday.*)
may, maiden, 10/18/1.
mayn, mean, speak, mention,—or moan, complain,—85/91 (see note !).
mean, mediatrix, intercessor, 61/14.
meladye, "melody," used in some figurative sense, = the 'golden mean' ? 28/8. [The same spelling, where it evidently means "melody," 11/20/6.]

mele-pok, 'meal-bag' (used by beggars to hold the meals received in charity), 116/38.
methe, 68/54,—? [rhyme *separet*!] moderation (O. E. *mǣðu*), hence domination, power?
mold, erth, 6/10/30.
montenance (for *montance,* "appar. simulating the form of maintenance"), amount, space, extent (used of time), 104/87/9.
more, most, in the old sense of "greatest," 1/18, 2/3/13. So *more and lesse,* great and small, 3/6/ headl.;—*most,* the greatest, mightiest, 6/35;—*more,* bigger, fatter, 120/34.
most, must, in the emphasizing formulas *so most* (or *mot*) *I goo,* etc. (*e. g.*, 46/55/headl.), appears in its old sense of "may"; the same in *blessyd mot þou be,* 49/61/1, 57/15.
musket, male sparrow-hawk, 3/4/7.
myllyan, million, 85/118.
myscheve, to bring to mischief, 75/121.
mysspent, made ill use of, 55/33.
mytis, mights, powers, virtues, 10/17/9.

ne, if not, 53/55.
nere hond, near, 48/57/10.
nesshe, soft, mild, 83/17 (O. E. *hnæsce*).
nete (O. E. *nēāt*), cattle, 121/38.
newell is the Balliol MS.'s usual spelling for *nowel* (the Christmas cry; Fr. *Noël,* Lat. *natalem*), 2/3/ burden, *etc.*
noll (O. E. *hnoll*), head, 119/101/17.
not, do not know, 89/11.
nyse, foolish, 36/46/1; fastidious, 115/3.

on for of: 8/14/5, 9/15/17, 65/69/10, *etc.*
overcaste, to overthrow, 72/12.

pare: *pared his crown,* cut off the crown of his head, 31/27 (cf. the quotation from J. Heywood in *N. E. D.*).
parla pompe = Fr. *par la pompe?* 117/100/headl.—But it gives no sense.
pay, *subst.*, contentment, satisfaction, 26/70, 34/4, 56/59.

per se, standing alone, by itself, unparalleled, 100/85/1.
peyse, weigh, 87/25.
pight, pitched, fixed, placed, put, 59/13; **ypyght,** 83/29 ("our tents are pitched in the wilderness").
plasshe, "to lower and narrow a broad-spread hedge by partially cutting off the branches, and entwining them with those left upright" (Halliwell), 110/22.
platis, from *plate,* "a Spanish money of account" (*Century Dict.*), used for coins, money generally (cf. Shakspere, *Ant. Cleop.*, V, ii, 92).
plight, *plyght,* 5/9/22, seems a mistake for (a)*lyght* (so Wright's text), "though *plyght,* 'promised,' makes a sort of sense." [H. B.]
poke, pocket, 128/1.
porte (Fr. *portée,* range or reach of a missile): *high of porte,* high of flight, ranging wide, 81/29.
portratowr, portraiture, 91/48 (referring to the funeral monuments in St. Paul's, on which see Stow's *Survey of London,* ed. Strype, 1720, I, 157–168).
prest, ready, 84/21, 86/2, 121/48.
presydent, precedent, 69/13.
preved, proved, put to the test, 47/18.
prophet, profit, 72/5.
prosellyng (other MSS. *precelling*), prominent, excellent, 101/23.
purches: *purches . . . þes prophettis for thy supplement,* acquire these profits to supply thee, 69/41.
purvey, provide, prepare, 91/52.
pyn, bolt of a door, 111/3.

quart, safety, health, 86/76/6.
quyte-rent, 'quit-rent,' "rent paid by the freeholders or copyholders of a manor in discharge or acquittance of other services," 138/106/16.

recure, recover, 69/10.
rede, to counsel, advise, 9/15/13; *sb.,* advice, 71/85.
rehersyng, report, indication, 68/9.
reke, *vb.,* reek (in burning), 81/21.
repyn, reaped, 35/44/7.
rest, *transit.,* lay to rest, lay low, 53/38.
rive, "speedily" (Halliwell), 123/198.
rode, cross, 2/3/16.

Glossary.

rolyon, a shoe of untanned leather; in Scotch also "a coarse, ill-made animal," a sense perhaps more fit for the passage (nonsensical as it intentionally is), 114/11.
rowght, 118/101/burden (rhyming with *a towt*), same as *run the rout*, "gad, run about," go round (Wright, *Dial. Dict.*, s. v. *rout, sb.*, 6). Cf. *lette the cupe go route* in st. 10 of "Lytyll Thanke" (Ritson), p. 187.
Roye, king, 100/85/13.
ryse (O. E. *hrīs*), twig; *rose of ryse*, rose on the bough (flower from the root of Jesse), 6/10/31.

say, to speak, recite verses, 106/79.
see, see, throne, 48/58/17.
semewes, sea-mews, 114/18.
sequens, *sequentia*, a Roman church hymn in rhythmical prose or accentual metre, sung after the Gradual and before the Gospel, 13/23/19.
seruyce, dish that is served, 33/42/8.
sese, to cease, stop; pret. *sest*, 4/8/6; *sees*, inf., 25/9; *seste*, pret.,48/58/14.
sew, sowed (O. E. *sēōw*), 6/8.
shake: *shrew shake*, shrewishly inclined, disposed? 110/93/7.
shent, disgraced, cónfounded, 3/4/7, 82/47.
Shere Thursday, Sheer Thursday, Maundy Thursday (in Easter Week), 35/15 (O.N. *skíriþórsdagr*).
shot, payment, contribution, 108/97.
shryll, clear, loud (of the Virgin Mary's voice), 5/8/28. (The form **shill**, *shyll*, also occurs, see Halliwell, and cf. 89/18.)
siker, certain, 34/27; *sikernes*, stability, 88/79/8 (burden).
skalde, scabby (Lat. *glabriosus*), 130/23.
skill, *skyll*, reason, right, 26/103; argument, 70/60; human reason, 61/*b*/4; ability, 112/95/28.
skuse, excuse, 109/27.
slake, slack, stop, cease, 95/15.
slipper (O. E. *slipur*), slippery, 73/48.
slo, slay; pple. *slone*, 85/117.
small, 101/46, means 'small in the waist,' not 'small of stature' (Schipper).
smater, to chatter, prate, 113/31.

solas, comfort, joy, pride, 6/6.
sond, message, sending, 6/7.
sort, assembly, company, 85/113, 106/2.
sowse: souse, pickle: *sethyng sowse*, cooking sauce, 110/92/1.
sparkyll, spark, 130/32.
sperling, sparling (a small fish), 114/13.
sprente, sprinkled, 69/16.
spurne, to stumble, 80/11.
spyll, *spill*, destroy, 89/20; perish, 8/10; *spill . . . wynde*, waste breath, 43/10.
stede, place, spot, 1/21.
sterne-vite (Lansd. MS. *treunytie*, and only Cotton MS. correctly *strenuytie*), strenuousness, strength, 101/19.
stie, *stye*, to mount, ascend, 66/31, 75/111 (*he stithe*).
stownd, while, 8/22.
stowr, combat, strife, struggle, 68/53.
streme, flow of light, ray, beam, 7/12/11; cf. Chaucer, *Merchant's Tale*, 976 : *Phebus hath of gold hise stremes doune ysent*. (*Cent. Dict.*)— Flügel alters to *sterne*, but preserves *the bryght strem*, ib. 18.
stroy, destroy, foil, 83/12.
sure, assure, 9/16/6.
swynk, to labour, 90/18.
syke, sigh, 29/49.
syne, since, 52/6.
synglar: *thy synglar plesure*, every single pleasure thou affordest (folio 1557 has *single*), 97/30.

take: *ys to hym take*, has joined him, bears him company, 27/8.—*toke*, gave, appointed, 36/8 ;—*the tyrtyll fro hym* (viz. *fawcon*) *tok a tre*, fled from him to the shelter of a tree, 85/104 ;—*I take me*, surrender, give up, betake myself, 89/23, 96/101.
tall, docile, obsequious, 124/273.
tarbox, "a box containing tar, carried by shepherds for anointing the sores of sheep" (*Cent. Dict.*), 18/59.
taxe, rate, estimate, assign, 79/249.
tende, give attention, 120/6.
tene (O. E. *tēōna*), 'teen,' pain, torment (in hell), 10/17/15; grief, anger, 115/8.

Glossary.

tent = *entent; take tent,* pay attention, 67/7.
thayre = *the ayre* (other MSS. *are*), oar, 101/29.
the (O. E. *þēon*), to strive, 111/31.
ther to : *I never synned ther to,* I never sinned to deserve it, 19/32/headl.
thowght : *with a thowght,* with the swiftness of thought (frail flesh yields to temptation), 63/49.
throw, while, moment, 112/94/21.
tight (M. E. *tihten*), devise, intend, 85/64.
till : *per-till,* thereto, also, 26/76.
to-torne, torne, lacerated, 13/24/2 ; *to-tere,* inf., 22/38.
towght, a variant of *tight* (Mod. E. *taut*), 118/24.
trist, confidence, 51/12 ; 63/63.
trow, trust, 95/21.
Troynouant, 100/85/9, according to Geoffrey of Monmouth a corrupt form of *Troja Nova,* the name originally given to London by its legendary founder Brutus.—The *Trinobantes* were a Celtic tribe in Essex (mentioned by Cæsar); the name of their capital [*Augusta Trinobantum* or *Trinovantum*] probably was brought into arbitrary connexion with *Troja Nova* by Geoffrey or somebody else, whose interpretation came by tradition down to Dunbar.
tryll, to turn, twirl, 111/3.
twayn, in too (two), separate, dissever, 55/20.
twyte = *twyghte,* from *twicchen,* to pull away, snatch, 53/61.

verament : *in verament* (the adverb being mistaken for a substantive), truly, in very truth, 7/11/3.
verey, true, 25/7.
vise, advise, 46/1.
vnbuxvmnes, disobedience, 55/29.
vnneth, scarcely, hardly, 120/33.
vnsiker, uncertain, 91/43.
vphold, to esteem, rate high, 6/39.
vplent, borne, brought upward, 71/83 (see *lent*).

vpsodown (this the normal old form, literally "up as down"), upside down, 91/35.

waryson, treasure, store, 84/44.
wede, garb, clothing, 38/8, 55/13.
weme, spot, stain, 8/14/6 ; spelt *wemb,* 12/22/10.
wene, to 'ween,' think, mean, 109/7 ; pret. *went,* 124/270; comp., pp., *a-went,* 111/9.
were, doubt, 83/37.
wheton, wheaten, 120/38.
wight, *wyght,* being, person, 12/21/2 ; 54/3.
will, fulfilment of wishes, satisfaction of wants, 55/13.
wisshe, washed, 66/22.
wite, to blame, 121/58 ; *wyte,* 96/92.
witsave (for *with-save*), to vouchsafe, 98/40 (see quotations from Wyatt and Palsgrave in *Century Dict.*) (fol. 1557 has *vouchesafe*).
witt, soul, quintessence ? Mary is called the 'well (*fons*) and wit' of all wisdom (59/6) and of mercy (60/37).
woddowes, wood-doves, 114/19.
wode, mad, 43/19.
won(n)e, dwell, 2/2/4; *sb.,* dwelling, abode, 85/116.
worled, hurled, 126/348.
worship, to do honour to—, 111/9.
worth: *take in worth,* take in good part, 98/59 ; see quotation from Latimer, in *Century Dict.* (*in good worth*).
wrechesse, wretchedness, 60/4.
wynne, to earn, 121/36.
wysse, to guide (O. E. *wīssian*), 51/6, 56/71.

yede, yode, went, walked.
yglent, O. E. *geglenged,* from *glengan,* M. E. (*3e-*) *glengen,* to adorn, trim ; 65/9 ("*yglent* for *ygleynt,* cf. *yment* for *ymeynt,* from O. E. *gemenged*" [H. B.]).—Flügel originally altered to *prevalent.*
yndefycyent, "unfailing, exhaustless, unceasing" (*N. E. D.*), 84/31.

RICHARD CLAY & SONS, LIMITED,
BREAD STREET HILL, E.C., AND
BUNGAY, SUFFOLK.